EurographicSeminars

Tutorials and Perspectives in Computer Graphics

Edited by W. T. Hewitt, R. Gnatz, and D. A. Duce

D. A. Duce M. R. Gomes
F. R. A. Hopgood J. R. Lee (Eds.)

User Interface Management and Design

Proceedings of the Workshop
on User Interface Management Systems
and Environments
Lisbon, Portugal, June 4–6, 1990

With 117 Figures

Springer-Verlag
Berlin Heidelberg New York
London Paris Tokyo
Hong Kong Barcelona

EurographicSeminars

Edited by W. T. Hewitt, R. Gnatz, and D. A. Duce
for EUROGRAPHICS -
The European Association for Computer Graphics
P. O. Box 16, CH-1288 Aire-la-Ville, Switzerland

Volume Editors

David A. Duce
F. Robert A. Hopgood
Informatics Department
Rutherford Appleton Laboratory
Chilton, Didcot, Oxon OX11 0QX, U.K.

M. Rui Gomes
Rua Alves Redol, 9–2°
P-1017 Lisboa Codex, Portugal

John R. Lee
EdCAAD, University of Edinburgh
Department of Architecture
20 Chambers Street, Edinburgh EH1 1JZ, U.K.

Organizer of the Workshop

Graphics and Interaction in ESPRIT
Technical Interest Group

ISBN 3-540-53454-7 Springer-Verlag Berlin Heidelberg New York
ISBN 0-387-53454-7 Springer-Verlag New York Berlin Heidelberg

Library of Congress Cataloging-in-Publication Data
Workshop on User Interface Management Systems and Environments (1990: Lisbon, Portugal). User interface management and design: proceedings of the Workshop on User Interface Management Systems and Environments, Lisbon, Portugal, June 4–6, 1990 /
D. A. Duce . . . [et al.] p. cm.
(EurographicSeminars)
Includes bibliographical references.
ISBN 0-387-53454-7
1. User interfaces (Computer systems) – Congresses. I. Title. II. Series.
QA76.9.U83W67 1991 005.1 – dc20 90-23984 CIP

45/3140-5 4 3 2 1 0 – Printed on acid-free paper

Preface

This volume is a record of the Workshop on User Interface Management Systems and Environments held at INESC, Lisbon, Portugal, between 4 and 6 June 1990. The main impetus for the workshop came from the Graphics and Interaction in ESPRIT Technical Interest Group of the European Community ESPRIT Programme. The Graphics and Interaction in ESPRIT Technical Interest Group arose from a meeting of researchers held in Brussels in May 1988, which identified a number of technical areas of common interest across a significant number of ESPRIT I and ESPRIT II projects. It was recognized that there was a need to share information on such activities between projects, to disseminate results from the projects to the world at large, and for projects to be aware of related activities elsewhere in the world. The need for a Technical Interest Group was confirmed at a meeting held during ESPRIT Technical Week in November 1989, attended by over 50 representatives from ESPRIT projects and the Commission of the European Communities.

Information exchange sessions were organized during the EUROGRAPHICS '89 conference, with the intention of disseminating information from ESPRIT projects to the wider research and development community, both in Europe and beyond.

The present workshop, organized by the EUROGRAPHICS Association and its Portuguese Chapter in conjunction with the Technical Interest Group, arose from the common interests in User Interface Management Systems, identified by a number of ESPRIT I and ESPRIT II projects, at the workshop in May 1988. Several ESPRIT I projects were concerned with developing or using the ideas of User Interface Management Systems (UIMS). Several of the foundational concepts in UIMS were established at the workshop held in Seeheim in November 1983 (*User Interface Management Systems*, edited by G.E. Pfaff, *EurographicSeminars*, Springer-Verlag). In the intervening six years, the development of windowing systems, object-oriented methodologies and AI-inspired techniques have proceeded on a scale which was hard to anticipate at that time. The ideas in the Seeheim model are beginning to show their age.

Several workshops organized by ACM Siggraph have addressed the topic of interactive systems, and it was felt that it would be timely to organize a workshop in 1990 to re-examine the basic notion of a User Interface Management System, to question its continued appropriateness in the context of current, and probable future, systems, entailing a proper attempt to relate it to the newer paradigm of "user interface development environment", and an assessment of the impact of "knowledge engineering" (both in the interface and in the application) on interaction strategies.

The format of the workshop was to spend the first half-day with presentations from a number of invited speakers. The aim was to highlight the major outstanding issues. The workshop participants then split into four groups. Membership of the groups was determined prior to the workshop on the basis of position papers submitted and the topic of each group may not have been fully representative of the interests of the group's members. Papers accepted by the Organizing Committee were briefly presented in the groups as a prelude to discussion. As a further stimulus to discussion, each working group was given a list of key questions for that area. Full papers and lists of questions were circulated to all participants for study in advance of the workshop. Plenary sessions helped to keep the individual groups informed of progress in the other groups. A closing plenary session was held on the third day to hear final working group reports and agree the conclusions of the workshop.

Part I of this volume contains the three invited papers, reports of the four working groups and the final conclusions of the workshop.

The remaining parts contain the papers accepted by the Organizing Committee which were presented at the workshop. These are organized by the working group in which each was presented.

The Organizing Committee, A. Conway (UK), D.A. Duce (UK), M. Rui Gomes (P), P.J.W. ten Hagen (NL), F.R.A. Hopgood (UK), A.C. Kilgour (UK), H. Kuhlmann (FRG), D. Morin (F), B. Servolle (F), G. Pfaff (FRG), chaired by J.R. Lee (UK); was responsible for the work prior to the workshop and special thanks are due to them, particularly David Duce for organizing the administration.

Particular thanks are due to Mario Rui Gomes and his colleagues at INESC who handled all the local arrangements for the workshop, especially Ana Freitas who provided secretarial support for the workshop. We also wish to express our thanks to Karel De Vriendt of DG XIII of the Commission of the European Communities for his support of the activity.

Mention must also be made of Nuno da Camara Pereira, whose restaurant, Novital, and Fado music, provided the setting for the workshop Dinner and much fruitful discussion.

However, the success of the workshop was due to the participants and we express sincere thanks to all who gave of their time in preparing papers and attending the workshop.

Lisbon, June 1990

D.A. Duce
M.R. Gomes
F.R.A. Hopgood
J.R. Lee

Table of Contents

Part I Invited Presentations, Discussions and Conclusions 1

Invited Presentations

1. Critique of the Seeheim Model 3
P. J. W. ten Hagen

2. The Reference Model of Computer Graphics 7
G. Faconti

3. The Architectural Bases of Design Re-use 15
G. Cockton

Working Group Discussions

4. Concepts, Methods, Methodologies Working Group 35

5. Current Practice Working Group 51

6. Multi-media and Visual Programming 57

7. Toolkits, Environments and the Object Oriented Paradigm 61

Workshop Conclusions

8. Conclusions 65

Part II Concepts, Models and Methodologies 69

9. Some Comments on the Future of User Interface Tools 71
J. Grollmann, C. Rumpf

10. Modelling User Interface Software 87
N.V. Carlsen, N.J. Christensen

11. GMENUS: An Ada Concurrent User Interface Management System 101
M. Martínez, B. Villalobos, P. de Miguel

12. Usability Engineering and User Interface Management 113
R. Gimnich

13. Designing the Next Generation of UIMSs 123
F. Shevlin, F. Neelamkavil

14. Intelligent Interfaces and UIMS 135
J. Lee

15. Assembling a User Interface out of Communicating Processes 145
P. J. W. ten Hagen, D. Soede

Part III Current Practice 151

16. IUICE — An Interactive User Interface Construction Environment 153
P. Sturm

17. Dialogue Specification for Knowledge Based Systems 169
C. Hayball

18. SYSECA's Experience in UIMS for Industrial Applications 179
J. Bangratz, E. Le Thieis

19. The Growth of a MOSAIC 195
D. Svanæs, A. Thomassen

20. A Framework for Integrating UIMS and User Task Models in the Design of User Interfaces 203
P. Johnson, K. Drake, S. Wilson

21. PROMETHEUS: A System for Programming Graphical User Interfaces 217
D. Ehmke

Part IV Visual Programming, Multi-Media and UI Generators 229

22. An Environment for User Interface Development Based on the ATN and Petri Nets Notations 231
M. Bordegoni, U. Cugini, M. Motta, C. Rizzi

23. Creating Interaction Primitives 247
L. Larsson

Part V Toolkits, Environments and the OO Paradigm 255

24. The Composite Object User Interface Architecture 257
R.D. Hill, M. Herrmann

25. An Overview of GINA - the Generic Interactive Application 273
M. Spenke, C. Beilken

26. The Use of OPEN LOOK/Motif GUI Standards for Applications in Control Systems Design 295
H.A. Barker, M. Chen, P.W. Grant, C.P. Jobling, A. Parkman, P. Townsend

27. The OO-AGES Model - An Overview 307
M.R. Gomes and J.C.L. Fernandes

List of Participants 323

Part I

Invited Presentations, Discussions and Conclusions

Chapter 1

Critique of the Seeheim Model

Paul J.W. ten Hagen

1.1 Introduction

The Seeheim Model will be discussed under the three headings:

(1) what is the Seeheim Model;

(2) critique of the Model;

(3) critique of the divergencies from the Model.

The aim is to show that the original Seeheim Model still has merit and many of the criticisms are due to an over-simplification of what the Model contains or a preoccupation with problems associated with current practices.

1.2 Seeheim Model

The basic diagram of the Seeheim Model that is frequently quoted is shown in figure 1.

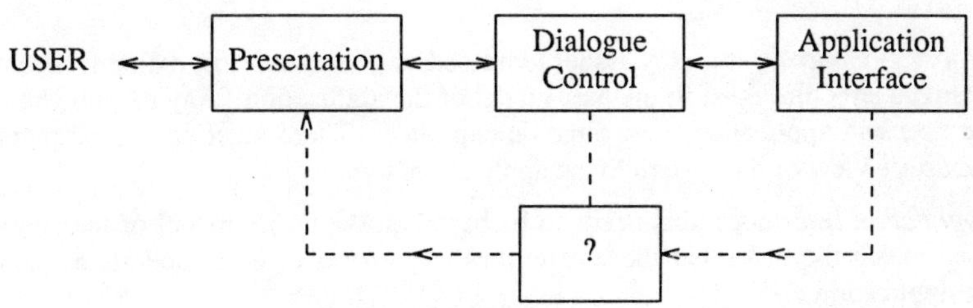

Figure 1: The Seeheim Model

The Model aimed to categorize the parts of the interface such that the designer of an Application Interface can describe what is going on between the user and the application program. The Model addressed three questions related to user interface descriptions:

(1) Specification;

(2) Human Factors;

(3) Classification or Notations.

1.2.1 Specification

From a specification view, the three parts can be described as:

(1) *Presentation*: responsible for the external to internal mapping of basic symbols. The device dependent input from the user is translated to a set of basic symbols (sometimes called tokens). To specify a dialogue, these basic symbols have to be defined.

(2) *Dialogue Control*: responsible for defining the structure of the dialogue between the user and the application program. It is responsible for routing the basic symbols to the appropriate part of the application. As this may vary in time, there is a need for internal state information which is updated by the Dialogue Control component. The dialogue itself is likely to have a syntax. The description of that syntax is likely to require internal state information also.

(3) *Application Interface*: this is a representation of the application from the viewpoint of the user interface. It defines the semantics of the application in terms of the data objects relevant to the user interface and the processes that can be initiated by the user interface. It is responsible for the communication between the user interface and the application in the form required by the application.

From the application's point-of-view, the UIMS is responsible for anything that the application wants to sub-contract. Examples are imposing constraints on the input from the user, defining the feedback required, low-level checking of the dialogue and other tasks that need to be moved to the User Interface for performance.

1.3 Human Factors

From the Human Factors view, the separation into components may be useful in giving design guidelines and in evaluation from a human factors point-of-view.

(1) *Presentation*: the key issue addressed is the name space for application objects and concepts. The Human Factors issues relate to the design of the symbol space accessed by the user, any structure imposed on that space and the effects of interactions between symbols.

(2) *Dialogue Control*: the key issue addressed is command and dialogue structure. The dialogue structure must fit the user model of the application. Any natural chunking from the user and application view must be exploited. There must be a good mapping from the user's view of the system to the application's view.

(3) *Application Interface*: this needs to be based on the user's model of the application. It must match the tasks that the user wishes to perform with the operations performed by the application.

1.4 Notations

Many classification schemes exist in UIMS. For each part of the Seeheim Model, several are required:

(1) *Presentation*: output notations must deal at least with text and graphics primitives. In the future this will need to be extended to media primitives. As hardware becomes more complex, the need for adequate abstractions becomes more important. Similar problems exist in the input area.

(2) *Dialogue Control*: this is the part that has been most highly developed so far with three major categories: state/transitions, grammars and events/handlers. All have notational peculiarities with different strengths and weaknesses. The major argument against states and transitions is that for non-trivial applications, they become much too complex. However, suitable techniques for defining sub-transitions can solve many of the problems. The grammar systems are the ones that have been looked at most intensely both before and after Seeheim. The usual complaint is that it can only handle directed graphs. However affixes to grammars allow much more flexibility. The adherents of the

events/handlers approach imply that it is the richest of the three approaches. However, complex interactions need some form and structure placed on the interaction. All that happens in event systems is that such structure has to be added by *ad hoc* techniques.

To some extent, which system to use is a matter of personal taste. There is a great deal of equivalence in the systems with the emphasis on different areas.

(3) *Application Interface*: most current systems use a procedural interface between the user interface and the application. Newer systems are likely to adopt a more object-oriented approach but this is not current practice at the moment.

1.5 Interrelationships Between Components

Two interfaces are well defined in the Seeheim Model:

(1) *Presentation Dialogue*: a major issue is the form of tokens between the two components. The current datatypes in use consist of a set of logical output primitives and logical input devices. The richness of these datatypes is not very great and more flexibility and richness is required. Many new problems arise when the dynamic characteristics of the interaction are considered.

(2) *Dialogue: Application*: A major question is whether the dialogue system has access to the application data. This is mainly a trade-off between efficiency and program modularity. Another question is how the application gives information to the dialogue handler concerning checking of input values for correctness. By allowing the dialogue manager to have access to the application data, significant semantic checking can be done and it avoids the copying of application data.

The third interface between the Presentation Component and the Application Interface is not defined in the Seeheim Model. However, it may well be needed for applications where the presentation component needs to navigate through the application data. The Seeheim Model did not really address performance issues and, probably, it is only then that there is a need for an interface. Conceptually, it can be defined by information passing through the Dialogue Control component.

1.6 Critique of the Seeheim Model

The major criticism of the Seeheim Model is that the Run-Time Model does not have sufficient detail. It needs to define how it relates to a window management system. It cannot assume that the resources it requires are available and has to negotiate with the workstation agent to get what it requires in terms of screen space, colour table access etc. This, of course, makes the Model much more complicated.

The Seeheim Model continues to be useful at specification time but too little attention was paid to:

(1) *Distributed applications*: the assumption in the Seeheim Model is that the physical system is not distributed.

(2) *Concurrency*: the Model assumes a simple interaction structure. It does not really cater for an environment where the processing of several events is outstanding.

(3) *Resource Management*: the Seeheim Model does not really address the problem of overloading. If the mouse click has several meanings dependent on context, how is it sorted out? In a window system, you need to define the focus of the application. How do you handle application specific echoing in a window management environment? Who has control of the keyboard? Is it controlled by the application or the user?

(4) *Performance*: the resource management issues described above all have performance constraints associated with them that complicate the interface and the associated Model.

A second criticism of the Seeheim Model is the lack of semantic support in the UIMS. It really does not address the issue of making application information available to the Dialogue Manager in order to improve the interface. This is a particular concern of the area of Direct Manipulation where appropriate feedback most of the time is essential together with sensible patch-up and undo strategies. The belief is that the user interface and the application are intimately connected and their definitions have to be more interrelated than at present.

1.7 Current Practice

The main criticism of current practice is the growth of toolkits based on top of window management systems. These tend to provide a useful set of facilities for building small simple interfaces. However, they normally contain little structure so that this is provided by hidden links that are not part of the toolkit.

For advanced applications, a well-defined structure is needed. The function of the UIMS is to provide that integrating module. For example, the toolkit approach does not have the ability to describe cut-and-paste between application processes. To achieve that, it is essential to have a Run-Time Model that is similar to the Seeheim Model.

1.8 Conclusions

The Seeheim Model has stood the passage of time well particularly if you read the complete description rather than only look at the main diagram.

The current trend of building simple interfaces using toolkits will not scale up to the needs of demanding application environments. The future is likely to be the simultaneous design of User Interface and Application based on a sound underlying model. The Seeheim Model may be incomplete but it is currently the best model to work from if you are building complex user interfaces. The current trend towards simpler models just emphasises the state of hardware and software developments today rather than concentrating on the basic understanding of the processes involved in user interface design.

Reference

(1) *User Interface Management Systems,* G.E. Pfaff (Ed), EurographicSeminar Series, Springer-Verlag (1985).

Chapter 2

The Reference Model of Computer Graphics

Giorgio Faconti

2.1 Introduction

This chapter discusses the Reference Model for Computer Graphics being developed within the ISO/IEC committee on Computer Graphics (ISO/IEC JTC1/SC24) and explores some relationships to User Interface Management Systems. The history of the development is presented first, as there are interesting parallels with the development of models for UIMS.

2.2 History

2.2.1 Introduction

Serious work on a Reference Model for Computer Graphics started at the ISO meeting at Timberline in July 1985. A Task Group with membership from the GKS, GKS-3D, PHIGS, CGI, CGM and language bindings working groups came together under the chairmanship of F.R.A. Hopgood to put forward a simple model for comment.

A major problem identified early on was the relationship between the workstation interface of the functional standards and CGI. While some believed the two were synonymous, the CGI Working Group believed they had a much wider remit.

The CGM Working Group had established an International Standard based on a clean concept of a *picture* to be captured and restored. GKS, on the other hand, had much more the concept of graphical information flowing to some subset of open workstations with the arrival of information at the workstation display being determined by a number of controls. Making a clean interface between the two standards was difficult.

PHIGS, designed as a structuring facility for computer graphics, had also made changes to the primitive set and the way operator attributes, such as highlighting, were controlled at the workstation. Although PHIGS could have been designed with GKS-3D as the viewing back-end to the system, this was not the case.

In consequence, a set of graphics standards had been produced over a 10 year period with a great deal of similarity and common concepts but with minor incompatibilities due to the different times at which they were produced and the different people involved. It was clearly going to be difficult to produce a Reference Model of the existing set of standards with clean concepts. The approach had to be to define a Reference Model having a distillation of the current concepts in use and use this as the basis for the next generation of standards. GKS, the oldest of the set of standards, would be coming up for its Review in a few years time.

2.2.2 Strand Model

An *ad hoc* Committee on Reference Models was established and this met in Frankfurt in February 1986. A major input to that meeting was a paper by Graham Reynolds [3] emanating from the Modular Graphics Systems Project [1] at the University of East Anglia. This defined a novel process oriented graphics system architecture for emulating a variety of computer graphics systems. It was proposed that this could be used as the basis for a Reference Model.

The underlying conceptual models of most standard graphics systems, in particular of those existing and proposed international standards for graphics, and of many existing graphics packages, are most often seen as being graphics processing pipelines. In the case of graphics output, graphics data is refined as it passes down the pipeline, by associating graphical attributes, transforming coordinates, clipping etc., until it reaches a form which is suitable for display on a particular workstation or device. Graphical input can be viewed as a pipeline of processes transforming the data resulting from some input interaction into a form suitable for use by the application. The input interaction may also involve processes from the output pipeline in order to achieve any desired prompts and echoes. Clearly, the composition of these pipelines and the order of components within them may differ widely between models, however there are often a reasonable number of components common to most. Examples of these are transformations, attributes, clipping, storage etc. These common components play an equivalent role in each model, even though the internal details of the components will most likely differ. It can be shown that a large number of the differences between graphics system models can be expressed in terms of the different orderings (or configurations) of these components.

The Reynolds abstract reference model of graphics data states developed this processing pipeline model by isolating the smallest incremental changes to the states of graphics information (or storage areas), and by defining when graphics data undergoes transitions between these states by the application of specialized processes.

The data states are grouped together to form strands of processing, where a particular strand is concerned with a subset of the overall intended graphical effects. Five major strands can be identified in most standard graphics systems, as follows:

(1) attribute strand;

(2) transformation strand;

(3) clipping strand;

(4) dimensionality strand;

(5) storage strand.

The processing strands are illustrated in figure 1, which also indicates how a specific graphics pipeline can be configured by ordering the state transitions on and between strands.

The Frankfurt meeting identified a list of concepts that needed to be included in a Reference Model:

(1) pipelines;

(2) levels/interfaces;

(3) multiplexing;

(4) attribute binding;

(5) elaboration;

(6) instantiation;

(7) language bindings and encodings;

(8) data coding versus procedural interface;

(9) resource sharing;

(10) input model;

(11) application interface;

(12) operator interface;

(13) primitives, attributes;

(14) storage structures;

(15) workstations;

(16) metafiles;

(17) raster graphics.

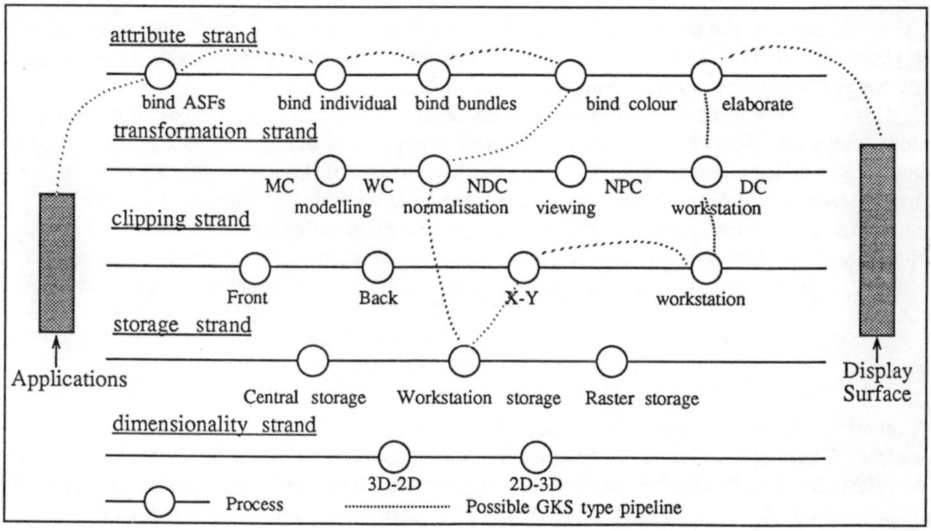

Figure 1: An example of the strand model

The strand approach was looked at as an alternative to the more normal pipeline description of computer graphics.

2.2.3 External Reference Model

After the Frankfurt meeting, two independent approaches were considered. The first concentrated on establishing a Reference Model that was primarily concerned with how other standards would interact with the computer graphics standards. The second concentrated on establishing an internal reference model for computer graphics showing how the various concepts in graphics should fit together.

The External Reference Model was based on the pipeline approach establishing a 7 stage pipeline for input and output. The output stages were seen as:

(1) *Conceptualization*: the mapping of the application's requirements into graphical terms.

(2) *Formulation*: the creation of graphical information.

(3) *Elaboration*: the mapping of graphical information onto the abstract picture on a workstation.

(4) *Generation*: the mapping of some part of the abstract picture onto a virtual display surface.

(5) *Realization* : the use of real attributes on the workstation to define the picture.

(6) *Production* : the process of causing the image to appear.

(7) *Visualization* : the process of inspecting the output by the operator.

A similar set of stages did the reverse process for input.

Work on the external reference model continued until January 1989 with several refinements of the document.

2.2.4 Components and Frameworks

The major input to the internal reference model came from BSI using the work of Arnold and Reynolds on strands and Duce on Formal Specification [2]. Out of these came a components and frameworks model for describing graphics standards.

Components can be thought of as basic concepts such as output primitives, attributes, pictures, views etc. Frameworks define how these components fit together in a particular standard. Thus a framework statement might be that pictures in this standard can only be constructed from a sequence of output primitives that have all their attributes bound to them.

As for the external reference model, the internal reference model went through a number of refinements with attempts at describing existing standards in terms of the model. As a separate activity, the relationship between components and abstract data types was established.

2.2.5 A Single Reference Model

A meeting was held in Paris in January 1989 to consider the two activities - external and internal. The major output from the meeting was a decision to merge the external and internal reference model into a single activity. The meeting elaborated the basic concepts or components in the Reference Model and attempted to define both the internal and external relationships. Four major concepts were agreed:

(1) *Pictures* : the current contents of a space.

(2) *Collections* : a storage structure associated with primitives and their related attributes.

(3) *Metafiles* : a mechanism for storing and retrieving pictures.

(4) *Archives* : a mechanism for storing and retrieving collections.

A Reference Model based on these 4 major concepts was seen as being both feasible and able to relate to existing standards. These concepts existed at 4 environment levels similar to the stages in the External Reference Model.

A subsequent meeting in Darmstadt provided further input to the Reference Model including a desire to have more symmetry between output and input and an ability to have attributes jointly owned by the output primitive and the associated input device.

The Single Reference Model approach was accepted at a full ISO Meeting in Olinda, Brazil in October 1989. The major change at Olinda was to increase the number of environment levels from 4 to 5, the additional level being concerned with the viewing operation.

2.2.6 Current state of the Computer Graphics Reference Model

Despite the CGRM developed at Olinda being significantly more detailed than the Seeheim Model for UIMS, it is deficient in describing the interactions that occur between input and output. As the support system for a UIMS has to incorporate a graphics system, the complication is that a UIMS probably needs a Reference Model of similar or more complexity.

The problem addressed by the latest attempt at a CGRM was to provide sufficient detail of data and processes operating on data that the complex interactions between input and feedback could be explained and the composition of basic input tokens into tokens for submission to a higher level. Again, the relevance to UIMS is because the tokens delivered by the graphics system to the UIMS may be quite complex. Also, the UIMS needs to describe to the graphics system how semantic feedback occurs and at what level in the graphics system.

The major concepts in the current model are:

(1) *Composition*: at some level of abstraction, the information to be presented to the user.

(2) *Collection*: the filing system of graphical information that may need to be used in the composition. Icons, for example, that do not currently appear, would be stored in the collection.

(3) *Aggregation*: the memory of input from the lower level of abstraction.

(4) *Token Store*: the input tokens composed for presentation to the next higher level. For example, a set of input values in the aggregation could be composed into a single gesture token for submission to the next higher level.

Associated with the main data entities are processes that transform these items or provide the linkage between output and input. The model is able to both describe and provide a methodology for such complex tasks as multi-level feedback. A picture of the complete description of a level is shown in figure 2.

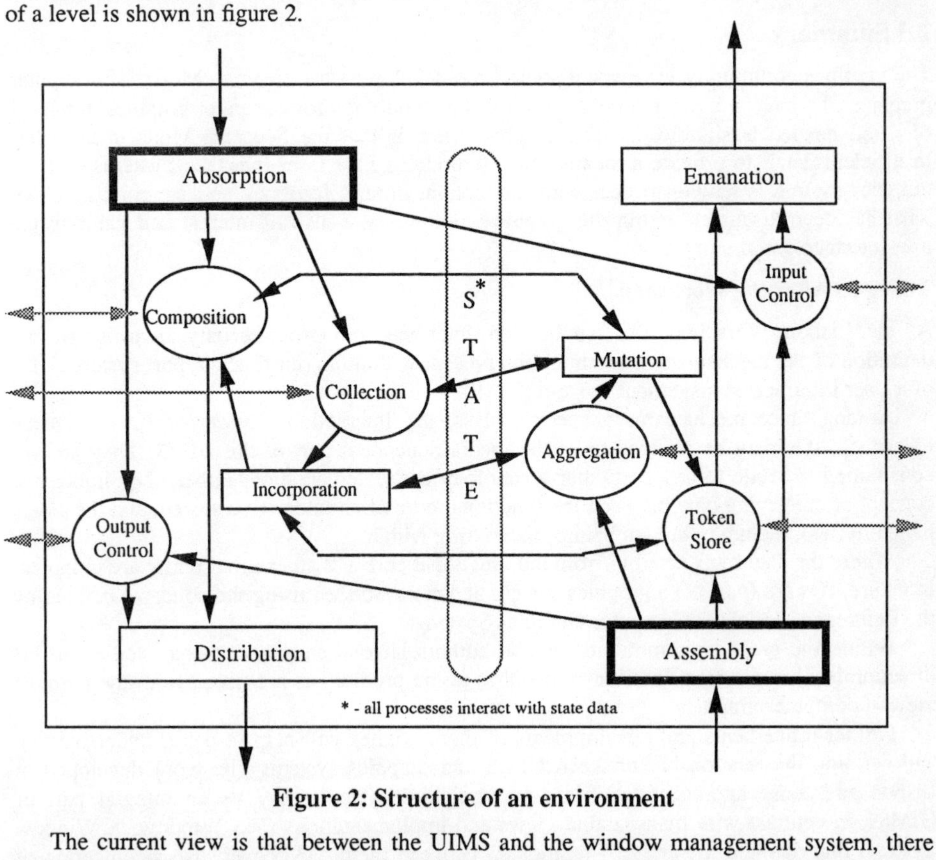

Figure 2: Structure of an environment

The current view is that between the UIMS and the window management system, there are conceptually five distinct levels of activity which are worth delineating and where picture capture may occur.

The five levels are:

(1) *Application*: the model of the output to be displayed is defined but the specific part to be displayed has not been bound.

(2) *Virtual*: the graphical output has been defined as a scene in a virtual coordinate space. This could be multi-dimensional (3 or more).

(3) *Viewing*: a particular view of the scene is taken as a picture to be displayed.

(4) *Logical*: aspects such as line thickness, colour are bound to the graphical picture to produce a device independent image.

(5) *Physical*: the virtual bit-map image is produced ready for the window manager to display.

Similar transformations occur as the input transforms from, for example, incremental mouse positions, via absolute location on a window to the integer representing the position of a menu hit.

Without this level of detail, it is not possible to define meaningful constraints and rules applicable to graphics. The position as far as UIMS are concerned is at least as complex. Consequently, the graphics community believe the Reference Model for a UIMS should be at least as complex as one level of the CGRM.

2.3 Summary

The graphics community have spent some time developing a Reference Model of computer graphics. To have sufficient detail to provide a methodology for computer graphics, the level of detail needed is significant. The graphics view is that the Seeheim Model clearly has insufficient detail to provide a meaningful Methodology for User Interface Systems. As the graphics system is having to deal with interaction, output, feedback and echoing, much of what has been discussed within the graphics community is also of interest and value to the user interface community.

Thoughts After the Workshop

At the Lisbon Workshop, the Application Interface Sub-Group briefly investigated the definition of the mechanisms that should be present within the run-time support system (UIS) of a User Interface Management System (UIMS) (see section 4.2).

Among those mechanisms a specific class, the Interaction Objects or IOs, has been identified. IOs may be referred to as the media dependent part of the UIMS. They are not constrained to relate to any particular technology or implementation; rather, they imbed the concept of conveying data between the functional core of an interactive system and the external entity(ies), including human beings, interacting with it.

Where the data transferred to/from the functional core and an external entity are graphical in nature, IOs are (part of) a graphics system and are described using the concepts defined by the Reference Model for Computer Graphics Systems.

Within the graphics community several authors have already undertaken studies in this direction [4,5], indicating possible approaches to the problem as perceived from the point of view of computer graphics.

Further refinements and developments of those studies will help in better understanding and defining the relationship between UIMS and graphics systems The work developed in Lisbon and those approaches indicate that graphics systems may be an integral part of UIMSs, in contrast with many actual views and implementations (MS Window, X Window System) that define a hierarchical relatioship between them. Moreover, the specification of such a relationship may definitely lead to the consideration that input/output data carried on over media such as voice and film recording are not in the domain of computer graphics but may be related to graphical data by transformation objects within the framework of UIMS.

References

(1) D.B. Arnold, G. Hall, G.J. Reynolds, "Proposals for Configurable Models of Graphics Systems", *Computer Graphics Forum,* **3***(3) pp. 201-208 (1984).*

(2) D.B. Arnold, D.A. Duce, G.J. Reynolds, "An Approach to the Formal Specification of Configurable Models of Graphics Systems", in *Proceedings of Eurographics 87,* ed. G. Marechal, North-Holland (1987).

(3) G.J. Reynolds, "A Token Based Graphics System", *Computer Graphics Forum,* **5***(2) pp. 139-146 (1986).*

(4) D.A.Duce, R.van Liere, P.J.W.ten Hagen, "An Approach to Hierarchical Input Devices" *Computer* Graphics **9**(1), pp. 15-26 (1990).

(5) G.Faconti, P.Paerno, "An approach to the formal specification of the components of an interaction", in *Proceedings of EUROGRAPHICS'90,* ed. C.E. Vandoni and D.A. Duce, North-Holland 1990.

Chapter 3

The Architectural Bases of Design Re-use

Gilbert Cockton[1]

1 Architectures: Attractive, Unignorable and (at Least) Four Dimensional

The architecture problem for interactive systems is a hard problem. Objective, rational and well-informed analysis of interactive architectures is rare. This is not all due to sloppy thinking. Much of it is due to the many obstacles to progress in the area of software for interactive systems. The topic is inherently slippery, because it is hard to get a grip with either our hands or our feet. The minute we think we have a grasp of the main issues, new technologies rain down on us and wash away the islands of firm ground on which we are standing. Part of the problem has undoubtedly been a lack of appropriate standards. The *GKS* standard took a conservative approach to interactive input (Rosenthal *et al.* 1982), and the *PHIGS* standard (Shuey *et al.* 1986) has added no significant developments for interaction[2].

The *de facto* X11 standard (Scheifler and Gettys 1986) has lead to some much needed stability, whatever its merits (increasing) and demerits (decreasing). Now that the ground under our feet has become firmer again, conceptual issues on requirements and design are more important. With all those X11 workstations and terminals out there there is a real chance that UIMSs *really will get used.* The motivation for getting architectures right is now stronger. We should not rely on random experimentation. We must be able to take a principled approach to tool design. There is a risk that the plethora of X11 terminals may result in something uncomfortably close to sitting thousands of chimpanzees in front of workstations to design and test the next generation of software tools for interactive systems. Principles must be articulated and consciously explored. They are not going to jump out of the next 700 user interface specification languages and stare us in the face.

Well-informed application and evaluation of principles requires concrete experience. Our experience of good User Interface Management Systems (UIMSs[3]) is limited. This is not due to a lack of systems. New ones appear every day, but like graphics systems at the time of the first Seillac workshop (Guedj and Tucker 1979), many systems have only one user site, and perhaps only one (occasional) user! Some of the key figures in the field have designed several very different systems over the last ten years. The conclusion must be that the best research groups have yet to produce something that they are really happy with. Thus potential users will not commit themselves to systems made obsolete through their developers' concentration of energies on new, radically different UIMSs.

The makers of UIMSs are making them rather than using them. The potential users of UIMSs are waiting for the technology to stabilise before committing themselves. This is not a situation in which hard facts about the benefits of different interactive architectures are going to emerge. Thus, for the moment, we can only bring analysis to bear on the problem. This is not ideal, but the process of testing even sketches of architectures against tricky examples *does* produce worthwhile results. Furthermore, as the list of things which a UIMS should and should not do grows, integrating principles become vital as organising concepts for this body of knowledge.

Only explicit principles can be accepted as evidence of progress in UIMS design. The key principles in UIMS design are architectural ones. The division of labour between tools in a UIDE (User Interface Design Environment) should be motivated by an attractive generic decomposition for interactive systems. An integrated tool set is impossible without a coherent architecture. Architectures are, of course, conceptual things, boxes and arrows on the page. They are not the hard code of an honest working system. So why should decent, hard-working toolsmiths be bothered with the flimsy architecture diagrams of those fancy city boys and girls?

---

[1] Author's address: Department of Computing Science, University of Glasgow, Glasgow, G12 8QQ, UK

[2] Pick paths are useful additions, but they were added because support for them already existed in the modelling hierarchy. They were not added as part of an intention to radically upgrade the GKS input model.

[3] The opinion of at least two working groups at Lisbon was that a UIMS comprises a run-time framework *and* a design environment (UIDE) — no design tools, no UIMS. This view was endorsed in plenary sessions and it is the original sense of the term as used at Seattle in 1982. Still, those who misuse the term UIMS will probably not read this volume!

Good short answers are not yet possible. Nor are definitive ones. A definitive answer would take the form of a commentary on some *good* architecture, but we do not yet have any architectures which are unreservedly good. Thus anyone who is willing to study architectures must take part actively in a research process — there are, as yet, few solid results which the software professional can consume passively. This chapter's main aim is to motivate the study of architectures for interactive systems as a proper object of explicit and separate study, independent of the implementation of specific UIMSs and interactive computer systems. As a preliminary, models must be distinguished from architectures.

A model is a starting point, an architecture is its first refinement. Both must be taken seriously. A tool set which is based on an architecture which is derived from a flawed model will have been inadequate from the very earliest stages of its design.

Models are the minimal form for software structures. An example is the *PIE* model used in formal methods work at York University (Dix and Runciman 1985, Dix 1988). The *PIE* model states that an interactive program is an *Interpretation* function which maps from *Programs* (command sequences) to *Effects*. The first refinement, the *RED-PIE* model, distinguishes between *Result* Effects and *Display* Effects. "So what?" is a common response! Well, what we can do is formalise a number of properties of interactive systems in terms of a *PIE* model. The *PIE* model thus has enough detail to express something useful.

Models are analytical devices (ten Hagen, chapter 1). They detail only what is needed for the purpose of some analysis. A model should be accurate and realisable, but not necessarily complete or detailed. Thus one model for separable interactive systems is *very* simple (Cockton 1987a) and doesn't do very much for the implementor with a UIMS to deliver at the end of the year. But implementors are beyond the analysis stage, and thus need to know the exact forms of components and their interfaces. These are generally left unspecified in a model. This avoidance of specific detail reduces the chance of premature commitment to assertions which cannot be justified or are obviously flawed in the general case.

It is a mistake to ask for too much detail from a model (and it is a sign that no distinction between models and architectures is in operation). There should be neither surprise nor disappointment that a model is inadequate for anything beyond the very earliest stages of tool set design. Clear identification of the requirements for algorithms, data structures and formalisms for each component is not possible in a general model. These requirements can only be derived from software structures with the detail which distinguishes architectures from models (Cockton 1990d).

Architectures detail component roles and inter-component interfaces. Models may be completely silent on the latter, or may only introduce examples of possible data flows in discussions outwith the model (e.g. Beech 1985). Detail, however, does not make architectures superior to models. Rather, models are logically prior to architectures. Most architectures bear some resemblance to existing models such as the Seeheim model (Green 1985a) or the *PAC* model (Coutaz 1989). Some issues can be explored at the model level, and thus *should* be explored at that level, since there is less detail to complicate the analysis. Other issues *must* be explored at the architecture level with its detailed roles for components and its initial detailing on inter-component interfaces.

The challenge is therefore to develop sound models and to use these models to design detailed architectures. Over-commitment is not the only problem. Under-commitment just pushes the real problems down from models onto architectures, and if the problems are not resolved there, then they could be pushed all the way down to the tool user, who must work around them or not use the UIMS.

The value and necessity of architectures are the themes of the next two sections of this chapter. The second half of the chapter explores these nice and needed structures.

2 Architectures Can be Attractive

The failures of the Seeheim model do not signal the failure of all re-usable software structures for interactive systems. What they do signal is the irrelevance of structures which are not accompanied by specific claims. Models and architectures should encapsulate one or more hypotheses about the consequences of using their structure. Such hypotheses do not concern the way things *really* are, but the way we want them to be.

The goal of UIMS research is to develop prescriptive structures. The cause of good design is not going to be helped by descriptive models alone, nor is computing research in the business of attempting a systematic induction of universal models from a large corpus of extant systems be they good, bad or indifferent. Such descriptive models as do exist are proposals (e.g. the *PIE* model) rather than systematic abstractions. Furthermore, the loss of detail in an empirical search for the lowest common denominator removes the bases for extending the model into an architecture.

Descriptive models need to fit the past, the present and the future. Desirable properties are expressed separately from the model as predicates (Dix and Runciman 1985) or rules (Coutaz 1989). The model itself must encompass the good, the bad and the ugly. Prescriptive architectures can be aloof. They are a means of changing the future. For architectures, properties should be 'hard-wired' into component and interface descriptions so that they are inherent in the prescribed structure. Re-usable architectures can thus package up good ways of decomposing a class of systems (here interactive ones). Software structures have the potential to guide designers along fruitful paths and away from the pitfalls of poor design decompositions. A good structure reduces the possibility of inflexible design and leaves designers free to concentrate on the important details of user interfaces. A bad structure forces the designer's hand, making it difficult to undo some design decisions and impossible to make others.

The use of prescriptive structures is a form of ***design re-use***. Normally, software design begins when the initial set of requirements has been gathered. At this point an intended system is decomposed into components. This decomposition involves problem solving. A model may guide problem solving. An architecture reduces the need for problem solving. System designers can select an existing pre-designed structure which is suitable for the intended system (because it was designed to so be). A universal architecture would completely remove the need for problem solving during the early stages of software design.

The alternative to a universal architecture is a family of re-usable alternative architectures. With such a family, the reduction in problem solving depends on the clarity of the pre-conditions for the selection of each architecture. If the choices are clear cut, architecture selection will not be much of a problem. If there are no grounds for choice, the architectures might just as well be ignored. Rather than waste time, a project team should design a custom architecture from scratch.

Re-usable structures can give every interactive system builder a head-start. In these structures, the top levels of the data-flow diagrams and structure charts (Sommerville 1989), or some object-oriented equivalent, have already been sketched out, if not filled out in their entirety[4]. Programming and command language implementors have long taken advantage of the classic decomposition of compilers into lexical analysers, parsers, code analysers and code generators. The viewing pipeline of computer graphics is another such stable architecture which has saved much effort for thousands of system designers (as may the new structures under development, e.g. Faconti, Chapter 2).

The existence of standard architectures in other parts of computing does not guarantee that they are feasible everywhere. In expert systems, the need for an application-independent inference engine remains a topic of some debate. The dialogue control component of many UIMSs has been subjected to similar doubt (Dance *et al.* 1987). Indeed, the possibility of re-usable architectures in ***any*** form is an open issue in HCI research.

Much of the quality of an interactive system can be traced to the software architecture which underlies it. It is this direct connection between quality and architectures which makes their study worthwhile despite the difficulties involved. R&D workers in a hurry to get tools out for interactive system construction may have little time for abstract arguments and discussions about the attractiveness of a few boxes with lines joining them together. Yet architectural issues cannot be ducked, even though discussions tend towards the slippery and the insubstantial. This is a reflection of our current ignorance and uncertainty. It is not an indication that re-use of architectures cannot be achieved.

3 Architectures Can't be Ignored

Anyone who decides to fiddle around with a bottom-up design of a UIMS is labouring under the illusion that computing is like botany and if we look around long enough wherever we happen to be we might find something new. Computer science is about deliberately making things, not finding them fortuitously. If we cannot talk about things before we make them, we are not engaging in design. If we do not engage consciously and publicly in design, then we are intellectually bankrupt.

A comparison of behavioural specification techniques will be used to illustrate the meaninglessness of any analysis of user interface design tools which lacks a full architectural context. Hill's Event Response Language (*ERL* — Hill 1987) is compared with a provisional notation for Generative Transition Networks (GTNs — Cockton 1990d). The details of either formalism are not important here — interested readers should consult the two references. Briefly, *ERL* uses a combination of production rules and boolean flags (with associated data). GTNs are networks which are described by a list of arc generators rather than a set of arcs. The format of a GTN arc generator is:

[4] One potential problem could be that existing ways of representing initial design decompositions from structured methods (i.e. data flow diagrams, structure charts) may be unsuitable forms of representation. It is interesting to note that several UIMS papers use alternative representations such as layer diagrams (Lantz 1987, Hill and Herrmann 1989). We may have to find new ways of representing generic software structures.

initial states: condition ⇒ actions
→ *next state expression*[5]

The *ERL* example used is a command interpreter which takes a command and single argument in any order (Hill 1987, p.245). Five *ERL* rules are used in the presentation of the example. Three GTN arc generators specify similar behaviour:

all: argEvent ⇒ setArg;
→ *same*

all: cmdEvent ⇒ setCmd;
→ *same*

all: gotArg & gotCmd ⇒ callLinkage; unsetArgAndCmd;
→ *same*

Behavioural specifications are generally the bridge between interactive media and semantic interpretation. The translation to a GTN specification[6] makes assumptions about the capabilities of other system components which manage input[7] and the interpretation of abstract commands[8]. Assumptions about command interpretation are implicit in the *callLinkage* action which passes the command and argument values to a linkage component and waits for the processing to complete. The *unsetArgAndCmd* procedure would then be called. This synchronisation results in one *ERL* rule needing no equivalent GTN arc generator. However, this implicit assumption is incompatible with the asychronous communication with interpretation components in the *SASSAFRAS*[9] example. Modelling this in a GTN specification would require an extra generator to respond to an end of processing event, as in the *ERL* specification. Alternatively, control of closure could be left to a linkage component leaving the behavioural control component to pass values from command, argument and 'ok' events straight to it. This would be specified in a single arc generator. However, other generators would be required to respond to the different error tokens which the linkage could pass back. Thus the central behavioural specification can be simplified by crude capabilities, and be complicated by sophisticated capabilities, in the same part of the architecture.

The translation from *ERL* to GTNs need not assume that input events are read sequentially from a queue. A list could also be scanned for groups of events. Access to a buffered event list lets us specify complete freedom of revision until a final 'ok' event. This can be described using only two generators:

all: okEventButIncomplete ⇒ notAllThereMessage; removeOk;
→ *same*

all: okEventAndComplete ⇒ removeEvents; passToLinkage;
→ *same*

The first generator traps early entry of 'ok' events when other inputs are missing, informing the user and removing the 'ok' event(s). The second generator uses a condition which is true when all three inputs are in the event buffer. In response, an action removes events and calls the linkage with the values of the last command and argument events. These operations show how sophistication in another component of an interactive systems' architecture reduces the behavioural specification. Here, the ability to search input media event lists and to remove arbitrary events has collapsed the behavioural specification[10].

There is considerable interaction between a behavioural specification, input management abstractions and the linkage abstraction. Sophistication or simplicity in any component may increase or decrease the complexity of control specifications. Conclusive comparisons of media, behavioural and linkage abstractions cannot be made if these abstractions are not placed in the context of a full interactive systems architecture. The fact that a behavioural component cannot achieve some function can only be discussed sensibly if we know whether another component can perform that function. The boundaries between appearance, behaviour and interpretation in interactive systems are such that it is not always essential that a specific component be allocated some specific function.

Progress in UIMS research is not just a question of homing up the capabilities of specific formalisms for display structures, for view management, for user interaction, and for linkage to underlying functionalities.

[5]I am currently exploring the use of regular expressions over node alphabets for specifying the endpoints of arc generators.

[6]The translation is not exact with respect to possible user action sequences in the *ERL* example — see (Cockton 1990d) for the equivalent version.

[7]Usually part of a presentation or graphical media component.

[8]Usually the function of a linkage, application interface model, semantic support or abstract command component.

[9]*SASSAFRAS* is the UIMS where *ERL* was first used (Hill 1986).

[10]The basic capabilities of the necessary rule-based event lists have been sketched elsewhere (Cockton and Sharratt 1987).

There is no shortage of candidates here (Cockton 1988, Cockton 1990b), but definitive comparisons are impossible without reference to an architectural context[11].

Scepticism about the attractions of re-usable architectures is thus not a sufficient reason for ignoring the architecture question. It cannot be ignored.

4 A Classification Scheme for Re-usable Architectures for Interactive Systems

The attractiveness and tenacity of re-usable architectures has been reflected in several attempts to compare and classify architectures. The first Seattle workshop (Thomas and Hamlin 1983) gave us the internal/external control distinction. Group reports at the Seeheim workshop (Pfaff 1985) further explored this distinction. The second Seattle workshop gave us several ways of relating a semantic support component to presentation and underlying application components (Dance *et al.* 1987).

The rest of this chapter introduces and applies a comprehensive scheme for classifying architectures for interactive software. Existing distinctions between architectures can be accommodated by this scheme. The comprehensiveness of the scheme is due to four broad dimensions:

orientation — this dimension concerns the levels of system decomposition which an architecture provides for directly. One level is the starting point for software designers, and thus orients them in a particular way.

topology — this dimension concerns the topology of component *inter-relation.* Architectures can be classified according to the graph structure of the allowed control and data flows between components.

component provision — architectures can be classified according to the rationale behind the choice of basic components.

control and data propagation — this dimension concerns the propagation of data exchanges between components. It differs from topology, as there the relationships which may exist between specific components are only *enumerated*. Here, the *nature* of the relationships which may exist between any two components are classified.

This scheme differs from others encountered in the literature. In one survey, user interface *tools*[12] are divided into toolkits and UIDSs (Myers 1989). Myers uses the (non-)provision of management facilities (for sequencing and integration with the underlying application) to discriminate between toolkits and UIDSs. Myers' other distinction rests on differences in approach to component configuration. However, the distinctions between language-based, graphical or automatic configuration are not architectural ones. They are two steps removed from architectures (Cockton 1990f). In the first step, we select abstractions for components (e.g. hierarchies for presentation, event-response systems for dialogue control). In the second step, we choose how to represent a chosen abstraction to the designer, and it is representational differences which organise Myers' survey. In other papers in this volume, both architectural and non-architectural dimensions are used to distinguish between UIMSs (e.g. Johnson *et al.* 1990). Issues of specification language, editing tools and other design facilities are orthogonal to architectural decisions. The scheme presented here therefore does not address differences such as configuration or design iteration in tool environments.

5 First Dimension — Orientation for Designers

Design is a problem solving activity. A software designer works within the structure provided by a software architecture. Good re-usable architectures reduce the need for problem solving at the earliest stages of design. The first dimension of architectures covers the nature of the residual design tasks which follow from adopting an architecture. The positions in this dimension represent different *orientations* for designers. These are due to the different levels at which components may be provided.

Figure 1 uses simplified structure diagrams to illustrate the differences between the levels at which components are provided. Components which are not provided by the architecture are unshaded. Light shading is used to indicate *basic* components which are provided directly by the architecture. Dark shading is used to indicate components which can be built using the components which are provided directly by the architecture.

[11] Another example of the problems with architectural uncertainty is the *Lean Cuisine* notation for menus (Cockton 1990e).

[12] Myers restricts UIMSs to *run-time systems* and thus does not divide UIMSs into toolkits and UIDSs, but a misreading that he does is becoming common in the literature. Myers' use of the term UIMS is not that used here.

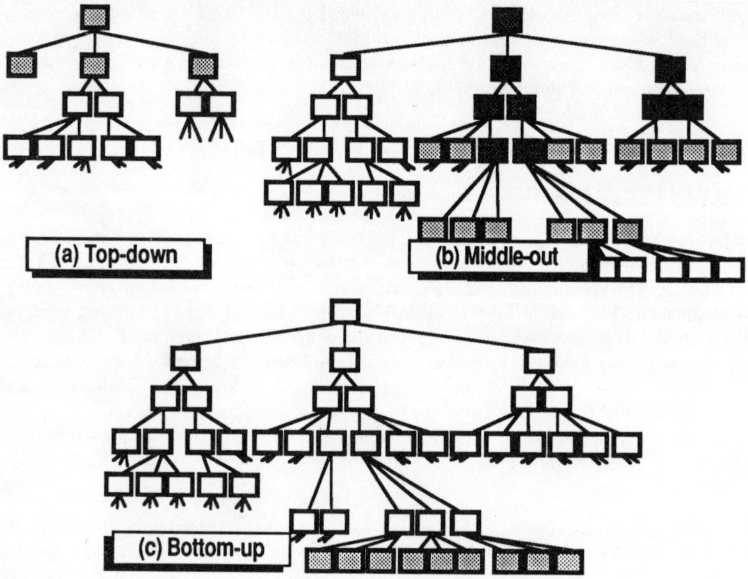

Figure 1: Forms of orientation with respect to software structure

In figure 1(a), the architecture provides a complete set of top level components. The orientation is *top-down.* In figure 1(b), the architecture supplies a set of lower level components and a high-level means of combining these components (perhaps recursively) to build up the components identified in a design for a specific application. The orientation here is *middle-out.* In figure 1(c), the 'architecture' provides a rich set of low to medium level components, but no fixed ways of combining them into higher level components. The orientation here is *bottom-up.* New components can be constructed, but a bottom-up orientation does not provide any means for this.

In a top-down approach, all the top level components are identified by the architecture, leaving designers with the task of configuring or instantiating them. Designers cannot (and supposedly do not need to) create new components, rather they only need to identify subcomponents. Where there can be more than one instance of a component in a top-down architecture (e.g. SERPENT's *View controllers* — Bass *et al.* 1990), designers have to decide how many instances of a component are required and when and how they will be created, and deleted. Such architectures are novel. Most top-down architectures allow only one instance of each component.

Generic top-down architectures, where new components cannot be created, are too restrictive for interactive systems design and construction. Their adoption has been due to the misplaced adoption of formal linguistic models (Kamran 1985). Lexical, syntactic and semantic elements are not the only elements of an interactive system and there would not be only instance of each of them. No honest analysis of a representative sample of interactive applications could *immediately* decompose each system into three homogeneous lexical, syntactic or semantic components. We can abandon the top-down view of the pipelined compiler architecture without renouncing the categories of formal language theory. Yes, there are lexical, syntactic and semantic components of interaction, but no, these are not the only principal components. This means that even where multiple instances of some components are allowed, a top-down architecture is going to be restrictive.

A middle-out orientation is more humble than a top-down one. It recognises that we cannot immediately decompose all interactive systems into a fixed set of top level components. Instead, the higher levels of the final software structure will reflect a specific design rather than embody an generic, application-independent architecture. In a middle-out approach, the designer builds up, rather than fills out, an interactive system. The designer is supported, but not coerced. The basic components may be combined in prescribed ways to form more complex components until the top levels of the application are reached.

A middle-out architecture need not support the construction of all higher level components. Instead it can provide the means for integrating 'foreign' components. In figure 1(b), the leftmost sub-tree is composed of 'foreign' components which are provided for, but given no further support, by the architec-

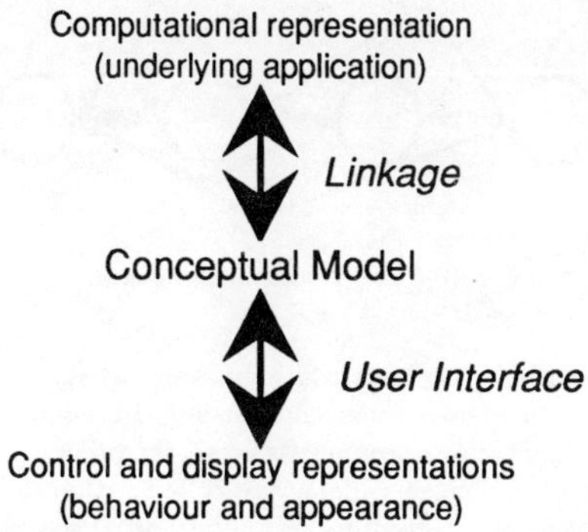

Figure 2: A software model which mirrors model-based design

ture. The most common foreign component in a UIMS-based interactive system will be the underlying application, but in R&D environments, intelligent user support components will be constructed using AI technologies rather than UIMS ones (Totterdell and Cooper 1986). An architecture must not prescribe the orientation of foreign components. They may be be built top-down (e.g. with DBMS tools), middle-out (e.g. with UNIX shell scripts) or bottom-up (e.g. with a library of statistical functions).

A middle-out orientation optimises the quality of high-level design, not its automation. For interactive system design, partially automated tasks which do not impair performance (i.e. quality of artefact) are preferable to full automation which does impair performance. Middle-out orientations let designers choose their own approach to design decomposition, rather than impose one which has no real legitimacy. Middle-out orientations are thus compatible with the common design approach of devising a conceptual model and then designing two representations: a computational one for the underlying application and a concrete one for controls and displays. Design methods which fit this pattern will be called *model-based*. Their key characteristic is the primacy which they give to the constructs which users will manipulate during planning and problem-solving. The actual concrete representation of these concepts is a secondary issue.

Figure 2 shows a model for interactive systems which is compatible with such design methods. The model has two explicit processes for mapping into and out from the components of the conceptual model (i.e. objects and actions). A *linkage* process maps between the conceptual model and the underlying application. A *user interface* process maps between the conceptual model and the control and display representations of the system image[13].

In model-based designs, all underlying computation and concrete presentations are related in some way or another to components of the conceptual model. These relations will be called *vertical* relations. They run along the processes (user interface and linkage) in figure 2. *Horizontal* relations, by contrast run across the components of the conceptual model and the processes in the interactive systems' model.

The principal components of a design are the components of the conceptual model, rather than the monolithic homogeneous components of top-down orientations. Generic top-down architectures introduce problems during the high levels of software design. They force designers to divide their designs immediately into processing categories rather than conceptual ones. Any initial model-based design must be restructured.

Object-oriented software design makes sense as it can respect the application-specific categories of a conceptual model. Architectures with a purely top-down orientation *must* cut across these application-dependent categories, since to be universal, top level decompositions must be application-independent. Such architectures force designers to factor out appearance, behaviour, interpretation and semantics within a rigid and monolithic structure. In the process, the logical lines of design, running outward in two directions from the components of the conceptual model to computational and user interface representations, are dismantled. This complicates the re-use of components which are common to several systems. In top-down architectures, the user-interface and functionality of each conceptual component must firstly be picked out of the donor system's processing components, and they must then be integrated into the top level components of the recipient system. With a middle-out orientation, complete objects can be slotted in and out of a system.

A middle-out system is superior to a purely top-down approach, but it is not without its limitations. For some adaptations to an interactive system, horizontal lines of integration are more advantageous. In a

[13] The underlying application is a third process. This gives us my three component model (Cockton 1987a).

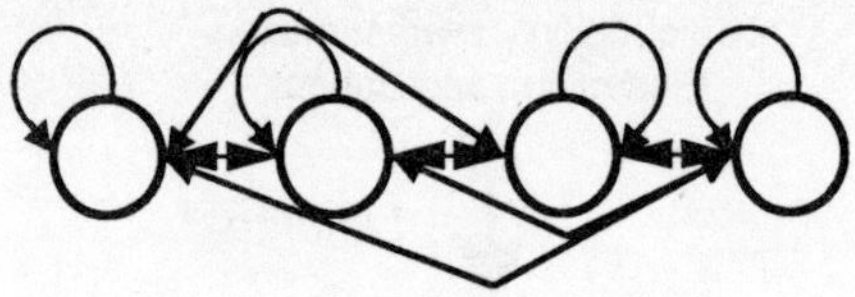

Figure 3: Fully-connected graph

layered top-down architecture, changing the presentations from one style to another can involve no more than straightforward changes to the presentation component. In a middle-out architecture, it may be necessary to pick through the presentation components of all the objects in the system.

There are design as well as maintainance problems associated with middle-out architectures. A system which is designed solely on the basis of representations of conceptual components is only suited for expert use[14]. Vertical lines of integration cannot capture the *coherence* of an interactive system. The components of a conceptual model are not mutually independent. A system is more than the sum of its parts. The weakness of object-oriented design is that the coherence of a system can only be emergent. There is no encouragement to encapsulate the logic of a system as a whole in specialised meta-objects. Only a top-down orientation can capture the way in which conceptual components mesh together to provide for the tasks which a system supports. If users can only see a system as its conceptual components, then the system is badly designed. Users need to know what they can *do* with a system — basic knowledge of the conceptual components themselves is not enough. Users may need on-line support to develop an appreciation of a system's potential. Architectures with a purely middle-out orientation do not provide well for this support.

A middle-out orientation lets designers build up to objects that combine the user interface and functionality for each conceptual component. Supportive systems need to incorporate knowledge of the *relations* between conceptual components (objects and actions). Such relations are horizontal rather than vertical. They cut across logical design decompositions. Use of these relations during an interactive session requires system components which can look at the states of several logical objects, perhaps on an *ad-hoc* basis.

An ideal architecture on the orientation dimension would combine top-down and middle-out orientations. Normal, user-driven and error-free interaction would be supported by the middle-out components of the architecture. Supportive components such as plan recognisers (Davenport and Weir 1986) would be top-down components with access to all the normal processing within the middle-out region of the architecture. Task-based or context-sensitive help components are a further example of components which need to exist at the highest level of a system decomposition.

In such a dual orientation, the application-dependent components of an interactive system would be configured and combined in a middle-out manner. However, re-usable components with a high degree of application-independence would be configured as top level components. The thorough integration of a system for the benefit of its users would thus be guided by a top-down orientation.

Nothing has yet been said about a bottom-up orientation. This is the approach of the *toolkit* and it provides not an architecture, but a builder's yard. For architectures we require more than an enumeration of components. Bottom-up orientations do not directly and explicitly support the *construction* of interactive systems. They thus have no place in the discussion of architectures for interactive systems (or in anything except discussion of run-time support in UIMSs). To be a software *structure*, a collection of development resources must be committed to some form of combination. Thus toolkits, which provide neither 'glue' nor patterns for combining their components (Coutaz 1985), are not structures. Rather they are aggregates and it is left to software professionals to devise an embracing structure for their application. The next section explores the forms of structure which re-usable architectures can provide.

6 Second Dimension — the Topology of Component Inter-relation

Two components are inter-related if there is a direct control or data link between them. The lexical analyser and the code optimiser of a compiler are thus not inter-related.

The inter-relations within a software structure can be modelled as a directed graph. The dimension of inter-relation is based on graph concepts (Carré 1979). Figure 3 illustrates the maximum extent of inter-relation — the fully connected graph. Each component is only linked to all the other components

[14] i.e. however simple the system, end-users must understand it fully to exploit it to the full.

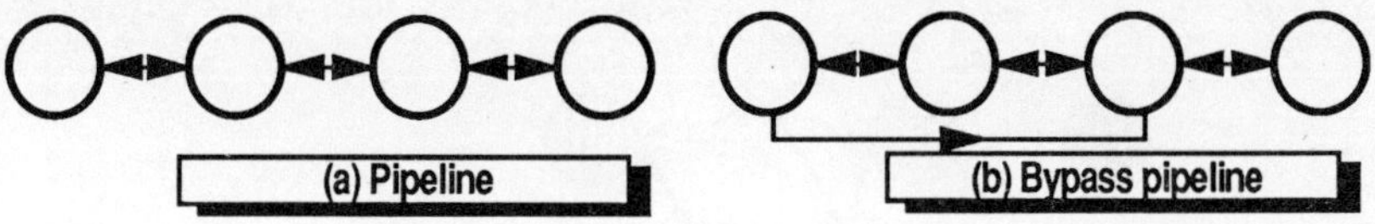

Figure 4: Pipeline structures

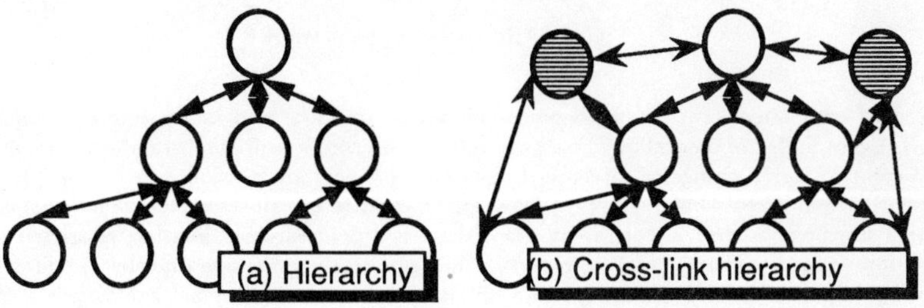

Figure 5: Hierarchical structures

(including itself) in the graph. Architecturally, fully connected structures are not satisfactory (Trefz and Ziegler 1990, discussion). If there are control and data links between all components, designers may be overwhelmed by the resulting choices. Such architectures do little to miminise problem solving during early design. Fully connected structures proscribe nothing and are thus bound to lead the unwary designer into problems. They are an example of a bad structure which pushes problems onto the tool user. They are free with any bottom-up approach which only provides components! The chances are that components can be combined in any way, even though some ways would be better than others.

Positions on the second dimension are due to different restrictions on the connectivity between components. The most restrictive graph structure is the *pipeline* (figure 4(a)). In a pipeline, there are two components which are only linked to one other component (the end points) and the rest are only linked to the two components adjacent to them. Pipelines are tied very closely to a top-down orientation, as it is difficult to imagine a middle-out architecture which could only build up to a simple pipeline at the top level. Pipeline components are *processing stages*. One can envisage an architecture which allows the creation of processing stages (as in the ANSA model), but it would be perverse to allow the creation of new stages while limiting their component inter-relation to a pipeline structure[15].

The first relaxation of restrictions on connectivity results in a *bypass pipeline* (figure 4(b)). A bypass pipeline is, roughly, a pipeline plus links between non-adjacent components. There is thus a partition of links into pipeline and bypass classes. This rough definition does allow fully-connected structures, but informally, every bypass requires a justification, and this will prevent a slide into full connectivity.

The next relaxation of connectivity restrictions allows components to be structured as a *hierarchy* (figure 5(a)). Each component except bottom (leaf) components has links to its child components, and all except the top (root) component have a single link to their parent component. There are thus paths from the root to each leaf via descendant components. Each leaf is at the end of only one path. It is this restriction which prevents cycles within the structure, and thus full connectivity.

Hierarchies are common in interactive systems' architectures. They follow immediately from a middle-out orientation. Building up by combining components into higher level components will result in a hierarchy, as each composed group results in an embracing parent component, which in turn can be a child of a higher level component. Recent toolkits which follow the device model of interaction (Anson 1980), such as *InterViews* (Linton *et al.* 1989), also result in a hierarchical topology based on only one component type — the widget.

A hierarchy is compatible with either a purely top-down orientation or a purely middle-out one. Pure hierarchies are not compatible with a dual orientation. That approach requires requires links from the generic top-level components into the application-specific components. Such links would result in a *cross-link hierarchy* (figure 5(b)).

Cross links allow integrating components (filled in figure 5(b)) to have direct links into the hierarchy of standard objects. No other cross-links are allowed (e.g. between unfilled components in figure 5(b)), and thus a fully connected structure is not possible. The restriction relies on a partitioning of components

[15] The ANSA model allows non-pipeline structures (Hoffner *et al.* 1990, discussion).

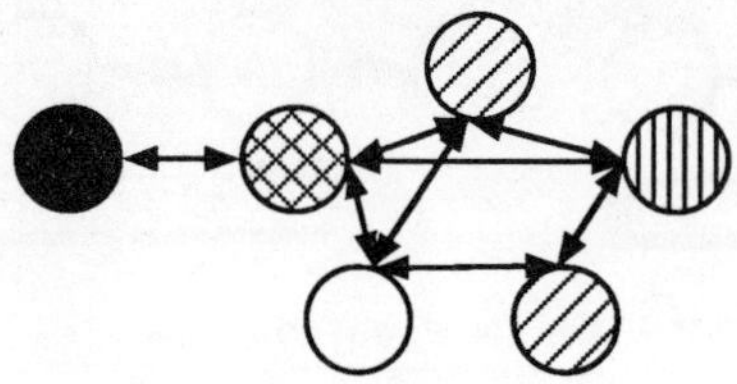

Figure 6: Restricted cycle network

into standard components (in the main design hierarchy, unfilled) and integrating components (at the top-level). Cross-links are only allowed between integrating components and standard components.

More complex partitionings or categorisations of components are possible which result in a restricted structure other than a cross-link hierarchy. These structures will be called ***restricted cyclic networks*** (figure 6), as there may be no underlying hierarchy. As with cross-link hierarchies, links are restricted on the basis of a partitioning or categorisation of components. In figure 6, there are five categories, represented by no fill, a solid fill and vertical, left slanting and right slanting hatching (diamond hatching is a combination of left and right slant). Solid filled components may only be linked to left slanting hatched components. Unfilled and vertically hatched components may only be linked to right slanting hatched components.

In existing architectures, there are linking rules that: interpretation components should not manage input events; control components should not twiddle with low level data structures in the underlying application; presentation objects should not manage gross task sequences. However, it is not easy to draw up well-defined rules which are not too restrictive. There are many examples where the responsibilities of each component are not clear. Should a behavioural component enable and disable parts of composite presentations or should a presentation manager do this? Should an interpretation component access display structures directly, or should all updates be explicit in a behavioural specification? How much feedback should be performed in a presentation component without involving a global controller responsible for the overall flow of interaction in a session?

Whatever the answers may be, the route to all answers is clear. It is by exploring different inter-connections within an interactive system that the appropriate links, and thus the requirements for any formalisms, can be determined. Yet, laying down rules on inter-component connectivity is not, currently, a straightforward task. The above analysis suggests that cross-link hierarchies seem preferable to more general restricted cycles, as they have one simple rule: non-hierarchical links should be justified by the need for integrating objects in interactive systems. There is also a close compatibility between a dual orientation and cross-link hierarchies. Architectures seem bound to contain hierarchical sub-structures and thus cross-link hierarchies with as few non-hierarchical links as possible are the preferred topology for component inter-relation.

7 Third Dimension – Component Provision

An architecture provides designers with a structure and an orientation. It also provides a set of components within its structure. The motives, analogies or theories behind the selection of basic components vary, and it is this variation which gives rise to the third dimension of component provision.

Two architectures may be identical with respect to orientation and component inter-relation, and yet differ in the components which they provide. The choice of components may be due to a single rationale, but it is possible to derive an architecture from several rationales. Positions on this dimension are thus sets of values rather than single values.

The most common approach to component choice arises from an information processing rationale. The basic components are distinct stages in the transformation of user input to application functions and their parameters, and from application results to media updates. The decomposition into processing stages may be motivated by a language metaphor, or by an abstraction of the structure of processing in interactive programs. Note that this choice is orthogonal to the choice of orientation. It is possible to combine either a top-down or a middle-out orientation with linguistic or other information flow components. The difference lies in the level at which these components come into operation.

Information flow architectures have an internal structure which bears no resemblance to anything which end-users perceive. End-users are not expected to have any understanding of the separate processing stages. The approach is wholly technical. What end-users experience will emerge from the designer's configuration. There will be no one-to-one correspondence between user concepts and system components at the information flow level (designers may build up to user constructs). Other component selection strategies are more closely tied to user phenomenology, and may thus be grouped under the heading of user-centred component provision.

7.1 User-Centred Component Provision

The earliest user-centred components were based on idealised *interaction cycles* (Benbasat and Wand 1984). In these structures, components manage a specific stage in a human-computer transaction: a prompt, an input, a validation, some feedback, an echo or a result. Such structures are very common in graphics standards for interactive input (Rosenthal *et al.* 1982). Other structures derived their components from global functions within an interactive system such as help, customisation, history, naming and security (Beech 1985). This *functional* approach (in the classical architectural sense) has form follow function — the components match the application-independent functions of the system. The interaction cycle and functional approaches result in two very different varieties of user-centred architecture.

The final variation on user-centred components is based directly on the objects which users can interact with or otherwise encounter. In the Macintosh environment, end-users encounter applications, documents, menus, radio buttons, printers and networks. These objects are supported directly by the components of the MacApp framework (Schmucker 1986). This component selection strategy can be called the *copycat* approach, as in its pure form it only provides components which correspond directly to entities which end-users encounter during their interaction. The Brown Workstation Environment provides a wide range of such components (Reiss and Stasko 1990).

This copycat approach is inherently conservative. It only provides for things which have already been designed. In its pure form, it cannot support the creation of radically novel interaction objects and support facilities. The functional and interaction cycle approaches are also conservative, in that only identified functions and points of the interaction are supported. Indeed, all user-centred approaches are limited to components which users have experienced. The possible configurations of components are limited by their providers' experience and imagination, as well as by parameterisation mechanisms which limit flexibility (Cockton 1987b).

7.2 Summary

The one criterium for choosing a purely technical or a user-centred approach to component provision is the extent of expected innovation. User-centred components increase productivity at the expense of innovation. Architectures for R&D environments need components at a level below the constructs which users encounter. Innovation is only possible if designers are building up from information flow or language processing components. Pre-fabrications of familiar objects are not a basis for innovation. A middle-out orientation can thus be heavily constrained by a specific provision of components.

8 Fourth Dimension – Propagation of Control and Data

The last main dimension identified in this analysis addresses differences in the way changes in state are propagated between system components.

The commonest form of inter-component communication is the subprogram call. Here one component directly requests a service from another. Message-passing in the object-oriented paradigm is essentially the same form of control (although it may be asychronous). This form of propagation will be called *direct request*. The normal relation between components is one where most components are servers that provide services to a client controlling component.

The first departure from direct calls in UIMS work was due to developments in knowledge representation languages from Artificial Intelligence work. *Active values* have been used in a number of systems in last five years (Henderson 1986, Hudson 1987, Myers 1988). By updating a *slot* (or *cell*), changes in control and data values can be propagated to interested components. This propagation is controlled by the slot. Slots often correspond to conceptual components. When this is the case, the slots form the interface between the user interface and the underlying semantics of a system. This form of propagation will be called *direct slot update*. The resulting inter-component links are more declarative than procedural, but the process of propagation is not completely automated in this style of communication.

An even less focussed form of control is *internal event* generation. Here a component may raise an event which another component responds to. The *SASSAFRAS* UIMS (Hill 1986) used a local event broadcast mechanism to manage the distribution of internal events. However, systems which use unaddressed events can be difficult to understand and more directed addressing schemes are now being explored (Carlsen *et al.* 1990). Even so, the flow of control may not be as clear as with direct slot updates, where a specific slot is named and the response to it is clearly associated with the slot.

The most declarative form of inter-component commmunication is based on constraints between the different components of an interactive system. Propagation is completely *automatic* in this approach. Constraints between conceptual components and their different concrete and computational representations are expressed as logical conditions. When a change of value causes a constraint to be broken, action is taken to restore the constraint (Borning and Duisberg 1986). Considerable processing may take place in order to restore a constraint. This may be due to the re-representation of a new conceptual value in either the underyling application or the user interface. It may also be due to the translation of changed values in the user interface or underlying application into updates to the values of conceptual components. Slot updates and constraints are clear about the flow of specific transfers, unlike the internal event approach.

The relationship between constraint managers and other components is a master-slave rather than a client-server one. Client-server and master-slave relationships are the current extremes of the propagation dimension. As inter-component communication becomes more declarative along this dimension, links become processing units rather than simple data channels. This results in architectures where the 'glue' between components may be more complicated than the components themselves. Client-server architectures have many simple links under the control of specific components and the links between components are inseparable from the configuration of the client component. In master-slave architectures, designers explicitly configure links instead of control components. The actual master constraint manager is driven by the link configurations and the current state of linked components.

Direct slot update and automatic propagation are the preferred positions on this last dimension for standard information and control exchanges. Global components could use several approaches. It is difficult to prefer one approach to another, as experience is limited. At present, more systems use slots than constraints, and I know of no reported problems with the slot approach. Constraints on the other hand, are associated with the specification problems which are common in rule-based systems (Bass *et al.* 1990, discussion). Rule-synergy has been a problem with expert systems and it is likely to be a problem in constraint-based UIMSs as well. However, there is something attractive about the possibility of treating constraints as objects in themselves which may be re-used in different designs. This dimension also has implications for configuration, since pre-defined constraints can be manipulated in a graphical environment (e.g *ARK*, Smith 1987).

Analytical comparison is thus equivocal, and therefore a better understanding of this dimension will only follow disciplined experimentation with each approach.

9 Applying the Classification Scheme

The scheme makes previous distinctions such as internal/external control seem detailed and narrow. For internal and external control, all control links between application and user interface components are unidirectional. The direction is from the underlying application to the user interface for internal control, and from the user interface to underlying application for external control. Mixed control results from bi-directional links which do not use a form of propagation which blocks (e.g. some direct request forms) requests in a component which is providing a service to another.

The relationships between semantic support, presentation and (underlying) application components which were discussed at the second Seattle workshop are not architectural. They involve the configuration and not the provision or inter-relation of components. The components which could be configured were fixed for the purposes of discussion. The analysis was based on different combinations of similar configurations in adjacent components (Dance *et al.* 1987).

The scheme thus places previous distinctions between UIMSs into a wider context. The applicability of the classification scheme will be further demonstrated by applying it to some well known examples. The examples are grouped, firstly, by orientation, and then secondly, by topology. Differences in component provision and control and data propagation are noted within each of these subsections.

9.1 Top-Down Oriented Architectures

There are no simple pipeline or cross-link hierarchy architectures with a top-down orientation. The former would be too restrictive. The latter could draw little advantage from its component structure as a top-down orientation would prevent that.

9.1.1 Bypass Pipelines

This group of architectures can be regarded as specialisations of the Seeheim model. In the Seeheim model, a single bypass is allowed which links the presentation component to the application-interface model (Green 1985a; ten Hagen, Chapter 1). Component provision is usually motivated by an information flow rationale, often based on language stages. Direct request propagation is the norm. Thus in the *RAPID*

UIMS (Wasserman *et al.* 1986), the dialogue control component calls the presentation and application interface components at different points in an interaction.

9.1.2 Hierarchies

Top-down hierarchies are more common in methods than architectures (e.g. *SUPERMAN* methodology — Yunten and Hartson 1985). It is difficult to imagine a fixed hierarchical structure of re-usable components which is more than a few levels deep. A component may subdivide into a hierarchy, and this is common in control components in Seeheim style architectures. *RAPID* uses Augmented Transition Networks, and thus has a hierarchical sub-component structure below the top-level dialogue control component (Wasserman *et al.* 1986). However, the other processing stages of top-down architectures do not have such straightforward decompositions. Component provision is usually motivated by an information flow rationale, but interaction cycles are used for user interface leaves of a *SUPERMAN* hierarchy (Hix and Hartson 1986). Direct request propagation is the norm.

9.1.3 Restricted Cycle Networks

MacApp (Schmucker 1986) is the best known example of a restricted cycle network with a top-down orientation. Links between all components are possible, but there is an advised structure which associates views with windows, windows with documents and documents with the application. As there can be multiple instances of each component (except the application component), these restrictions do not result in a pipeline structure. MacApp uses direct request propagation between copycat components drawn from the Macintosh style guide (Apple 1985).

9.2 Middle-Out Oriented Architectures

Combining a middle-out orientation with a pipeline structure would be perverse. Full exploitation of a middle-out orientation requires a hierarchical structure or a restricted cycle network. There are no examples of the latter in the literature with which I am familiar.

The *PAC* model made an early break with top-down orientations (Coutaz 1987). The best of current practice (e.g. *TUBE*, Hill and Herrmann 1989) follow the *PAC* model in combining a middle-out orientation with a hierarchical structure. The components provided are based on an information flow analysis (presentation, control and abstraction for *PAC*, appearance, behaviour and semantics for *TUBE*).

The *PAC* model does not address control and data propagation. *TUBE* uses two approaches for control and data propagation. Behavioural modules, written in *ERL* (Hill 1987), use internal events for communication via the local event broadcast mechanism. Other parts of the system may be related via constraints.

9.2.1 Cross-Link Hierarchies

The *DIAMANT* UIMS combines standard media manager hierarchies with a global dialogue manager, a representation manager and an underlying application. Links are not allowed between media managers and the underlying application (Trefz and Ziegler 1990). In the case of graphics, objects in the media-managers are built from user-centred components based on the *InterViews* toolkit (Linton *et al.* 1989). *DIAMANT* thus combines copycat and information flow approaches to component provision. Direct requests are used for control and data propagation.

9.3 Comments on the Classifications

Existing systems can be described economically using the scheme developed in this chapter. A complete survey has not been attempted (but is left as an exercise for the reader!) Still, the examples do indicate that the scheme can be applied to existing systems and models.

10 Yet Another Structure for Interactive Systems

The classification scheme can be used to sketch out the beginnings of a new architecture for interactive systems. This move from classification to generation is made possible by the prescriptions made for some dimensions. As far as the individual positions adopted on each dimension are concerned, there is little originality. What is original is the combination of choices.

By adopting positions on orientation, component inter-relation and component provision, the structure goes beyond a descriptive model. The basic components of user interface objects (UIOs) are identified,

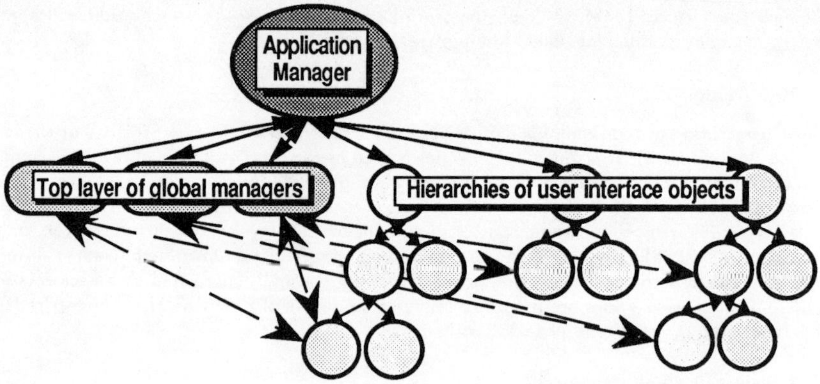

Figure 7: A prescriptive structure for interactive systems

but there is no commitment to specific global managers. The motivation behind component provision can be heterogeneous, and thus partial decisions are possible with respect to this dimension.

By failing to enumerate global managers, and by failing to to adopt a position on control and data propagation, the structure is not an architecture. Decisions on these dimensions must be made before an architecture can be completed. Components cannot be firmly defined until inter-component interfaces are defined, and this is not possible while there is equivocation on control and data propagation.

The new structure is presented in figure 7. There is a dual orientation, with middle-out hierarchies of user interface objects (UIOs) and a top-down layer of global managers. Each UIO hierarchy corresponds to a separate thread of end-user control. Components are inter-related within a cross-link hierarchy. Possible global components with cross-links into the UIO hierarchy are:

a view manager which maintains consistency between user interface representations and objects in the underlying application. The application manager notifies the view manager of changes. The view manager then communicates with each relevant UIO. How view updates are propagated is undecided in the structure, as there is no committment to direct slot update, internal events, automatic propagation, direct requests, or even, for that matter, to view managers themselves.

a tailoring manager which supports end-user modification of the user interface. While each UIO could have its own tailoring mode (e.g. *metaViews* in ***InterViews***, Linton *et al.* 1989), this may be inefficient and result in inconsistencies. Without some central facility, there is no way of propagating representational changes to new instances of UIOs. Tailoring facilities are thus best centralised in a group of control panels in a UIO hierarchy dedicated to the tailoring manager.

a passive help manager which provides context-sensitive help and therefore must refer directly to the current state (and ideally appearance) of UIOs in help screens or windows. As users may be able to alter the appearance of UIOs, the passive help manager needs to be able to access tailoring information. This manager may also provide help which is specific to the current state of the system. This requires cross-links to UIO hierarchies. A passive help manager would need its own UIO hierarchy to provide an interface for end-users.

a passive recorder which provides for history-based user support. Object specific history mechanisms do have their uses, but they are not enough. A global history facility requires a passive monitor which records user actions on all UIOs in the active hierarchies. Undoing, journalling and playback could also exploit the monitoring facilities of a passive recorder. Journalling may have to take place at a number of levels from the key-stroke level up to the conceptual level. This would require considerable processing within this component. A passive recorder would need its own UIO hierarchy to provide an interface for history and playback commands.

an active monitor for mixed-initiative dialogues (Carbonell 1970). History and passive help facilities are user-driven. Experimental systems provide active support for users. Users need not ask for this help, it will be offered automatically. Such 'intelligence' requires monitors which process information, rather than merely store or classify it. Active monitors detect patterns of end-user interaction, such as common errors, misconceptions, inefficient usage and abandoned commands. Active monitors may use task models (Johnson *et al.* 1988) or application models (Adhami *et al.* 1987).

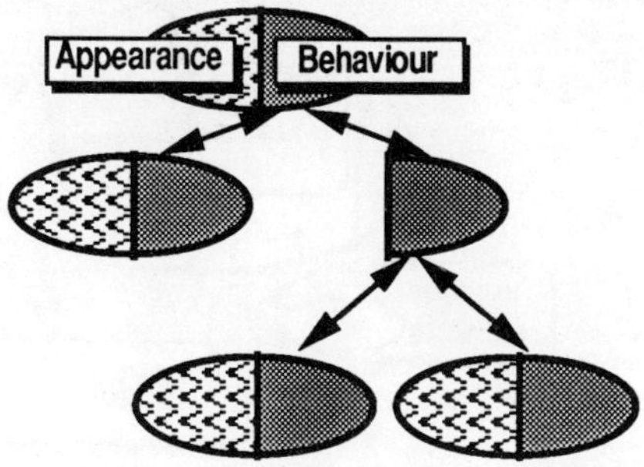

Figure 8: Basic components in the user interface object hierarchy

an active helper which uses the knowledge bases in the active monitor to provide active support for end-users in difficulty. System-initiated dialogues may assist users in completing a task sequence, instruct them about system functions, draw their attention to short cuts (Owen 1986), or explain the causes of repeated errors. Such a component needs full access to UIO hierarchies to allow it to refer to current and previous states of the system and the representations of objects.

All these components except the first are concerned with user support. Experimental user support features usually require non-standard architectures with monitors and modifiers tapping the normal flow of interaction (Cockton 1990c). The provision of global managers in a cross-link hierarchy represents a compromise between the unique architectures of AI-based systems (e.g. Benyon 1984) and the modeless instance hierarchies of existing object-oriented architectures.

As much work on user support is still experimental, the structure only provides support for global monitoring and modification. No specific provision of global components can be recommended at the moment. Even view management could be delegated to the UIO hierarchies. The structure supports both distributed and centralised strategies rather than one or the other. What is common to all global managers is that they will perform specific functions, and so in this part of the architecture, a functional approach to component provision is taken.

Within the UIO hierarchy, only two basic components are sketched out. Their provision is motivated by an information flow rationale. UIOs have two major components (Figure 8). Their appearance (as regards both input and output) is orthogonal to their behaviour. Appearance can be controlled by specific media managers. The provision of components here follows the existing categories such as audio, speech, graphics, video and haptic media. Behaviour involves state and time. The behaviour of a UIO is a sequence of state transitions in time. The state and the transitions between states need to be supported by the behavioural components in UIOs.

The adoption of an information flow rationale does not rule out some copycat provision of components. Widgets and other such components could be provided as 'black box' UIOs which may be slotted into a UIO hierarchy, but not further decomposed. However, there seems to be neither architectural nor design advantages in this, since widgets can just be regarded as re-usable UIOs. Access to their internal components allows more flexibility than is possible with simple parameterisation mechanisms (Cockton 1987b). However, commercial considerations may require support for 'black box' widgets and display mechanisms (Frankowski *et al.* 1990, discussion), even though this may preclude their being monitored by global components.

In figure 8, UIOs are composed via their behavioural components. This follows the *PAC* model (Coutaz 1987), where hierarchies are formed by delegation by control components to subordinate PACs. There is at least one other possibility, and it is not proscribed by the structure: constraints between appearance components may augment the global view manager, as in the TUBE system (Herrmann and Hill 1989).

The TUBE composite object architecture distinguishes behaviour from semantics. This current structure makes no such distinction in the UIO hierarchy. All functional interpretation of user actions takes place in the application manager. This interpretation is a mapping to the underlying semantics which are invariant across alternative user interface representations. Immediate interpretation for the purposes of semantic feedback takes place in the UIO hierarchies, but this is regarded as part of the *behaviour* of a UIO. A component is 'semantic' if and only if it implements the ultimate meaning of a user action or system presentation. Feedback, while meaningful, may indicate states which are not legal in the underlying application. The only clean cut-off between interactive behaviour and underlying semantics is the set of conceptual components. No provision is thus made for 'semantics' in the user interface. The user

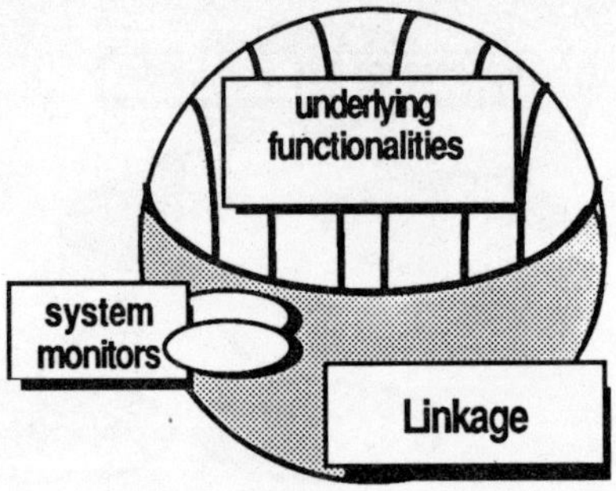

Figure 9: Possible subcomponents for application managers

interface delegates the full and final meaning of all significant user actions to the application manager, although what happens there may be modelled in the global monitoring and modification components[16].

UIO hierarchies are enabled and disabled by both the application manager and parent UIOs. Each hierarchy corresponds to a thread of user control. These are either enabled at start up, or in response to user actions. Threads are also disabled in response to user actions.

As a structure for *interactive systems* rather than just their user interfaces, subcomponents of the application manager are also outlined. Figure 9 presents an application manager as a linkage, a set of system monitors, and a collection of underlying functionalities.

The linkage is structured around the conceptual components of the system. UIO hierarchies are associated with specific objects or actions when they are enabled. The linkage also associates conceptual components with objects, functions or procedures in the underlying functionalities[17].

The final subcomponents of the application manager are *system monitors*. These perform the same holistic functions as global components in the user interface. Specific functions such as *integrity* and *security* cannot be provided by isolated conceptual components. The integrity of the system is a function of the state of all the conceptual components. Thus, following a deletion of the last object in a document, there should be no currently selected object, otherwise the system could fail on the next delete or other operation on the currently selected object. Another example is the disabling of global defaults (such as plain text) when a specific selection (such as bold style) is chosen. This enforcement of implicit deselection is one of the roles of an integrity monitor. In general, enforcement of post-conditions is one responsibility of an integrity monitor, as is enforcement of pre-conditions — for example, certain statistical functions would not be allowed on empty data sets.

System monitors manage relationships which exist independently of the control and display representations of conceptual components. A document-based system may be command, menu or icon driven, but the interaction between quit actions and unsaved changes will be the same. Users need to confirm quitting without saving changes. Enforcing this is an example of a responsibility of a *security* monitor.

As with global user interface components, no specific system monitors are prescribed as essential subcomponents of application managers. They are merely provided for, and how this is done is not considered here.

10.1 Wot! — No Window Managers?

A concern of the second Seattle workshop was the relationship between UIMSs and window managers. The structure presented here is silent about this relationship. Window managers and window systems are just one of many workstation resources. Underlying functionalities, linkages and media managers will interface with these low level resources as and when needed. It should be possible to handle events from window managers in specific appearance components or in the application manager. The handling of events depends on their nature. Quitting a window is not the same as typing a character into it. The latter is a low level event for a UIO, the former is an application event for the application manager. Cut and paste operations will be high or low level according to the way in which data is transferred. Character

[16]this does *not* duplicate semantic information in the user interface. An underlying application and a model of it for a specific purpose are not one and the same. What is modelled may have not have an explicit representation in the modelled program code (Rich 1982).

[17]These are *applications* to those who have to call a part of a system by this name. The structure thus allows integration of several underlying applications by a single user interface.

streams can be handled by média managers. Structures in memory need to be handled by application managers which will update underlying applications and user views accordingly.

No detailed relationship between window systems, window managers and interactive systems can be prescribed. Models and architectures should be able to interface in any sensible way to a workstation resource manager, and as such there is nothing to detail about these relationships at the higher levels of software structures for interactive systems.

11 Conclusions

Architectures guide software construction. They may be implemented directly for an individual application. They can also be implemented as the core structure of a UIMS, and thus the implementation, as well as the concepts of an architecture may be re-used.

Design re-use can take two forms. We can distinguish between the content of a design, such as the functions which a system will support or the way in which menu options will be named, and the *software form* of a design, which is the way in which the content of the design will be realised. Architectures are concerned more with the re-use of software forms than with the specific design content with which ergonomists and human factors specialists concern themselves. Even so, some architectures are better than others at supporting re-use of the detailed design of interactive systems.

Each of the four identified dimensions addresses different aspects of software form and they thus each influence different aspects of software design re-use:

orientation — the orientation may maximise or reduce re-use at the level of immediate decomposition, as well as easing re-use of whole parts of a design across several applications;

topology — the allowed inter-connections direct designers towards re-using separation and co-operation strategies in interactive systems;

component provision — the components provided allow re-use of software mechanisms such as display hierarchies, event-response systems and constraints, and specialised support components;

control and data propagation — re-use is limited for procedural forms of propagation, but declarative forms allow re-use of both the software mechanisms and specific configurations of links.

There is only a potential for re-use here. To realise this potential, *good* architectures must be developed. The analysis of architectures for interactive systems can expose what is good in current systems and also what cannot yet be classified as good, bad or ugly. Such an analysis is a necessary preliminary to any serious study of interactive architectures. Conclusive experimental comparisons are going to require considerable effort. The space of worthy architectures must therefore be pruned as much as possible before such an endeavour.

The space can be generated by a four dimensional classification scheme and pruned by rejecting positions on each dimension. This approach allows a more disciplined focus than has been apparent in other surveys of this area.

The classification scheme has been used to adopt positions where prescription or proscription is possible, and to leave things open where analysis alone cannot settle the issues. The new structure embodies the following decisions on each dimension:

orientation — a dual orientation was adopted, with a middle-out orientation in the main hierarchies and a top-down orientation in the cross-link global monitors and modifiers;

topology — a cross-link hierarchy was adopted;

component provision — information flow rationales were used in the UIO hierarchies and within the application manager, and a functional rationale was adopted for global managers and system monitors, but there was no commitment to any identified components[18];

control and data propagation — no position was adopted here: direct slot update, constraints or both could have been chosen for most of the links, but direct requests may be the best form of link for some control and data exchanges between global managers and UIOs.

[18] copycat and interaction cycle approaches were not adopted, as UIOs can be used to prefabricate such components which could then be used as if they were basic components.

The architectural inadequacies of the new structure are thus due to some uncertainty on the third dimension and complete indecision on the fourth dimension. This narrows the focus for experiments on architectures for interactive systems, but convincing experiments are not going to be easy to design and implement. Building one UIMS is difficult enough. No one has yet built several for the purpose of controlled comparisons[19]. Without such experimentation, we will not progress beyond the inconclusive positions which can be reached by analysis alone.

A Note on the Workshop Presentation

Only my presentation slides were distributed at the workshop, as I had not finished my draft. Consequently, this chapter combines thoughts from before, during and after the workshop. The main changes after the initial draft are due to detailing and a restructuring of my presentation around four dimensions rather than the three groups of example models and systems which I used in Lisbon. These were:

1. the Seeheim and IFIP WG2.7. CRL Reference Models (Green 1985a, Beech 1985);
2. the PAC model (Coutaz 1987) and the TUBE architecture (Herrmann and Hill 1989);
3. the MacApp framework (Schmucker 1986).

My new structure was presented as a fusion of the top-down components and functional rationale of WG2.7's model and the incomplete framework of MacApp. A framework of global managers left gaps for the main part of an interactive system's design. PAC style hierarchies were proposed as a structure for building up to fill the gaps at the top levels of an interactive system. Cross-links would join the hierarchy to the global components.

As a transformation on the Seeheim model, the new structure pushes the information flow components down to the bottom of the hierarchy and limits global components to view consistency and user support.

The conclusions and recommendations in my presentation, which were my input to the workshop, have not been changed in this chapter. The classification scheme is new, but all it does is reduce the reliance on specific examples by developing explicit principles rather than raiding existing systems for good ideas.

Acknowledgments

The ideas in this chapter developed during the year before the Lisbon workshop. They have been presented with varying clarity at the Olivetti Research Centre in Menlo Park, Hewlett-Packard Research Laboratories in Palo Alto, a panel session at the 4th IFIP TC2/WG2.7 working conference (Napa Valley 1989) and to the long suffering Graphics and HCI group at the University of Glasgow. I would like to thank the many people at these presentations whose questions have helped me to clarify (and modify) my ideas.

I would like to thank the organisers of the ESPRIT workshop on UIMS for inviting me to present my ideas on architectures for interactive systems. Peter Johnson's comments on the lack of precision in my original classifications (components, agents and frameworks) prompted me to look deeper into the differences between architectures.

References

Adhami, E, D.P. Brown and S.K. Mitra. (1987), "Application modelling for the provision of an adaptive user interface: a knowledge-based approach" in *Human-Computer Interaction — INTERACT'87*, eds. H.-J. Bullinger and B. Shackel, 981–987, North-Holland: Amsterdam

Anson, E. (1980), "The Semantics of Graphical Input" in *Methodology of Interaction*, eds. R.A. Guedj, P.J.W. ten Hagen, F.R.A. Hopgood, H.A. Tucker and D.A. Duce, 115–126, North-Holland: Amsterdam.

Apple Computer Inc. (1985), *Inside Macintosh*, volume 1, Addison Wesley: Menlo Park.

Bass, L., E. Hardy, R. Little and R. Seacord (1990), "Incremental Development of User Interfaces" in *Engineering for Human- Computer Interaction*, ed. G. Cockton, 155–175, North-Holland: Amsterdam.

Beech, D. (ed) (1985), *Concepts in User Interfaces: A Reference Model for Command and Response Languages*, LNCS 234, Springer-Verlag.

Benbasat, I. and Y. Wand (1984), "A structured approach to designing human-computer dialogues," *International Journal of Man-Machine Studies*, 21(2), 105–126.

Benyon, D. (1984), "Monitor: A Self-Adaptive User Interface" in *Proceedings of the 1st IFIP Conference on Human-Computer Interaction*, ed. B.Shackel, 1:307–313 (participants edition), Elsevier/IEE: London.

[19]Green has reported an attempt (Green 1985b).

Borning, A. and R. Duisberg (1986), "Constraint-Based Tools for Building User Interfaces," *Transactions on Graphics*, 5(4), 345–374, ACM.

Carbonell, J.R. (1970), "AI in CAI: An Artificial Intelligence Approach to Computer-Assisted Instruction", *Transactions on Man-Machine Systems*, MMS-11(4), 190–202, IEEE.

Carlsen, N.V., N.J. Christensen and H.A. Tucker (1990), "An Extended Event Model for Specifying User Interfaces" in *Engineering for Human-Computer Interaction*, ed. G. Cockton, 473–491, North-Holland: Amsterdam.

Carré, B. (1979), *Graphs and Networks*, Oxford University Press: Oxford.

Cockton, G. (1987a), "A New Model for Separable Interactive Systems" in *Human-Computer Interaction — INTERACT'87*, eds. H.-J. Bullinger and B. Shackel, 1033–1038 (participants' edition), North-Holland: Amsterdam.

Cockton, G. (1987b), "Some Critical Remarks on Abstractions for Adaptable Dialogue Managers" in *People and Computers III*, eds. D.Diaper and R.Winder, 325–344, Cambridge University Press: Cambridge.

Cockton, G. (1988), "Interaction Ergonomics, Control and Separation: Open Problems in User Interface Management Systems," *Scottish HCI Centre Report*, AMU 8811/03H, Scottish HCI Centre, Heriot-Watt University, Edinburgh, Scotland.

Cockton, G. (1990a), "Models and architectures (introduction)" in *Engineering for Human-Computer Interaction*, ed. G. Cockton, 107–111, North-Holland: Amsterdam.

Cockton, G. (1990b), "Formalisms: abstractions and their representation (introduction)" in *Engineering for Human-Computer Interaction*, ed. G. Cockton, 331–332, North-Holland: Amsterdam.

Cockton, G. (1990c), "User support (introduction)" in *Engineering for Human-Computer Interaction*, ed. G. Cockton, 253–255, North-Holland: Amsterdam.

Cockton, G. (1990d), "Designing abstractions for communication control" in *Formal Methods in Human-Computer Interaction*, ed. M. Harrison and H. Thimbleby, 233–271, Cambridge University Press: Cambridge.

Cockton, G. (1990e), "Lean Cuisine: no sauces, no courses!," *Interacting with Computers*, 2(2), 205–216.

Cockton, G. (1990f), "Engineering for Human Computer Interaction: Architecture and abstraction" in *Engineering for Human-Computer Interaction*, ed. G. Cockton, 3–8, North-Holland: Amsterdam.

Cockton, G. and B. Sharratt (1987), "Dialogue Specification and Implementation" in *HCI'87 Tutorial Notes*, British Computer Society: London.

Coutaz, J. (1985), "Abstractions for user interface design," *Computer*, 18(9), 21–34.

Coutaz, J. (1987) "PAC, an object oriented model for dialog design", in *Human-Computer Interaction — INTERACT'87*, eds. H.-J. Bullinger and B. Shackel, 431–436 (participant's edition), North-Holland: Amsterdam.

Coutaz, J. (1989), "UIMS: Promises, Failures and Trends" in *People and Computers V*, ed. A. Sutcliffe and L. Macaulay, 71–81, Cambridge University Press: Cambridge.

Dance, J.R., T.E. Granor, R.D. Hill, S.E. Hudson, J. Meads, B.A. Myers, and A. Schulert (1987), "The Run-time Structure of UIMS-Supported Applications," *Computer Graphics*, 21(2), 97-102, ACM .

Davenport, C. and G. Weir (1986), "Plan recognition for intelligent monitoring" in *People and Computers: Designing for Usability*, ed. M.D. Harrison and A. Monk, 296–315, Cambridge University Press: Cambridge.

Dix, A. (1988), "Abstract generic models of interactive systems," in *People and Computers IV*, ed. D.M. Jones and R. Winder, 63–77, Cambridge University Press: Cambridge.

Dix, A.J. and C. Runciman (1985), "Abstract Models of Interactive Systems" in *People and Computers: Designing the Interface*, ed. P. Johnson and S. Cook, 13–20, Cambridge University Press: Cambridge.

Frankowski, E.N., W.T. Wood and J. Larson (1990), "Concurrency and Multi-Threaded Interaction in the Task-Script User Interface Model" in *Engineering for Human-Computer Interaction*, ed. G. Cockton, 359–382, North-Holland: Amsterdam.

Green, M. (1985a), "Report on Dialogue Specification Tools" in *User Interface Management Systems*, ed. G.E. Pfaff, Springer-Verlag: Berlin, 9–20.

Green, M. (1985b), "The University of Alberta User Interface Management System," *Computer Graphics (SIGGRAPH '85)*, 19(3), 205–213, ACM.

Guedj, R. A. and H. A. Tucker, eds. (1979), *Computer Graphics Methodology*, North-Holland: Amsterdam.

Henderson, D.A. (1986), "The Trillium User Interface Design Environment," *Proceedings of CHI'86*, 221–227, ACM.

Herrmann, M. and R.D. Hill (1989), "The Structure of Tube — A Tool for Implementing Advanced User Interfaces" in *Eurographics '89*, ed. W. Hansmann, F.R.A. Hopgood and W. Strasser, 15–25, Elsevier Science Publisher B.V.: Amsterdam.

Hill, R.D. (1986), "Supporting Concurrency, Communication and Synchronisation in Human-Computer Interaction — The Sassafras UIMS," *Transactions on Graphics*, 5(3), 179–210, ACM.

Hill, R.D. (1987), "Event-Response Systems — A Technique for Specifying Multi-Threaded Dialogues," *Human Factors and Computing Systems — CHI+GI'87*, 241–248, ACM.

Hix, D. and H.R. Hartson (1986), "An Interactive Environment for Dialogue Development: it's Design, Use and Evaluation — or — Is AIDE Useful?," *Proceedings of CHI'86*, 228–234, ACM.

Hoffner, Y., J. Dobson, and D. Iggulden (1990), "A New User Interface Architecture" in *Engineering for Human-Computer Interaction*, ed. G. Cockton, 113–136, North-Holland: Amsterdam.

Hudson, S.E. (1987), "UIMS support for Direct Manipulation Interfaces", *Computer Graphics*, 21(2), 120-124, ACM.

Johnson, P., H. Johnson, R. Waddington and A. Shouls (1988) "Task-related Knowledge Structures: Analysis, Modelling and Application" in *People and Computers IV*, eds. D.M. Jones and R. Winder, 35–62, Cambridge University Press: Cambridge.

Kamran, A. (1985), "Issues Pertaining to the Design of a User Interface Management System" in *User Interface Management Systems*, ed. G.E. Pfaff, Springer-Verlag: Berlin, 43–48.

Lantz, K.A. (1987) "Multi-process Structuring of User Interface Software," *Computer Graphics*, 21(2), 124–130.

Linton, M.A., J.M. Vlissides and P R Calder (1989), "Composing User Interfaces with Interviews," *IEEE Computer*, 22(2).

Myers, B.A. (1989), "User-interface tools: Introduction and survey," *IEEE Software*, 6(1), 15–23, IEEE.

Owen, D. (1986) "Answers first, then questions" in *User Centred System Design*, eds. D.A. Norman and S. Draper, 361–371, Lawrence Erlbaum Associates: New Jersey

Pfaff, G.E., ed. (1985), *User Interface Management Systems*, Springer Verlag: Berlin.

Reiss, S.P. and J.T. Stasko (1990) "The Brown Workstation Environment: A User Interface Design Toolkit" in *Engineering for Human-Computer Interaction*, ed. G. Cockton, 215–231, North-Holland: Amsterdam.

Rich, E.A. (1982) "Programs as data for their help systems," *Proceedings of the AFIPS Conference*, 481–485, AFIPS/ACM.

Rosenthal, D.S.H., J.C. Michener, G. Pfaff, R. Kessener, and M. Sabin (1982), "The Detailed Semantics of Graphics Input Devices," *Computer Graphics*, 16(3), 33–38, ACM.

Schmucker, K. (1986) "MacApp: an application framework," *Byte*, 11(8), 189-193.

Scheifler, R.W. and J. Gettys (1986) "The X Window System," *Transactions on Graphics*, 5(2), 79-109, ACM.

Shuey, D., D. Bailey and T.P. Morrissey (1986), "PHIGS: A Standard, Dynamic, Interactive Graphics Interface," *Computer Graphics and Applications*, 50–56, IEEE.

Smith, R.B. (1987), "Experiences with the Alternate Reality Kit: an example of the tension between literalism and magic," *Human Factors and Computing Systems — CHI+GI'87*, 61–67, ACM.

Sommerville, I. (1989), *Software Engineering*, 3rd edition, Addison-Wesley.

Thomas, J.J. and G. Hamlin (1983), "Graphical Input Interaction Technique (GIIT). Workshop Summary," *Computer Graphics*, 17(1), 5–30, ACM.

Totterdell, P. and P. Cooper (1986), "Design and evaluation of the AID adaptive front-end to Telecom Gold" in *People and Computers: Designing for Usability*, ed. M.D. Harrison and A. Monk, 263–295, Cambridge University Press: Cambridge.

Trefz, B. and J. Ziegler (1990), "The User Interface Management System DIAMANT" in *Engineering for Human-Computer Interaction*, ed. G. Cockton, 177–195, North-Holland: Amsterdam.

Wasserman, A.I., P.A. Pircher, D.T. Shewmake and M.L. Kersten (1986) "Developing Interactive Information Systems with the User Software Engineering Methodology," *IEEE Trans. on Software Engineering*, SE-12(2), 326–345.

Yunten T. and H.R. Hartson (1985), "A SUPERvisory Methodology And Notation (SUPERMAN) for Human-Computer System Development" in *Advances in Human-Computer Interaction*, volume 1, ed. H. R. Hartson, 243–281, Ablex.

Chapter 4

Concepts, Methods, Methodologies Working Group

4.1 Participants

P.J.W. ten Hagen (Convenor)
L. Bass
N.V. Carlsen
G. Cockton
G. Faconti
R. Gimnich
J. Grollmann
R. Guedj
E. Hollnagel
F.R.A. Hopgood
J. Lee
M. Martinez
F. Neelamkavil
F. Shevlin
D. Soede
B. Villalobos

Paul ten Hagen opened the session on Monday afternoon by saying that the Working Group should concentrate on looking at existing concepts, methods and methodologies and see how we can develop ideas from these. Six papers were to be presented and the authors should concentrate on answering the two questions:

(1) Which design techniques, toolkits, environments, UIMS are currently in use?

(2) Who uses them, how and for what?

The presentations should concentrate on the relationship of their work to the aims of the Working Group.

Four papers by Carlsen, Grollmann, Shevlin and Gimnich were to be presented and the presentations should address these issues in particular:

(1) Graphics Sub System/ Reference Model requirements.

(2) UIMS and API: Separation possibilities.

(3) Intelligence in the User Interface.

(4) Future Systems and Techniques (multi-media, multi-threaded, object-oriented, standards).

(5) User's model (human factors, style, look and feel).

The Working Group continued on Tuesday morning with three short presentations from Lee, ten Hagen and Martinez.

After the paper presentations, a list of possible areas of work was presented by the Chairman:

(1) Define Terms.

(2) Application Interface.

(3) Objects, Types and Graphics in UIMS.

(4) Intelligence in UIMS.

(5) Futures (multi-media, multi-threading etc.)

(6) User definition.

(7) Define UIMS

(8) Scope of Methodology.

The two areas chosen for study by two Sub-Groups were:

(1) Application Interface;

(2) Methodology.

4.2 Application Interface Sub-Group

4.2.1 Introduction

This a report of the work done by the working group on the Application - UIMS Interface. This was a subgroup of the working group on Concepts, Models and Methodology. The chairman was Paul ten Hagen and the remaining participants were: Len Bass, Niels Vejrup Carlsen, Gilbert Cockton, Giorgio Faconti, Margarita Martinez, Fergal Shevlin, Bonifacio Villalobos. The authors of this report are Niels Carlsen, Len Bass, Gilbert Cockton and Paul ten Hagen.

The group was asked to discuss the interface between the application domain and the UIMS. We were asked to focus on run-time issues such as how applications are interfaced to a UIMS and what facilities a UIMS should provide for an application programmmer. Special attention was to be paid to the unambiguous definition of the terminology used.

4.2.1.1 Levels of Abstraction As the discussion progressed it became clear that we had to distinguish between several layers of abstraction in order to relate our aims and results to the existing body of work within the user interface software community. The layers were also extremely helpful in resolving several arguments during the discussions. We explicitly identified 3 layers of abstraction used when modelling or defining software systems:

(1) *The Conceptual Level* - where the different mechanisms or functionalities that should be present in a system are identified.

(2) *The Architectural Level* - where it is determined how a collection of system agents or a set of system components implementing these mechanisms or functionalities are combined to form the system. This defines a system architecture.

(3) *The Realization Level* - where the implementation of these agents or components is decided. At this level interfaces between the agents or components are defined and the way in which they are to communicate is determined.

Several software architectures may be used to structure the mechanisms of a system and several implementations may realize a given architecture.

It was decided that the aim of the working group would be to provide a framework at the conceptual level for interactive software systems. This could be the basis for building software tools or environments for developing and managing interactive systems. Furthermore, it would give a common frame of reference for discussions or for comparing the capabilities of different architectures and implementations.

Within this framework we should then identify the interface between the application domain and the user interface functionality. Such an architecturally independent definition would be useful for all in the user interface software community regardless of their choice of system architecture.

4.2.1.2 Basic Terminology In recent years the terminology used to describe interactive systems and prototyping environments for developing these systems has grown increasingly diffuse and ambiguous. When the subgroup started up, there were disagreements to the meaning of basic terms. This lead us to (re)define a number of these in order to clear the confusion. In doing so we tried to retain the original intent of the terms and only introduce new ones when absolutely necessary.

We want to set a framework for discussing the design of an Interactive (Software) System. The end user perceives an interactive system as the entity he/she works with to achieve some goals associated to a specific task domain. It consists of all the application specific and user interface specific functionality needed to support the user in achieving the goals.

We define a *User Interface Management System* (UIMS) to be an environment for constructing (prototyping) and managing interactive systems. A UIMS is comprised of a run-time support system and a set of design, specification and evaluation tools plus maybe other tools we haven't yet thought of. Thus a UIMS is not merely a tool kit, but has design-time components.

The *User Interface Design Environment* (UIDE) was determined to denote the collection of tools within the UIMS. Thus, a UIDE has no run-time component. This contradicts some existing use of the term as almost synonymous to UIMS [13].

The *User Interface System* (UIS) was the term we decided to use for the run-time support system. Other authors have called it User Interface Framework [5] or User Interface Management System. The reason for our choice has been the original and still prevalent analogy between UIMSs and Database Management Systems (DBMSs) [24]. A DBMS includes a set of database definition tools for data modelling and data entry and furthermore a database system for handling the defined databases.

4.2.1.3 The User Interface System The UIS is responsible for managing the dialogue between end users and the applications at run-time. The UIS supplies a framework in which the dialogue designer using the UIDE may instantiate the user interface functionality desired for a given interactive system. Thus, an instantiation of a given UIS plus the functionality of a given application yields an interactive system. The UIS comprises three categories of mechanisms that allow differing degrees of design control:

- *Fixed Mechanisms* - that are imposed on the designer.
- *Parameterized Mechanisms* - that allow a designer to configure user interface functionality that conforms to a given model.
- *Interpretation Mechanisms* - that allow for the interpretation of functions defined by a designer.

It is the way the support for user interface functionality is distributed between these three categories of mechanisms that determine the level of predetermined user interface design (imposed look & feel) in a given UIS implementation.

The fixed mechanisms of a UIS supply the basic functionality which is the same for all the user interfaces supported by the UIMS. A certain look & feel may be imposed through this functionality if these mechanisms are at a high level. They might also restrict the way applications are linked to the UIS.

The parameterized mechanisms support the design of user interface functionality that must conform to some model employed by the UIS but which may be configured to allow different instantiations of this model. These mechanisms restrict the designer to a certain grain of control in the design of a user interface. Examples could be the inclusion of standard graphics systems or window managers within a UIS. The interaction techniques supplied by the graphics system may be configured within a range of predefined feedback and prompt options. Similarly the window manager may impose a certain style of interaction (window management policy) and allow configuration of layouts.

Another example of a parameterized mechanism could be a finite state automaton for handling dialogue control within the user interface. If arbitrary procedures and internal state were allowed this automaton would be one example of a framework for supplying interpretation mechanisms. These give the designer full freedom of expression within the functional domains covered by the mechanisms.

The aim of the working group was to provide a conceptual framework for an interactive system. That is, at the conceptual level the aim was to determine the mechanisms of the UIS (the services it should provide for an interactive system) and the application domain, thereby defining the interface between the two domains. We were not concerned with the architecture or the implementation of the UIS which determines the structuring of the mechanisms and whether these are supplied as fixed, parameterized or interpreted functionality.

The following two sections contains a description of the conceptual framework we propose. During the discussions we found that a controversial point was how design-time relates to run-time issues. Therefore, each of these sections contains a discussion of this.

4.2.2 Defining the Application Domain

In order to determine the services of the UIS it is necessary to have a reasonably unambiguous definition of the application domain. That is, we would like to define what functionality we consider to be external to the UIS. Much disagreement exists as to what constitutes an 'application', the term is clearly overloaded. Users perceive the entire interactive system as an application, a dialogue designer employs a conceptual model of an application which may collide with the systems designer's software oriented view [6]. The group therefore decided that a new term with a clearer definition was needed.

4.2.2.1 Functional Core The Functional Core is that part of the interactive system which is invariant to change in the media used for interacting with the user (definition from [2]). An interactive system is thus comprised of the functional core and the user interface which is an instantiation of the given UIS defined through use of the tools within the UIDE, see figure 1. It is important to note that the functional core is not defined as independent of the functionality of the user interface. This implies that to a given functional core we may not design any user interface even though the UIS supports it. Some interface functionality may require extra functionality within the functional core to work. An example could be a monitoring capability (percent-done indication) in the user interface. This requires functionality within the functional core that supplies the monitoring data to the user interface.

Our definition of functional core is not equivalent to the prevalent use of the term 'application' in the user interface software community as being user interface independent, [21,22]. However, it was also proposed at the second Seattle workshop [20] that the separation between the application and the user interface domains be defined as a media independent interface [18]. A further refinement of the concept of functional core could be to try to isolate

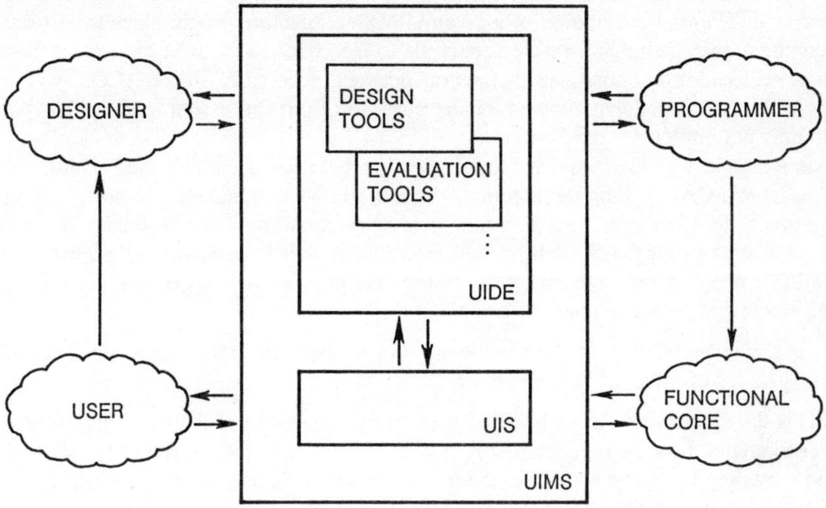

Fig.1. A UIMS is an environment comprised of a set of tools, the UIDE and a run-time support system, the UIS

the user interface independent and the user interface dependent functionalities, but we were not sure this would be fruitful.

We do not think it is a problem that the functional core may need to be modified if a new type of user interface is to be designed for it. One of the long forgotten advantages of the UIMS as a prototyping environment is that it will allow rapid prototyping of both the domains of interactive systems. The environment allows rapid design or redesign of user interfaces to a given functional core. This implies that a replacement or a modification of the functional core is also easily dealt with.

Our definition puts an end to the discussion on whether UIMSs can be developed such that the large mass of existing applications with tele-type or batch-job user interfaces may easily be modified to fancy direct manipulation interactive systems. The answer is no! It should be possible to redesign user interfaces to existing systems within a UIMS, but if a radically new user interface design and not just a change of media is asked for then the functional core also needs to be modified. A UIS may provide some facilities for 'semantic repair' [8], but this will not cover everything.

4.2.2.2 Conceptual Objects In the following we will be taking the liberty of using the term 'object' with its original English semantics as an entity or a thing. Thus, an object is not necessarily an abstract datatype, it may be anything. One could perhaps substitute it with the equally vague 'mechanism' to avoid confusion.

Conceptually we may regard the functional core as a collection of objects. The functional core wishes to make some of these objects visible to the user through the UIS. An implication is that parts of the functional core may be invisible to a UIS! This leads to the definition of conceptual objects:

- *Conceptual Object* (CO) is the user interface accessible media independent representation of an object the functional core wishes to make visible.

COs are resident in the user interface domain, within the frame of the UIS. This is a conceptual decision. The implementation of a given UIMS architecture, might place the COs within the functional core such that they are accessible to the UIS, see the next section on the application interface. Furthermore, the distinction between accessible objects (COs) and visible objects within the functional core is, for the purpose of our discussion, conceptual. A given system may not implement the distinction.

One example that clarifies why the distinction between accessible and visible may be valuable is: in a CAD system the functional core might wish to make a geometric object visible. Internally this is represented in a complex representation (B-rep or other) that contains information on topology, materials, database attributes and information on geometry. However, all that needs to be made accessible to the user interface is the geometrical information and the associated presentational attributes.

- It is the responsibility of the functional core to maintain integrity of the COs and the consistency of relations between them.

The CO is the mechanism for embedding parts of the semantics of the functional core within the user interface. It is the functional core that decides which objects are currently made visible and how they may interact within the user interface. It is thus, its responsibility to create and delete COs within the user interface, inform the user interface when they are accessible and whether they are modifiable or read only objects.

The functional core is responsible for maintaining the integrity of COs such that they give a true picture of the current state. That is, if changes happen in the internal state that affect visible objects the corresponding COs should be notified of this or vice versa if a CO has been modified by the user and the change is accepted then the corresponding visible object should be notified. Furthermore, if a change in one CO affects others this should be propagated via the functional core to maintain the consistency between the COs. After all, it is the semantics of the functional core which is the basis for this sort of interaction.

- The COs may be composite, but this information is handled in the functional core. It is the functional core that knows how and why they are composed.

An example of this could be a user selection of a CO representing a folder in a MacIntosh like interface which implies making the contained file COs visible. This is handled by the functional core. The relations between COs could be defined within the COs themselves as attribute values (object references). But it is still up to the functional core to control this. Otherwise, a lot of predefined handling of the semantics of composition will be needed within a UIS, see the example in section 4.2.3.2.

4.2.2.3 The Application Interface to the UIMS The section title is actually misleading, but it refers to the charter of the working group. We are in this section defining the interface between the functional core and the UIS. The collection of COs defined for a given functional core may be regarded as the external specification of this core. It is the functional core as seen from the UIS point of view. It is also a representation of the functionality within the user interface as seen from the functional core. This leads us to the following definitions, see figure 2:

- The *Application Conceptual Interface* (ACI) is the collection of COs defined for a given application.
- The *Application Programmers Interface* (API) is the mechanism available for information and control transfer between the functional core and the collection of COs (the ACI).

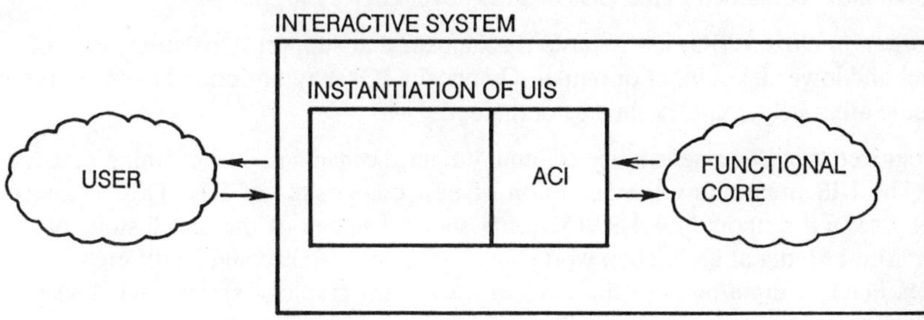

Fig.2. An interactive system with the functional core and instantiated UIS which incorporates the ACI

The way visible objects from the functional core are made accessible to the user interface through exporting, describing or sharing COs and how these are controlled depends on the architecture and implementation strategy chosen for the UIS. The nature of the API thus depends on the choice of 'separation model' [5]. The COs could be shared between the functional core and the UIS, as proposed in [9], in which case the information transfer is straight forward. Another approach could be to have the functional core in some way map its visible objects onto UIS resident COs through event passing or function calls.

4.2.2.4 Design-time vs. Run-time The ACI may be seen as a run-time representation of the user interface designers conceptual model of the functional core [6]. However we did not discuss how the ACI is actually defined. This might be through a high level description of the visible parts of the functional core which is interpreted by a tool in the UIDE. We could also imagine that they were implemented directly by the application programmer according to some standard protocol defined by the UIS. This depends on whether the UIS allows COs as parameterized or interpreted functionality.

Although the group did not adress questions regarding design methodology, we could summarize the above into a two-step design process for interactive systems: 1) The functional core is designed with a given style of user interface in mind. 2) To create the user interface within the UIS the set of COs is designed. In parallel the user interface functionality may be designed within the UIS to match this ACI.

4.2.3 Defining the User Interface Domain

This section will focus on our definition of the mechanisms we believe should be present in the UIS apart from the COs. This was actually a subject the working group spent little time on, but it was needed for completeness of our conceptual framework for interactive systems and we think that some novel ideas arose from our discussion.

In the definitions we have abstracted away from implementation and architectural problems such as resource management, constraint management, couplings between input and output and so on. We are dealing with functionalities at a conceptual level.

4.2.3.1 Mechanisms We need a transformation mechanism to translate between the low level device inputs and high level inputs understood by the COs and vice versa between high level information contained in the COs and low level device output.

- *Interaction Object* (IO) is the basic mechanism that support translation between higher level and lower level input or output. Composite IOs may be formed from simple IOs to handle arbitrarily complex threads of dialogue.

It is recognized that the extensibility of input/output mechanisms is something that is fundamental. The UIS must allow the definition of new composites of IOs. This has been established by several authors [1,3,4,10,15,16,17] and it was one of the conclusions of the subgroup on Multi Media at the Lisbon workshop. Examples of IOs could be different interaction primitives [11,12], input/output primitives of a standard graphics system, window presentations in a window manager or the handling of a command language syntax.

The composite IOs handle the threads of dialogue from which a user interface is constructed. They represent the transformation of information between the user action level and the CO level of abstraction. We now need a mechanism which will enable us to manage the mapping between COs and IOs. This mapping is a many to many relation. One CO can have a representation in many threads of dialogue handled by different IOs. Similarly, one IO may be connected to several COs.

- *Transformer Object* (TO) is the basic mechanism for managing the relations between the different objects of the UIS.

TOs are used to maintain and manage the integrity of the mapping between COs and IOs such that the IOs at all times represent a true picture of the semantics expressed by the COs. This not necessarily just a question of update management to

maintain the consistency between the two information representations. We could have TOs for handling metadialogue control, that is, switching between dialogue contexts controlled by different composite IOs. The latter would include the creation and deletion of IOs and it might be driven by some state mechanism which is maintained by monitor objects which are introduced below, see figure 3. Another use for TOs is the maintenance of consistency between the different IOs in the UIS. This may involve constraint management to maintain the relations. The TO concept was discussed at some length by the working group and one of the tentative conclusions were that TOs might not only be used for the above mentioned integrity relations between COs and IOs and the consistency relations between IOs. We could also envision that TOs might be used for controlling relations between different TOs. For example, a dialogue context switch might have consequences in the management of constraints.

We need a third kind of functionality in our UIS for the UIS to support the design of supportive user interfaces. These might include user support in the shape of default handling, active help systems, undoing and error recovery.

- *Monitor Object* (MO) represents the mechanism for monitoring and perhaps modifying relations and transactions between the different objects within the UIS. MOs could also be called user support objects.

An MO could be used for collecting the history of user interactions for a thread of dialogue handled by a composite IO. Such an MO would be attached to the TO(s) implementing the mapping between COs and this IO and it could supply information to a state mechanism within the UIS, see figure 3. The state mechanism which can be used in connection with for example dialogue context switching, error recovery, undoing and active help systems could be maintained by another MO. This MO not only monitors the TOs which handle the mapping between COs and IOs but it also affects these in accordance with the state. Thus, MOs are the objects which enable the entire user interface to be glued together. They are the integration mechanism.

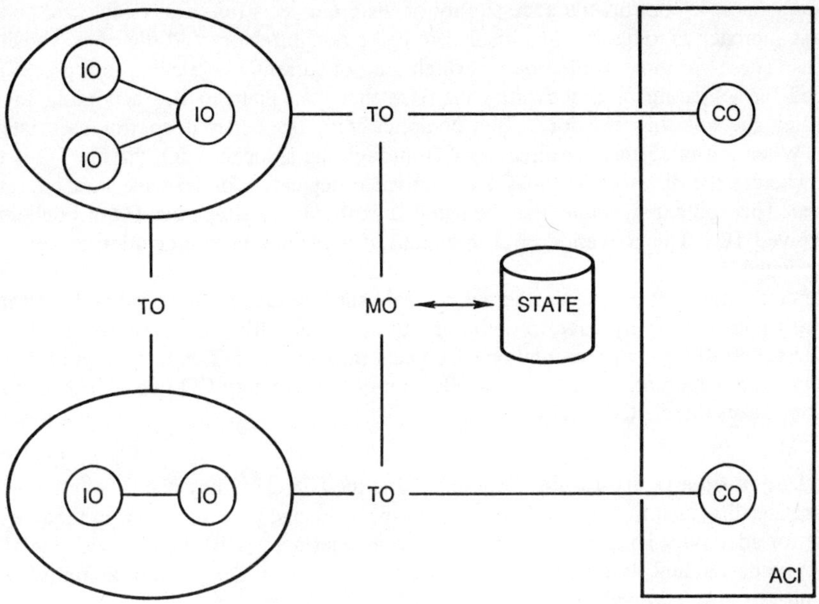

Fig.3. How TOs may be used for the CO-IO mapping and the maintenance of consistency between IOs. An MO is used to monitor and affect the information flow

4.2.3.2 A Small Example To illustrate how the above concepts might be used to decompose the functionalities of an interactive system we improvised a small example of a dialogue thread in a user interface: The user may at a given time interact with a file directory which contains a collection of files. The directory name and the file names are the objects that the functional core wishes to make visible and these names are embedded in separate COs. The relation between the directory and the files is maintained entirely within the functional core. Furthermore, some of the files are marked by the functional core as illegal choices at a given point in time. The media independent representation of this is some flag within the file COs. We cannot just make these illegal choice COs invisible since we still might wish the file IO to represent them as discussed below.

TOs define the mapping between the media independent COs and the user level IOs representing media dependent interaction and presentation techniques. We might imagine one TO handling the mapping between the directory CO and an iconic or textual IO for representing the directory name. Another type of TO maps the collection of simple file COs to an IO which could implement a textual or iconic menu interaction technique or a command language parser which accepts a set of legal commands that correspond to the filenames. In a given user interface we would perhaps like all the filenames of the directory to be displayed but with an indication of which ones are illegal choices at the time. The TO associated with the simple file COs must now cover the transformation of this information as well. The TO could tell a menu IO not to accept the choices represented by illegal COs and to gray them out. A language parser IO would perhaps simply be informed not to accept these choices as part of the language.

The dynamics of the user interaction may be handled in at least two different ways depending on who controls the accessibility of visible objects (external or internal control): The first approach is to let the functional core make both directory and file objects visible at all times. There are thus visible objects which are not currently accessible to a user. This is managed by activating or deactivating the TOs that map them to IOs according to some (meta)dialogue control behaviour. This complies with the external control user interface model. When a user selects the directory CO through the associated IO, the file TO is made active whereas the directory TO may be deactivated depending on how the user interface is designed. This context switching may be handled explicitly by a separate TO or implicitly by the involved TOs. The activation or deactivation of a TO implies the creation or deletion of the associated IOs.

We could however model an internal control user interface using the same abstractions. In the example we merely have to define the directory and file TOs as active all the time. Now the accessability and presentation of objects through these TOs is only guided by the functional core which for example upon selection of the directory CO makes it invisible and thereafter makes the file COs visible.

4.2.3.3 Design-time vs. Run-time Many feel that the UIS should by itself include user support functionality such as help facilities, history mechanisms, error recovery and maybe even support for adaptivity in user interfaces (intelligent interfaces [19]). Others wish the UIS to incorporate design and style rules in order to ensure consistent designs and to impose a look & feel proven to be acceptable [14].

However, we decided that a UIS should support the design of all kinds of user interfaces. In principle it should not impose any design restrictions, it must be possible to design bad as well as good user interfaces within its framework. This implies that a UIS does not provide any of the above mentioned facilities automatically. But, it must provide mechanisms that allow for the construction of these. We believe that our three categories of objects plus the COs are sufficient for this.

The definition of a UIS should be independent from design concepts and the choice of specific design tools in the UIDE. The UIS must aim to support all user interfaces instead of the ones conforming to an existing set of design rules. It must facilitate experimentation with new kinds of design otherwise a UIMS based on such a UIS will be useless for prototyping new kinds of interactive systems. It should be invariant to changes in 'fashion', ie. if new design concepts were formed, new techniques were developed or task requirements rule out consistent look & feel across all applications. We believe that design rules should be embedded in the tools of the UIDE and that these tools must be either modifiable or easily replaced.

We are exploring the mechanisms of the UIS at the conceptual level. Therefore, they must be independent of any choice of UIS architecture and implementation. A given implementation of a UIS may still supply design oriented abstractions through supplying high level fixed and parameterized mechanisms.

Some questions arose on the feasibility of constructing a UIS that is essentially independent from the UIDE. If the UIS should support all kinds of user interfaces, do we then end up with a general purpose programming language such as C? If so, we will have gained nothing by this system decomposition! The idea is of course to supply the right high level constructs within the UIS such that the construction of user interfaces are facilitated while still retaining fine grain control. However, this discussion concerns implementation issues that we did not address further.

The architecture and implementation of a given UIS will probably affect the architecture and implementation of the tools of the UIDE. However, these effects might be hidden through an intermediate representation of design between the tools of the UIDE and the UIS [23].

4.2.4 Discussion

The proposed conceptual framework for interactive systems may be seen as the top level of a taxonomy of models, the definition of the universe of discourse. The next level could be a categorization at the architectural level of UIS models and models for the functional core. One such tentative categorization of UIS models may be seen in [5] and this could be refined by including the categorization of design architectures as presented by Cockton [7].

An architectural taxonomy for functional cores was hinted at in comments made by Hollnagel during the discussions of the working group on Concepts, Models and Methodology. He suggested that several categories of 'applications' existed that are not covered by existing research within the UIMS community. Examples are time critical control and monitoring systems which guide the user and do not necessarily allow the user to be in control. Such systems may require other types of UIS architectures than those used in non time critical office automation systems.

We hope that our conceptual framework for interactive systems could be a step towards a common frame of reference which we believe would be helpful to the community. The framework needs to be refined and tested but we think that we have defined a set of abstractions that do not restrict us unnecessarily in the choice of UIS architecture and implementation. This could be checked by confirming that the abstractions are adequate for categorizing the functionalities present in the models proposed for UISs at the architectural level.

Because of the limited time at the workshop we did not address this issue thoroughly. However, we considered whether the functionality of the Semantic Support Component (SCC) in the architectural proposal in [9] could be expressed using our abstractions. The SCC provide information and support for semantic operations such as feedback, defaulting, error checking, help information and interface adaptivity based on application state. It defines application specific viewing methods and what parts of the semantic objects that are visible.

The way we would categorize these functionalities within our framework is: feedback, error checking, help information and viewing/visibility support are functionalities encapsulated in the COs defined for a given application. Defaulting is controlled by the information gathered by MOs monitoring user interactions. Interface adaptivity is also controlled by MOs attached to COs representing the state of the functional core. The viewing and the feedback methods are embedded in IOs controlled by attributes in the COs. Parts of the functionality that might be included in an SCC is in our framework placed in the functional core. This is the maintenance of consistency between COs and the handling of composite COs.

Another issue we tried to cover was the implications of our definitions of functional core and its interface to the UIS. As previously mentioned the functional core of an interactive system may need modification if a new kind of user interface functionality is wanted. This has implications for the way existing systems can be redesigned within a UIMS.

An example: We wish to redesign the user interface to an old FORTRAN application which has a teletype interface that read and write strings exclusively. The existing application is regarded as the functional core. The strings are then the conceptual objects we can work with and the API consists of the read and write statements. The only possible user interface to such a functional core is some sort of pseudo-terminal with either textual or iconic representation of the strings. Alternatively, the application code could be changed to use more complex conceptual objects. The ACI could consist of higher level data structures matching the internal structures of the application. This would give the UIS the possibility of representing and manipulating these higher level objects freely and thus perhaps allow a direct manipulation style interface. A third approach is needed if other types of functionality that were not originally considered is also wanted in the user interface. For example, if a percent-done of job indication is needed, the functional core should be extended with such a monitoring function.

4.3 Methodology Sub-Group

4.3.1 Methodology

The Sub-Group started by defining its meaning of Methodology. It had two different views from one which saw a methodology as a set of high level principles to another which saw it more as a set of design rules for specifically solving a problem.

The usage in the Working Group was:

METHODOLOGY OF 'X' is a systematic approach which includes guidelines and principles to the development of 'X'. Development includes requirement specification, design and test.

4.3.2 UIMS

There was a concern at the use of UIMS to describe a system which both designs user interfaces and provides run-time support. It was agreed to itemize the functions expected of such a system and then name it once the included functionality was specified.

It was agreed that the four major areas of the system were:

(1) Model of User Characteristics (preferences).

(2) Support communications between user and applications (note plural).

(3) Designing user interfaces.

(4) Function Distribution between Human and System.

4.3.3 Support Communications Between User and Applications

The main subtopics were:

(1) *Record of Communication*: for replay, inquiry etc. it was believed that a record of communication was needed. An obvious ordering would be temporal, but, it would not be the only possible ordering.

(2) *Navigation*: the user needed to have support for where he was in a complex dialogue and what options were available.

(3) *Communication support between applications*: the need to provide meaningful 'cut and paste' support between applications at a level relevant to both applications.

(4) *Control*: different types of control needed to be supported.

(5) *Feedback*: the user needed to have response to actions.

(6) *Query*: the ability for the user to inquire the state of the system and *vice versa*.

4.3.4 Designing User Interfaces

The main headings reflected the activities of the design process:

(1) Requirements capture.

(2) Specification of Interface.

(3) Prototyping (this does not imply mock-up).

(4) Test.

(5) Delivery (production of delivery system from prototype).

(6) Maintenance.

(7) Style.

(8) Mode.

(9) Scenarios: the need to provide dialogue sequences for user training and system evaluation.

4.3.5 Model of User Characteristics

The major headings were groupings of a large number of characteristics:

(1) *Preferences*: user choice not dependent on his characteristics;

(2) *Permanent user features*: these are features that a set of users are born with or are permanent (left handedness, colour blind etc.);

(3) Inherent Features (short term memory is limited);

(4) Skills (typing ability etc.);

(5) Environmental Factors (hot room, low light);

(6) Physical State (tired);

(7) Mental State (depressed);

(8) Ability to Use without Understanding (user has ability to use system without really having a correct model of the system);

(9) Knowledge of System (user understands the underlying conceptual model of the system).

4.3.6 Name

The Group considered what would be an appropriate name for a system of this type. It was agreed that UIMS was inappropriate. Instead it was suggested that:

Development
Environment for
Human
Computer
Interaction
Systems

DEHCIS was more appropriate.

4.3.7 Final Session

The Group returned to discussion of the essential features of an interface design support system. Were *all* the factors previously identified always important? It was agreed that the central concept for interactive system design is that of *task*. This should be understood not 'normatively', as an externally imposed exercise (cf. German *Aufgabe*, French *Tache*), but 'descriptively', including an account of methods for achieving it. The usage is related to the notion of 'task' in the GOMS model, described in Gimnich's paper and discussed earlier during his presentation.

Interactive system design should identify the relevant tasks, then illustrate them through a set of *scenarios*, needed both to clarify objectives and for use in teaching future users. Methodology is thus directed to the design process only - no general decomposition can be given for run-time systems. Designing interfaces is itself a task, which can be differently described in different cases.

Interactive system design is constrained by the following:

(1) task;

(2) tools (and other software modules);

(3) situation.

Tools (2) includes window managers and graphics systems, as well as application software in cases of retrofitting, and other possible items of software methodology that might be useful in analysing the task or implementing the design.

Any of these may be arbitrarily imposed on the designer, and form a space within which he has creative freedom (different designers might produce very different - but equally 'good' - interfaces). The situation (3) includes characteristics of intended users, nature of the organization context, issues of 'house style', etc.

References

(1) Anson, E., "The Device Model of Interaction", *Computer* Graphics **16**(3), 1982.

(2) Bass, L.; Coutaz, J., "Developing User Interfaces", to be published by Addison-Wesley, spring 1991.

(3) Borufka, H.G.; Kuhlmann, H.W.; ten Hagen, P.J.W., "Dialogue Cells: A Method for Defining Interactions", *IEEE* Computer

(4) van den Bos, J.; Plasmeijer, M.J.; Hartel, P.H., "Input-Output Tools: A Language Facility for Interactive and Real-Time Systems", *IEEE* Transactions **9**(3), 1983.

(5) Carlsen, N.V.; Christensen, N.J., "Modelling User Interface Software", in this volume.

(6) Cockton, G., "A New Model for Separable Interactive Systems", in *Proceedings of the INTERACT'87*, North-Holland, 1987.

(7) Cockton, G., "Components, Agents & Frameworks - the Architectural basis of design re-use", in this volume.

(8) Coutaz, J., "Architecture Models for Interactive Software: Failures and Trends", in *Engineering for Human-Computer Interaction*, Cockton, G. (ed), North-Holland 1990.

(9) Dance, J.R.; Granor, T.E; Hill, R.D.; Hudson, S.E.; Meads, J.; Myers, B.A.; Schulert, A., "The Run-time Structure of UIMS-Supported Applications", *Computer Graphics* **21**(2), 1987.

(10) Duce, D.A.; ten Hagen, P.J.W.; van Liere, R., "Components, Frameworks and GKS input, *Proceedings of EUROGRAPHICS '89*, North-Holland, September 1989.

(11) Faconti, G.P.; Paterno, F., "An Approach to the Formal Specification of the Components of an Interaction", *Proceedings of EUROGRAPHICS '90*, North-Holland, September 1990.

(12) Foley, J.D.; Wallace, V.L.; Chan, P., "The Human Factors of Computer Graphics Interaction Techniques", *IEEE Computer Graphics & Applications*, November 1984.

(13) Foley, J.D; Gibbs, C.; Kim, W.C.; Kovacevic, S., "A Knowledge-Based User Interface Management System", *Proceedings of the ACM CHI'88*.

(14) Grollmann, J.; Rumpf, C., "Some Comments on the Future of User Interface Tools", in this volume.

(15) Hill, R.D.; Herrmann, M., "The Structure of Tube - A Tool for Implementing Advanced User Interfaces" *Proceedings of EUROGRAPHICS '89*, North-Holland, September 1989.

(16) Herrmann, M.; Hill, R.D., "Some Conclusions about UIMS design based on the Tube experience", *Colloque sur l'ingeniene des interfaces homme-machine*, Sophia-Antipolis(France), May 1989.

(17) Huebner, W.; Gomes, M.R., "Two Object-Oriented Models to Design Graphical User Interfaces", *Proceedings of EUROGRAPHICS '89*, North-Holland, September 1989.

(18) Lantz, K.A.; Tanner, P.P; Binding, C.; Huang, K.T.; Dwelly, A., "Reference Models, Window Systems and Concurrency", *Computer Graphics* **21**(2), 1987.

(19) Lee, J., "Intelligent Interfaces and UIMS", in this volume.

(20) Olsen, D.R. (chair), "ACM SIGGRAPH Workshop on Software Tools for User Interface Management", *Computer* Graphics **21(2)**, 1987.

(21) Pfaff, G. (ed), *User Interface Management Systems*, Springer-Verlag 1985.

(22) Prime, M., "User Interface Management Systems - A Current Product Review", *Computer Graphics Forum*, March 1990.

(23) Shevlin, F.; Neelamkavil, F., "Designing the Next Generation of UIMSs", in this volume.

(24) Thomas, J.J.; Hamlin, G., "Graphical Input Interaction Technique (GIIT) Workshop Summary", *Computer Graphics* **17**(1), 1983.

Chapter 5

Current Practice Working Group

5.1 Participants

D. Morin (Chairman)
J. Bangratz
R. Castaleiro
D.A. Duce
D. Ehmke
C.C. Hayball
P. Johnson
L. van Klarenbosch
E. Le Thieis
P.H. Munch
P. Sturm
D. Svanaes
S. Wilson

5.2 Discussion

Dominique Morin opened the Working Group on Monday afternoon, saying that there were six papers for presentation and two lists of questions as a starting point for discussion. The two key questions presented to the Working Group were:

(1) Which techniques are currently used and why?

(2) Who uses them, how and for what?

Papers by Sturm, Hayball, Le Thieis, Svanaes, Johnson and Ehmke were presented on Monday afternoon and the first part of the Tuesday morning session. Five UIMS systems were described in the presentations, IUICE, KHS, RAID, MOSAIC and PROMETHEUS, and one other (DICE) described at the Workshop. As a result of discussion during the presentations, a number of questions were identified which were subsequently answered for each system described. The questions and responses are given below.

(1) *Identification of the types of users of the tools (expert/non-expert).*

IUICE: non-expert end users; UI designers have to be expert.

KHS: expert UI designers or applications programmers.

RAID: programmers.

MOSAIC: anyone can use the tool, e.g. children, students.

PROMETHEUS: expert - programmers.

DICE: systems programmer for adding new tools, programmers for interaction application.

(2) *Have the tools been evaluated, if so on what criteria?*

IUICE: only performance of UI code generated has been evaluated.

KHS: no evaluation has yet been carried out, though this is planned.

RAID: no formal evaluation has been carried out.

MOSAIC: no evaluation has been carried out.

PROMETHEUS: system has been evaluated.

DICE: see the survey paper by Prime [1].

(3) *Environment (platform, window system, toolkit, ...)*

IUICE: SUN cluster on top of X windows, using own toolkit.

KHS: SUN or ICL DRS 6000, X, XView and PCE toolkit.

RAID: UNIX workstation, X windows, Motif toolkit.

MOSAIC: MS-DOS (IBM PC), version for Microsoft Windows 3.0 under development.

PROMETHEUS: X with Athena, Motif toolkits, also DecWindows. Runs on UNIX and VMS.

DICE: Unix workstation, X Windows, GKS-3D like graphics system.

(4) *Languages used:*

(a) *for UIMS tools development*

IUICE: C/IUICE (bootstrapped)

KHS: C++.

RAID: C, UIL.

MOSAIC: Turbo Pascal.

PROMETHEUS: C.

DICE: C, C++.

(b) *to capture UI specifications*

IUICE: IUICE language.

KHS: KDL.

RAID: RAID.

MOSAIC: Prolog.

PROMETHEUS: widgets.

DICE: DICE specification language.

(c) *run-time*

IUICE: C.

KHS: interpretive.

RAID: C.

MOSAIC: interpretive.

PROMETHEUS: C code generated.

DICE: C code.

(5) *UI specification techniques and notations used (ATNs, scripts, etc.):*

IUICE: visual programming language offering events and objects and object hierarchy.

KHS: object hierarchy and event state transition rules, scripts.

RAID: extended ATNs, ATNs (Navigator tool), extended UIL (Explorer tool).

MOSAIC: objects with event actions, object hierarchy, script-like.

PROMETHEUS: specification of events in C, C callback for semantic feedback.

DICE: context free grammar, resource declarations, trigger expressions, C interface to application.

(6) *Application areas addressed:*

IUICE: visualization of scientific data.

KHS: interactive decision support systems (especially knowledge-based systems).

RAID: CIM.

MOSAIC: education software and simulation (Mac-like).

PROMETHEUS: software engineering environments, office systems, highly interactive graphical systems.

DICE: CAD/CAM and video games.

(7) *Use of explicit User Task Model? If yes, based on what?*

IUICE: does not have a UTM.

KHS: does not have a UTM. Tool is a part of the KADS KBS Design Methodology.

RAID: does not have a UTM. Tool fits with Foley's methodology.

MOSAIC: not constrained by tool.

Prometheus: none.

DICE: extension of SADT during conceptual/functional design.

(8) *Characterization of the application interface and the relationship between UI design and application design (precedence, simultaneity, ...).*

IUICE: the application interface uses sockets and files. There are no restrictions on the relationship between application and UI design.

KHS: application interface is message passing across UNIX pipes. UI design usually precedes application design.

RAID: application interface is sockets and IPC. It is preferable for application and UI design to proceed in parallel.

MOSAIC: application interface is a message interface. Application design and UI design are normally simultaneous, but UI can also be retrofitted to existing programs.

PROMETHEUS: application interface is a procedural C interface. UI design normally comes first.

DICE: application and user interface done together. User interface linked to application as a set of C routines.

(9) *What is the role of prototyping in the design process (place in the lifecycle, exploratory vs. evolutionary, etc.)*

IUICE: prototyping is used in a 'game-playing' manner. There is no constructive way to arrive at the answer.

KHS: prototypes are used to demonstrate concepts to customers. The approach is evolutionary with evaluation by the customer at each stage.

RAID: evolutionary prototyping, with reuse of UIL files and architecture.

MOSAIC: prototypes can be throw-away, but are normally evolutionary. Prototypes can be used as specification tools in order to obtain user feedback.

PROMETHEUS: prototypes are used for evaluation by designers.

DICE: can use empty application calls and high level interaction units not yet decomposed.

(10) *Development effort (man years), size, number of projects in which it has been used.*

IUICE: 2 MY, 30K lines of code, 3 applications projects.

KHS: 7 MY, still under development, PCE used in 100 projects.

RAID: 1 year so far, 5K lines of code, used for prototype of scheduling package.

MOSAIC: 5MY, 30K lines of code, 100 systems produced are in use (represents about 1000 systems if throw-away prototypes are included).

PROMETHEUS: 20 MY, large volume of code, used for 5 real applications (external use).

DICE: 12 MY, 1M byte code including graphics system, used in 2 major applications (database and CAD/CAM).

These results were presented to the Plenary Session. It was suggested that the Working Group should look at the problems encountered in the development of these systems and the test cases which caused significant design revisions and the reasons for these. The Group was also asked to look at how the systems fit in with the Seeheim Model and the reasons for divergences.

(1) PROMETHEUS: development of the system started in 1985 and it was based on the Seeheim Model. The application defines objects which the user can interact with. The application cannot define *how* the user manipulates the objects and sometimes *how* turns out to be important.

(2) MOSAIC: the inspiration for MOSAIC was MacResources rather than the Seeheim Model. MOSAIC follows the Seeheim Model in putting a wall between the UI and the application.

All members of the Group concerned with direct manipulation interfaces agreed that the Seeheim Model could not support direct manipulation interfaces because of its inability to handle fine-grained semantic feedback.

The need for each *object* to have presentation and action components was noted. The distinction between a design framework and the components of a run-time system was also noted.

(3) IUICE: this system might be expressed in the Seeheim Model, but the author preferred and had thought of it as an object description. Each object can be decomposed into presentation, dialogue etc. components. This discussion led to the following view of design being proposed by Morin.

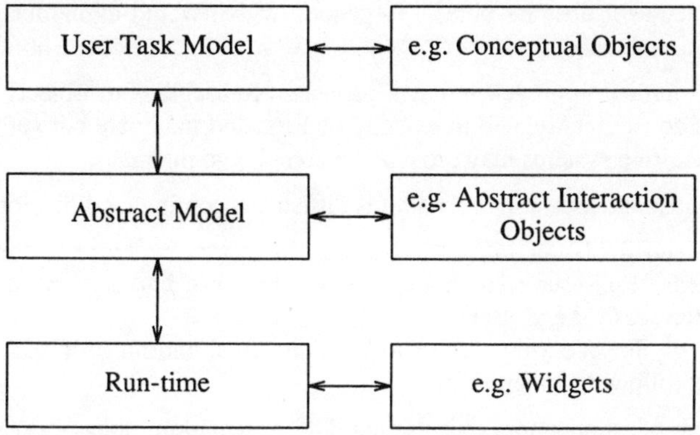

The above diagram shows schematically one possible relationship between the user task model, abstract model, run-time model and interface design components such as 'conceptual objects', 'interaction objects' and 'widgets'.

It was realized that there is a spectrum of divisions in architectures between the vertical divisions of the Seeheim Model to the horizontal divisions of the object-oriented approach. Four system components were identified in the Seeheim Model: presentation, dialogue, application interface and application. The Seeheim Model represents a vertical division between each. Object oriented approaches, for example PAC, are creating horizontal divisions, meaning that objects contain elements of more than one component. Characterizations of the systems discussed in the Working Group were given as follows.

(1) KHS: this system has a vertical separation between application interface and application, but alides presentation and dialogue. There is a clear application interface component.

(2) IUICE: presentation and dialogue can be composed, as can application interface and application. The structuring is similar to KHS, but provides more flexibility in the application interface.

(3) MOSAIC: every object has presentation, dialogue and application interface components. For conceptual design, all components can be mixed in every object, but for implementation the application components are separated out and implemented in Pascal.

(4) RAID: a distinction is made between dialogue local to an object and global dialogue common to all objects, leading to splitting of the dialogue component. Presentation and local dialogue can be horizontally divided; other components are vertically divided.

(5) PROMETHEUS: this system has a vertical division between presentation and dialogue with horizontal divisions of dialogue and the components of the application responsible for semantic feedback.

In summary, the Group's feelings about the Seeheim Model were that the model does provide a reasonable abstract view of an interactive system but the run-time system need not contain distinct dialogue or presentation components. There were some concerns that the notions in the Seeheim Model are too vague rather than too abstract, and some reservations were expressed about the adequacy of the linguistic interpretation of the model for modern direct manipulation interfaces.

Some observations from the final session of the Working Group were:

(1) There is a need for an abstract representation of widgets, so that at the abstract level, implementation issues can be avoided. There is a parallel here to the conceptual views provided by database management systems, which avoid low-level detail.

(2) There is a need for abstract objects in general which would allow designers to ignore implementation details.

(3) The object-oriented approach is not a panacea. Reusability of objects implies acceptance of the constraints related to existing objects, and many are not yet ready to accept this. The resulting systems may prove to be complex to maintain.

(4) Objects encapsulate look and feel and it is difficult to confine modifications to one place.

(5) There is a need for better integration of human factors expertise in the user interface design process. End-user opinion also needs to be taken into account to allow customization of interfaces for end-users.

A subgroup of the Working Group met on the final morning of the Workshop and emerged with the following conclusions.

(1) The division of application objects and UI presentation objects is important. The counter example is HyperCard where a card is a card and a button is a button. This makes it very difficult to develop systems with multiple views on a data structure.

(2) Application and presentation objects are each complex and dynamic and the relations between these objects are also complex and dynamic, leading to difficulties of maintaining consistency.

(3) There is a need for a language to express these relationships (possibly constraint-based). Flexible and extensible design environments are required. Object-oriented design is helpful, but is neither necessary nor sufficient.

References

(1) M. Prime, ''User Interface Management Systems - A Current Product Review'', *Computer Graphics Forum*, **9**(1), pp. 53-76 (1990).

Chapter 6

Multi-media and Visual Programming

6.1 Participants

A. Kilgour (Chairman)
M. Bordegoni
U. Cugini (for part)
W. Doster
N. Guimaraes
G. Howell
W. Huebner
L. Larsson

6.2 Introduction

Papers by Bordegoni, Larsson, Grant, Herrmann, Spenke, Gomes and Howell were presented to this Group and to the participants in the Working Group on Toolkits, Environments and the Object Oriented Paradigm (see Chapter 7) in common. Then the groups divided to work in parallel.

The Working Group first looked at Multi-Media as it saw this area as being of major concern. It followed this by a discussion of Visual Programming and its relationship to User Interface Management Systems. The major papers of relevance to this Group were those by Bordegoni, Larsson and Howell.

6.3 Multi-media

6.3.1 Definition

The Working Group used the following definition of multi-media:

(1) Multi-media is concerned with both input and output (including their combination called interaction).

(2) For output, multi-media is concerned with multiple streams operating in parallel (for example, vector graphics, raster graphics, text, video, sound, etc.). Streams may not be the best word, channels tracks or modes were alternatives.

(3) For input, multi-media is concerned with simultaneous input events generated by one or several different devices (for example key chords, foot pedals, spoken command, data-glove, datasuite, five-finger-mouse, touch screen, eye tracker, musical instruments etc.) all being used in parallel.

(4) On input, it is concerned with the composition of higher level input tokens in terms of more primitive input events. For example, gesture input could be derived from a set of dataglove positions.

Each output stream is of a specific medium. It may be connected to any media source (for example, speech synthesiser, computer graphics generator, video disc, CD-ROM drive etc) and routed to any presentation destination (graphical devices, bitmap, video etc.). There may be multiple graphical channels (for example, outputting to different windows on the same screen or to different screens) simultaneously with sound (speech or music), tactile feedback (for example, variable resistance), and even smell! On the input side, it should be possible for keyboard, dataglove, mouse and foot pedal all to be working in parallel. The synchronization of different output channels, of parallel input events and of input and output is a characteristic problem of multi-media.

6.3.2 Interface Requirements

On the output side, the designer needs to be able to:

(1) Specify the connections between streams and media sources, and the transitions between episodes on the same source and another.

(2) Control the characteristics of each episode on a channel (for example, output destination, speed of playback, interrupt events).

(3) Combine two or more streams into higher level logical streams.

(4) Specify *synchronisation* constraints between different channels.

On the input side, the designer needs to be able to:

(1) Extend the list of primitive events recognised by the system.

(2) Compose primitive events into higher level input *tokens* such as gestures, hand-drawn symbols etc.

(3) Recognise simultaneous events when they occur.

(4) Specify synchronization constraints between input events.

(5) Use a basic media manager that must be very exact in timing (better than X Windows) for defining synchronisity and parallel events.

(6) Set up parallel event monitors.

(7) Handle new input modes and devices.

(8) Dealing with several users in parallel.

On the interaction side, the designer needs to be able to:

(1) Specify routing of event (queues) to different output channels. Not only the window that contains the position of the mouse cursor but more sophisticated rules are necessary.

(2) Specify synchronization constraints between input events and output channels.

(3) Provide meaningful feedback in the context of relevant output objects (for example, when an object is grasped with a dataglove).

(4) Combine input and output to interaction objects.

6.3.3 Implications for Design Environments

The primary implications are:

(1) That *full concurrency* (not just interleaving) must be supported and synchronisation controls provided for activities on different streams.

(2) That input handling must be extensible, so that new primitive event types can be added by connecting new input devices and drivers and translating input operations into input events.

(3) That composition mechanisms must be available for defining higher level event classes in terms of primitive events and for composing complex interactions by a meaningful coupling of input, output and application semantics.

Mechanisms to allow the composition of input events into higher level tokens could be based on logical and temporal operators and should rely on the knowledge about the application semantics; those mechanisms have not been discussed in detail within the Working Group.

6.3.4 Relevance of Seeheim Model

The Working Group concluded that the requirements of multi media, as well as the evidence from their own experience, highlighted the unsuitability of the Seeheim Model if applied at the macro level, that is if taken to imply that there must be single identifiable monolithic software components dealing with presentation, dialogue control and application interface.

If taken on the micro level to describe the internal structure of interactions the components are applicable. Therefore a composition/decomposition along all dimensions towards a recursive (or distributed) Seeheim Model was discussed for multi-media applications. Nevertheless, no single alternative architecture (Lisbon=Seeheim++) was proposed or believed to be appropriate. Rather the Working Group supported the multi-faceted approach proposed in the opening session, in particular:

(1) Decomposition at the top level based on design, encapsulating application abstractions.

(2) Complementary to this, the identification of generic functional components such as media managers, session managers, etc. Instances of these would be found in specific interfaces.

(3) The application of the Seeheim Model to the design of the individual objects arising from these decompositions.

The question was not resolved as to whether the Seeheim breakdown of presentation, control and application linkage was sufficient in all cases. Should more aspects be flagged for the designers attention in refining individual components?

It was felt that these architectural requirements were in accord with the object-oriented approach but that:

(1) Some objects need to be concurrently active (for example, media handlers).

(2) Both synchronous (*message passing*) and asynchronous (*event-based*) communication between objects must be supported.

These requirements go beyond the capabilities of conventional object-oriented systems such as Smalltalk.

6.4 Visual Programming

The Working Group did not feel that this raised any special problems or requirements for interface design environments or architectures. The user interface development process consists of several design tasks at different levels of abstraction. For those design tasks which describe information that can be graphically expressed, visual design tools should be integrated. These are restricted areas: at the presentation level some graphical appearance can be designed with visual tools (for example icon editor, menu builder, graphics editor etc.). At the dialogue control it is useful to describe abstract information like flow of control with graphical formalisms (for example ATN- or Petri-net editors). For other tasks, for example to develop the application level or textual information at the presentation level or to say 'width = 2 × height' non-visual programming techniques are more adequate. Therefore the Working Group concluded that it is not an issue whether to use visual programming or not but to integrate these techniques in the user interface design process. In this case the general visual programming problems arise also in user interface design but no additional issues appear. However, the following points were noted:

(1) Generic tools for the production of specific visual programming systems would be desireable.

(2) Users need to understand the domain concepts. Visual programming should not be thought of as avoiding the need for application knowledge.

(3) Visual programming gets harder to do the lower the level (and so narrower the abstraction) of the operations being addressed.

(4) Different formalisms have different degrees of suitability for generation by visual programming. In some cases, visual programming may be more cumbersome and opaque than textual specification.

(5) Visual programming systems work best when targeted at specific and restricted tasks.

(6) Program visualization systems may provide visual programming capabilities if the visualization can be edited by the user.

(7) Visual programming should be encouraged as a research area where imagination and ingenuity in finding effective representations and metaphors can yield rich rewards in improved functionality.

Chapter 7

Toolkits, Environments and the Object Oriented Paradigm

7.1 Participants

M. Gomes (Chairman)
B. David
P. Grant
M. Herrmann
R. Hill
K. Molander
M. Spenke
P. Townsend

7.2 Introduction

The Working Group defined a target family of applications, Graphical Direct Manipulation Human Computer Interaction Systems.

The Working Group saw as its two main areas of activity:

(1) *Relevance of Object Oriented Programming to UIMS*: including how these approaches help throughout the life cycle of Human Computer Interaction Systems.

(2) *New Architectures, Models and Methodologies:* the main areas to be considered were the identification of new components and the relations between them.

The major papers of relevance to the Group were those by Ralph Hill, Michael Spenke, Peter Townsend *et al*, and Mario Gomes.

7.3 Object Oriented Methodologies

The Working Group started by looking at the use of Object Oriented Methodologies and related techniques. A major comment is that Inheritance and Polymorphism, although important parts of the technique, were infrequently used due to lack of knowledge and experience of OO technology amongst the professional community. The Group also believed that current OO techniques were not sufficient for UID and should be extended in two directions: constraint solvers and support for actors. It was identified that Object Orientation is a good approach for the definition of semantics: constraints can be used for Presentation and actors for Dialogue, with Object Orientation as the 'glue' between all the elements.

The Working Group believed that the specification and implementation of a Human Computer Interaction system is a multi-dimensional problem incorporating all the major requirements identified in the Seeheim Model and many others besides, including support for Help, Undo, Test and Dynamics.

The Group looked at some Object Oriented UID systems on the market for assessment. MacApp was seen as good for a limited family of applications. HyperCard Next Interface Builder is just a compose tool that gives no support to the creation of new interaction techniques.

It was also concluded that the OO approach helps:

(1) the inheritance of generic properties;

(2) to define abstractions (data plus operations);

(3) to increase the support of properties important in software engineering such as modularity and code reuse;

(4) to extend the user interaction abstractions;

(5) to model Human Computer Interaction Systems.

The approach does not help:

(1) to define a good OO structure (bad structures are particularly difficult to change!);

(2) to define the system dynamics including the behaviour of each class and the relation between objects of different classes. Dynamic definition of both classes and relations is needed.

At the language level the strengths and weaknesses of both prototyping languages (weak typing) and OO languages (strong typing) were discussed, but no consensus was reached. The relation between standard programming and visual programming was also discussed and the Group agreed that programming by demonstration is not enough even for programming low level control structures.

7.4 Seeheim

The Working Group spent some time assessing the Seeheim Model and deciding where it was not appropriate.

The major points in its favour were:

(1) as a means of educating people in the components of a UIMS;

(2) it had been shown to be useful in the area of command-based dialogues;

(3) it had provided a concrete definition which could be used as a focus for criticism;

(4) the Model was appropriate for simple static interfaces such as form filling.

The major criticisms were:

(1) The breakdown into only three components gave very little structure in the model and was only just useful.

(2) If the components were modules in the run-time system, it would almost certainly imply an unacceptable performance penalty.

(3) If separation was to describe abstract concepts, it was inferior to other possible formalisms.

(4) If the Seeheim model was a run-time model, it was unlikely to be able to provide efficient semantic feedback.

7.5 CASE Versus UIMS

If a UIMS is seen as a design aid, the major criticism is that designing the user interface is only one part of the complete design process. The system may be using a set of CASE tools that force a certain discipline on the design process. In this case, the UIMS must inter-work with the CASE tools and it is important, therefore, to provide an integrated CASE/UIMS design environment.

7.6 Models and Methodologies

The Working Group looked at the needs of the community in terms of a Human Computer Interaction System and decided to concentrate on looking for a model and methodology which encompassed what was believed to be the most generalized family of user interfaces, the direct manipulation family.

The Working Group's view was that a model based on object orientation methodologies was the correct approach to follow and that Tube and PAC are examples of these models. But new methodologies and architectures should be defined to cope with the problem of defining the internal structure of each object and the relationships between objects.

Some application dependent advice was given:

(1) Use a toolkit to implement low level User Interaction Techniques. (XToolkit was used by eight of the people in the Group and Open Look by four.)

(2) Find and use higher level tools such as Forms Managers.

(3) Use an extensible and integrated environment for the composition of high level User Interaction Techniques. Heterogeneous techniques should be used. In any case, roles must be defined first and secondly relations between objects.

The Working Group concluded that:

(1) new methodologies, models and architectures for families of applications must be studied;

(2) new formalisms for the definition of intra and inter object structure must be defined;

(3) the integration of object support, actor support and constraint solving support should be achieved;

(4) new development environments for the creation of Human Computer Interaction Systems, not only for User Interfaces, must be specified, developed and used.

7.7 Answers to Questions

The Working Group attempted to give answers to the list of questions issed to inaugurate discussion.

(1) *Should we define a set of interaction tools needed by a UIMS (rubber-band lines, icon dragging, browsing, scrolling, zooming)? Which of these are equivalent?*

It is good to have those low level interaction techniques but they do not fulfill the requirements of a Graphic Direct Manipulation Application.

(2) *Should we define a set of interaction objects for the operator (menus, icons of various types)? If so what are they and what attributes should be associated with them?*

Even the Look and Feel should be family dependent.

(3) *Are 'Look and Feel' standards necessary and practical? If so, how should such standardization be provided and what should be covered?*

Yes if you are building a product, no if you are conducting research.

(4) *What are the requirements of a HELP tool in a UIMS?*

Insufficient experience to answer.

(5) *What are the requirements of a rapid prototyping tool in a UIMS?*

The development of a product should be a task which integrates all the phases in the life of the product. So the requirements of rapid prototyping should be the same as the requirements of the product development environment. The last prototype should be the product. The emphasis should be not on prototyping but on updating.

(6) *Would a properly-designed UIMS be easier to use than a toolkit (for the interface designer)? Would it be easier to create a better interface?*

Depends on the tasks.

(7) *Should toolkits only be used by the best interface designers?*

No comments.

Or does the OO paradigm ensure the enforcement/encouragement of good design principles?

No.

(8) *Using an UIDS is it already possible to define the relationship between objects (to define a society)?*

Yes.

Is it possible to define also the behaviour of each object?

Yes with knowledge representation at the class level, but this is still an open question.

(9) *Should we continue to see interaction techniques mainly as a procedure or should we see them also as a data type that is produced (like the GKS input model)?*

This is the wrong question if objects are multi-dimensional.

(10) *What will be the importance of the future object-oriented operating systems, OOOS to the UIDS and UIMS? what will be the UIMS on an OOOS?*

Wait and see!

(11) *How can an OO UIMS interact with existing applications written in Fortran?*

This is an application dependent problem. No general solution exists.

(12) *Is there any emerging consensus on object hierarchy from current OO systems?*

Not as yet. There are both heterogeneous and homogeneous approaches.

(13) *What society (set of objects) should be used for the architecture of a UI?*

Open question.

(14) *What are the best features of an AI language and of an OO language to satisfy the requirements of an interactive graphic application.*

Not enough experience yet to answer the question.

(15) *Can we use OO programming for the implementation of any kind of dialogue specification technique, including transition networks, grammars and event models?*

Yes.

Chapter 8

Conclusions

The result of the Workshop was a set of general conclusions and some pointers for future research. The conclusions detailed below received general support across the Working Groups, which had achieved striking convergence on a number of issues.

A notable tendency during discussions in the Workshop — including the plenary sessions — was a shift from talking of 'user interfaces' to talking of 'interactive systems'. This reflects one of the strongest themes in the conclusions, which is that the emphasis should be on system *design*, and that design of the interface to an interactive system cannot be divorced from the design of the 'application' itself. It was recognised that these distinctions are always artificial, even when 'retrofitting' an interface to an existing system. In these circumstances, existing application software forms an environmental constraint on the design that has to be taken into account in the same way as policies enforcing the use of existing window managers, graphics systems, etc.

If there is a coherent message from this Workshop, it must be that to create high quality user interfaces the old conception of a UIMS as a monolithic component, portable to various back-end applications, was overly optimistic. One of the goals of a UIMS as seen at the Seeheim Workshop (according to Mark Green, in Pfaff (ed) 1985, p. 9) was 'the automatic (or semi-automatic) construction of user interfaces'; this Workshop leaves it much less clear that such a goal makes sense. However as originally presented, the Seeheim Model was explicitly abstract:

> This model does not represent how a UIMS should be structured or implemented, instead it represents the logical components that must appear in a UIMS. (Green, ibid.)

It is now being recognised that the distinction between UIMS and application is supportable only as a logical abstraction. The concept of an interactive system must incorporate both the user interface and the application.

8.1 Conclusions

(1) *The conceptual decomposition of the Seeheim Model does distinguish aspects of interaction which can be analysed separately.*

Discussion of the Seeheim Model had naturally been a theme of the Workshop. The Model was generally agreed to be highly abstract and in a certain sense crude. It could provide little *guidance* for implementation of systems. On the other hand, it was found that even Object-oriented systems can be *described* in terms of the Model, and in some cases this provides a useful conceptual framework, for example for evaluation. However it is not the only model that can be used and more recent work has proposed alternatives.

(2) *Run-time architectures need not reflect a conceptual model directly.*

All the Working Groups observed that it is very often either unhelpful or impossible to apply the decomposition of a model to the architectures of run-time systems. It must be firmly established that the model provides at most a tool for analysis.

(3) *An object-oriented approach is often flexible, effective and efficient ...*

Several Working Groups concluded that one or other of a family of object-oriented or 'actor'-based approaches would provide the best model for various kinds of systems. A great variety of dialogue styles can be supported, and it was felt to be particularly promising for multi-media integration.

(4) *... but it is not always either necessary or sufficient*

There was also a common feeling that in many cases an object-oriented approach, even though it might work, would be no *better* than an alternative (for example a grammar-based specification). The Working Group on Current Practice, in particular, pointed to the Procrustean restrictions that can be introduced by excessive commitment to the properties of existing objects.

(5) *A design-oriented approach is best.*

A remarkable concensus emerged, that to look at run-time issues ahead of design is unprofitable. Nothing completely general can be said about run-time systems, except at the level of abstraction of the Seeheim Model itself. Therefore, methodological principles should be be sought only for the *design* of interactive systems, placing the needs of the user in the context of his/her task domain firmly to the fore. This applies equally to the design of new systems and to retrofitting interfaces to existing applications.

(6) *Constraint-satisfaction is an important issue and should be supported in any design environment.*

At several levels, from communications between software objects or modules, to global aspects of the system user's environment, satisfaction of constraints is a crucial aspect of interactive system design. These constraints form the boundary of the space within which an interface will emerge as (part of) a solution. But how the constraints at different levels interact remains a research problem.

8.2 Research Issues

(1) *What are the generic components?*

Reflections on the Seeheim Model, combined with Gilbert Cockton's paper, prompt this as an issue about architectures. *Are* there, in fact, any generic components, common to all interactive systems? The Workshop leaves this question wide open. Perhaps generic decompositions can happen only at the Seeheim level of generality, and all more specific architectures are bound to be restricted to certain tools, certain users, certain designers, etc.

(2) *Composition methods for components.*

Whatever components there are, even at a relatively specific level, their methods of composition are still unclear. For example, the PAL model uses similar components to the Seeheim model, but composes them in a radically different way.

(3) *Support for concurrent object-oriented approach.*

It was clear from discussion, and from a number of participants' papers, that concurrency is increasingly an issue in object-oriented design. But often it has little or no specialized support, for example at the levels of operating systems and window manager.

(4) *Formalisms.*

There is still much doubt about what formalisms are well-adapted for various tasks, for example defining compositions of events. Much discussion surrounded Petri nets, ATNs, and several other less standard devices, but many of the issues remain unresolved, especially in the context of concurrent systems.

(5) *Equivalences between systems (and formalisms).*

Though common in other areas of theoretical computer science, detailed examination of formal equivalence is not often undertaken with respect to interactive systems. Time is often spent in debating the differences between systems and formalisms which might well turn out, on deeper examination, to be equivalent in the sort of way that competing grammar formalisms often turn out to be, i.e. in terms of computational complexity, generative power, etc. Where differences are essentially on a surface level, or better approached as psychological or human factors issues, this should be clearly recognized.

(6) *Human Factors, HCI and Interactive System Design.*

Starting with the 'traditional' notion of a UIMS, the Workshop (especially the Methodology Subgroup) rapidly began to focus on the importance of seeing the design of interactive systems as an activity that should take special account of the needs of the *user*. This suggests that many aspects of discussion of 'UIMS' should pay much more attention to ongoing work in generalized HCI and human factors areas.

Part II

Concepts, Models and Methodologies

Chapter 9

Some Comments on the Future of User Interface Tools

Joachim Grollman and Christoph Rumpf

Abstract

The goal of this paper is to point at some of the more important deficiencies of current user interface tools. Our point of view is an industrial one. Therefore, many of the requirements to user interface tools formulated in this paper are results from experience made with customers and real use of such tools. Let us mention already here the most eminent deficiency we currently see: the missing experience with the application of user interface tools, in contrast to the large number of tools that have been developed thus far. Also, it needs to be observed that workstations in office environments are not the only field where user interfaces exist. In detail we discuss the following areas: AI-inspired techniques, multi-media dialog, the evaluation of user interface and distributed computing.

1. Introduction

This paper is not so much meant to be a technical paper on user interface (UI) tools, nor does it describe specific features of any such system. But, sometimes we make references to existing or planned systems as examples. The goal of this paper is to point at some of the more important deficiencies of current UI tools. Our point of view is an industrial one. Therefore, many of the requirements to UI tools formulated in this paper are results from experience made with with customers and real use of such tools. Let us mention already here the most eminent deficiency we currently see: the missing experience with the application of UI tools, in contrast to the large number of tools that have been developed thus far.

Currently, nobody seems to be able to give a definitive formal answer to the following question: "What precisely is a UI?" In the following we will assume that we have some common feeling about what a UI is, in spite of the lack of a formal definition.

Now, why is it necessary to discuss UIs and tools for their design at all? There are several reasons for doing this:

- Social reasons. More and more non-experts use computers. Our society is moving into a fully computerized society. We can no longer afford to fit man to machines; instead we have to fit machines to man. This was already recognized in 1963 (!) by Mills, cited in (Bullinger et al. 1987):

  "The future is rapidly approaching when professional programmers will be among the least numerous and the least significant system users."

- Technical reasons. More and more possibilities exist for interaction with computers. The relative portion of programs which is responsible for human-computer interaction grows constantly. New interaction techniques and the higher degree of interactivity of programs are responsible for this. We need the means to cope with the growing complexity.
- Research reasons. Hardware ergonomics by now is well established, but software ergonomics is not yet.

In the early years of data processing, the typical users of computers were computer scientists, trained experts. This has very much changed over the last years. Therefore, one of the most important goals of research on UIs is to make systems accessible also for non-experts, and to hide the complexity of todays software. Buzzwords like user friendliness, software ergonomics and adaptability of software to its end users characterize the changing situation.

Designing UIs for software systems based on ergonomical principles in general demands much effort. The simpler the UI of an application appears to the end user, the more complex is its design. There are also no general design strategies ensuring that the designed UIs fulfill all user requirements. Currently, there is only one reliable strategy for achieving high acceptance of applications and user-friendly UIs, namely, the iterative design and test in close cooperation with future users. Developing applications with good UIs is expensive and time consuming if only the basic graphics and windowing software are provided. The purpose of a UI design environment must be to ease the iterative task of UI design. With such an environment, UIs should be designed rationally; the design should be carried out in parallel with the design of the application's functionality.

Sometimes these environments were called "UI management systems", but there is no general agreement on which notions to use. In Chapter 2 we discuss notions and features of systems which are used for design and management of UIs. Chapter 3 discusses AI-inspired techniques, Chapter 4 multi-media dialog, Chapter 5 evaluation problems, and Chapter 6 distributed environments, in each case in the light of UI tools. Chapter 7 contains a summary and list of the most important open questions and problems.

2. Current Concepts and Notions

There has been much discussion on the term "UI management system". Several people tried to design such a system, and several others then typically claimed: "No, this is none!". Now, what is a "UI management system"? In (Betts et al. 1987) we find the following definition:

> *"A User Interface Management System (UIMS) is a tool (or a tool set) designed to encourage interdisciplinary cooperation in the rapid development, tailoring and management (control) of the interaction in an application domain across varying devices, interaction techniques and user interface styles. A UIMS tailors and manages (controls) user interaction in an application domain to allow for rapid and consistent development.*
> *A UIMS can be viewed as a tool for increasing programmer productivity. In*

this way it is similar to a fourth generation language, where the concentration is on specification instead of coding. A UIMS can be described from two different viewpoints: the viewpoint of the software developer and the viewpoint of the end user."

From this definition we conclude that a UIMS consists of two main components:
- a design component which can be used for the design or adaptation or modification of a specific UI by either the software developer (in this role also called a "dialog designer") or by the end user himself (these components have been called "Interactive Design Tools" in (Atlas et al. 1989)
- and a run-time component which handles and manages the dialog between end user and application at run-time.

We call the first component a UI design system, and the second a UI management system. The combination of the two will be called UI design and management system (UIDMS). We will use these terms in this paper; but, we believe that it does not make much sense to discuss the confusion about such terms too long: this does not at all help the end user or the dialog designer! And to help the end user and the designer is our fundamental goal, or isn't it? Instead, we believe that it makes more sense to define the functionality of such systems, to implement them and *to get experience with them*!

What is the functionality of a UIDMS? We recall some of the fundamental tasks, without going into detail. A UIDMS has to support
- rapid prototyping of UIs, with intelligent support, and parallel to the development of the functionality of a system; this includes graphical design of UIs, with on-line evaluation; perhaps even an automatic mechanism for the design of a first UI prototype
- reusablity of UI components; this together with graphically-interactive design should help rationalizing the software development process
- different kinds of control (internal, external and mixtures)
- homogeneous UIs for different applications, and homogeneity inside one application
- adaptability or even (self-)adaptivity of a UI to different end users of an application
- different styles of interaction, especially direct manipulation and multi-threaded dialogs - parallel methods of working with free choice of input possibilities (mouse, keyboard, etc.); more general: openness to new developments; most current systems for design and support of UIs have been monolithic software packages rather than open extensible architectures allowing integration of additional components to support, e.g., new interaction techniques. An alternative approach, offering an open extensible architecture while permitting close coupling of input, application semantics and feedback, would be that of object-oriented programming
- mechanisms for error-handling, undoing, redoing
- user guidance, even "intelligent assistance"
- modification of the UI at run-time.

We claim that this all can only be managed when UI code and functionality code are separated. Separation, however, leads to quite a lot of problems, e.g., provision of semantic feedback is yet unclear. Our feeling is that this is essentially a technical problem, and by itself no reason to give up the separation principle. The separation principle is not more than just a weakened version of the principle of writing software in a modularized way.

The Seeheim model (Green 1983) demands a very strict separation between UI and functionality. Let us call the interface between the two "dialog interface", or, shortly, "DIF". It also demands that all user input passes through the "dialog control component", and the same should hold true for output. This yields insufficient performance, at least with current machines. But, we should obey the separation principle, in spite of performance considerations. Nearly nobody nowadays uses assembling languages, although they could often lead to better performance; we prefer the clarity of high-level languages.

Separation sometimes demands to keep the same information twice, namely, to keep semantic information about the application inside the UI portion *and* inside the functionality portion. Data managed by the complete system can be seen from two points of view: the one of the UI and the one of the application functionality. E.g., a form is seen from the UI's point of view as a representation with a specific screen position, colour, etc., while from the application's point of view it is seen as a record. Common data can either be hold only in the UI portion, or only in the functionality portion, or in both. The first two solutions avoid redundancy, but make explicit data transfer necessary, while the last solution makes the data efficiently accessible to both, but leads to redundancy and consistency problems. The first two solutions become hard if UIMS and functionality run in two seperate processes, perhaps even on two different machines. The final solution is mandatory, e.g., if a graphics terminal is used for accessing a mainframe. The fundamental principle should be this: try to separate the complete set into UI and application portion such that the UI by itself can handle as much as possible and such that the DIF becomes as "thin" as possible.

This issue needs clarification. Obviously, the question here is what precisely the DIF is. And here, again, we see that we need experience with the use of UIDMSs. Still, it is absolutely unclear, and only solved for special (and mostly trivial) cases, how the DIF looks. (Hudson 1987) proposes a model in which application and UI keep some common data. This model contains presentation and application views on data. What we really need is some kind of formalism for describing the DIF.

3. User Interface Tools and AI-inspired Techniques

The use of AI-techniques is now widespread; examples are circuit design and medical analyses. Are AI-inspired techniques also helpful for UI design? Several applications for their use are conceivable. Basically, they can be used for the dialog designer and for the end user of a system. In other words, we might try to construct intelligent UI design tools and intelligent end user systems. There has already been a tutorial at CHI '88 called "Intelligent Interfaces" (Miller 1988). This delt with the latter aspect - "clever" interfaces for end users. More specifically, but not exhaustive, AI-techniques should prove useful, e.g., for

- integration of design rules into UI tools
- intelligent design assistance for UI designers, in general
- active help systems for end users
- intelligent presentation of data
- intelligent support of the end user, in general.

For these different tasks, the system has to collect and manage knowhow on

- software ergonomics, e.g., it should keep a catalogue of design rules
- the goals of the respective user. What does he want the system to do for him? The system must be able to offer strategies for solving the user's problems. Often, the user himself does not exactly know his goals at the beginning of a session; in such cases the system must infer the goal from his actions.
- the application, e.g., how it is used, what tasks can be carried out with this application, what are the expected results, what kind of help is offered
- current and previous system states, i.e., some kind of dialogue history (also used for undo- and redo-strategies)
- end user characteristics, i.e., models of "the" end user; examples are the user's response times, preferred interaction techniques, kind and number of commands used, kind and number of different errors.

The last point mentioned seems to us the most important. We mean here embedded models, i.e., user models which the system has of the user characteristics. Such user models play an important role in the development of adaptive UIs and on-line help systems. They are helpful during the design process for evaluating and improving the system design as well as during the actual use of the system to adapt its "look and feel" (automatically) to the individual user's needs. A user model describes the behavior of an individual user who is interacting with a computer system and represents the amount and structure of knowledge which is relevant for using the system. This includes modeling of tasks, goals, plans and methods. One of the best known approaches to user modelling is the GOMS model (Card et al. 1983), but one still has to examine whether this approach is appropriate for an embedded user model.

Why do we have to use AI-techniques here? An important characteristic of most types of knowhow mentioned above is that they are not always *a priori* available. A typical example: there is really no model of "the" user; instead, we always deal with individuals, and the only way to know the current user is to monitor him while he is using the system. Put another way, in order to serve the user well (this is the purpose of a "good" UI!) we must learn something about him while he uses the system. We cannot in advance place the user in some catagory and hope that it will fit him. A rather simple, but to our knowledge never really implemented, example is this: the system monitors the kind of help the users tries to get. Does he, e.g., need detailed help? After a while, the system offers by itself the desired kind of help. Error analysis is another obvious application area for AI-techniques, much related to help systems. Finding out erroneous concepts which the user may have, and correcting them, is a yet much harder problem which cries for AI-techniques. The system X-AiD (Thomas et al. 1987) is one of the few examples where "courses of action" can be defined according to which the user can solve specific tasks. Courses of action offer a structured description of a set of actions through which certain goals can be reached. A specific course of action is compared with the actions of the user, and once the system "knows" the users goal, it can give him advice. Thus, the course of action is the base for active support. However, much research is still needed; it is, e.g., yet unclear how to extract the user's goals from his actions. If the system's guesses are often wrong, the user will be irritated.

Thus, in general, the use of AI-techniques allows the design of *active* systems in contrast to *passive* systems that simply react but never apply what they could learn from being used. AI-based systems can offer in a specific situation several different reactions; somehow they are nondeterministic. Only acquired user specific knowledge lets the system react deterministically. Thus, these systems adapt themselves to the user and to his goals.

Do we want such a "self-adaptive" system? This is much more than simply an "adaptable" system, which can be modified only from outside in order to better fit the user and his needs, i.e., in order to provide him with a personalized UI. In this case, no knowledge about the user has to be kept inside the system. A self-adaptive system, in contrast, makes it very easy to monitor the user, to watch how fast he works (and, whether he works at all!). This is something employees do not always want their employers to know! These remarks may sound a little too cautious, but we heard them quite often in discussions with researchers and users.

Besides implicit ways of knowledge acquisition explicit ways may be used (the system may ask the user specific questions in order to understand his reasoning).

One severe problem is the association of a "new" user with some user model. The user never used the system before, so, how should it know *anything* about him?

Thus far, we mentioned mostly applications of AI-techniques for the end user. However, also the designer of a system may heavily use AI-techniques. The term "intelligent design assistant" is coined for this purpose. It means that the UI designer gets some help during the design process. The least he should expect is that design rules are integrated into the system. E.g., the Smith-Mosier-guidelines (Smith et al. 1986) contain about 1.000 (in words: one thousand) different rules. It is not at all conceivable that the designer of a UI is able, or only willing, to know them all. But what is a computer-based system for UI design good for if after design someone sits down for a couple of days (in case of the Smith-Mosier-guidelines probably years) in order to check whether the design obeys all ergonomic rules?

Integration of rules does not necessarily imply the use of expert systems from the beginning on. There is a very specific problem with rules, namely, they must be formulated and formalized. We do not know any software ergonomist who would be able to formulate ergonomic rules in Prolog or any other computer language. Instead, he could design some exemplary "good" and "bad" UIs, and let the system find out what the rules are behind these examples. And again, AI comes into the game. Knowledge acquisition is the problem here.

We see more applications for AI-techniques. One is the presentation of data, sometimes also called "scientific visualization". Computers are tools able to produce gigantic amounts of data; the end user is interested in some specific aspects of these data, but surely not in seeing them, one or several per line, as digits. Instead, he wants to "see" the semantics of these data. In some cases, this is nothing more than a binary value; sometimes, it is a qualitative assertion, not a plain quantitative number. We do not go into more details here; the point is that UI tools must also handle these problems; at least, tools to handle them must be integrated with UI tools. Such a filter for the presentation of data is described in (Rouse et al. 1987) where an expert system used by jet pilots is given as example.

4. User Interface Tools and Multi-Media Dialog

Traditionally, human-computer interfaces are limited to keyboard and mouse input and to output of text and graphics on the screen.

The channels of human communication are manifold. Especially skills in visual and audio perception are very strong. The visualisation of complex data makes medical and scientific data understandable and gives access to (for an individual user) new information and insight.

Easy access to documents containing text, graphics, video, sound, speech, computer generated animation, and photorealistic pictures has to be provided by a homogeneous UI, that is easy to learn and use. To achieve this, support for multimedia interaction such as graphics and voice has to be incorporated in the design of the UIDMS. ACHILLES (Naffah et al. 1984) is an example for a UIDMS with such features. It has been used for the multi-media document filing system MUSE (Constantopoulos et al. 1986). Work on ACHILLES and MUSE was carried out in the ESPRIT projects MULTOS and IWS. Although already existing tools for speech and motion processing are in use, we have to see that a complete multi-media dialog is much more than just a sum of different singular communication styles. It will even offer completely new application areas. In the following sections we present some examples for areas where we see great need for more research.

Lingual Channel

For the recognition of fluently spoken words (in contrast to the "single word mode") currently systems for handling up to 1 000 words are being developed. They use simple speech models for increasing the rate of recognition. These models make assertions about the probability for a certain word to follow a sequence of words that has already been recognized. These systems are speaker dependent, and achieve a recognition rate of 80 to 90 %, depending on the speech model. The vocal input of short (otherwise typed) commands is feasible today. But a more "natural" dialog with the computer needs a larger thesaurus and more so the understanding of semantics. Semantic analysis, however, is limited to phrases with very simple content and is not yet developed as far as syntactical analysis. The representation of complex sentences is not easy. In particular, problems where a sentence contains temporal and local references or the scope definition of quantors (e.g. how many, some, these) are still unsolved. The semantics of a word often cannot be found in a single sentence, but in the context of several. The solution and representation of such references in texts and dialogs is understood very poorly so far. Finally, a good user and task modelling is necessary to provide a guidance and to understand misconceptions.

Haptic Channel

There are alternatives next to mouse, joystick and touch screen for specific needs. Light pen and tablet allow handwritten input. To define location and direction in an artificial 3-D space, there are developments for a special mouse (Ware et al. 1988). Another way to interact with objects in 3-D space is the data glove (Zimmerman et al. 1987) that gives you the sensation of reaching with the hand into this space. Other systems use special sensors to understand gesture input. Some recognize where the user's finger points, others follow the eye movements. This has the advantage that no device needs to be in direct contact with the user. All this points in a direction where currently the space suit is the ultimate thing to interact very closely with a virtual reality. Today used in special areas only, like pilot and astronaut training, the entertainment industry might pick this up soon. The overexposure to unrealistic virtual worlds might cause unwanted effects on the social behavior, much worse than those caused by television consumption today.

Video and Animated Scenes

Ignoring the amount of data involved, the handling, i.e. editing of video clips and computer animated scenes is still a very young field. Techniques and UIs developed so far, like MUSE (Hodges et al. 1989) or Intermedia (Yankelovich et al. 1988), have had no chance to be tested thoroughly. New ones will come up, i.e. standardization rules for UI design are still far away in this area. The same is true for hypertext or hypermedia structures, although activities to standardize data structures have started already (Intern. Organiz. for Stand. 1989). With the hypertext idea, more interactivity is possible. The user can be more active and the communication gets richer. The problem is, not to get lost in this hyperspace of information. Again intelligent user guidance is wanted.

When books, pictures and movies are available in digital form, it is important to provide a good browsing support. The art of presenting multi media information requires trained designers and authors. Animation draws from graphics layouters and movie directors. New job descriptions will be generated, that will influence UI design principles substantially.

5. What is a "Good" User Interface?

Actually, this title covers only one half of the problem. Namely, as soon as we know what a "good" UI is, we will have to design tools that allow to decide this question for specific UIs. Even more, we will have to provide tools that are used at design time and that from the very beginning on prevent people from doing old well-known design mistakes again and again. Hence, these tools must be integrated into the UI design tools.

Since we do not know how to answer the first question, we will from now on concentrate on the second one. For that purpose it is necessary to evaluate the UI that has been or is currently being designed.

One of the advantages of the separation principle really is that it allows to use methods for analytical evaluation. (Olson 1987) says:

> *"It is not reasonable to expect extensive human factors analyses to be performed on every user interface. The demand far outstrips the resources. Tools for performing such analyses may assist in bridging this gap. Such tools become possible within a UIMS because of the extensive amount of information about layouts and command syntax that a UIMS already has in order to perform its function."*

And (Cockton 1987) mentions:

> *"The final challenge in UIMS development lies in incorporating human factors guidelines and psychological knowledge into the interaction techniques implementations packaged into UIMS. Only when this challenge is met can we guarantee that end users will see the full benefit of UIMS."*

Different ways for evaluation of UIs can be conceived. Typically, analytical and empirical evaluation are distinguished. Empirical evaluation carries out tests with "real users", while analytical evaluation tries to get conclusions without users being involved. Analytical evaluation assumes that the quality of a UI can be decided by measuring its conformity to a catalog of design rules (whatever these are), and to come to a corresponding conclusion. Sometimes, the empirical basis for these rules is rather vague in spite of numerous studies.

The analytical method is the one of choice in the context of design tool integration. Its main advantage is that it can be carried out without an implementation of the UI. Namely, it suffices to have a formal description of the UI. Because analytical evaluation can be supported by tools and does not need "test users", it costs much less than empirical evaluation does. Also, it enables the use of objective criteria for UI quality. (Many experts claim, however, that analytical evaluation can never fully replace empirical evaluation (Reisner 1987). Nevertheless, when discussing UIDMSs, this is what we have to provide.)

Todays analytical evaluation is mostly based on cognitive models of man-machine interaction, i.e., models that try to explain the process of problem solving with computers. A prominent example is the GOMS model (Card et al. 1983). Sad to say, but nearly all of these models are unsuitable for analytical evaluation in an industrial environment. Some reasons:

- Many UI aspects are very subjective, like the "beauty" of icon layout, or the consistency of colour use.
- Most rules depend on the user, but *the* user does not exist.
- Current models for human-computer interaction assume error-free behavior of the system; this is highly unrealistic.

Once the need for analytical evaluation is recognized, and useful models and rule catalogs have been developed, one must integrate the evaluation into the UI design process. This essentially means to have a formalism for design rules and a useful interface between a database containing the formalized design rules and the UI design tools. The final goal must be the automatically designed ergonomic UI. This would follow the rule that errors must be avoided as early as possible in the software design process. This is, what the software architecture BASAR (Waldhör 1989) tries to achieve. In contrast, most of the current UIMDSs can be used for "bad" UIs just as well as for "good" UIs. Such UIMDSs are not really helpful. However, when trying to formalize design rules, we meet some problems:

- What is a good formalism for design rules? Many rules and guidelines for UI design can easily be interpreted by humans, but are hard to be formalized.
- How to convince software ergonomists to formulate their rules according to this formalism?

Currently, we do not know a satisfying answer to the first question, i.e., an answer that also solves the *hard* problems. The second question might be solvable with the help of artificial intelligence, see Chapter 4. We also cite (Green 1987) here:

> *"Another area where future research is required is in codifying our knowledge of user interface design. This codification is particularly important at the presentation level. This codification would contain rules for laying out menus and screens, selection of input techniques, selection of output techniques, and the best way of designing dialogues for particular classes of users. This type of research could lead to the development of expert systems for user interface design."*

At the end of this chapter we mention some interesting approaches for evaluation: (Young et al. 1989) describes a system which includes a "Programmable User Model (PUM)". After specifying a UI, the dialog designer can define with PUM a hypothetical user, and let him "work" with the system. This leads to information about conflicts between the UI and certain parameter values of PUM. I.e., the dialog designer receives information like "users with this specific characteristic will not be able to handle that specific aspect of the system". Another interesting approach is the "Cognitive Design Aid (CDA)", described in (Byerley et al. 1986). More approaches have been investigated, but none ever received much attention from industry.

6. Distributed User Interfacing

Meanwhile, support of distributed systems is state of the art for windowing systems in the following sense: clients and servers can be distributed across a network. This does not necessarily mean that windowing systems support distribution of one application across a network. What about UIDMSs, at least at run-time? I.e., we concentrate on the management system part, or the run-time support portion, of a UIDMS, in the sense defined in Chapter 2. There has been a German conference on this specific topic (Kapsner 1989); the discussions showed that the topic is recognized, but fundamental solutions are still missing except for very specific cases. Distribution is important also for an integration of different media for communication (multi-media dialog). We currently see that television, telecommunication and computing approach each other. Soon, one single piece of hardware will replace the telephone, the TV and the computer. One consequence of this is that traditional help systems with fixed help messages will be replaced by flexible smart help agents. It will even be possible to reach a system administrator in order to receive direct help from him in situations where nothing else can help.

Traditionally, UIMS and application are linked; they form one single program. The interface then consists of procedural function calls. Data of the functionality need, e.g., not be copied if the UI needs them, but the UI can access them via pointers. This architecture, however, has some disadvantages:

- The UIMS code exists in every application, yielding heavy paging and memory use. With some operating systems, shared libraries can avoid this problem.
- A UI description cannot be used at one time for more than one application.
- If several applications run at one time, an additional synchronization mechanism is necessary for output.
- Different UIs exist for different applications, confusing the user.

Quite similar to windowing systems, there is today a trend towards distributed UIMSs, where UIMS and application can run in different processes. In this case, the interface between application and UIMS is realized via a protocol. The access of the application to the protocol is implemented through a library that is embedded in the respective programming language environment. Thus, applications in different languages can work together with one UIMS. Such a client-server architecture allows easy use of *one* UIMS for several applications at the same time. It is reasonable, however, not to use a classical unsymmetrical client-server architecture, but instead a symmetrical one, where UIMS and applications have equal rights. For more details, see (Kühme 1989).

An interesting question arises on the type of protocol to be used between UIMS and functionality. This could either be a static protocol (like the one X uses), or a dynamic one (like the one NeWS uses). But, it is obviously not possible to define a fixed set of interaction objects and techniques that could be used as a basis for any style of dialog. The system must be open, and hence the protocol must be dynamic, it must be extensible.

7. Summary, and More Open Problems

In the previous chapters we mentioned some of the currently disputed topics for UI tools: How to formalize the DIF? Why and how to use AI-inspired techniques? How to design UIDMSs that support multi-media dialog? How to evaluate UIs? What are influences of distributed environments? Now, we briefly list some more problems.

(Rosenberg 1989) mentions that current UIDMSs handle only UIs that are "old-fashioned", and not todays state of the art, the reason for this being the long development time of UIDMSs. Our conclusion is that we have to accelerate UIDMS development. Too many systems today exist; many of them try to do exactly the same. From an industrial point of view, tiny differences in the functionality do not matter. More important is the stability of the system, and even more important is experience with the use of such systems.

Well-known problems come from the interplay between UIDMS, application, windowing system and graphics package. Probably, for graphics output, sneak paths are necessary.

The next problem area to be mentioned is the prototyping of dynamic aspects of UIs. Many current commercial systems only treat static aspects, i.e., the layout of a UI. They do not care much about reactions on mouse clicks, menu choices, etc., i.e., they only treat the appearance of an application, but not its behaviour. At least, most systems only allow prototyping the direct reaction on events. But this reaction could be rather complicated; it could be the execution of a complete course of action. It seems to us that this more complex dynamics is so close to the functionality level of an application that textual prototyping is unavoidable. (Jacobs 1989) claims that as well. There has been research on language approaches for prototyping dynamics; others concentrated on transition nets, on Petri nets or on automata.

Another important remark in our opinion: workstations are not the whole world of computing! They are by far not a mass market, and it is only this market segment that is touched by UIDMSs. What is even worse: current systems are useful only for applications that are to be designed from scratch. What about the thousands of applications that already exist? Many of them need new UIs, and our tools must be able to provide new UIs for such applications without throwing away most of the existing code. We could "hide" the application in a process which is not allowed to make any output on screen, and we could add in another process a new UI for such an application. This is far from being efficient, and we think it is extremely worthwhile to put some thought into this problem. Customers will be delighted to see some results there. This is actually an interesting research area. By the way, our customers are also always delighted when we use standards. Speaking about them does not suffice; we have to devote ourselves honestly to using them.

Let us also take a brief look at toolkits in the sense of the X-toolkit, e.g. This is the basis on which we should build UI tools, at least if we do not want to implement monolithic systems that integrate toolkit and UI tools. Also, such monolithic systems do not use standards.

From our specifc point of view, the biggest deficiency with toolkits is that all current toolkits only support applications for office environments. None supports applications for factory automation. Such applications impose rather specific requirements on toolkits. Some examples:

- Factory environments demand the use of specific normed symbols, e.g., for drills, for NC-machines, robots, etc.
- In factory environments it must be possible to control the whole system without mouse as well as with mouse.
- Typical factory software controls a large number of separate machines and a large number of separate communicating processes. The communication is time critical; it is often necessary to respond in real-time on some external event. These events quite often demand a complete update of some presentation on the screen, e.g., the representation of the temperature of the cooling system of a nuclear reactor. It must therefore be possible to distribute applications onto several different processes.

- Asynchronous montoring processes must be supported, although in certain clusters of processes it must be possible to work in synchronous mode. There are some problems with such an approach: sometimes objects in different processes which do not know each other have to exchange messages; also, sometimes objects have to be instantiated where the corresponding class is defined in a different process.
- It must be possible to exchange messages inside processes as well as among different processes in a transparent way.

This all is heavily different from office environments where the only external events are things like notifications on the arrival of e-mail; and nobody is urged to respond in real-time! Partner processes in office environments are typically passive. Communication there is more like the exchange of files than like external events. The only external events come from the end user.

SX/Tools (Kneißl 1989) is a toolkit currently developed at Siemens which meets the above requirements. SX/Tools is based on X. Use of standards is mandatory in an industrial environment! SX/Tools also allows the simultaneous access from several different processes to one screen object. Other toolkits associate a widget to a specific process only. Then, only this one process can communicate directly with this object. This restriction is not good enough for systems used in factory environments. SX/Tools will be implemented in an object-oriented language as an open extensible and customizable toolkit. Reusability and inheritance are important features of SX/Tools. Features for rapid prototyping of UIs will be integrated into SX/Tools.

Another problem comes from different treatment of the interior and exterior of windows. Some of todays UIDMSs only treat elements of toolkits like windows, menus, scrollbars. Others do not care for these object classes, but only treat application objects inside windows. In contrast, SX/Tools (Kneißl 1989) will allow both. E.g., it manages the contents of a window just as it manages a set of windows. In this respect it is similar to THESEUS (Brandt 1989). We need systems that treat both aspects in an integrated way. It is, by the way, sometimes really hard to get information out of publications on which of these aspects is treated by the respective UIDMS!

What about the UIs of UI tools? It is nice to hear "this was our first application!" But, usually the tools do not impress by their own UI. It does not suffice to offer a fantastic functionality. Remember, these tools are supposed to be used by software ergonomic experts, which usually do not know or care much about computing. They need easy access to the functionality of the tools, otherwise they will not use them at all.

Finally, we claim once again that discussion on notions does not promote research in this exciting area any further. Let us shortly come up with some agreeable definitions, let us try to define the notion of a "good" UI, and then *let us get experience with the tools we have developed or are currently developing*!

References

Atlas, A., et al. (1989) OSF User Environment Component - Decision Rationale Document. OSF, Cambridge MA

Betts, B., Burlingame, D., Fischer, G., Foley, J. D., Green, M., Kasik, D., Kerr, S. T., Olsen, D., Thomas, J. (1987) Goals and Objectives for User Interface Software. Computer Graphics 21, 73-85

Byerley, P. F., Leiser, R. G., Saffin, R. F. (1986) Kognitive Konzeption zur Entwicklung von Mensch-Maschine-Schnittstellen. Elektrisches Nachrichten-Wesen 60, 294-302 (in German)

Brandt, J. (1989) Die Konstruktion von Benutzungsoberflächen mit Hilfe eines UIMS und Resource Files. In: Kapsner, F. (Ed.) GI-Fachgespräch Dialoggestaltung mit verteilten Fenstersystemen, Stand und Perspektiven. München, 17-23 (in German)

Bullinger, H.-J., Fähnrich, K.-P., Ziegler, J. (1987) Software Ergonomie: Stand und Entwicklungstendenzen. In: Schönpflug, W., Wittstock M. (Eds.) Proc. Software-Ergonomie 87, Nützen Informationssysteme dem Benutzer? Teubner, Stuttgart, 17-30 (in German)

Card, S. K., Moran, T. P., Newell, A. (1983) The Psychology of Human-Computer Interaction. Lawrence Erlbaum, Hillsdale NJ

Cockton, G. (1987) Interaction Ergonomics, Control and Separation: Open Problems in User Interface Management. Information and Software Technology 29, 176-191

Constantopoulos, P., et al. (1986) Office Document Retrieval in Multos. Proc. ESPRIT Technical Week

Green, M. (1983) Report on Dialogue Specification Tools. In: Proc. User Interface Management Systems, Seeheim. Springer Verlag, Berlin, 9-20

Green, M. (1987) Directions for User Interface Management Systems Research. Computer Graphics 21, 113-116

Hodges, M. E., et al. (1989) A Construction Set for Multimedia Applications. IEEE Software 6, 37 - 43

Hudson, S. E. (1987) UIMS Support for Direct Manipulation. Computer Graphics 21, 120-124

Intern. Organiz. for Stand. (ISO) (1989) Coded Representation of Picture And Audio Information, Draft ISO-IEC7JTC1/SC2/WG8 N MPEG 89/046.

Jacob, R. J. K. (1989) NRL, Washington DC, Private Communication.

Kapsner, F. (Ed.) (1989) GI-Fachgespräch Dialoggestaltung mit verteilten Fenstersystemen, Stand und Perspektiven. München (in German)

Kneißl, F. (1989) Ein Toolkit auf X-Windows für die Automatisierungstechnik. In: Kapsner, F. (Ed.) GI-Fachgespräch Dialoggestaltung mit verteilten Fenstersystemen, Stand und Perspektiven. München, 129-149 (in German)

Kühme, Th. (1989) Kommunikationsschnittstellen in verteilten graphischen Dialogsystemen. In: Kapsner, F. (Ed.) GI-Fachgespräch Dialoggestaltung mit verteilten Fenstersystemen, Stand und Perspektiven. München, 115-128 (in German)

Miller, J. R. (1988) Intelligent Interfaces. Tutorial, CHI 88

Naffah, N., et al. (1984) Intelligent Workstation in the Office: State of the Art and Future Perspectives. Report

Olson Jr, D. R. (1987) Larger Issues in User Interface Management. Computer Graphics 21, 134-137

Reisner, P. (1987) Discussion: HCI, What Is It, and What Research Is Needed? In: Carroll, J. M. (Ed.) Interfacing Thought. Cognitive Aspects of Human-Computer Interaction. MIT Press, Cambridge London, 53-78

Rosenberg, J. (Moderator) (1988) UIMS: Threat or Menace? Panel CHI '88. In: Soloway, E., Frye, D., Sheppard, S. B. (Eds.) Proc. CHI 88, ACM, New York

Rouse, W. B., Geddes, N. D., Curry, R. E. (1987-88) An Architecture for Intelligent Interfaces: Outline of an Approach to Supporting Operators of Complex Systems. Human-Computer Interaction 3, 87-112

Smith, S. L., Mosier, J. N. (1986) Guidelines for Designing User Interface Software. The MITRE Corporation, Report ESD-TR-86-278

Thomas, C. G., Kellermann, G. M., Hein, H.-W. (1987) X-AiD: An Adaptive and Knowledge-Based Human-Computer Interface. In: Proc. INTERACT 87, 1075-1080

Waldhör, K. (1989) Wissensbasiertes Generieren von Benutzerschnittstellen. In: Maaß, S.,Oberquelle, H. (Eds.) Proc. Software-Ergonomie 89, Tagung des German Chapter of the ACM und der GI. Verlag Teubner, Stuttgart, 294-303 (in German)

Ware, C., et al. (1988) Using the Bat, A Six-Dimensional Mouse for Object Placement. IEEE Computer Graphics & Applications 8, 65-70

Yankelovich, N., et al. (1988) Intermedia, The Concept and the Construction of a Seamless Information Environment. IEEE Computer 21, 81 -96

Young, R. M., Green, T. R. G., Simon, T. (1989) Programmable User Models for Predictive Evaluation of Interface Designs. In: Proc. CHI 89. ACM, New York, 15-19

Zimmerman T., et al. (1987) A Hand Gesture Interface Device. In: Proc. CHI and GI, Canadian Information Processing Soc. Toronto, 189-192

Chapter 10

Modelling User Interface Software

Niels Vejrup Carlsen and Niels Jørgen Christensen

Abstract

Though a considerable effort has been spent on designing environments for the development of user interfaces no consensus has been reached on how to construct these. We feel that the lack of a common terminology has been one of the hurdles. Therefore we suggest a user interface model taxonomy could be a step towards agreeing on such a terminology.

Second, we present a model of user interface software according to this taxonomy. This model is employed by a UIMS currently being developed at the department. It attempts to meet the requirements posed by the state of the art direct manipulation user interfaces and prepares for the requirements of future user interface designs. The model uses a hybrid of the existing user interface software abstractions and incorporates new approaches to the application interface model and the interaction model.

1 Introduction

Since the beginning of the 1980's a considerable effort has been spent on the construction of environments for the development of user interface software. This has been motivated by the desire to incorporate human factors in the user interface design process which requires a prototyping process. Therefore user interface prototyping tools called User Interface Management Systems (UIMS) are needed.

We consider a UIMS to be an environment comprised of a set of design tools and a run-time support component, the user interface framework. The design tools allow a dialogue designer to specify the behaviour of a user interface to a given application using high level design notations tailored to the different aspects of user interface functionality. The user interface framework supplies the support functionality for the specified user interface and handles the application interface. Thus, a UIMS is used for rapid construction of user interfaces and for managing the run-time execution of the specified system.

This informal definition identify several issues we have to deal with to construct a UIMS. How do we in general define a logical separation between the application domain and the user interface domain? How do we model user interface software such that a user interface framework based on the model may support the widest possible range of designs? These problems have been discussed at several workshops [31,32,37] and in many papers, but there is still little consensus on how to solve them. We feel that one of the hurdles has been the lack of a common terminology based on an accepted user interface model taxonomy. We therefore suggest such a taxonomy in section 2 as a step towards a common terminology. After that, we will focus on our proposed model of user interface software presented according to this taxonomy.

1.1 Directions for User Interface Design

The requirements a user interface model has to meet, originate from the range of user interface designs we want a UIMS to allow. Furthermore, if the UIMS is not to lag a generation behind [20] we should also make some assumptions on the future user interface designs we want it to support.

Direct manipulation interfaces [35] are generally considered to be the state of the art in user interface design [15] so their requirements should be considered. But, as pointed out in [20], there are different kinds of direct manipulation. The usual direct manipulation interfaces only allow direct manipulation of the symbolic objects of the interface such as icons or menus. Other interfaces allow direct manipulation of application specific objects such as geometric presentations or formatted text. This is one desirable direction for user interface design since it seeks to achieve optimum 'feeling of directness on the part of the user' which means maximum engagement, minimal articulatory distance and semantic distance [23].

Especially reducing articulatory distance ('the degree to which the form of communication with the system reflects the application objects and tasks involved', [23]) is an interesting direction. It could lead to 'task specific' interface design which not only involves different user interface software (different look & feel) for each kind of application but also different hardware configurations.

New kinds of user interface hardware will be developed and integrated into such interfaces. We could imagine a text editor having a large interactive table [38]. One may directly edit the text with a pen or define new sections of text using a keyboard or a voice input device. We could have multiparameter devices used for manipulating designs in a CAD system or 3D viewing devices used for walking around in architectural designs. This multimedia future was also envisioned in [27], which added increased networking and concurrency in user interfaces to the expectations.

1.2 Implications for User Interface Modelling

Most existing UIMSs support a limited class of user interface designs. They are based on a coarse grain user interface model that leaves many aspects of the user interface to the fixed mechanisms of the user interface framework. Thus, the framework look & feel is imposed on the designs. To allow fine grain control in the design of user interfaces, which is essential [3,18], we need a user interface model that covers 'all' aspects of user interface behaviour.

If task specific user interface designs are to be supported by a UIMS it should allow easy integration of new devices. It must be maintainable with respect to the hardware configuration. This implies that the user interface model has to incorporate an input/output model and a revised window concept based on a very flexible device abstraction.

Apart from extensibility and flexibility, direct manipulation interfaces pose specific requirements that must be met by a user interface model [23]. Free format interaction (no syntax) which includes multithreaded dialogue must be supported. Continuous feedback [25] and semantic feedback should be handled. However, to avoid an imposed look & feel, the model should still support interfaces like command language interpreters. Finally, networking implies that the model must support physical separation between applications and the user interface on a given server [27].

The user interface model presented in this paper is an attempt to model the full functionality of user interface software such that the above requirements are met. A UIMS based on this model should support fine grain control in the design of state of the art and future user interfaces. The model and the user interface framework based on it is presented in the sections following our taxonomy proposal.

2 A User Interface Model Taxonomy

A user interface model taxonomy attempts to delimit the domains that has to be modelled to adequately specify how user interface software is structured. The taxonomy can therefore be used as a guideline for the specification of a UIMS and as a framework for a common terminology. At the most abstract level our taxonomy contains two 'orthogonal' models that define user interface software.

- The Separation Model
- The User Interface Model

2.1 The Separation Model

The separation model specifies how we intend to separate application code from the user interface software. It involves modelling of the two aspects of this separation.

- The Control Model
- The Information Distribution Model

The control model defines the distribution of global control between the application and the user interface software in the system. Several models have been proposed [11,15]. 1) Internal control - the user interface software is a set of application controlled abstract interaction devices. 2) External control - the application is regarded as a set of attached semantic functions controlled by the user interface. 3) Mixed control - both application and user interface software may influence the flow of control. This strategy might be implemented by having a separate global control component, yielding 'balanced' control [15].

One of the most difficult problems in the construction of UIMSs is finding an adequate model for the data separation between the application domain and the user interface. The discussion about the feasibility of separation [16,19] is about this information distribution model. It should define how application specific output is handled and whether the user interface has direct access to the application data for handling semantic echo or undoing. Once this model has been decided on we can discuss how the information is actually handled within the user interface.

We have currently identified three categories of such models. 1) Symbolic vs. Direct Data, proposed in [11], specifies that only symbolic information such as icons and menus is the responsibility of the user interface. Direct data, application specific output and inputs coupled to it, is handled by the application using the graphics subsystem. Several of the older UIMSs used this model [4,26,28]. 2) Shared Data, used in Higgens and Mike [22,30], propose that all application information relevant to the user interface is placed in a shared database. This facilitates semantic echo but restricts the application to the supplied data modelling facilities and is a problem in a distributed system where a physical separation is needed. 3) Distributed Data, used in GRINS and UofA UIMS [13,29], propose that these application data are distributed. The application defines a relevant view of its internal database through a set of mapping functions. Updates in the view are communicated between user interface and application. This facilitates distribution and does not constrain the application datamodel. Semantic echo demands careful design of communication protocol and the internal structure of the interface database.

2.2 The User Interface Model

Once we have chosen the separation model we can determine the structure and functionality of the user interface framework by specifying the user interface model. It involves

- The Architectural Abstraction
- Component Models

The architectural abstraction [15] (user interface model [12], reference model [27]) specifies how user interface software can be partitioned into components handling different aspects of the user interface functionality. It should specify the way they are controlled and how they communicate within the user interface. Wellknown abstractions are: 1) The Seeheim Model [9,12] which divides a user interface into three components: A presentation component dealing with physical appearance and direct interaction with the user; a dialogue control component, dealing with the syntax of the interaction; and an application interface component. 2) The Seattle Model [27] also consists of three components: The workstation agent equivalent to the presentation component and the dialogue manager which is a combination of the dialogue control and the application interface components. The handling of the metadialogue such as switching dialogue context is separated from the dialogue manager and handled by a separate workstation manager component. This is important in a distributed multiuser, multiprocess environment.

A third type of architectural abstraction is represented by PAC [8], COA [16,17,20] and the Active Semantics Data Model [22]. These are attempts to model the user interface as a homogeneous object space [9]. A user interface is seen as a composition of objects all having the same microarchitecture. In PAC and COA the user interface objects all embody presentation aspects, dialogue control and possibly an interface to the application.

The component models describe the functionality of each of the components defined in the architectural abstraction. The detailed user interface model determines the functionality of the user interface framework which provides the run-time support for the components and handles the communication between them. The models should cover the entire spectrum of 'behaviour' for each component. This allows design tools within the UIMS to give a designer fine grain control in the specification of them. Fine grained design may be very complex, but simplicity can be achieved by supplying abstractions in the design tools.

3 The UIMS Platform

Two important factors influencing our system design is the operating system and the choice of language platform for the user interface framework. These establish the abstractions we can use at the lowest levels of modeldefinition such as data or control structuring and communication constructs. Furthermore, they affect the models at higher levels. An object oriented language platform is an obvious choice when designing a system based on a homogeneous object space abstraction whereas traditional programming languages would make this difficult. If we need direct access to the resources of a workstation in order to give a designer fine grain design control we need an operating system that allows this. If our user interface model is based on a multiprocessing paradigm, the operating system should support this to achieve efficient execution [36].

This operating system dependency point to an interesting development. For some time now window systems have been integrated into the workstation environment almost as a part of the operating system. This is a natural development since window systems and operating systems both manage the resources of a workstation. The obvious extrapolation of this is the integration of a UIMS into the workstation environment. The same development could apply to database management systems thus giving an application programmer access to both high level storage manipulations and high level interface constructs [33]. In this paper we do not deal with the operating system dependency.

To efficiently meet the multithreading and networking requirements previously discussed we need a language platform that support parallel independent processes and asynchronous communication between these. The systems designed using the language must be maintainable, extensible and flexible to support the direct manipulation paradigm which favours a high level language. At the same time however, we need a language supporting direct access to hardware making hardware maintainable systems feasible. This would enable implementation of maintainable support for the flexible input/output model and the window concept based on a variable hardware configuration. We discussed this in [5,6] with the result that an extended event language was chosen. This language is based on an extended version of the event model as presented in [14].

An 'event-oriented' system consists of a dynamic set of independent concurrent processes called event handlers, a global state and a set of templates from which event handlers are instantiated. All communication between event handlers is through asynchronous passing of events which contain data values, the type of which is defined by the event type. Each event handler has an internal state and a set of event responses. The event responses define the event protocol, the set of events that the event handler may respond to. An event response may manipulate the local and the global state, create or destroy new event handler instances or send events to event handlers. An event queue is associated to each event handler which handle one event at a time. An event sent specifically to a given event handler is always added to the queue, the event handler then ignores the event if no response is defined for it.

Structuring of event handlers in event systems is done through event handler references in the local state. These references may be used within an event handler to determine the destinations for emitted events. By manipulating these references different event flow structure may be constructed. This may be used to define control structures in a system or for data structuring through the local states of the connected event handlers.

To allow event handlers to act as filters or pipelines we have added an optional exception response to the template specification. If an event is received to which the event handler has no response this exception response is invoked. Within the response the 'unknown' event may be referred to symbolically.

A strong analogy exists between event languages and object oriented languages. The templates resemble classes, event handlers resemble objects, the events resemble messages and the event responses resemble methods. The basic difference is that our event handlers are intrinsically parallel processes which communicate asynchronously while objects are not necessarily parallel and communicate synchronously. Currently we do not support event or template inheritance but we are researching this area.

4 Modelling the User Interface

According to the taxonomy we have to define the separation models before modelling the user interface functionality which determine the user interface framework of our UIMS. We would like to regard a UIMS as a language environment giving the application programmer access to very high level input/output abstractions [10,33]. This implies an integration of general purpose programming languages with UIMSs and as a consequence also with operating systems. Very much in line with what the designers of Smalltalk foresaw [24].

Given this UIMS concept, the application would submit data structures to the UIMS for input, output or editing purposes using the available abstractions. This implies choosing the information distribution model we named the distributed data model. Furthermore, we have chosen the mixed control model which allows the application to be user controlled but lets it intervene when necessary.

These separation models and the event language platform define the guidelines for the user interface model presented in this section. The architectural abstraction is introduced whereupon the component models are described. The cornerstone of our model - the symmetrical translation model - is presented in more detail in section 5.

4.1 The Architectural Abstraction

Our architectural abstraction is a hybrid of the 3 proposals summarized in section 2.2. Each of these have their own problems. The Seeheim model impose a strict layering of interfaces which is a problem when dealing with direct manipulation interfaces [20]. The Seattle model does not deal with the problem of interfacing applications to the user interface and also impose some layering. Finally the homogeneous object space models lack ways of representing metadialogue control [27] and they assume that the information distribution model is the shared data model.

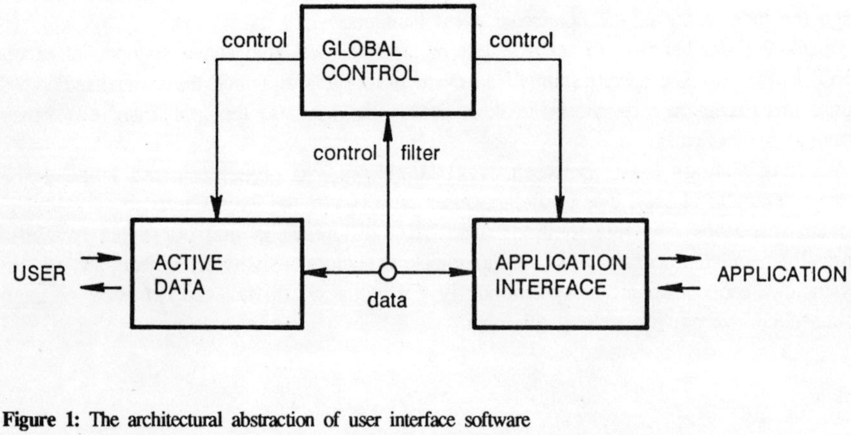

Figure 1: The architectural abstraction of user interface software

Fig.1. shows our architectural abstraction dividing the functionality of user interfaces into three components; the active data component, the global control component and the application interface component. The active data component is responsible for all local dialogue handling which removes the artificial layering between lexical and syntactical dialogue control in the Seeheim and Seattle models [20]. We assume that this component encapsulates a homogeneous object space. That is, the dialogue is handled by the intrinsic behaviour of active data objects [23]. This approach is excellent for providing continuous and semantic feedback.

The global control component is responsible for the metadialogue control, switching between dialogue threads and active application processes. This component mirrors the workstation manager in the Seattle model. Finally, the application interface component resemble the application interface model component of the Seeheim model. It should support application structuring of the active entities modelling the dialogue in the active data component. There is a direct data linkage between the application interface component and the active data component monitored by the global control component which filters out requests for dialogue switching.

4.2 The Active Data Component

The active data component comprises a collection of windows each handling a thread of dialogue between the user and the application. They are controlled by the dialogue threads in the global control component, which monitor the communication between the windows and the application module controllers described below. Each window is associated to one dialogue thread.

We have introduced a new flexible window concept to meet the flexibility and maintainability requirements. A window is merely defined as a set of active objects. These objects are the units of the user - application dialogue. An active object might handle a menu, a pickable application specific geometric entity, a command entry syntax or a rubberline. The active objects are the cornerstone of our user interface model and they are based on a symmetrical input/output model which is described further in section 5. The collection of active objects encapsulated by a window may vary at run-time through the creation of new objects by the application module controllers or by the dialogue thread.

The resource requirements of a window such as access to screen space or mouse events are determined by the requirements of the active objects. If a window has a presentation on some output device and some associated intrinsic functionality such as moving or resizing, this must also be handled by the encapsulated active objects. This gives us a very flexible uniform window model not tailored to any device configuration. The window control model resemble that of X [34]. The windows are arranged in a hierarchy which facilitate resource protection and enables the automatic assignment of priority values to determine overlaps. The placement of the windows in the hierarchy is managed by the global control component.

The framework support for this component, described in [6], includes a resource manager which handles the window hierarchy, the overlaps and the resource allocation to the different windows. The windows are realized through window controllers. Such a controller handles the entrypoint to the set of active objects encapsulated by the window and it has a protocol for manipulating this set.

4.3 The Application Interface Component

We currently view an application as a set of functions. These may be grouped into modules of mutually exclusive functions which have the same effect in the semantic domain but accept different sets of input parameters. For example, functions in a CAD application generating the same object but from different inputs. Functions may submit objects or structures of objects to the user interface for input, output or for editing purposes. The types of structures supported by the user interface framework defines the input/output abstractions available to an application programmer. This is very similar to the philosophy in [10].

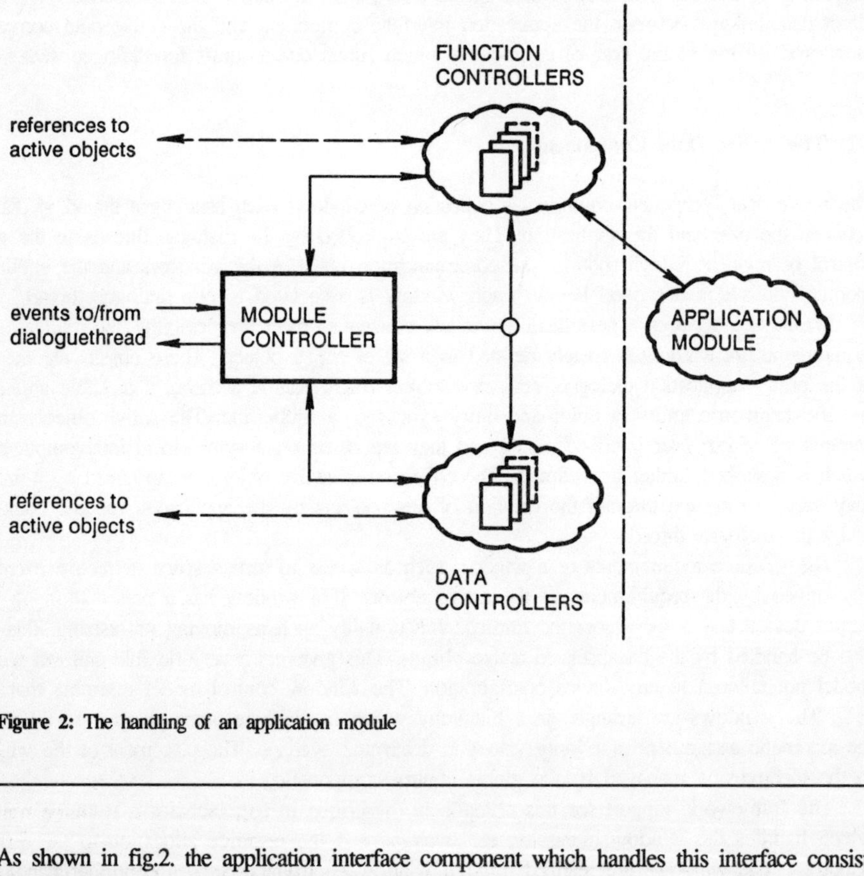

Figure 2: The handling of an application module

As shown in fig.2. the application interface component which handles this interface consists of three kinds of controllers. The module, function and data controllers. A module controller handles an application module of mutually exclusive functions. The entire flow of data and control between the module and the windows associated to it pass through this controller. A module controller is linked to exactly one dialogue thread in the global control component which may be linked to several windows, see below.

The module controller is responsible for instantiating the active objects in the active data components that are to produce the input parameters for the different functions integrated by a module. It does so under the request of the function controllers. Each function in the application is controlled by a separate function controller which handle the accumulation of the input parameters. It checks the input pre-conditions and informs the module controller whether it has finished accumulating and is ready to pass the information on to the function or if it has received an erroneous input. The module controller handles the mutual exclusion of the functions by flushing the other function controllers if one of them is finished. Upon receiving an error message it checks to see if any function controllers are still accumulating. If none, the user inputs are incompatible with all function parameter sets and we have an error. This is reported to the global control component.

A function may at run-time submit data to the user interface for input, output or editing purposes in the windows connected to it. This is handled by the function controller which informs the module controller that a data controller for these data should be created and that the references to active objects being instantiated are to be handled by it. Specific data controllers are defined for each input/output data abstraction supported by the user interface. A list data controller could handle a list structure of references and support the logical operations on a list. These operations are accessible to the application through the function controller. When an object in such a structure has been manipulated (picked by a user or defined through the input syntax embedded in the object) the application is notified by the module controller.

The framework for the application interface component supplies a set of data controller templates for the different data abstractions supported such as simple elements, records, arrays, lists, trees and sets. The framework may easily be extended by defining new types of data controllers. The module controllers are constructed by modifying a generic template to integrate the relevant function controllers. Finally, the function controllers are specified through pre-conditions on the input parameters to the functions of the application. They are tailored to collect the exact parameters of their associated functions.

4.4 The Global Control Component

The global control component handles the metadialogue control [27] through a set of controllers, dialogue threads. All communication between the user and the application functions pass through these. This communication is filtered such that control information may be received by the dialogue thread itself. Such information could be error messages from a module controller or it could be a message from an active object in a window signifying that a state change in the user interface is wanted. This is used to activate new dialogue threads and/or deactivate old ones. In this way switches between dialogues, starting new dialogues or closing old dialogues is handled.

Several application modules may be utilized by the user in a single thread of dialogue. Therefore several module controllers may be linked to the same dialogue thread in the global control component. The same module may also be used in different threads, but not simultaneously which is a restriction in our current model. We can also have several windows associated to the same dialogue thread as in X [34] where a window as perceived by the end user may be constructed from several windows. But a window may not be connected to several threads. Thus, a dialogue thread handles a many-window to many-modules linkage.

The framework supplies a generic template for the dialogue thread controllers. This may be tailored to the different templates needed to structure a given user interface. In such a controller the communication between windows and modules is handled by the exception response, the filtering is done by defining specific interception responses capable of catching the relevant event messages.

5 An Extensible and Symmetrical Translation Model

All handling of physical presentation, direct interaction with the user and local dialogue control in the user interface is embedded in active objects. These are based on an extensible input/output model, 'the symmetrical translation model' described in greater detail in [7].

The symmetrical translation model is based on a uniform low level device interface and a hierarchical composition facility, the translation handler [6]. Devices are regarded as event handlers emitting and receiving events. All the facilities of a device are available through its event protocol. Active objects represent compositions of these low level events yielding an arbitrarily high level event protocol. We have fine grain control when designing active objects since we have access to the low level device protocol. The model provides easy maintainability with respect to the hardware configuration because it is not based on a fixed low level event protocol.

5.1 The Translation Handlers

The translation handlers are event handlers having a common internal structure but not defined by the same generic template since they may embody widely different functionalities. A translation handler contains two independent processes, the input and the output process. Both are finite state automata handling the temporal composition of events emitted to or to be received from lower level translation handlers or the resources of the system. These automata may share data in

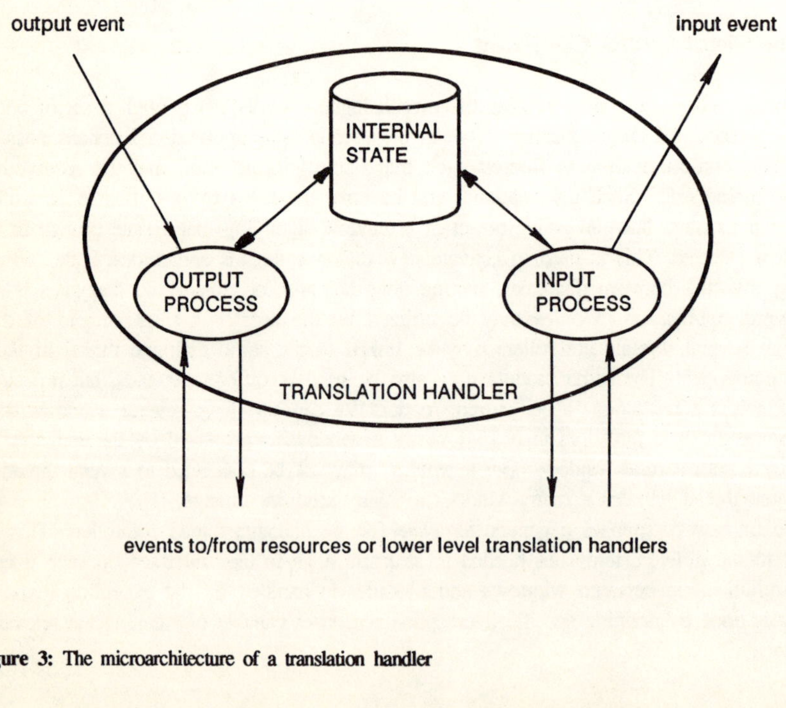

Figure 3: The microarchitecture of a translation handler

the internal state of the translation handler and the actions associated to state transitions involve manipulations of these shared data and of the data associated to the received or emitted events. Thus, the transitions of the finite state automata represent the temporal behaviour of an object while the spatial relationships within the object are maintained through the actions.

The output process handles the decomposition of output events while the input process handles the composition of input events. Since each translation handler is bidirectional we get active objects capable of handling decomposition of high level output and composition of high level input simultaneously. They represent the units of a two-way symmetrical translation process. The output process is triggered by a specific output event sent to the translation handler from the owner of it which may be a window or a higher level translation handler. When the process terminates it awaits a new output event. The input process is triggered by the activation of the translation handler. It emits a resulting input event to the owner of it upon termination. The input process is then started up again, see fig.3.

There are two categories of translation handlers, simple and composite. The simple translation handlers are the leaves of an active object hierarchy whereas the composite translation handlers are the nodes. The simple translation handlers represent compositions of device events, the composite translation handlers are compositions of lower level translation handlers which may be simple or composite. Examples of simple translation handlers are rubberlines, menuitems or tokens of a command language. Composite translation handlers could be menus or a command entry syntax recognizer. The resource requirements of an active object is determined by the resource requirements of the simple translation handlers in the hierarchy.

The shared internal data implement a strong coupling between input and output and the translation model also allows the processes to share lower level translation handlers. These couplings between input and output is necessary when using the model for implementing direct manipulation user interfaces where most input is output related, like picking and cut & paste operations. It is also essential for continuous feedback [29]. A menu object could exemplify this coupling. The output process of a menu generates a set of items from the data describing the menu. The input process responds to select events from these items and inform the owner of the selection.

We see our model as the natural extension of Anson's Device Model of Interaction [1] which is also based on hierarchical composition of a low level device dependent event protocol. But his model did not include output and coupling between the two data streams. Other related approaches to input/output modelling include the UIO's in [17,20], the Dialogue Cells in [2] and the two object oriented models presented in [21]. The three latter are all based on extending the input model of GKS to allow input/output coupling and composition of higher level interactions. They impose a certain dialogue structure on all interactions which tailors them to graphical dialogues thus imposing a look & feel. Both the UIO's and the models in [21] incorporate semantics into the interactive objects which we have avoided in our model.

5.2 The Model Framework

The framework support for this model within the active data component is described in [6]. For each device integrated into our system the framework supplies a device handler which interface the device to the event system such that it may be regarded as an event handler.

The resource manager which handles the windowing on the devices, is comprised of a main resource manager handling the window hierarchy and a set of sub resource managers each tailored to a specific resource. Output retention is handled by defining virtual resource handlers for the resources for which retention is meaningful. For each window on the resource an instance of the virtual resource handler is created. It contains a representation of the output to this resource.

Thus, to integrate new devices into our framework we just need to implement these three templates. This will create a modified device event protocol which may be utilized by the translation handlers. The translation handler templates are created using a design tool which allows a designer to specify their functionality in a syntactically sugared notation. A global library database keeps track of the translation handlers currently present in the system.

6 Conclusion

We have used the proposed model taxonomy as a framework for relating the different user interface models presented in the literature and found it helpful. It has furthermore aided us in delimiting the different problem areas to be dealt with when constructing a UIMS.

The user interface model we have presented allows the construction of a UIMS giving a designer fine grain control in the design of user interfaces. It supports multithreaded, direct manipulation user interfaces by a flexible windowing model and a strong coupling between the input and output data streams in the symmetrical translation model. It furthermore gives an application programmer higher level input/output abstractions to work with.

The framework for this user interface model is maintainable with respect to the hardware configuration and has an extendible translation handler library of active dialogue objects. The status for our system is that the framework for the active data component is finished and we are finishing an interactive graphical tool for specification of the translation handlers. The rest of the framework is currently under construction.

References

[1] Anson, E., 'The Device Model of Interaction', Computer Graphics 16(3), 1982.

[2] Borufka, H.G.; Kuhlmann, H.W.; ten Hagen, P.J.W., 'Dialogue Cells: A Method for Defining Interactions', IEEE Computer Graphics and Applications, July 1982.

[3] Buxton, W., 'Lexical and Pragmatic Considerations of Input Structures', Computer Graphics 17(1), 1983.

[4] Buxton, W., Lamb, M.R., Sherman, D., Smith, K.C., 'Towards a Comprehensive User Interface Management System', Computer Graphics 17(3), 1983.

[5] Carlsen, N.V.; Christensen, N.J.; Tucker, H.A., 'An Extended Event Model for Specifying User Interfaces', IFIP WG2.7 Working Conference on Engineering for Human-Computer Interaction, Napa Valley, August 1989.

[6] Carlsen, N.V.; Christensen, N.J.; Tucker, H.A., 'An Event Language for Building User Interface Frameworks', ACM SIGGRAPH Symposium on User Interface Software and Technology, Williamsburg, November 1989.

[7] Carlsen, N.V.; Christensen, N.J., 'A Symmetrical Input/Output Model', submitted for publication, March 1990.

[8] Coutaz, J., 'Architecture Models for Interactive Software: Failures and Trends', IFIP WG2.7 Working Conference on Engineering for Human-Computer Interaction, Napa Valley, August 1989.

[9] Dance, J.R.; Granor, T.E.; Hill, R.D.; Hudson, S.E.; Meads, J.; Myers, B.A.; Schulert, A., 'The Runtime Structure of UIMS Supported Applications', Computer Graphics 21(2), 1987.

[10] Dewan, P.; Vasilik, E., 'An Approach to Integrating User Interface Management Systems with Programming Languages', IFIP WG2.7 Working Conference on Engineering for Human-Computer Interaction, Napa Valley, August 1989.

[11] Enderle, G., 'Report on the Interface of the UIMS to the Application', User Interface Management Systems, Springer Verlag, 1985.

[12] Green, M., 'Report on Dialogue Specification Tools', User Interface Management Systems, Springer Verlag, 1985.

[13] Green, M., 'The University of Alberta User Interface Management System', Computer Graphics 19(3), 1985

[14] Green, M., 'A Survey of Three Dialogue Models', ACM Transactions on Graphics 5(3), 1986.

[15] Hartson, H.R.; Hix, D., 'Human-Computer Interface Development: Concepts and Systems for its Management', ACM Computing Surveys 21(1), 1989.

[16] Herrmann, M.; Hill, R.D., 'Some Conclusions about UIMS design based on the Tube experience', Colloque sur l'ingeniene des interfaces homme-machine, Sophia-Antipolis (France), May 1989.

[17] Herrmann, M.; Hill, R.D., 'Abstraction and Declarativeness in User Interface Development: The Methodological Basis of The Composite Object Architecture', IFIP XI'th World Computer Congress, San Fransisco, August 1989.

[18] Hill, R.D., 'Supporting Concurrency, Communication and Synchronization in Human-Computer Interaction - The Sassafras UIMS', ACM Transactions on Graphics 5(3), 1986.

[19] Hill, R.D. (in panel), 'UIMS: Threat or Menace', SIGCHI'88, Washington, May 1988.

[20] Hill, R.D.; Herrmann, M., 'The Structure of Tube - A Tool for Implementing Advanced User Interfaces', Eurographics'89, Hamburg, September 1989.

[21] Hübner, W.; Gomes, M.R., 'Two Object-Oriented Models to Design Graphical User Interfaces', Eurographics'89, Hamburg, September 1989.

[22] Hudson, S.E.; King, R., 'A Generator of Direct Manipulation Office Systems', ACM Transactions on Office Information Systems 4(2), 1986.

[23] Hudson, S.E., 'UIMS Support for Direct Manipulation Interfaces', Computer Graphics 21(2), 1987.

[24] Ingalls, D.H.H., 'Design Principles Behind Smalltalk', BYTE, August 1981.

[25] Kamran, A., 'Issues Pertaining to the Design of a User Interface Management System', User Interface Management Systems, Springer Verlag, 1985.

[26] Kasik, D., 'A User Interface Management System', Computer Graphics 16(3), 1982.

[27] Lantz, K.A.; Tanner, P.P.; Binding, C.; Huang, K.T.; Dwelly, A., 'Reference Models, Window Systems and Concurrency', Computer Graphics 21(2), 1987.

[28] Olsen, D.R.; Dempsey, E.P., 'SYNGRAPH: A Graphical User Interface Generator', Computer Graphics 17(3), 1983.

[29] Olsen, D.R.; Dempsey, E.P.; Rogge, R., 'Input/Output Linkage in a User Interface Management System', Computer Graphics 19(3), 1985.

[30] Olsen, D.R., 'Editing Templates: A User Interface Generation Tool', IEEE Computer Graphics and Applications, November 1986.

[31] Olsen, D.R. (chair), 'ACM SIGGRAPH Workshop on Software Tools for User Interface Management', Computer Graphics 21(2), 1987.

[32] Pfaff, G.E. (ed), User Interface Management Systems, Springer Verlag 1985.

[33] Rowe, R.A.; Shoens, K.A., 'Programming Language Constructs for Screen Definition', IEEE Transactions on Software Engineering SE-9(1), 1983.

[34] Scheifler, R.; Gettys, J., 'The X Window System', ACM Transactions on Graphics 5(2), 1986.

[35] Shneiderman, B., 'Direct Manipulation: A Step Beyond Programming Languages', IEEE Computer, August 1983.

[36] Tanner, P.P.; Buxton, W.A.S., 'Some Issues in Future User Interface Management System (UIMS) Development', User Interface Management Systems, Springer Verlag 1985.

[37] Thomas, J.J.; Hamlin, G. (chairs), 'ACM SIGGRAPH Workshop on Graphical Input Interaction Technique', Computer Graphics 17(1), 1983.

[38] Wolf, C.G.; Rhyne, J.R.; Ellozy, H.A., 'The Paper-Like Interface', HCI International '89, Boston, 1989.

Chapter 11

GMENUS: An Ada Concurrent User Interface Management System

Margarita Martínez, Bonifacio Villalobos and Pedro de Miguel

Abstract

This paper presents a concurrent User Interface Management System (UIMS) developed in Ada. Application and UIMS modules are constructed as Ada tasks, providing high flexibility and independence of control and communication. Several dialogues can be simultaneously maintained on different windows.

The dialogue model is based on state-transition diagrams which we have extended with behaviour properties. By using these properties sophisticated interaction techniques can be built. They also provide another level of concurrency inside a dialogue, thus allowing several states to be active at the same time.

Separation between user interface and application is enforced by means of linkage modules, called Application Dialogue Managers.

1. Introduction

The cost and difficulty of creating and maintaining good user interfaces have led to the development of specific tools, called User Interface Management Systems (UIMS). Most of the current working environments involve the use of multiple windows, each one associated with a different process, related to one or more application programs. Such environments require complex UIMS architectures. It has been pointed out [6][8] that this kind of concurrent systems can not be constructed basing either on an external control strategy or an internal one. However, application, dialogue control and presentation processes should be at the same level and synchronized with multitasking facilities. This parallel processes-mixed control UIMS model has been relatively unexplored, except in the field of object-oriented systems. Since the object-oriented approach is not always suitable for application programs, it is still interesting to explore this model with more conventional programming and design techniques.

This paper presents a system that has been built taking into account these concepts, using Ada as the implementation language. This work, which has been developed at the "Departamento de Arquitectura y Tecnología de Sistemas Informaticos", constitutes the graphical subsystem of a major project[1] whose original objective was to build a concurrent application with interactive graphical user interface.

1 This project has been supported by SEIDEF S.A., Spain

The graphical subsystem was designed as a UIMS, rather than an application embedded graphical component. This approach was followed because it was expected that the user interface requirements would evolve all through the life-cycle of the system. Ada was chosen as the development language because of the large size of the project and the need of concurrency. This election brought out other advantages such as data abstraction mechanisms and modularity. As far as we know, this has been the first complete UIMS developed in Ada, although a limited prototype has been reported and some guidelines have been proposed by Burns [3][4][17]. Portability was a major goal to be achieved, so it was also decided to use a graphical standard, GKS, thus avoiding the lower levels of graphics programming.

This paper focuses on the description of GMENUS, the dialogue manager component of this graphical subsystem. A paper about another component of this subsystem, the scheduler that allows concurrency over GKS, has been presented to the Ada-Europe Conference'89 [16].

2. Overview of the Graphical Subsystem

The architecture of the subsystem follows the well-known proposal made at the Seeheim workshop [6][8]. As shown in Figure 1, three levels can be identified: presentation, dialogue control and application level.

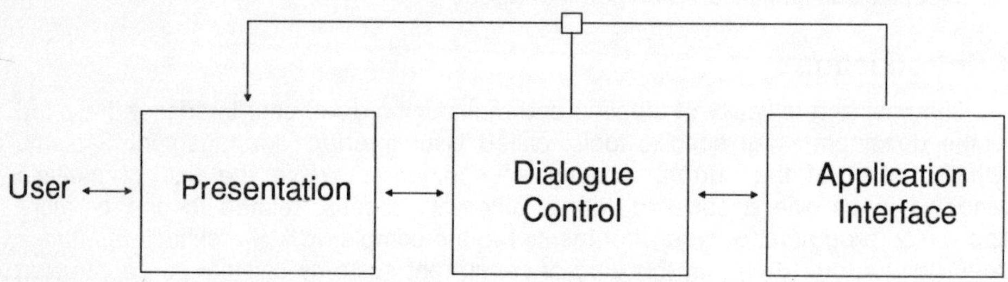

Figure 1: Seeheim model for an UIMS

The presentation level is responsible for the external presentation of the user interface. This level manages the windows on the screen, displays application data and reads physical input devices, translating the input data into forms accepted by the rest of the modules. The presentation level is composed of several processes which deal with the different windows.

The dialogue control level manages the interaction between the user and the application modules. It can support several dialogues that involve one or more windows and application modules.

Each dialogue sequence is described by a graph. Each vertex of the graph represents a place where the user is allowed to make a choice. We call these places *User Interaction Points (UIP)*. Every possible choice is represented by an arc, that leads to another UIP.

The application level establishes the interface between the UIMS and the application. It is mainly composed by the Application Dialogue Managers (ADM) and the Hierarchical Data Model (HDM) (Fig. 2).

The Application Dialogue Managers link the dialogue and presentation layers to the application modules. In particular, they make the correspondence between the UIP graph and the application functionality.

In order to display the application data, they are viewed by the graphical subsystem as a hierarchy, regardless of the structure they have for the application programs. The HDM is a tree-structure that models these hierarchical relations and contains references to the application data themselves and to the description of its graphic representation. It is used to control concurrent access to the data and to group data for representation or selection. The presentation level can represent any subtree of the HDM or update its representation upon modification. When data are modified by an application module, the corresponding nodes are marked as modified

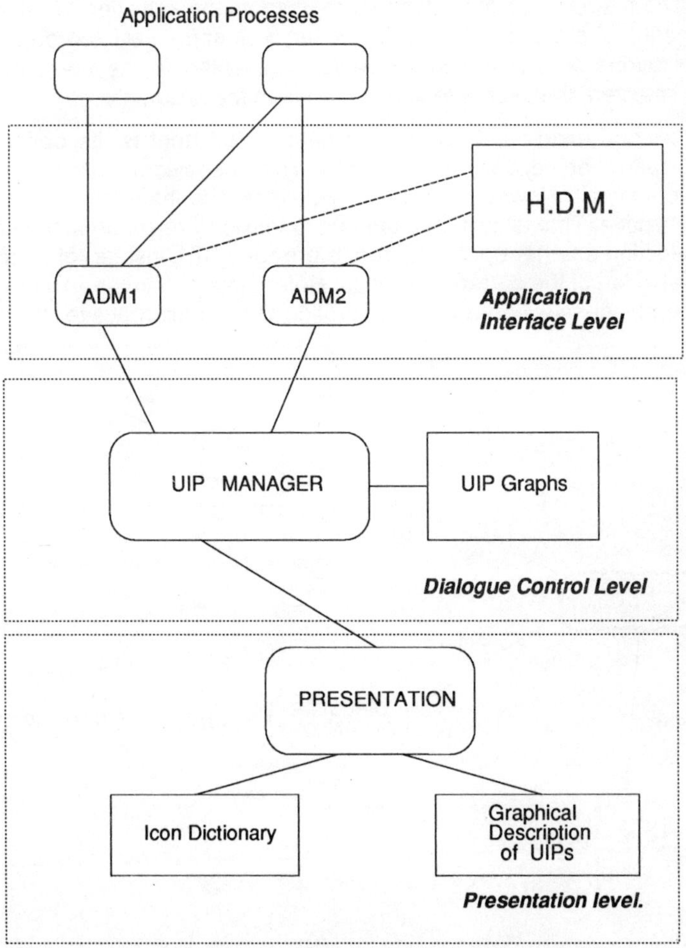

Figure 2: The graphical subsystem

in the HDM, but the updating of its graphic representation can be done in another moment by the presentation level under control of the ADMs.

The following sections of this paper will be devoted to the dialogue control level and the part of the application interface level more strongly related to the dialogue, the ADMs.

3. Dialogue Description: The User Interaction Point Graphs

A User Interaction Point represents a place in the dialogue where the user can make a choice of some type. Examples of UIPs are a displayed menu, an object selection or a value of a command parameter. After the selection is made, the associated application function is performed. Once this function has been executed, the dialogue sequence proceeds by proposing another choice to the user. This is reflected, in the dialogue description, by an arc which connects the current UIP with the following one. This arc is labeled according to the option it represents.

Figure 3 shows a simplified subgraph of a dialogue description of a command interpreter. The first UIP (object selection) represents the selection of an icon on the screen by means of a mouse. Depending on the type of the selected object, a menu with the operations allowed on that object is presented to the user. If the delete operation is selected, the user is required to confirm the action.

In the previous example, each UIP is deactivated (that is, its options became non-eligible) after an option is selected. This behaviour follows the classic state-transition model. However, in some situations it is interesting to maintain the previous UIP active. That allows for example, to implicitly reject an initiated operation by simply selecting another operation from a previous UIP, instead of completing the parameter selection of the current operation. Referring again to the example of Figure 3, should the object-selection and the operation UIPs remain active, the user could

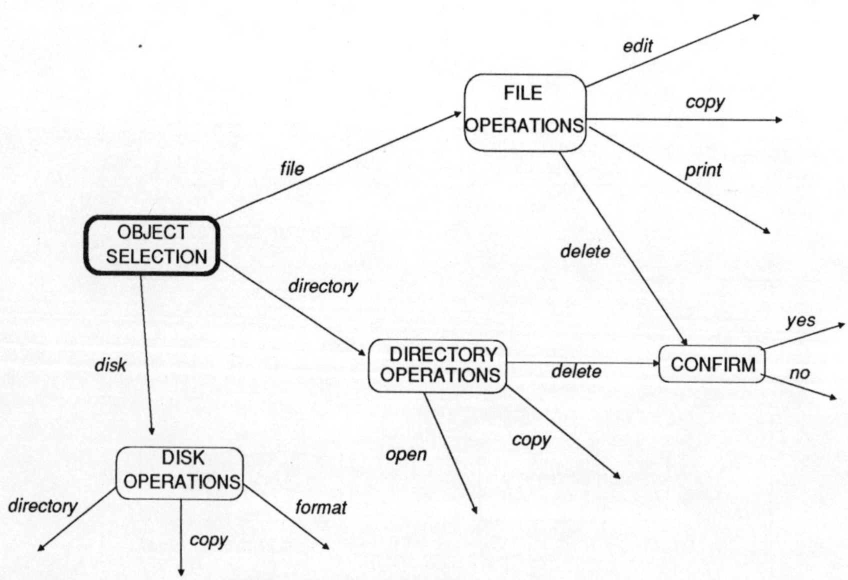

Figure 3: An example of a UIP graph

reject the deletion of the file by simply choosing another object or another operation, rather than only by giving a non- confirmation answer.

This is represented in the graph by adding to the UIPs some properties that reflect the behaviour that follows the selection of one of their options [13].

Our experience has reflected that, with a small set of properties, it is possible to obtain many different styles of interaction. The properties selected for GMENUS are the following:

- *Closed-by-next:* The UIP representation, if any, disappears from the screen when a descendant UIP is activated.
- *Deactivated-by-next:* When a descendant UIP is activated, the options of the current UIP become non-eligible; but its representation, if any, does not disappear from the screen.
- *Several-descendants:* The UIP may have several active descendants at the same time. This is possible only if the UIP remains active after the election.
- *Autoinhibited-options:* Whenever an option of the UIP is selected, the option becomes non-eligible until the UIP is reactivated or the descendant UIP is closed.

By using these properties different UIP behaviours can be easily defined, for example pull-down, pop-up or stair-arranged menus.

Figure 4 shows an example of how to construct pull-down menus with UIP properties. It is composed by five UIPs that are represented graphically as menus of strings. The first one, MAIN, whose options are disposed horizontally, is the parent of

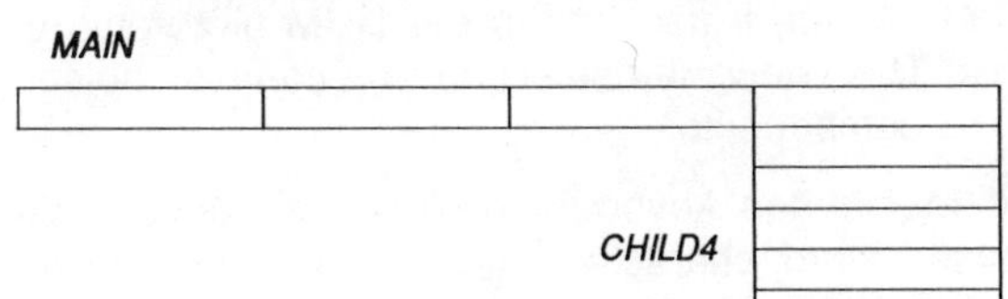

a) after the selection of one option of MAIN

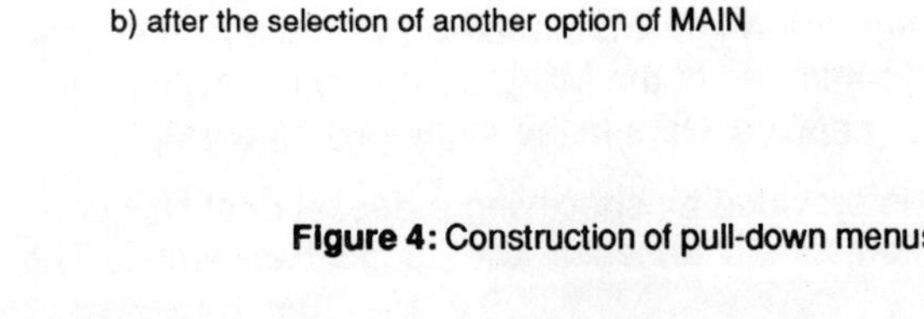

b) after the selection of another option of MAIN

Properties of MAIN:

closed-by-next = FALSE
deactivated-by-next = FALSE
several-descendants = FALSE
autoinhibited-options = FALSE

Figure 4: Construction of pull-down menus using UIP properties

the other four. When one of its options is selected, the corresponding descendant UIP is activated and the menu that represents this UIP is displayed under the option. The properties of MAIN determine the behaviour of the whole set as pull-down menus. First, closed-by-next and deactivated-by-next need to be set to FALSE, so that its options remain elegible after the activation of any of its descendants. Second, several-descendants is also set to FALSE, causing the UIP Manager to close any other active descendant when activating a new one. So, as shown in Figure 4, if the fourth option of MAIN is selected when CHILD2 is active, CHILD2 will be closed before the activation of CHILD4. The autoinhibited-options property should also be FALSE, since a UIP should not be activated if already active.

As a consequence of behaviour properties, several UIPs may be active at the same time. Here, therefore, UIPs do not represent states of the dialogue, as in dialogue control models based in Transition Networks [9][11][14], but rather places in a Petri Net, allowing another level of concurrency inside a dialogue.

4. Specification of an UIP

The descriptions of the UIPs can be divided in three main parts. The "syntactic description" details the type of the UIPs, their options, behaviour and their adjacency in the graph. There is also a "semantic description", that specifies the relation between the dialogue graph and the application modules. For each UIP that has a graphical representation, there is a separate "graphical description".

The syntactic description of a UIP is composed by:

- *Header:* Contains an identifier, the properties, the UIP type and a reference to its graphic description.
- *List of options:* Each option has an identifier, its option-type and the adjacency in the graph.

Five types of UIP are available: text, icon, point-location, node-selection and command-token.

Text and *icon* UIPs correspond to menus presented on the screen, with its options represented, respectively, as text strings or as graphic icons.

Node-selection UIPs are used to pick up graphic objects. Only those objects that correspond to nodes of the HDM and are displayed on the screen can be selected. Nodes are divided into classes. Each option of a node-selection UIP enables the selection of nodes of one class. When a node is picked up, the UIP Manager first checks if its class has been activated. If not, it ascends in the HDM hierarchy to check if any of its ancestors is eligible. This allows the selection of a complex object or a group of object by picking any of its components.

Command-token UIPs are used to manage keyboard entries. The options of these UIPs may be of the following types: word, character, integer, real and error (for example, a misspelled number). By combining command-token UIPs it is possible to define not only single keyboard entries but a complex command-language described by a graph similar to Conway's diagrams. Figure 5 presents, as an example, the description of the "change directory" command of the MS-DOS operating system. It is also possible to merge keyboard and graphical UIPs in the same dialogue graph.

The adjacency in the UIP graph is provided by specifying a descendant UIP to be activated when the option is selected, or an ancestor UIP to go backwards. The

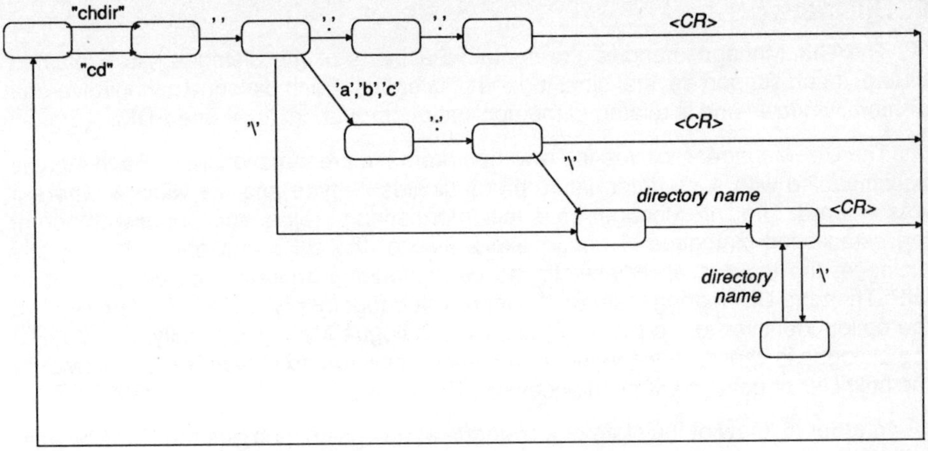

Figure 5: A command described by command-token UIPs

go-backwards destination can be defined with a UIP identifier or with a number of steps to move back.

The <u>semantic description</u> consists of an activation function and an application interface procedure associated with every option of each UIP.

The *activation function* indicates whether an option is eligible at a certain moment or not, depending on the semantic context of the application. These functions must be written by the dialogue designer in Ada, according to the specific application constraints. A run-time module is automatically generated from the set of activation functions of all UIPs. This module is used by the UIP Manager to calculate the state of each option whenever a UIP is activated.

The *application interface procedure* is the set of operations to be executed when the option is selected. This procedure embodies the communication with application modules and the housekeeping of the dialogue (for example, recording of context to handle cancel operations or updating the data presentation). The Application Dialogue Managers are automatically generated from the procedures of each dialogue graph.

Each UIP with graphical representation (text or icon) has a <u>graphical description</u>, which specifies characteristics such as: the number of rows and columns, the text strings or references to an icon dictionary (for text and icon UIPs), or the echo-type for point-location UIPs. For keyboard entries (command-token UIPs) a window is opened, with the characteristic of its graphical description.

An interactive graphical editor, that enables the description of the UIP graph in a friendly way, has been developed. This tool facilitates the definition of the graph connections and the behavioural and graphical characteristics of each UIP. It also checks the consistency of the UIP properties and the type of the UIPs and the type of their options. It is complemented with an interactive icon editor.

5. UIP Manager

The UIP Manager handles the syntactic aspects of the dialogue. As explained before, it can support several simultaneous dialogues. Each dialogue can involve one or more windows and is related to the application through at least one ADM.

The UIP Manager receives the raw input from the presentation level. Each input is accompanied with some information that indicates its type and the window where it was entered. The UIP Manager uses this information to relate each input with one of the established dialogues. Through exploration of the UIPs that are active for this dialogue, the input is associated to the corresponding option of the corresponding UIP. Then the UIP Manager sends the input value together with the UIP identifier and the option identifier to the proper Application Dialogue Manager. Finally, the state of the dialogue is changed according to the input received and the UIP graph, activating the next UIP or going back to an ancestor UIP.

In order to know of the state of a dialogue at any given moment, the UIP Manager builds a UIP tree, which is a subset of the UIP graph. When a dialogue is initiated, the UIP Manager is given an initial UIP that is taken as the root of the tree. Whenever a UIP is activated, it is inserted in the tree as a child of the UIP whose option was selected by the user. In this way, the tree contains all the active UIPs as well as the paths that lead from the initial UIP to each active UIP. These paths are used when returning to previous steps of the dialogue.

Each node of the dialogue tree contains one UIP and its corresponding state. A UIP can be in one of the following states:

- *open:* the UIP has a node in the dialogue tree, but the user can not select anyone of its options. If the UIP has graphical representation, it remains on the screen.
- *active*: the UIP has a node in the dialogue tree and its options are available to the user. If the UIP has graphical representation, it remains on the screen.
- *closed:* the UIP has a node in the dialogue tree, its options are not available to the user and it is not displayed on the screen.

When a UIP is activated, the state of the rest of the UIPs in the tree is updated according to their own properties. If the parent UIP is closed-by-next or deactivated-by-next, it is closed or deactivated, but it remains in the tree as a step of the path. If the parent UIP is not allowed to have several descendants, then any active descendant, except the one just activated, has to be closed.

The state of the options of each UIP is also kept in the corresponding node of the tree. This state is evaluated by means of the activation functions whenever the UIP is activated. This state is also influenced by the auto-inhibition property of the UIP as explained before.

The dialogue sequence is modified whenever an error is detected. The detection can occur both at the presentation level (for instance, a misspelled command) and in the UIP Manager (such as an input that does not correspond to any eligible option). In these cases the dialogue sequence returns to an ancestor UIP, that can be specified in the UIP. It is considered as if it was another option, the error option. If no error option has been specified, the sequence goes back to a default UIP (defined for each dialogue).

Errors can also be detected by the application. These errors are reported to the UIP Manager by the proper ADM, together with the target UIP to step back. If the ADM does not include this UIP, the dialogue default error UIP will be used.

6. Application Dialogue Managers

Every time an application module wishes to initiate a dialogue, an ADM process is created to act as an interface between the application on one side, and the dialogue and presentation levels on the other. The connection among ADMs and application processes is quite flexible, because an application process can be related with several dialogues, or an ADM can communicate with various application processes.

The role of the ADMs is, in conjunction with the HDM, to make the application functional core independent of the user interface. The ADMs contain the necessary knowledge about both the application and the dialogue in order to act as a link between them. The HDM is more related to the data presentation, while the ADMs participate in the dialogue as well as in the presentation.

This participation is achieved by means of the application interface procedures. These procedures collect all the parameters for an operation, call the application modules to carry it out, and then update the presentation of the modified data on the screen. They also support cancel and undo operations as well as feedback and prompting.

The code of the ADMs is automatically produced from the application interface procedures included in the description of the UIPs. ADMs are supposed not to depend on the paths of the dialogue graph, but only on the whole set of options. This hypothesis enables the ADMs to have a regular structure as shown in Figure 6. However, the hypothesis may fail, or other problems may arise, for instance, in the communication with the application processes. In these cases, a more complicated

```
loop
    UIP_MANAGER.READ_OPTION (UIP, OPTION, ENTRY);
    case UIP is
        when UIP1 =>
            case OPTION is
                when OPTION11 => PROC11 (ENTRY);
                when OPTION12 => PROC12 (ENTRY);
                    .
                    .
                when ERROR => . . .
            end case;
        when  UIP2 =>
            case OPTION is
                when  OPTION21 => PROC21 (ENTRY);
                    .
                    .
                when ERROR =>
            end case;
        .
        .
    end case;
end loop;
```

Figure 6: Code automatically generated for an ADM

scheme, that can be achieved by modifying the generated ADMs manually, is necessary.

As figure 6 shows, the basic cycle of an ADM consists of reading an input and then executing the correspondent application interface procedure. It should be pointed out that the UIP Manager does not advance the dialogue sequence until the execution of the interface procedure has concluded.

7. Comments About the Ada Implementation: Advantages and Drawbacks.

In this project, the most exploited features of Ada have been data abstraction and concurrency. The possibility of an object-oriented design and implementation was considered [1], but the most important characteristics of object-oriented design that play a key role in user interfaces (property and method inheritance, and dynamic binding [14]) are not sufficiently supported by Ada.

In order to achieve a high degree of independence and communication flexibility among the application, dialogue control and presentation levels, they were constructed using Ada tasks. With this approach, one of our main goals was achieved: the control flow of the application was separated from the user interface one.

The UIP Manager, which represents the dialogue control level, acts as a passive task. It collects inputs from the presentation level, relates every input with its corresponding dialogue and stores them. When the application waits for an input, the corresponding Application Dialogue Managers request it from the UIP Manager. If there is an input, it is processed by the UIP Manager before giving it to the ADM. If there is no input for that dialogue, the ADM must wait until the user provides it. To allow the application to proceed with other operations in the meantime, each ADM is

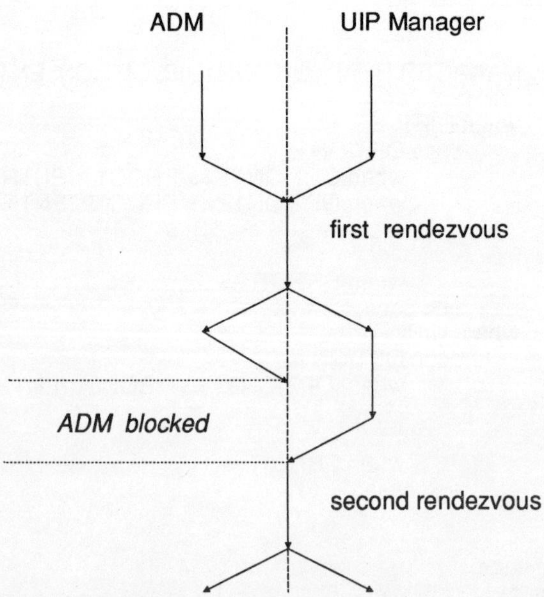

Figure 7: Diagram of the interaction between an ADM and the UIP Manager when waiting for an input

also a task. The UIP Manager needs to know the identity of the requesting ADM to check if there is any input for it, thus the ADM has to provide a parameter with its identification. At this point a difficulty arises: in Ada it is not possible to know the parameters of a queued task before the rendezvous, nor to select an specific task from the queue. So, it was necessary to build a family of entry-points together with a double rendezvous mechanism [2][7]. In the first rendezvous, the ADM gives its identifier to the UIP Manager, which records that this ADM is waiting for an input. Then the ADM performs a second call to the proper entry-point of the family, where it remains blocked until there is an input available. As an entry-point family has a fixed number of entries, this also imposes a limit to the number of active dialogues.

A problem was also found in the generation of the ADMs. It would have been desirable to have a dynamic binding (similar to C pointers to functions) between the options of the UIPs and the application interface procedures. The adopted solution is based on the less flexible *case* structure.

It would have also been interesting to exploit Ada exceptions to handle dialogue errors at any of the three levels. This mechanism is used within tasks but could not be used to propagate error information among different tasks, due to the restrictions imposed by the language.

8. Conclusions

Starting from a simple dialogue model like a UIP graph, a great description power can be achieved by adding a representative group of properties. A wide variety of interaction styles can be defined in this way. Although the behaviour of the final model is complex, it is easy to define and understand. The proposed properties have proved to be fairly complete, but new ones could be added without difficulty. Another suitable extension to the model would be the possibility to define parametrizable subgraphs.

The tree used to maintain the status of the dialogue could also serve to add interaction ergonomic techniques [5]: sideways viewing, selection history, etc.

The concept of ADM enforces the separation between the application and the user interface. A further development of the current version may be worthy in order to reduce the effort in dialogue definition. The most exploited features of Ada within this system have been its modularity and concurrency. Nevertheless, some obstacles have been encountered, mainly the lack of dynamic binding and task communication facilities.

We are now working in a new version of GMENUS in the UNIX environment, built in C language and using the OSF Motif interface standard.

9. References

1. Booch, G: Object-Oriented Development. IEEE Transactions on Software Engineering, vol. SE-12, no. 2, Feb. 1986.
2. Burns, A: Concurrent programming in Ada, Cambridge University Press, 1985.
3. Burns, A.; Kirkham, J.A: The Construction of Information Management System Prototypes in Ada. Software-Practice and Experience, vol. 16, no. 4, Apr. 1986, pp 341-350.
4. Burns, A.; Robinson, J: A prototype Ada dialogue development system. Ada UK News, vol. 5, 1984, pp. 41-48.
5. Cockton, G: Interaction ergonomics, control and separation: open problems in user interface management. Information and Software Technology, vol. 29, no. 4, May 1987, pp. 176-191.

6. Enderle, G: Report on the Interface of the UIMS to the Application, Proc. Works. User Interface Management Systems Eurographics (1983) (Ed.Pfaff) Springer-Verlag (1985), pp. 21-30.

7. Gehani, N.H: Rendezvous Facilities: Concurrent C and the Ada Language, IEEE Transactions on Software Engineering, vol. 14,no. 11, Nov. 1988.

8. Green, M: Report on Dialogue Specification Tools. User Interface Management Systems, Proc. Works. User Interface Management Systems Eurographics (1983) (Ed.Pfaff) Springer- Verlag (1985), pp. 9-20.

9. Green, M: A survey of Three Dialogue Models. ACM Transactions on Graphics, vol. 5, no. 3, July 1986, pp. 244-275.

10. Kasik, D.J: A User Interface Management System. ACM Computer Graphics, vol. 16, no. 3, July 1982, pp. 99-106.

11. Koivunen, M.; Mantyla, M: HutWindows: An Improved Architecture for a User Interface Management System. IEEE Computer Graphics & Applications, Jan. 1988, pp. 43-52.

12. MacLean, A: Human factors and the design of user interface management systems: EASIE as a case study. Information and Software Technology, vol. 29, no. 4, May 1987, pp. 192-201.

13. Martínez, M.; Villalobos, B.; De Miguel, P.: The Gmenus UIMS: State-Transition Diagrams with Behavioural Properties for the Specification of Human-Computer Interaction. Proc. of the 8th IASTED International Symposium on Applied Informatics, Innsbruck (Austria), February 1990, pp.475-478.

14. Myers, B.A: User Interface Tools: introduction and survey. IEEE Software, Jan. 1989, pp. 15-23.

15. Olsen, D.R: Editing Templates: A User Interface Generation Tool. IEEE Computer Graphics & Applications, Nov. 1986, pp. 40-45.

16. Perez, F.; Carretero, J.; Gomez, L.; Perez, A.; Zamorano, J: Ada Mechanisms To Obtain Concurrency in GKS. Proc. of the Ada-Europe Conference, Madrid (Spain), June 1989, pp.266-273

17. Robinson, J.; Burns, A: A Dialogue Development System for the Design and Implementation of User Interfaces in Ada. The Computer Journal, vol. 28, no. 1, 1985, pp. 22-28.

Chapter 12

Usability Engineering and User Interface Management

Rainer Gimnich

Abstract

Development environments for planning, designing, implementing, and testing user interfaces from a usability point of view become of growing importance. This paper outlines some anticipated cornerstones of a user interface development environment incorporating cognitive aspects. An estimate of realistic progress in the near future is given on the basis of a sample current software development process. One significant problem area deals with elaborating usability test methods and related tools for current user interface technology, focusing on direct-manipulation interfaces. As an example, the aims and present status of the Software Ergonomics project at IBM Germany's Heidelberg Scientific Center are presented.

1. Usability Processes

In response to the growing demand for software products, the software development cycles have to become shorter and shorter. This holds, in particular, for user interface software. Current techniques in user interface development make use of object-oriented design and programming, and aim at producing highly interactive, direct-manipulation user interfaces. According to (Shneiderman 1987), *direct manipulation* can be characterised by the following features:

- ongoing presentations of relevant objects and operations on these objects,
- physical operations (e.g. by means of pointing devices, or function keys) instead of complex syntax,
- incremental and reversible operations, providing direct and visible feedback for the user.

Graphical, direct manipulative user interfaces have introduced new opportunities for the use software systems by a more general community of users. In particular, direct-manipulation interaction may be helpful for end-users who have little computer knowledge but are experts in their specific application fields. Thus, casual users may easily learn and remember interaction principles which are perceived as "more direct" in their daily work.

The example of direct manipulation clearly shows the importance of inventing new interaction devices, techniques, and languages, of evaluating their usability in various applications, and of accessing the resulting knowledge in the software development cycle.

Advanced process specifications for software development will incorporate usability activities at each development stage. *Usability* is meant here as the ability of a software product/prototype to interact easily and effectively with the user, in order to fulfil his/her needs and expectations (Nocentini 1987). There is some consensus that, trying to measure usability, the following factors are important (per user and per task): learning time, performance time, error rate, subjective satisfaction, and retention over time. Generally, activities which aim at ensuring a high level of software-ergonomic quality have to start as early as possible in the development cycle, by defining the usability goals that the product is to meet. Ways of implementing these goals are developed and manifested, for instance, in usability planning and usability testing activities.

Usability planning includes analysing the characteristics of potential users of the proposed product: the users' background and experience, culture, education, computer knowledge. The analysis may also comprise more detailed information such as preference of guidance/non-guidance, preferred problem-solving style, etc. Such *user profiles* have to be developed and treated with caution in order not to restrict the community of users unnecessarily, but still provide useful planning information. For instance, it will be crucial to know that a certain product is intended exclusively to, say, skilled system administrators with several years of experience.

Another activity in usability planning aims at defining *scenarios* of system use. As a prerequisite, the workplace environments of typical users have to be analysed. A comprehensive task analysis will account for the current organisation of work, the co-operation in teams, and kinds of objects and actions dealt with. This activity clearly points out the need for "contextual" research (Shackel 1985; Whiteside et al. 1988) in that the user's natural work context has to be taken as the basis for defining usability goals and related measurement criteria.

Usability testing comprises all activities concerning field or laboratory experiments with end-users as test subjects. Hypotheses, usability criteria (variables), and evaluation methods have to be defined, the tests have to be planned and run, the results have to be analysed. Further activities deal with communicating the results to the development teams, in order to interpret them (jointly) and to find constructive solutions if usability problems are encountered.

Although only a few usability activities have been mentioned, it is apparent that the usability process cannot be conducted in a linear sequence. It is iterative and cyclical in nature.

2. Usability Engineering

There are various research projects investigating engineering approaches for supporting usability processes and their relationships to other development processes. Some of these approaches are characterised by the term *usability engineering* (Bennett 1984; Shackel 1985; Gould 1988; Whiteside et al. 1988; Mack 1989).

Engineering, in general, aims at developing products according to a functional specification, within a certain space of time, and at limited costs. Engineering approaches typically apply well-planned and approved principles and methods. In a way that software engineering has emerged from "hard" engineering disciplines, usability engineering is emerging from a general software engineering basis.

In the approach presented here, usability engineering is positioned in the following way: Usability engineering is seen as a natural extension of software engineering (Figure 1). It reflects new directions in software development (e.g. user-centred design, Norman and Draper 1986) and attempts to solve the methodological problems in such new directions (e.g. predicting and supporting various users who perform various tasks at various times in various environments). In particular, early prototyping and empirical investigations are essential requisites. Thus, reliable usability work is time-consuming, iterative, and expensive.

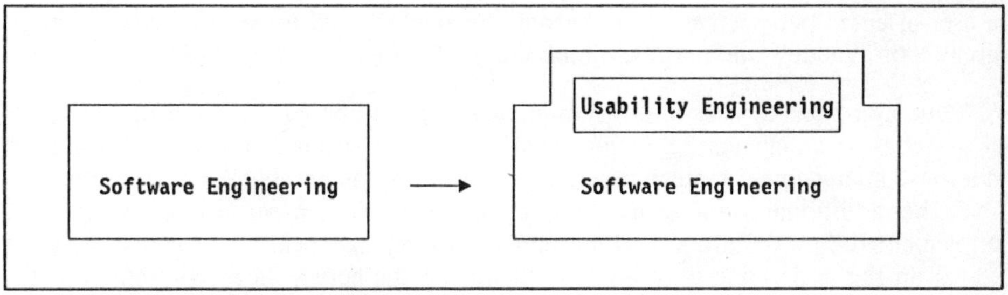

Figure 1: Positioning usability engineering

The main objective of usability engineering, in accordance with software engineering in general, is to provide principles, methods, and tools for supporting the work of user interface developers and of usability specialists. This will entail further improvements of their productivity as well as of the quality of their work.

Usability engineering principles are basic guidelines for user interface development. Such guidelines should be derived from empirical investigations and the results of controlled experiments. Examples of sets of guidelines can be found in the West-German DIN 66234/8 (Principles of Dialogue Design), and in the Working Paper of the ISO 9241/10 (Dialogue Principles for Human-Computer Interaction) (ISO 1990). As their titles indicate, these principles are applicable mostly for dialogue aspects in user interface design. The ISO standard draft – and, similarly, the DIN – include descriptions of general usability principles such as suitability for the task, self-descriptiveness, controllability, conformity with user expectations, error tolerance, ability for individualisation, and learnability.

More detailed, directly applicable descriptions are given in various design guides. As an example, the Common User Access within the IBM System Application Architecture (SAA) includes an Advanced Interface Design Guide (IBM 1989a). In this document, detailed descriptions of user interface elements are given.

Usability engineering methods are procedures and planned actions to aid user interface development and usability assurance. They may be especially helpful in achieving the previously defined usability objectives. In order to be of practical use and accepted by the development and usability teams, usability methods should be accompanied by related *tools.* A generally important aspect in the use of tools is their *integration.* It may be frustrating to find that certain functions cannot be performed just because the data produced by one tool cannot be processed by another, and there is no automatic way of transforming the data. Frameworks for integrating different tools by means of different views on common data have been developed, one example being AD/Cycle (IBM 1989b).

3. User Interface Design and Management

Usability engineering will support the development of user interface software from a user-oriented perspective. User-centred approaches need to be reflected in suitable architecture models and specification methods for their implementation.

One approach to user interface management may be gained from the evolution of database management. Starting from simple file systems, the main benefits of database management systems are the separation of the access system from the data and the additional data structuring capabilities. A general access system (i.e. implemented data definition and manipulation languages) can be provided, which is based on the underlying data model, but not on the actual data represented in the system.

Transferring this idea to user interface management, a *user interface management system* supports separating the user interface from the "application" and includes general access techniques only dependent on the "user interface model", not on the application. Here, we arrive at questions of a suitable architecture for user interface management systems, i.e. which components with which data/control flow are adequate. We also arrive at questions of how these components reasonably can be specified, with a view to interpreting the specifications for "animating" purposes. This may mean to produce working prototypes from the given descriptions. It may also mean to parameterise existing framework code.

In usability engineering, the *rapid prototyping* perspective is extremely important. Since usability processes should accompany the early development stages, it is vital that working user interface code, i.e. a prototype, be available for the usability test. The usability test results may cause revisions of the design specifications. Therefore, the results should be available before the design phase is completed. Later changes, i.e. after the implementation phase has started, are costly and often error-prone.

On the basis of these requirements, the ideas expressed in the Seeheim Model (Pfaff 1985) are still of great value. In particular, the basic structuring approaches relying on the Seeheim architecture model have proved useful. Introducing a constructive specification language for abstract data types, particularly for the presentation and application interface aspects, provides concise and problem-oriented expressions (Gimnich 1990). Such an approach also leads a way to embed the "generative" aspects of user interface management into an overall software prototyping methodology. For instance, a specification of a presentation component may be transformed, i.e. interpreted into executable code in much the same way as specifications in other application areas are treated, except that the set of base functions to be linked is different. In the case of presentation specifications, the base functions may be those provided by a standard window system, for example.

Even for advanced user interface management approaches, the structuring capabilities of the Seeheim Model may be used as a reference in understanding various user interface aspects. For instance, in direct-manipulation user interfaces, it is important to interrupt some activity represented by an icon, to perform some other work and later resume at the processing state before. Here, coroutine concepts and object-oriented techniques are helpful, as (Jacob 1986) showed. Since direct-manipulation user interfaces play an important part in today's user interface technology, there is an obvious benefit of incorporating object-oriented methods in an architecture model for user interface management.

4. User Task Descriptions

An important extension to the Seeheim architecture model would be the inclusion of a task description layer. This layer could be oriented towards concrete users' needs and influenced by the application considered. Tasks are sets of actions to be performed by the user in a goal-directed way in order to reach a defined goal state from a given starting state. Descriptions of tasks, whose performance is to be supported in the user interface, will influence the specification of the interface components. Here, a task description method and an associated language may aid in finding explicit ways of stating the *pre-design* phase of user interfaces. If this is feasible in an integrated way, user interface management may be put at higher conceptual level.

Task description approaches have been developed, such as Task Action Grammar and the GOMS (Goals - Operators - Methods - Selection rules) approach. They will be discussed separately below. These task description approaches are mainly oriented towards command language interaction and their related, transformable, direct-manipulation equivalents. However, beyond icon-oriented dragging of symbols and handling menus, direct manipulation has an essential structural aspect in that it provides a means for representing structural relationships of objects in a both abstract and direct way.

The GOMS approach (Card et al. 1983) suggests the description of tasks through four information components:

- **G**oals which the user has in mind,
- cognitive **O**perations of the user (e.g. reading the contents of a window or pressing a key),

- Methods of organising sequences of operations for reaching goals (or subgoals; a hierarchical organisation of goals is assumed),

- Selection rules applied by the user when deciding which method to use for attaining a goal.

A key concept of GOMS is that of "unit tasks", which are independent of each other. However, the specification of such tasks and their modular use in higher level tasks is not clearly defined.

Several extensions of GOMS have been proposed, one of them being GOMS* (Arend 1989). It offers a more concise treatment of goals and operations by introducing a set of base functions, such as "get", "move", "press". Further, the control flow is made more explicit by using ALGOL-like control structures. Arend has used GOMS* successfully for analysing the consistency of user interfaces and for predicting users' learning times.

A different task description method is given in Task Action Grammar (TAG) (Payne and Green 1986). In contrast to the intent of predicting user performance times (as in GOMS, Card et al. 1983), the TAG approach concentrates on the user's competence, i.e. on modelling the user's knowledge of a system and evaluating the consistency of user interfaces. TAG is a grammar-oriented description method, including a dictionary of simple tasks. Thus, TAG has a more solid mathematical basis than GOMS, with the consequence that tools for processing TAG descriptions can be developed more easily. Various kinds of consistency are defined within TAG, which allow to predict possible sources of user errors.

Tauber's extension of TAG (ETAG, Tauber 1989) is motivated by the idea that, with a view to direct manipulation, presentational aspects should be incorporated in a task description method. Visualisations, e.g. spatial constellations of objects, should be expressible in an adequate way, and not by simply translating graphical operations to equivalent commands and neglecting the object structures they operate on. While Tauber's approach is powerful, ETAG descriptions seem to become difficult to handle when complex applications are considered.

A practical task description method suitable for the complete range of today's direct-manipulation approaches still needs to be developed. This is one of the goals of the Software Ergonomics project at IBM Heidelberg Scientific Center. This research project has been set up in 1989 and is conducted in cooperation with the IBM Development Laboratory at Böblingen, Germany. The project is named InterUse and has two basic aims: developing criteria for assessing future human-computer **Inter**action modes, and, for its main part, developing a well-defined **Use**ability test method which is suitable for advanced user interface technology, with focus on direct manipulation.

The method will imply an analysis of the requirements and functions which are necessary for powerful test support, e.g. for choosing usability test procedures. Besides, the method has to account for measurable units of users' actions. For instance, in a direct-manipulation user interface, there is no consensus as yet on *what* exactly to measure. This is partly due to the fact that actually no task description technique adequate for testing direct manipulation has been developed so far. This type of user interface involves the modelling and visual presentation of the user's information space and of the (direct) operations to be provided for the user in this model. While operations have been investigated intensively, this is not true for the underlying complex object structures which are manipulated by them.

We have developed guidelines which will form the basic elements of a method for designing and testing user interfaces. Most of the guidelines have been drawn from generalisable results of empirical investigations in the field. The work relies on numerous investigations reported in the literature, and on several experiments of our own. Interaction styles other than direct-manipulation, such as menu selection or command input, have also been considered, since direct manipulation may include techniques which are more thoroughly investigated in their specific areas. In order to analyse a large amount of reports economically, a classification scheme has been developed in a formal notation. This has helped considerably in comparing the contents and condense them to concrete guidelines.

The guidelines will form the basic knowledge for designing and testing direct-manipulation user interfaces. This knowledge will be applied in a controlled way in the framework of a usability test and design methodology suitable for direct-manipulation interaction. The basic architecture is depicted in Figure 2 and will be employed for two purposes:

- *Usability testing:*
  Starting from given implementations of a user interface and an application, the user interface specification can be structurally related to a user-oriented task description which is developed independently.

- *User-centred design:*
  Starting with task descriptions, the user interface and even the functional parts of the software system can be specified and implemented subsequently.

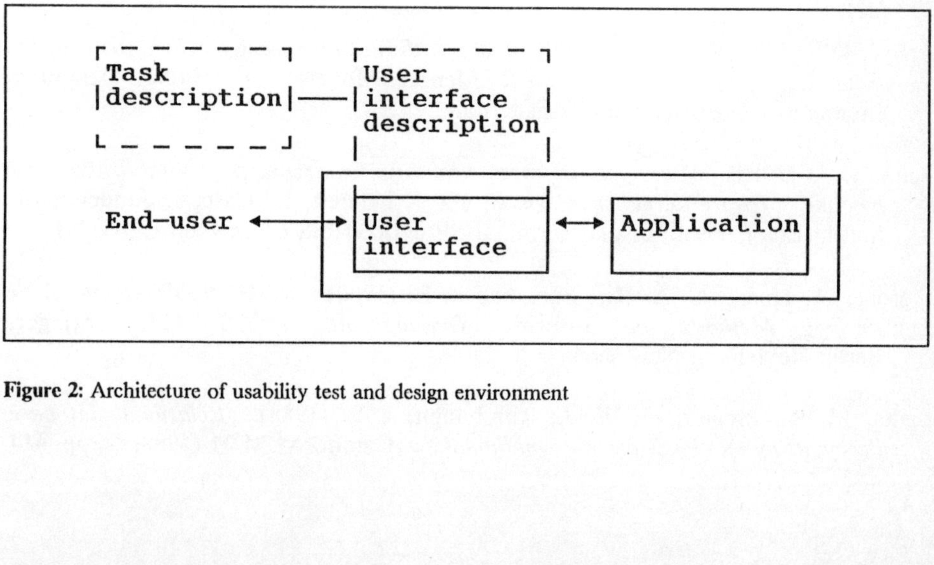

Figure 2: Architecture of usability test and design environment

While we mainly concentrate on usability testing in the scope of our project, the planned description methods have to account for both of these purposes.

Adequate user interface specification methods have already been developed. For graphical user interfaces, most of these methods root in object-oriented approaches. However, suitable task description methods require more research effort. Such a method and its associated language are currently under development. They benefit from experience with existing task description methods (GOMS, GOMS*, TAG, ETAG). Further, they will draw from

- advanced task analysis approaches (Diaper 1989),
- database design methods, e.g. OMT (Object Modelling Technique; Blaha et al. 1988), and
- model-theoretic software development methods, e.g. VDM (Vienna Development Method; Jones 1990; Bjørner et al. 1990).

The task description method under development will form the central reference in a usability test method for direct-manipulation user interfaces. Then, support tools for the test method will be designed, e.g. a syntax-oriented editor for the task description language and a structure checker. The idea is that this planned usability test environment will be a first experimental setting, in order to understand how task-oriented user interface development environments could be realised.

Acknowledgements

I would like to thank my colleagues Klaus Kunkel and Thomas Strothotte for constructive discussions. Special thanks go to Jürgen Ebert, Koblenz University, for carefully reading an earlier version of this paper.

References

Arend, U. (1989). *Analysing complex tasks with an extended GOMS Model,* in: D. Ackermann, M. Tauber (Eds.), Mental Models and Human-Computer Interaction, North-Holland, Amsterdam.

Bennett, J. (1984). *Managing to meet usability requirements: establishing and meeting software development goals,* in: J. Bennett, D. Case, J. Sandelin, M. Smith (Eds.), Visual display terminals, Prentice-Hall, Englewood Cliffs, NJ.

Bjørner, D., Hoare, C. A. R., Langmaack, H. (1990). *VDM'90: VDM and Z – Formal Methods in Software Development,* LNCS 428, Springer, Berlin Heidelberg New York.

Blaha, M. R., Premerlani, W. J., Rumbaugh, J. E. (1988). *Relational database design using an object-oriented methodology,* Comm. ACM 31 (1988, 4), pp. 414 - 427.

Card, S. K., Moran, T. P., Newell, A. (1983). *The psychology of human-computer interaction,* Lawrence Erlbaum, Hillsdale, NJ.

Diaper, D. (1989). *Task analysis for human-computer interaction,* Ellis Horwood, Chichester.

Gimnich, R. (1990). *A unifying view on interaction styles and their implementation in a user interface management system,* Ergonomics 33 (1990, 4), pp. 509 - 517.

Gould, J. (1988). *How to design usable systems,* in: M. Helander (Ed.), Handbook of human-computer interaction, North-Holland, Amsterdam, pp. 757-789.

IBM (1989a). *Common User Access: Advanced Interface Design Guide,* Doc. No. SC26-4582-0, 1989.

IBM (1989b). *AD/Cycle Concepts,* Doc. No. GC26-4531-0, 1989.

ISO (1990). *Dialogue Design Criteria,* Working Paper of ISO 9241 Part 10, 1990.

Jacob, R. J. K. (1986). *A specification language for direct-manipulation user interfaces,* ACM Trans. on Graphics 5 (1986, 4), pp. 283 - 317.

Jones, C. B. (1990). *Systematic software development using VDM,* 2nd edition, Prentice-Hall, London.

Mack, R. (1989). personal communication.

Nocentini, S. (1987). *The mission of the IBM Human Factors Competency Centres,* Proc. SEAS (SHARE European Association) Conference (Edinburgh, Scotland; Sept. 28 - Oct. 2, 1987), pp. 241 - 247.

Norman, D. A., Draper, S. W. (1986). *User centered system design,* Lawrence Erlbaum, Hillsdale, NJ.

Payne, S. J., Green, T. R. G. (1986). *Task-action grammars: a model of the mental representation of task languages,* Human-Computer Interaction 2 (1986), 93-133.

Pfaff, G. E. (1985). *User interface management systems,* Springer, Berlin/Heidelberg/New York, 1985.

Shackel, B. (1985). *Human factors and usability – whence and whither?* in: H.-J. Bullinger (Ed.), Software-Ergonomie '85, Teubner, Stuttgart.

Shneiderman, B. (1987). *Designing the user interface: Strategies for effective human-computer interaction,* Addison-Wesley; Reading, MA., 1987.

Tauber, M. (1989). unpublished manuscripts, Institut für Informatik der Universität Paderborn.

Whiteside, J., Bennett, J., Holtzblatt, K. (1988). *Usability engineering: our experience and evolution,* in: M. Helander (Ed.), Handbook of human-computer interaction, North-Holland, Amsterdam, pp. 757-789.

Chapter 13

Designing the Next Generation of UIMSs

Fergal Shevlin and Francis Neelamkavil

Abstract

Some new suggestions are made relating to the structure of User Interface Management Systems (UIMS) which may be beneficial in enhancing their functionality, both with respect to the User Interface (UI) developer, and the eventual UI end-user. Advantages to the developer stem from improved specification facilities that may be provided with the new UIMS architecture, while the end-user can benefit from easier to use UIs with better response times. An explanation of UIMS model hierarchies is given, and different types of UI separation : Physical, Logical, and Virtual, are introduced. The advantages of Virtual Separation and the requirements introduced by it are outlined. The specification of the UI is discussed in relation to the new concepts involved. These issues have an impact on the architecture of the Interactive Application created with the UIMS, this is discussed along with some ideas for UI code generation.

1 UIMS

A UIMS is a utility oriented towards easing the burden of Interactive Application development by providing facilities that enable the User Interface to be designed and implemented separately from the application-specific computational parts of the system. Separation of the two main aspects of an Interactive Application into distinct components is regarded as desirable for the reduction of development complexity, but it has its associated problems. The UIMS should provide separation, but also aim to minimize the disadvantages, such as the inter-component communication (control and data transfer) overhead. The user of a UIMS would primarily be a UI Developer, this is a person whose job is to implement User Interfaces, as opposed to a UI Designer who need not necessarily have any detailed knowledge of software.

1.1 UIMS Model Hierarchies

Several UIMS logical models have been proposed, and more are appearing as the popularity of the field increases. Perhaps the most well known is the Seeheim Model [Pfaf 1985]. This structures the User Interface into three parts :- Presentation Component (PC), which deals with implementational details of input and output (this corresponds to the Lexical level of the interaction model proposed by [Fole 1989]); Dialogue Control (DC) Component, which deals with sequencing of interaction (the Syntactic level); and Application Interface (AI) Component, which integrates the User Interface with the application-specific computational component of the Interactive Application (the Semantic level). This model has come under criticism for a number of reasons, perhaps most especially for assuming that a clear separation of Interactive Application functionality is possible. Although few UIMSs have been developed rigidly using this model, it is important because it explicitly specifies the areas that must be considered in the design of any UIMS. We take the view that a UIMS need not necessarily partition an Interactive Application into these physical components, but the functionality of these components must be encompassed in the UIMS model. This model is shown in Figure 1, termed the Generic Level because of the generality of its relationship with other UIMS models.

Other UIMS models (mostly based on the Seeheim one) which have been suggested share the same aim of providing the User Interface designer with a framework that can be used for the easy specification and implementation of a wide variety of interfaces. The designer must specify the desired interface in terms of the logical model, and then the code-generation part of the

Authors' Address : Department of Computer Science, Trinity College, Dublin 2, Ireland.

UIMS processes these specifications to produce the User Interface source code and assemble the Interactive Application. A typical UIMS model is shown in the Logical Level of Figure 1. The term Logical Model is used because a wide variety of different models which map onto the generic model are possible, these could be considered a logical level of abstraction below the generic model.

An idea that could have an impact on the next generation of UIMSs, but which has not received much notice to date, is that Interactive Application code generated by UIMSs need not necessarily bear any close similarity to the UIMS logical model that the User Interface designer adhered to in specification. The functionality should be the same, but details of physical implementation could be different to the logical model. The advantage of this approach is that the major UIMS problems of component separation, communication, and control [Hill 1987] may be reduced because at run-time, the components need not actually be separate from each other, so the problems caused by separation do not occur. This is represented in Figure 1 by the Run-Time level.

Figure 1 highlights how different models can exist at different logical levels. In the past the Run-Time architectures of Interactive Applications generated by UIMS have inherited their structure from the logical UIMS model. This close relationship is not actually required, and could change as better logical UIMS models and more efficient Run-Time Architectures are developed - enabling the best of both worlds, logical simplicity with run-time efficiency.

2 Virtual, Logical, and Physical Separation

The separation of UI from application-specific computational aspects of the Interactive Application is the most important function that a UIMS should aim to provide [Myer 1989]. There are different types of separation, and some are more useful than others for easing the development of Interactive Applications.

Physical Separation is where the code for application-specific computation and the UI code are implemented in separate procedures/functions and possibly located in separate modules. These different types of code can be stored in different files and references to each other can be resolved by compilation and linking to produce the executable application. This is quite a common form of separation and should occur in all systems of professional-quality, most Windowing Systems, Graphical Toolkits, and User Interface Management Systems provide this level of separation by allowing the UI and the application to communicate (passing control and data) through parameterised and non-parameterised function calls. Figure 2 shows the physical separation of functions/routines, with the lines linking them representing communication.

When separation is discussed in relation to UIMSs, the advantages that are often mentioned are not based on the physical separation of code, since this is not too difficult to achieve, rather they are based on the simplification of the complex interaction that occurs between the two components. It is this complex relationship that is primarily responsible for the difficulty in programming Interactive Applications. It is difficult to reduce this complexity, but if achieved, it can be regarded as Logical Separation. Figure 3 shows how *Logical* Separation lessens the complexity of the relationship between the components more so than Physical Separation. Despite the fact that most of the well-publicised advantages of separation are based on Logical as well as Physical, few UIMSs have implemented logical separation so as to provide these advantages.

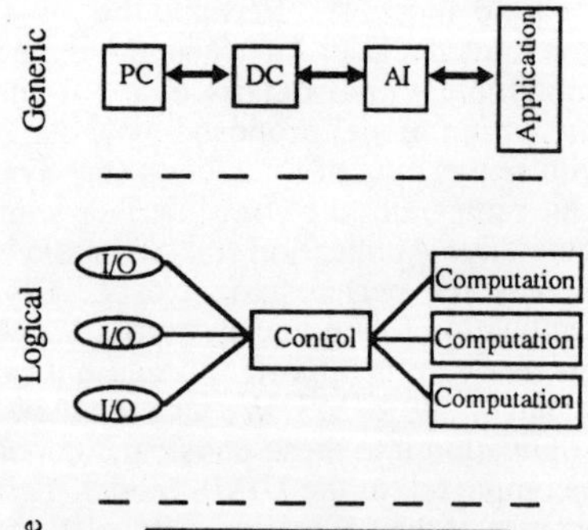

Figure 1. A Hierarchy of UIMS Models

Failure to provide Logical Separation is demonstrated by the fact that the Application Interface (which is the part primarily responsible for the implementation of separation) has often not been given as much attention as other components. This may be because separation of User Interface parts from the computational parts of the application is extremely difficult, the UI and the application can be linked in so many subtle ways that attempted separation may impair rather than facilitate development [Manh 1989]. In order to avoid dealing with this possibly insoluble problem, what is needed may not be actual separation of code, but rather an apparent separation, provided through a UIMS. This would give Interactive Application developers the impression that they are specifying a separated system, but this would not really be the case at the physical level. The UIMS could manage all links between the User Interface and the application to make them look as separate as possible to the UI developer.

This could be regarded as *Virtual* Separation where the UIMS transforms the Logical Model specifications into the Physical Architecture. Figure 4 shows the role of the UIMS in this case - it allows specification to be performed with simple concepts, and transforms this into the complex physical application. This is compatible with the ideas of having different models on different levels described earlier, the UIMS could provide virtual separation at the logical level and an efficient physical implementation. The PAC (Presentation, Abstraction, Control) model [Cout 1987], also counters the argument for physical separation.

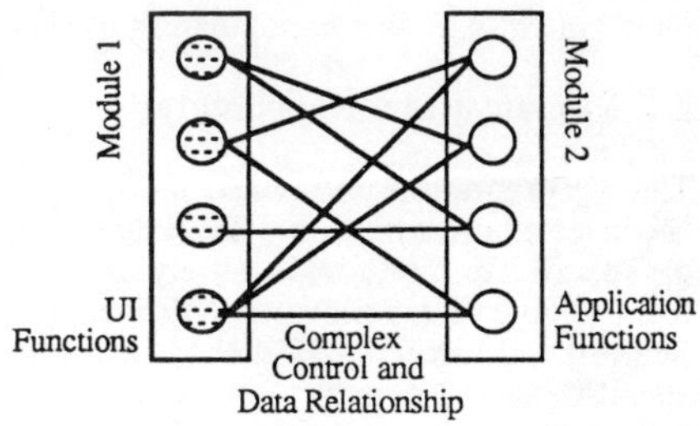

Figure 2. Physical Separation of Interactive Application Code

PAC advocates the *suppression* of a single clear boundary between the main components of an Interactive Application. It provides a recursive logical model which distributes the semantics and the syntax at various levels of abstraction, and explicitly introduces the notion of Control which reconciles the Presentation with the application-specific computation. This allows delegation and modification of semantics. This concept can be reconciled with the idea of virtual separation, the UIMS could transform specifications (possibly done with reference to another model) into this type of model and provide the required distributed semantics management functionality.

2.1 Logical Models with Virtual Separation

Different Application areas can have very different interaction requirements, eg. the requirements for Real-Time Process Supervision and Control Systems may not be similar to those for Office Automation systems. These different requirements imply that different specification paradigms might be more suited to different areas. Alternative specification paradigms would be quite difficult to implement with conventional UIMS architectures, but if the concept of Virtual Separation has been applied, there is no problem in changing Logical Models for specification, without altering the rest of the UIMS. Many different logical models can be supported by the UIMS in this manner, all that is required is a specification utility for the desired model/paradigm with which the designer can describe the desired UI.

In order for different logical models to be understood by the UIMS, specifications should be converted into the same format so that they can be processed in a similar manner. This common format could be termed an *Intermediate Representation* (Section 2.2) because it plays an intermediary role between the logical specifications and the physical architecture of the code. It should be the responsibility of the Logical model specification utility to perform the conversion into Intermediate Representation. This means that the UIMS code generator does not need to have any knowledge about the model through which the UI was specified, it need only deal with the

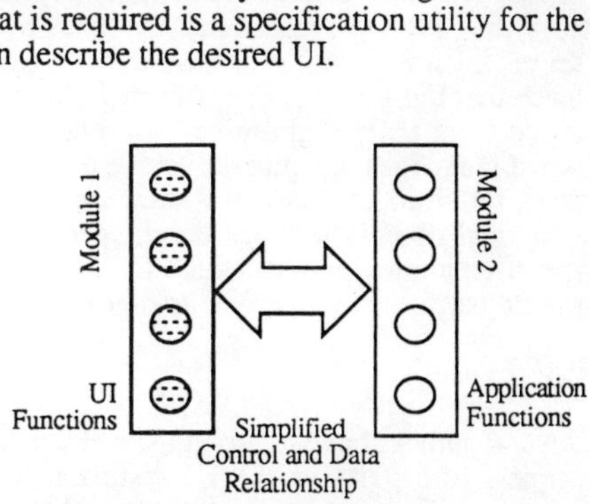

Figure 3. Logical Separation of the Interactive Application

Intermediate Representation input. In addition to avoiding the problems of UI separation, another example of how different logical models can be applied in practice is that a non-expert application end-user could specify simple UIs or small alterations to existing UIs through the use of a simple Logical Model, designed for ease of use and which has minimal functionality. A general purpose application programmer could specify a reasonably complex UI through the use of a Logical Model that is sophisticated, yet did not have a high learning overhead associated with its use. A UI specialist programmer could use a comprehensive, expert-oriented model that enabled specification of complex interfaces. It could be argued that if one logical model is good enough, then others wouldn't be needed. This is possibly true, but it is probable that models tailored to different application areas and implemented at different levels of complexity would be more suited to a diverse population of UIMS users.

2.2 Intermediate Representation

The representation into which the specified UI is converted must be complete enough to handle the specification of a wide variety of interfaces. It is possible that (following the concepts of the Seeheim Model) different intermediate specification languages are most suited for different aspects of UIMS functionality : Presentation, Dialogue Control, and Application Interface. In investigating these languages, the emphasis should be on functionality and completeness as opposed to readability. This is because the Intermediate Representation should be generated automatically from the graphical specification, without UIMS-user involvement.

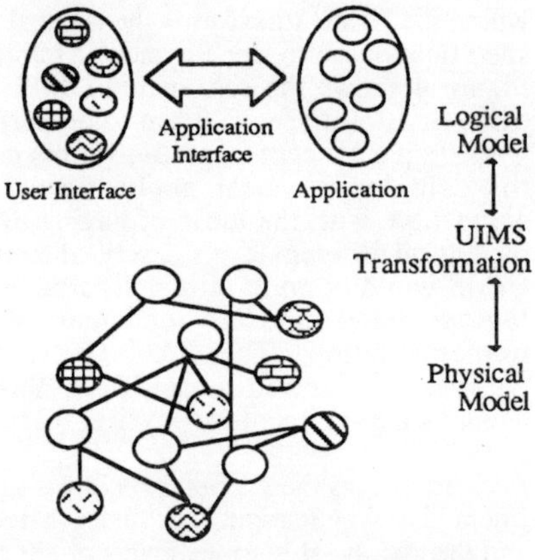

Figure 4. Virtual Separation by UIMS transformation

This concept is similar to that used in some programming language compilers, different language source code is compiled into the same intermediate language/representation by different initial-phase compilation procedures. A single final-phase compilation procedure can then convert intermediate into machine-specific code. In the field of compilers, this approach has been proven to be flexible and effective [Aho 1986], and it should be equally applicable in the area of UIMSs. Much research has been done on Specification Techniques/Languages for User Interfaces [Gree 1986], [Hopp 1986], [Harr 1989], it is most likely that the best Intermediate Representation would be found from this body of work.

3 UI Specification

After a suitable Interactive Application logical model has been designed, (i.e. intuitive and providing logical separation), the focus of UIMS development must turn to the provision of a set of UI specification techniques. It is important that they are easy to use, since it is through these that the UI developer has most interaction with the UIMS. Specification techniques can range from textual grammar-based languages to interactive graphical techniques. Grammar-based languages are generally not easy to use, since they need to be complicated to perform the tasks required of them, and they are at least one level of abstraction away from the visual, graphical objects that are being specified. It is desirable that UIMSs provide graphical UI specification techniques which UI Developers would find more intuitive, and through which it should be easier to specify a graphical interface since they enable visualisation of UI objects .

3.1 Presentation

Several authors have reported their research on techniques for the description of UI Presentation aspects (the parts of the UI visible to the user). Much of this work has concentrated on windowing system environments and the presentation specifications proposed are based on higher levels of abstraction than the basic ones currently provided in those environments. For example, UIL [DEC 1989], and WINTERP Lisp [Maye 1989] are based to some extent on levels of abstraction above the X Toolkit, which is itself a level above the basic Xlib of the X

Window System [Sche 1989]. The separation of UI functionality is not rigidly adhered to in these systems so that Dialogue Control and Application Interface issues may also be specified with these techniques, but the emphasis is on Presentation aspects. In general, these specification languages are effective for windowing environment-related issues, but they lack facilities when it comes to the more complex problem of application-specific input/output. Many seem to be too confined to the windowing framework and are not flexible enough to deal completely with what goes on inside the windows. Although current Presentation Specification techniques do not provide all the functionality that is desirable of them, they are effective for most Presentation tasks required in UIs.

3.2 Dialogue Control

Dialogue Control is probably the most well-researched area of User Interface specification and there are many techniques and representations available, such as those mentioned in [Gree 1986], [Hopp 1986], [Harr 1989]. There may be arguments about the applicability of a particular type of Dialogue specification to a particular application, but there is little doubt that Dialogue Control can be specified effectively using both textual and graphical specification techniques.

3.3 Application Interface

The Seeheim Model highlights the need for an effective Application Interface (AI) to link the UI with the application-specific computational component. This requirement has since been re-iterated and re-emphasised [Cock 1989]. There have been a limited number of suggestions for Application Interface Specification techniques, mostly proposing the implementation as a database of shared Interactive Application data [Alla 1989], [Shin 1989].

Despite the well-publicised requirement and the amount of interest shown in the other areas of the Seeheim model, little work has been done in accordance with the spirit of AI requirements - that the AI component is responsible for the resolution of issues resulting from the separation of the UI from the application. Perhaps the reason for this, and hence the resulting lack of AI Specification Techniques, is that the problem is more involved and more difficult than was first imagined. An exploration of these difficulties might enhance understanding and make the provision of AI specification techniques more likely.

The role of the AI was initially assumed to be for the initiation of application specific functions and the associated data transfer when the dialogue entered certain states. In reality, the task of the Application Interface is more difficult than this because AI issues arise in all areas, not just in Dialogue Control. Semantic Feedback about the meaning of what is being done at the lexical level of interaction must be provided through the Presentation Component. Since the meaning of what is being done is the responsibility of the Application, a link is required between Presentation and Application to provide this feedback, which is an AI issue. The AI is also involved when Dialogue Control needs to access Application semantics to see if transitions are allowed between certain states. Obviously, the Application is more closely involved with Presentation and Dialogue issues than may have been initially assumed. The complexity of this relationship is probably the reason why few effective AI specification techniques have been proposed.

3.3.1 Possible Approaches to Application Interface Specification

The AI has been shown to be difficult to specify, and few facilities have been provided for this task. It has been admitted that in practice, the whole User Interface is not normally specified at a high level with grammar rules, and that a lot of technical expertise in conventional programming is still required to integrate the UI [Hopp 1986], this does not fit in with UIMS aspirations. The aim of a UIMS is to reduce UI development difficulty through the provision of Logical Separation, the AI component is responsible (more than any other) for the implementation of this separation, so the UIMS should provide facilities for AI specification to eliminate the need for conventional coding. In general, windowing systems do not tackle this issue because the separation they provide is mainly physical.

A form of specification that the UIMS could provide without the necessity of a formal technique is an interactive utility that enables the UI designer to resolve AI issues. This UIMS AI specification utility could process the specifications of Presentation and Dialogue Control so that it is aware of Application Interface issues that need to be resolved. These issues can then be organised and the UI designer interactively involved in their resolution, by prompting for responses to particular problems, and enabling designers to use their expert knowledge of both UI and application areas to specify what needs to happen in the Application Interface.

This AI specification approach could use many of the concepts of graphical object-based interaction in the solution of the Application Interface problem. The UIMS AI utility could graphically display issues that the UI Developer could interactively resolve, using knowledge about the task that the Interactive Application is required to perform. Issues such as semantic involvement in Presentation and Dialogue Control levels, and transfer of control/data between components can be identified by the UIMS through processing Presentation and Dialogue specifications, and displayed via the AI specification utility so that the help of the UI developer may be invoked to handle them. Such a specification utility could solve the problem of having to build the application around the UI [Alla 1989], [Shin 1989], or having to resort to conventional coding methods [Hopp 1986] in order to implement a functional AI that provides Logical UI separation.

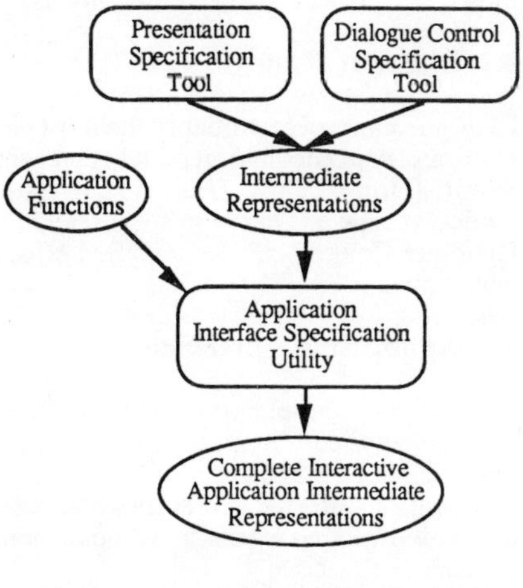

Figure 5. Possible Specification Scenario

Figure 5 shows how AI specification can fit in with what is required for the other components.

4 UIMS Functionality

The requirements for tools that a UIMS should provide can be divided into two categories [Alla 1989]. The first comprises of tools that enable the Interactive Application developer to specify the Presentation, Dialogue Control, and Application Interface in accordance with the Logical Model. The second category is made up of tools that take the specifications and generate the Interactive Application code. The application is generated by resolving all Application Interface issues and linking the Presentation Techniques / Dialogue Control code with the application-specific computational components. Figure 6 summarises functionality and structure for a comprehensive User Interface Management System, this is similar to the structures outlined in [Alla 1989], [Prim 1989].

4.1 Specification Processing

The primary function of a UIMS is to process the specifications of the desired UI to generate the Interactive Application. This requires generation of code to provide the specified UI, as well as integration of that code with the application-specific computational functions. If the approach of having different logical and run-time models is taken, then this processing can be even more complex and demanding than in the approach used to date.

Many current UIMSs rely on run-time interpretation of events to create and control the UI. This is an overhead that slows the speed of execution. It would be better if there is little interpretation at run-time and if event-response issues are resolved in the specification-processing phase of UI generation. The types of issues that arise at run-time, and which would require significant interpretation unless dealt with in the specification-processing phase, are Flow of Control and Semantic Support. The notion of a run-time Semantic Support Component has been raised in

[Danc 1987]. The functionality provided by this component is to integrate the application-specific computational parts (the semantics) with the UI.

This functionality is desirable, but it would be better if little run-time computation was required to support it. Therefore, one of the aims for UIMS specification-processing should be to provide as much semantic support as possible by resolving issues at code generation time, instead of leaving them for interpretation at run-time. It would be more difficult to provide semantic support functionality at generation-time, given that less information about the state of the dialogue is available. Some of the difficulty could be alleviated by the possible participation of the UI developer in the process. The developer could be prompted for responses to application-specific issues that are difficult to resolve automatically so that as many decisions as possible can be made before the execution of the program.

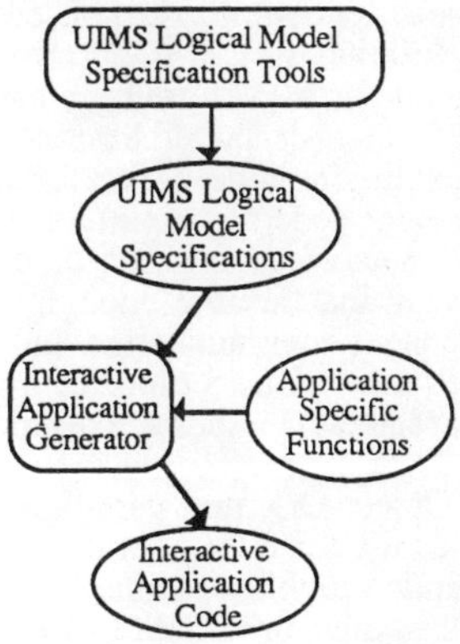

Figure 6. UIMS Structure and Functionality

This functionality could be included in the Application Interface Specification Utility that was outlined earlier, since Semantic Support is an issue closely related to the Application Interface itself.

Run-time interpretation of Dialogue Control information and run-time inter-process communication are both similar to Semantic Support in the sense that they need significant computation during execution, and hence worsen response times. Many UIMSs have some kind of run-time interpretative controllers present, eg. GRINS [Olse 1985], AIH [Feld 1982], ADM [Schu 1985], Sassafras [Hill 1986], HIGGENS [Huds 1988], DIAMANT II [Koll 1988], and LUIS [Manh 1989]. While these fulfill the controlling functionality required of them, it would be better if flow of control decisions were determined at code generation time. There is much difficulty associated with this flow of control determination, especially where the dialogues being implemented are multi-threaded or asynchronous. But even if all issues cannot be resolved in advance for reasons of practicality, it is worthwhile trying to clear up as many issues as possible in advance.

A similar motivation can be used for the minimisation of inter-process communications. Some of the more well-known UIMSs implement components of Interactive Applications as various processes, for example, Sassafras and LUIS. Each process communicates with the other via inter-process communication facilities. To reduce this overhead, it is necessary to facilitate component communication through techniques such as function calls or shared memory, as opposed to message-passing. This implies structuring the application as one large executable image, as opposed to many different individually executable components.

4.2 UI Code Generation

When the UI specifications have been converted into the intermediate representation by UIMS specification utilities, the UIMS Interactive Application generator must then process them to produce UI code in accordance with the run-time architecture. The UNIX tools LEX and YACC have been shown to be efficient for the implementation of UI code generators [Hopp 1986], they are a widely available means of conversion from formal specification to source code. YACC (parser generator) will produce a parser for a grammar, given its specification. LEX (lexical analyser generator) produces code that recognises specified regular expressions. The UIMS code generator should produce conventional (Third Generation) language code from the Intermediate representation. This code can then be compiled by a conventional compiler and linked with the application to produce the executable Interactive Application.

5. Implementation Issues

It is obviously desirable that UIMS-generated Interactive Application code should be as fast and efficient as possible. The concept of efficiency (at the expense of maintainability) is contrary to conventional software engineering principles, but this is not a major issue here since no programmer is ever going to have to deal directly with the generated code. Any changes that need to be made should be done at the specification level, which adheres to the Logical Model. An intelligent code generator (eg. Human Programmer) could produce highly application-dependent code of maximum run-time efficiency, but short of this level of competence, the UIMS needs a generic run-time architecture to follow. The Run-Time Architecture should be efficient and flexible enough to be the basis for a wide variety of interfaces. If all inter-component communication and control issues are not to be resolved at generation-time, then some form of UIMS run-time management component needs to be included in the architecture to manage these issues at execution-time.

The Object-Oriented paradigm has been shown to be effective for the implementation of graphical User Interfaces [Smit 1986], [Gros 1987], [Hubn 1989], [Youn 1987], and it could be applied to this run-time architecture definition problem. It has been reported [Hubn 1989] that the convenient UIMS Model of strict separation and modularisation between the Lexical, Syntactic, and Semantic levels is inappropriate and insufficient for graphics dialogues, whereas the Object paradigm is suitable. This is relevant to the central issue being discussed here; the model that is appropriate for specification is inappropriate for implementation, it does not mean that either the physical or logical model needs to be compromised - each can be used where it best suits and a (UIMS) transformation utility can convert from one to the other.

For the scenario described in this paper, with different logical and physical models tailored for a wide variety of applications, the most important items to be provided in a run-time architecture framework are complex application input and output facilities. Output facilities would ease the task of displaying complex output, (eg. Three-dimensional Graphical images, Speech, Multi-Media, and other non-trivial device control functions). Input facilities provided by current windowing systems (eg. X Window System) are fairly simple in terms of possible Interactive Application complexity. They provide a predetermined framework and facilities for interaction (Windows, Buttons, Scroll Bars) and do not really provide an application with the support required for various forms of input that are specifically application dependent (eg. user input from a three-dimensional graphics editor). These input and output requirements are very similar - which suggests that the Run-Time Architecture requires good inter-component communications facilities. Figure 7 shows a Communications Interface (CI), which could be considered as a module in the run-time architecture that manages/coordinates communications between all other modules in the system (this communication could involve transfer of control or data). Once the CI has initiated data transfer, the transfer can proceed without any more CI management/supervision.

Building UIs around this architecture (or others following similar concepts) could result in increased levels of UI quality. This is because both response times and levels of semantic feedback are enhanced since communication between the application and the UI is made more efficient. It is widely accepted that run-time configurability is desirable, so that some UIMS controlling functionality should be present although execution efficiency may suffer as a direct result. This control could be part of the Dialogue Control module, enhancing the role of this module to take run-time alteration into account. This is as well as the usual task of guiding the Interactive Application through the static, predefined set of dialogue states.

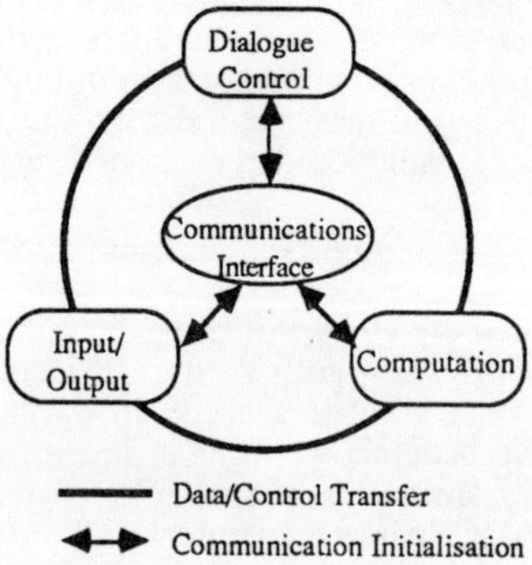

Figure 7. Communications Interface

6. Concluding Remarks

One of the main advantages of a UIMS is that it enables the User Interface to be developed separately from application-specific functions, in such a way that the complexities of both components do not make development as difficult as it has been in the past. In order to achieve this separate development, the UIMS provides an Interactive Application logical model, which the UI developer uses for specification. An issue which has not received much attention, but which could be of use in UIMS design, is that the logical model which the UIMS supports for specification and the actual Run-Time structure of the generated Interactive Application need not be the same. This means that the well-documented problems of component separation (inter-component communication and control) need not actually be encountered, while the advantages (reduction of Interactive Application development complexity) are provided by the UIMS in the form of virtual separation.

User Interface separation can mean several things, the most basic interpretation is that UI source code is physically separate from application-computation source code, so that they can be written separately, held in different object modules, and linked together. This is the level of separation that is provided by most windowing systems and graphics toolkits. A more advanced interpretation is not just physical separation, but logical separation. This is the level of separation that is implied when considering the advantages of a UIMS, and it requires that the complex relationships and interactions between the components of the Interactive Application be simplified, not just spatial separation of the components. Virtual Separation means the UIMS supports Logical Separation at the specification level, while implementing a non-separated, integrated system at the physical level.

The desired UI must be specified in accordance with the logical model , the specification can be considered in terms of the Seeheim Model - Presentation aspects, Dialogue Control aspects, and Application Interface aspects. There has been much work done on the first two of these, but very little Application Interface specification work has been carried out with the aim of achieving Logical separation - this is undoubtedly because it is so complicated. A possible solution to AI specification (but which may not be rigourous or complete) is for the UIMS to provide a graphical utility which enables the UI Developer to interactively resolve AI issues that the UIMS identifies after processing the specifications of the Presentation and Dialogue Control components. This would incorporate the knowledge and skill of the Developer with the syntactical analysis power of the UIMS to produce a powerful specification method that is more likely to result in Logical UI Separation.

To implement Virtual Separation, the UIMS code generator must convert the functionally-separated logical model specifications into possibly complex, non-separated, physical code. Since automatic code generation techniques are not good enough to generate the most efficient applications from specifications, some kind of framework for the Interactive Application is required, around which the code generator can build the code. The design of this framework (or Run-Time architecture), is important since it directly affects application execution efficiency and hence the user's perception of application quality. The most important qualities considered in the design of Run-Time architectures are flexibility and efficiency during execution, good inter-component communication is required to provide these.

7. References

[Aho 1986] Aho A.V., Sethi R., Ullman J.D., Compilers. Principles. Techniques. and Tools. Addison Wesely.

[Alla 1989] Allari S., Rizzi C., Hagemann T., Tahon C., System Builder Area of VITAMIN Project Description : Major Achievements. ESPRIT '89 Conference Proceedings. Kluwer Academic Publishers, Dordrecht.

[Cock 1989] Cockton G., Interaction Ergonomics, Control and Separation: Open Problems in User Interface Management Systems. Tutorial Note 12, Eurographics '89, Hamburg.

[Cout 1987] Coutaz J., The Construction of User Interfaces and the Object Paradigm. Proceedings ECOOP '87, Third European Conference on Object-Oriented Programming.

[Danc 1987] Dance J.R., Tamar E., Hill R., Hudson S.E., Meads J., Myers B.A., Schulert A., The Run-Time Structure of UIMS-Supported Applications. ACM Computer Graphics, Vol. 21, No. 2, pp. 97 -101.

[DEC 1989] User Interface Language Reference Manual. Ultrix Worksystem Software V2.1. Digital Equipment Corporation.

[Feld 1982] Feldman F.B., Rogers G.T., Towards the Design and Development of Style-Independent Interactive Systems. Proceedings ACM Human Factors in Computer Systems, Maryland, pp. 111-116.

[Fole 1989] Foley J., Summer School on User Interfaces '89, Tampere, Finland.

[Gree 1986] Green M., A Survey of Three Dialogue Models. ACM Transactions on Graphics, Vol. 5, No. 4, pp. 244-275.

[Gros 1987] Grossman M., Ege R., Logical Composition of Object-Oriented Interfaces. ACM OOPSLA '87 Proceedings, pp. 295-306.

[Harr 1989] Harrison M., Thimbleby H., Eds., Formal Methods in Human-Computer Interaction, Cambridge Series on Human-Computer Interaction, Cambridge University Press.

[Hill 1986] Hill R.D., Supporting Concurrency, Communication, and Synchronisation in Human-Computer Interaction - The Sassafras UIMS. ACM Transactions on Graphics, Vol. 5, No. 3, pp. 179-200.

[Hill 1987] Hill R.D., Some Important Issues in User Interface Management Systems, ACM Computer Graphics, Vol. 21, No. 2, pp. 116-119.

[Hopp 1986] Hoppe H.U., Tauber M., Ziegler J.E., A Survey of Models and Formal Description Methods in HCI with Example Applications. ESPRIT Project 385 HUFIT, Report B.3.2a.

[Hubn 1989] Hubner W., de Lancastre M., Towards an Object-Oriented Interaction Model for Graphics User Interfaces. Computer Graphics Forum (8), North Holland, pp. 207-217.

[Huds 1988] Hudson S.E., King R., Semantic Feedback in the Higgens UIMS. IEEE Transactions on Software Engineering, Vol. 14, No. 8, pp. 1118-1206.

[Koll 1988] Koller F., Trefz B., Zeigler J., Integrated Interfaces and their Architectures. Working Paper B3.4/B5.2, November 1988, ESPRIT Project 385 - HUFIT.

[Manh 1989] Manheimer J.M., Burnett R.C., Wallers J.A., A Case Study of User Interface Management System Development and Application. Proceedings ACM Computer-Human Interaction '89 , pp.127-132.

[Maye 1989] Mayer N.P., WINTERP. User Contribution with X11R4 Distribution.

[Myer 1989] Myers B.A., User Interface Tools - Introduction and Survey, IEEE Software, Vol. 6, No. 1, pp. 15-24.

[Olse 1985] Olsen D.R. Jr., Dempsey E.P., Rogge R., Input/Output Linkage in a User Interface Management System. Proceedings SIGGRAPH '85, ACM Computer Graphics, Vol. 19, No. 3, pp. 191-197.

[Pfaf 1985] Pfaff G., Ed., User Interface Management Systems. Springer-Verlag, New-York.

[Prim 1989] Prime M., User Interface Management Systems - A Current Product Review. Tutorial Note 12, Eurographics '89, Hamburg.

[Sche 1988] Scheifler R.W., Gettys J., Newman R., X Window System C Library and Protocol Reference. Digital Press.

[Schu 1985] Schulert A.J., Rogers G.T., Hamilton J.A., ADM - A Dialogue Manager. Proceedings ACM SIGGCHI 1985, ACM Computer Graphics, Vol. 19, No. 3, pp. 177-183.

[Shin 1989] Shingler K., SERPENT. User Contribution with X11R4 Distribution. Carneige-Mellon University Technical Report Reference CMU-SEI-89-UG-2.

[Smit 1986] Smith R.G., Dinitz R., Barth P., Impulse-86 A Substrate for Object-Oriented Interface Design, ACM OOPSLA '86 Proceedings, pp. 167-176.

[Youn 1987] Young R. L., An Object-Oriented Framework for Interactive Data Graphics, ACM OOPSLA '87 Proceedings, pp. 78-90.

Chapter 14

Intelligent Interfaces and UIMS

John Lee

1 Introduction

This position paper draws attention to some fairly abstract issues concerning the relationship between the notion of a User Interface Management System (UIMS) and the requirements of advanced intelligent interfaces for Knowledge Based Systems (KBS). It addresses possible future human-computer interaction (HCI) systems, especially those integrating both natural language (NL) and graphical interaction. Interfaces like these are likely to become increasingly important, and we should be prepared to take them into account sooner rather than later. Of course, such issues will for some time remain relatively peripheral, outside the "mainstream" of interface research; but this is no excuse for ignoring them, and many of the problems are closely related to mainstream problems.

The term "intelligent interface" is taken to have two main connotations: the interface should be based on an explicit representation of its own semantics relative to the "application domain", and by exploiting its access to this it should be able dynamically to mould its behaviour to the requirements of the user. No more is attempted here than to sketch some of the implications of these points, and some possible approaches to dealing with them.

2 Semantically-based Graphics

Much of the potential of existing interaction techniques is often missed by failing to make use of possibly informative features of a graphical display and of interaction with it. This is bound up with the fact that there is normally only a rather restricted connection between the interface and an application's semantics. Relaxing this restriction rapidly turns a graphical interface into a visual language which, for intelligent applications, needs to be highly flexible.

On the familiar Macintosh screen, for example, we typically see icons. These have a certain referential role; they act as names, *e.g.* for folders, documents and application programs. An interaction event in the context of an icon — *e.g.* double-clicking on it — has a certain effect depending on the type of thing the icon refers to: it opens a folder, or starts the appropriate application with a document. Many other properties of an icon have little or no significance. Its size and shape are irrelevant to the system. Its position in relation to other icons is ignored; grossly, its position conveys only the location of its referent within the file structure by containment within other areas (windows). An icon can be dragged, and the interpretation of this depends on where it is dragged to: it may be moved (to another folder), copied (to a different disc), or removed from a disc (into the wastebasket). In this case the "application" behind the interface is of course the machine's operating system. One might claim that its comparatively simple functionality is exhausted by the interface, so that no further representational power is needed. In more complex kinds of operating system, *e.g.* where there is multi-tasking, with the possibility of constructing pipelines, the need to describe interprocess communication, I/O redirection, *etc.*, it would be natural to use many more dimensions in the potential informativeness of an interface. The more this happens, the more the interface starts to resemble some kind of diagram, a picture of a situation. And at the same time, the more the meaning of a collection of graphical objects depends on their mutual relationships — their collective structure — the more obviously they function as an expression of a (visual) language.

Such visual languages can be very expressive, even when using only very simple constructions. But this is possible only because there are clearly understood conventions relating their expressions to a semantics given in terms of some application domain. Where constructions are simple, they must often be re-used to express different things; hence these conventions have to be alterable during an interactive dialogue. A visual language as conceived of here consists not only of graphical *constructions*, but also of *interactions* — in general, operations which allow changes to constructions, or permit references to parts of them. These operations also require a (malleable) semantics in the application domain (their meaning cannot always be captured simply by interpreting some resulting change in the state of a construction).

Interface systems supporting this kind of functionality clearly stand in need of some means for the user to communicate about the interpretation of the graphics, *i.e.* to communicate at a very high level of conceptual abstraction, with the ability to refer both to graphical representation features and features of the domain. Moreover, it is important to provide this in a way that can be used without acquiring a great deal of unusual expertise. Natural language is one of very few obvious candidates for such an expressive system (Lee and Zeevat 1990).

As a simple example, a user might be enabled to draw shapes and say things like "This square is London; this triangle is Edinburgh; their sizes show their populations; this arrow shows that they are linked; its length in cm shows the distance between them at scale 1:10 million". He should then be able to have the system draw a simple map from some existing data using the implied "visualisation" conventions. (Although this discourse obviously mentions only token objects, a generalisation might be derived by inferencing over a lattice structure of types in background knowledge, which suffices to establish *e.g.* the connection between cities and polygons as the least upper bounds of the London/Edinburgh and square/triangle pairs respectively.)

This is one possibility. Another may be that we can replace NL by a visual language (VL) treated analogously to NL. This is apparently paradoxical, since the whole point of introducing NL was to provide a natural means of expression at the high conceptual level needed for semantic definition. The conventions behind the use of NL are stable and universal enough for this to work. However, we can imagine a situation where the interpretation system for a VL is itself made available to the user through a VL; perhaps even the same VL. In this latter case, the language is functioning as its own metalanguage in describing its own semantics. This is analogous to metalinguistic uses of NL, *e.g.* in defining meanings of words with respect to some knowledge domain ("Dunedin" is Edinburgh, "herbivorous" means vegetable-eating). If $S(d, english)$ is a semantics for talking about some domain d in English, then we may want to have $S(S(d, english), english)$, which will allow us to define that semantics itself in English.

A customised VL system can be evolved from default visualisations of the structure of a knowledge-base (k) and the structure of the VL itself (l). A visualisation V is a semantic mapping between whatever it visualises and l; hence we have $V(k,l)$ and $V(l,l)$. It is assumed also that a visualisation defines the range of meaningful interactions that can occur with respect to depicted items. The *contents* of the KB — $cont(k)$ — includes (at least) domain information (in this case about cities: $dom(k)$) and a specification of the visualisation of that information, including *e.g.* what kinds of graphically-mediated updates can be made and how — $V(dom(k), l)$. It is one thing to visualise the domain of a KB (*e.g.* as a map) and quite another to visualise the KB itself (*e.g.* as some kind of entity-relationship diagram). $V(k,l)$ allows modification of k — and hence $cont(k)$ — so as to define or redefine $V(dom(k), l)$; this definition will allow direct updating of $dom(k)$ without the use of $V(k,l)$ at all.

It will be necessary to define $V(V(dom(k), l), l)$, *i.e.* a specific interface for modifying the visualisation of domain information, although we might assume that an advanced IKBS will also want to do such modification automatically, in order to present more clearly or appropriately the information it contains (recalling several aspects of the "Advanced Information Presentation System" of Zdybel *et al.* 1981.) In an NL-based system, it should of course be possible for the user to achieve this himself without graphical access to the visualisation mapping: in that case, the mapping needs to be seen as a distinct semantic domain for the interpretation of NL, *i.e.* we need $S(V(dom(k), l), english)$, which is likely to presuppose $S(l, english)$. (Presumably we have $S(dom(k), english)$ already.) On the other hand, there's no reason in principle why a visual interface for the redefinition of NL semantics should not be provided: $V(S(dom(k), english), l)$. V and S are both relations of the same *kind* — semantic mappings — only for different languages; all these cases presuppose explicit representation of that relation, and what we need is something flexible enough to provide for all of them. Fig. 1 attempts to convey the feeling of these relationships (perhaps taking liberties with what counts as graphical!).

GRAFLOG (Pineda *et al.* 1988, Pineda 1989) presents a knowledge representation for parts of such a system. Application objects, their properties and relations are mapped onto basic graphical objects, their properties and relations, using an explicit "translation" function. In its most recent version, this exists as a formal theory quite closely modelled on denotational semantic theories for NL, the details of its implementation being left flexible enough to fit a number of paradigms. Whereas an existing implementation based on it has used Prolog to implement a fact- and rule-base KB, extending the

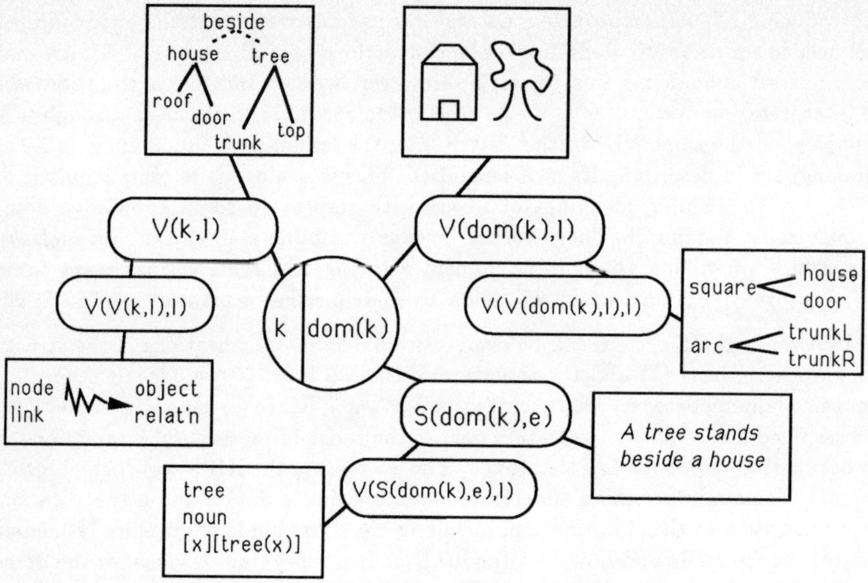

Figure 1: Several possible semantic mappings

scope of the knowledge representation and the integration with NL will be facilitated by moving to a more frame-like or object-oriented architecture. At the level of semantics, this would still be accountable in terms of the same theoretical approach.

The NL/VL question is whether the necessary structures and mappings need to be derived from NL/graphical interaction, or whether some default visualisation can present them for specification without NL. The latter can work, of course, only if there is some base level at which the interpretation of the VL is implicitly fixed. It is not yet clear whether VLs can be created which are general and natural enough to allow an easily usable base that would not require as great a learning effort as most formal languages, and that would permit the natural definition of alternative visualisation conventions. The approach is likely to be always less natural than NL for casual users, but probably very useful to habitual users of such a system. It is therefore probably appropriate to combine the two.

It is often argued that NL interaction is not particularly effective in HCI terms. Indeed, much of the development of graphical interfaces, especially the use of menus and icons, is promoted on the basis that any kind of textual interface is slow and unwieldy by comparison. This is probably true of unaided NL, especially without speech I/O, but the point here is that the integration of NL with various kinds of graphics offers the potential both to overcome the shortcomings of NL and to remove or reduce certain restrictions of traditional interface tools.

3 What About UIMS?

3.1 Interfaces and Design

The discussion thus far has introduced some important features of an intelligent interface: but how do these features relate to the existing idea of a UIMS? What we notice is that the intelligent interface system at least needs to contain something like a UIMS, because anything that supports the definition of $V(dom(k), l)$ is a kind of UIMS — especially, in the classical "Seeheim" sense, if it does this for arbitrary k.

A UIMS is normally thought of as having two quite distinct, though related, areas of functionality. On the one hand it is a system intended to *manage* a user interface. On the other, it is a system intended to help *construct* or *design* a user interface. This means that there are two classes of user for such a system: there is the "interface designer" whose job is to create the specification for an interface to some application program, so that the UIMS can then manage the operation of that interface in conjunction with the "end-user" of the application.

These two classes of user are normally thought to require quite different kinds of support. The interface designer needs a set of operations for specifying the syntax of the interaction — menus, dialogue windows, icon dragging, *etc.* — of which the end-user need know nothing beyond the final result. The end-user requires a clear and consistent set of appropriate actions through which he can create, access and modify information relevant to the application. The clarity, consistency and appropriateness of these actions is typically the responsibility of the interface designer.

UIMS have always been dogged by the semantic integration problem: in complex cases it often seems that the UIMS must be so sensitive to the application as to cease having an independent existence as a system. Whereas it is easy to provide within a UIMS itself a complete and coherent model of an interaction at the lexical and syntactic levels, semantic integration with the application is a natural cause of tension. There's a special problem here with applications that have a particularly graphical nature — *e.g.* CAD systems — where the interface seems fundamentally inseparable. It is only partly wrong to think of the discussion of the previous section as being about such an application. In fact, the notion of "visualisation" employed is general enough to encompass the entire interface specification. There are, of course, different semantic domain areas to be addressed. There may be "system" functions concerning files, folders, *etc.*, to be addressed by one part of the interface, with areas more specific to some particular use of the system (such as drawing maps) appearing elsewhere. And the different parts of the visualisation may also become semantic domains to be visualised (or talked about) and interactively modified. An obvious implication is that the distinction between the two different kinds of user falls away: the end-user is his own interface designer and has the same access to the specification of his interface as he has to his application domain.

In many cases, the idea of a unitary UIMS has been abandoned in favour of that of a "toolkit" of interface functionalities allowing an interface to be built up in a range of different ways, but with no clear policy of interaction management. An intelligent interface system is more of a UIMS in that it has a unified structure and centralised control strategy. The price for full flexibility is that the user must be, if not an application programmer, then at least very familiar with the representation of the target domain. However, a useful compromise is to consider the application as part of an intelligent system which decides its own presentation and interaction strategies, but flexibly, in response to the changing needs of the user. The role of the interface designer is now not to design, but to state rules for the design of effective interfaces; the "application" will need to contain a small expert system for the actual design task.

This idea seems to have been previously approached mainly in the area of presentation of particular kinds of information (*cf.* Gnanamgari 1981, Mackinlay 1986), but will have to be extended to include the whole interface. Notably, several of the old UIMS issues crop up here again, especially with regard to "fast prototyping" and reconfigurability. The activity of the designing system might be thought of as a continuous process of refining a prototype interface, or generating new ones for new types of material. This has to happen very quickly, and be very responsive to indications that the user finds a particular feature unsatisfactory. Only some of the large range of techniques being examined in the field (*e.g.* as surveyed by Hartson and Hix 1989) are likely to support the needs of these kinds of systems, and the criteria are obviously going to be very different from those which apply to evaluating techniques for use by humans.

We have conceived of visualisation as specifying not only the depiction of something, but also the range of meaningful interactions available through that depiction. An especially interesting development is the UIDE system of Foley *et al.* (1988). This proposes the idea of automatically generating alternative interfaces with equivalent functionality, which relates closely to the ability of Mackinlay's system to produce different presentation designs with the same semantics, some being more communicationally effective than others. Putting these together yields the idea of a combined visualisation specification with a clearly-defined semantics, which can be varied *e.g.* in response to differing strategies suggested by a user-model. We need to see progress towards more integration between such approaches to intelligent support for interface design.

3.2 Interaction and Semantics

Systems of these kinds will depend on effective exploitation of AI-related techniques at lower levels, *e.g.* the interpretation of complex interactions in a way that complements the interpretation of graphical structures. An approach currently under investigation is to use techniques imported from NL research. This has led to the adoption of an event-stream parsing approach, developed within the ESPRIT project ACORD (Lee *et al.* 1989). A KB is interfaced through a dialogue manager (DM) which maintains information about the visualisation of domain information, including a representation of the semantics of any current graphical state in terms of the domain objects depicted, and is capable of relating it to the semantics of NL sentences (Fig. 2). Interaction event tokens, parameterised by the object involved and a location, are submitted to a parser which produces a representation of the semantics of the action, using grammar rules that include semantic constraints and actions to be performed *e.g.* to update the graphical state and to provide feedback. The objective is to get a semantics for graphical interactions which is identical to, or at least compatible with, NL semantics. For example, moving an object might depend on the following (rather simplified) rules,

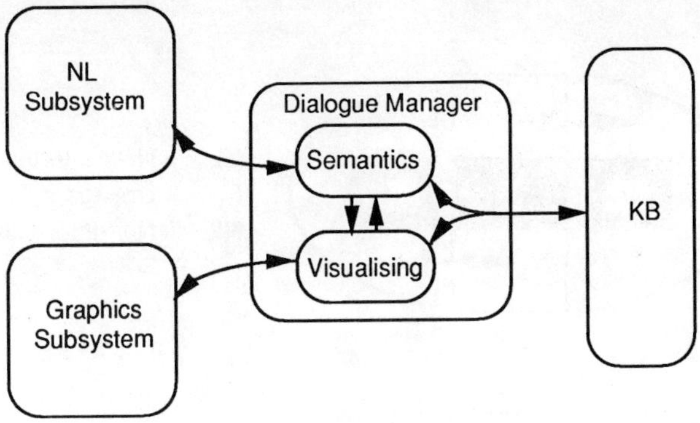

Figure 2: Architecture of the ACORD system

given in a Prolog-inspired format:

```
move([move(Object), Source, Dest]) <-->
    rule grab_object(Object, Source),
    rule drag_object(Object, Dest),
    action move_object(Object, Dest).

grab_object(Object, source(Src)) <-->
    token button_down(Object, Src),
    constraint movable(Object).

drag_object(Object, dest(Dst)) <-->
    token drag_out(Object),
    action ghost_follows_cursor(Object),
    token button_up(Dst).
```

In the context of an appropriate map, these rules allow us to derive the interpretation for such an action as "truck1 moves from Berlin to Paris", while giving suitable feedback to the user.

We find this grammar format somewhat clumsy and limited, however, and now hope to improve it by exploiting unification grammars (Zeevat *et al.* 1987) and by allowing the effect of constraints to be achieved through sortal restrictions on object types. This will also allow us to develop a combined lexicon for NL sentences and graphical interaction sequences, so that various different combinations of these can produce the same semantic representation. Either way, interaction is semantically based inasmuch as, for instance, the knowledge that a particular icon represents a vehicle, or more specifically a truck or a car, determines what range of actions are appropriate to it.

A visualisation mapping can be thought of as rather like the *linkage* component in Cockton's (1987) "new model" for separable interactive systems (Fig. 3), which sits between the "application" proper and the interface, and explains how the two are linked. This is roughly the job done by the ACORD DM, which is supposed to "download" a

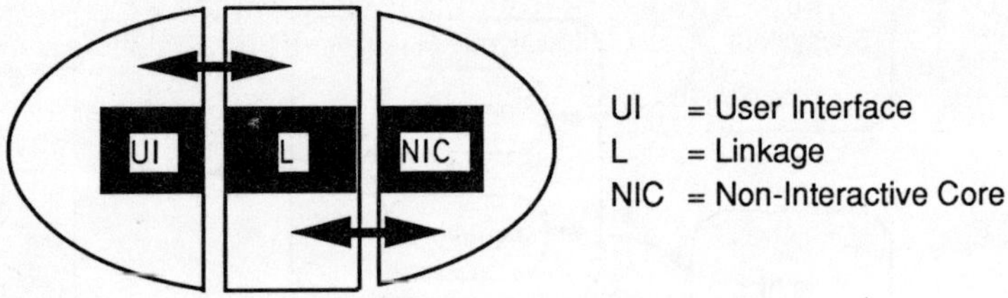

Figure 3: Cockton's New Model

description of allowable interactions to an otherwise application-independent graphics interface subsystem. Although this is a good logical model, we suspect that in an intelligent interface there are serious limits to the amount of modularity which is achievable, especially when efficiency becomes a consideration. Its real utility in this context is that it allows room for an intelligent linkage system to reconfigure the interface if new kinds of knowledge arise or new user desires have to be accommodated. An attraction of the unification-grammar formalism, being based on graph data-structures, is that it can be directly represented in a frame-like knowledge base and thus more easily integrated with semantic information. The theory of GRAFLOG gives us a starting point from which to formalise in these terms the representation of graphical objects and the notion of visualisation. Hence, we hope to arrive at a uniform representation for graphics, NL, domain knowledge and visualisation.

The UIDE system, mentioned above, usefully addresses several of the issues presented here. Its "preconditions" and "postconditions" surrounding interface functionalities bear an obvious resemblance to the constraints and actions of the ACORD system; on the other hand, it appears to have a less clear relationship to the domain-relative semantics of users' actions. Perhaps also UIDE's removal of responsibility for bottom-level details of interface syntax from the designer is less appropriate for an automated system, although it's somewhat unclear where the boundaries between these various aspects should lie. What both systems provide is a characterisation of the interface, but what both require is integration with a more principled approach to visualisation (done in a rather unsophisticated way in the ACORD system).

4 Conclusion

Some of the traditional objectives of UIMS, such as constructing interfaces for arbitrary applications, are evidently incompatible with an approach which implies a very tight semantic integration at all levels. We cannot expect to have an intelligent interface that attaches to just any KBS. It may well be that some of these objectives cannot effectively be met at all, which explains the popularity of "toolkit" systems, but in any case it is not plausible that the strong separability of interface and application can be supported in what we have called intelligent interfaces, except to the extent that an intelligent "linkage" component is provided between them. In other respects, however, there is more commonality: the abstraction of details of presentation and interaction from the application, and the provision of a centralised control strategy are characteristic of both. There is therefore substantial scope for convergence between developments in intelligent interfaces, on the one hand, and UIMS on the other.

5 Thoughts After the Workshop

The Workshop conclusions emphasise the importance of user interface design and the appreciation of a host of influences from considerations of human factors and many other aspects of the user's environment. A fully-functional "intelligent interface" would have to take this on board, and be able to react sensitively to these issues. Needless to say, such functionality would have to depend on very comprehensive background knowledge (as usually turns out to be the case with advanced AI functionality). There will be severe problems with the formalisation and representation of such knowledge.

From this point of view, the optimism of the above conclusion may be unjustified, in that work on UIMS (or ISDEs) intended to support system design by humans (who already have the necessary knowledge), with much less emphasis on management, may well diverge substantially from work on management systems dependent on capturing and encoding that knowledge. On the other hand, ISDEs may also include many "intelligent" tools to aid good interface design.

A discussion with Dag Svanæs brought home to me the importance of the word "intelligent" as used above. It is really only being used in the old-fashioned sense of indicating devolved functionality. There are many serious issues, unaddressed in this paper, concerning how much functionality, and of what kinds, it is either possible or desirable to devolve to an interface system. The point about the distinction between end-user and interface-designer being lost is important. The path forks here: either we can (try to) build the designer into the system, or as Bijl (1989), and perhaps Svanæs, would advocate, we can go rather for a "dumb" system which gives the user total control and total responsibility (but at the cost of the user's needing total expertise). Both of these routes, however, presuppose an increased explicitness about semantics and the relationships between different levels of representation.

Acknowledgements

Some of the research mentioned has been supported by the CEC ESPRIT programme (P393 ACORD). Its continuation is supported by the UK Joint Research Councils' Initiative in Cognitive Science and HCI, grants SPG8826213 and SPG8919793 on *Foundations for Intelligent Graphical Interfaces* and *Structure of Drawings for Picture-Oriented HCI*. The author is indebted to everyone working on these projects.

References

Bijl, A. [1989] "POINTER: Picture Oriented INTERaction – a programme for ICAD/HCI research", in *proc. 3rd. Eurographics Workshop on Intelligent CAD*, Texel, Netherlands.

Cockton, G [1987] "A New Model for Separable Interactive Systems", in *proc.* INTERACT '87, 1033-1038, North-Holland.

Foley, JD, Gibbs, C, Kim, WC, and Kovacevic, S [1988] "A Knowledge-Based User Interface Management System", in *proc. ACM CHI'88 Conference on Human Factors in Computing Systems*, 67-72, ACM.

Gnanamgari, S [1981] "Information Presentation through Automatic Graphic Displays", in *Computer Graphics '81*, Online Publications.

Hartson, HR and Hix, D [1989] "Human-Computer Interface Development: Concepts and Systems", *ACM Computing Surveys, 21, 1*, 5-92.

Lee, JR, Kemp, B and Manz, T [1989] "Knowledge-Based Graphical Dialogue: A Strategy and Architecture", in *ESPRIT '89*, ed. CEC-DGXIII, 321-333, Kluwer Academic Publishers.

Lee, JR and Zeevat, HW [1990] "Integrating Graphics and Natural Language in Dialogue", to appear in proc. INTERACT '90.

Mackinlay, J [1986] "Automating the Design of Graphical Presentations of Relational Information", *ACM Transactions on Graphics, 5, 2*, 110-141.

Pineda, LA, Klein, E and Lee, JR [1988] "GRAFLOG: Understanding Drawings through Natural Language", *Computer Graphics Forum 7*, 97-103.

Pineda, LA [1989] *GRAFLOG: A Theory of Semantics for Graphics with Applications to Human-Computer Interaction and CAD Systems*, PhD Thesis, University of Edinburgh.

Zdybel, F, Greenfeld, NR, Yonke, MD and Gibbons, J [1981] "An Advanced Information Presentation System", in *Computer Graphics '81*, 19-36, Online Publications.

Zeevat, H, Klein, E and Calder, J [1987] "An introduction to Unification Categorial Grammar" in *Categorial Grammar, Unification and Parsing*, ed. NJ Haddock et al., Working Papers in Cognitive Science, vol. 1, Centre for Cognitive Science, University of Edinburgh.

Chapter 15

Assembling a User Interface out of Communication Processes

P. J. W. ten Hagen and D. Soede

1 Introduction

The motivation for our interest in the workshop lies in the fact that we plan to build a new, second generation User Interface Management System (UIMS). In this paper it is our aim to indicate the direction we take. The central concept in our UIMS is concurrent processes and the semantics of their communication, described as transactions among these processes. This presumably offers an effective basis for describing user interfaces.

First the design aspects of user interfaces are considered. We emphasize the experimental nature and identify building blocks from which a user interface can be assembled. Then the role of concurrency in user interfaces is discussed. The next section gives an informal introduction to Transaction Cells, as the currently existing basis for this UIMS. This is clarified by an example of a railway yard design system.

2 General Design Aspects of a User Interface

The process of developing and maintaining a graphically-oriënted user interface has still a number of unresolved issues. The resulting product should act as an intermediary between a human being and an application which supplies some kind of functionality. Although the functionality of the algorithmic part of the application may be rather explicitly defined, various aspects of human cognition have not been explored enough to result in straight-forward design rules for optimal user interface design. Furthermore, there will always be differences in taste among people. The conclusion that can be drawn from this is that, since there are no cookbook prescriptions, trial and error must be the substitute for knowledge. This may in the end produce some kind of guidelines, but for now experimentation in construction and fine-tuning of user interfaces is indispensable.

Thus a UIMS must offer a flexible way for developing and maintaining a user interface. By flexibility we mean the ability to modify only a part of the application and having to know as little as possible about the rest of the application. The word application should be interpreted as the whole product: both the algorithmic part and the user interface part.

One way to realize this, is to make agreements of how a part communicates with the rest of the system or, in other words, establish the interface with the outside world. This idea can be found in object oriënted programming also, where the interface to an object determines how it can be used. As long as the interface is left unchanged, it is possible

Authors' address: Centrum voor Wiskunde en Informatica (CWI), Kruislaan 413, Amsterdam, The Netherlands

to restructure the internals of an object. Of course establishing an interface usually also implies some sort of semantics.

At higher levels of a program, there are good reasons to do the same type of thing. For instance, it is often useful to separate the computational part from the user interface part so that multiple interfaces can be linked to the same functionality. Other reasons for splitting up an application are maintainability and the existence of dedicated specialist areas like user interface programming. When and where to split up will depend on the situation and there are no rules which are applicable to all cases.

3 New Building Blocks for Interactive Programs

In the second generation user interface management systems the distinction between user interface design and interactive applications design will disappear. Both the application and the user interface are assembled from building blocks where each block already may combine application functions and user interface. Since we are talking about the design stage, it is still possible that the final run-time result will consists of one user interface module and one application module for the whole program.

This approach will bring several characteristic improvements over the first generation systems. We will briefly introduce these now. As a preliminary remark we emphasize that experimentation in real user interface design will remain a major requirement for second generation systems. We will support this in a fundamental way by maximizing the possibilities for (partly) disassembling an existing design and reassembling it from adjusted building blocks.

The building blocks can be one of three kinds: input, output, or input *and* output. A building block of type input not only performs the input but also executes the application processes responsible for dealing with the input. If such processes are already executing (active) as a result of previous inputs, such a building block would minimally direct the inputs to this process. Similar requirements hold for the other type of building blocks. Combining building blocks creates units capable of doing input and output. We will call a transaction an action which is either input, output or input *and* output exchange. In general we deal with building blocks capable of doing transactions. We describe applications as transaction configurations, including user interfaces transactions.

Hence the first improvement is that we are capable of specifying transaction expressions rather than input (tool-)expressions. This among other things allows the same design method to include large closed (i.e. non-interactive) application modules as well as highly interactive modules.

The second improvement will be that information can be very easily treated in chunks, almost without having to merge the various processes that independently deal with elements in the chunk. Such chunking is essential for consistent visualization of related and/or constrained values. The transaction based treatment of chunks creates maximal directness of user communication if so desired. Last but not least several chunking structures may exist simultaneously. This provides multiple views and access mechanisms as well as concurrent application processing.

The advanced facilities sketched here have an application domain far beyond user interface programming. In this paper we will only discuss it in the context of interaction. In a later stage we will address the more general issue of providing a flexible overall application control structure.

4 Processes in a User Interface

There are several reasons for using processes as building blocks of a user interface. First the nature of human computer interaction already suggests it. For example, in current user interfaces it is usually possible to choose from a number of different parallel interaction units like buttons and menus.

In future user interfaces temporal aspects will become even more important. For instance when video or sound is incorporated in the application one needs synchronization mechanisms. In an environment of autonomous processes synchronization can be introduced naturally.
But apart from this, there is another motivation. Seen from design viewpoint, the use of autonomous processes functioning as self-contained program elements adds to the flexibility of the application. In an earlier research project called Dialogue Cells (DICE) (see [4]) we gained experience with the use of concurrency. DICE is a UIMS in which a user interface is built as a hierarchy of processes called cells. At the leaves of the hierarchy are basic cells which perform actions like monitoring the pointer device for collecting input values. The higher level cells are constructed by combining other cells. One of the things that became apparent with DICE, is that a hierarchical communication structure is too limiting.

We believe that in principle this idea of crafting together cells into higher order cells is a fruitful one and should be elaborated further. We plan to do this by a specification language called Transaction Cells. In this language special attention is given to the inter-process communication. By detailed description of what symbols a process accepts and will react to, the responsibility of how it actually operates can be left to the process itself. This will result in a very flexible specification method in the higher levels of aggregation of applications.

5 Transaction Cells

The key idea of Transaction Cells is the ability to describe the so called process configurations. A process configuration is an expression about transactions among processes. A transaction between two processes is the exchange of a unit of information from one process to the other. In general a transaction among processes is the exchange of such a unit (or chunk) of information in such a way that each process in the transaction either contributes to, or consumes (part of) the unit. For instance a menu selection process can transact the result of a selection to a command interpretation process.

Expressions can describe transactions taking place in sequence, simultaneously, conditionally, etc. The ordering can be logical, temporal or by other means. A further basic notion is that a process configuration has a lifetime, during which the processes mentioned, behave according to the transaction expression. What they do beyond this lifetime cannot be concluded from this expression. Nothing in principle, forbids processes to be engaged in more than one process configuration at the same time.

Almost any kind of entity can be represented by a process. We have been made aware that in a similar way almost anything can be seen as an object. Using the concept of processes rather than objects is done to stress the relative independence of processes and the concept of explicitly defining their cooperation by means of transaction configurations. In the example that will be introduced next, points are seen as processes. A point process not only maintains a point as a geometric entity but also as a semantic entity because it can have access to the interpretation of point e.g. as a defining position of a railroad track. So a point process will act in the transaction rules that make up the semantics of a track (in the track process). As a result of this the user is given the possibility to address individual points as well as complete tracks. The same process set-up can make the point act in all visualizations of the concepts it is part of (e.g. tracks).

6 An Example: A Railway Yard Design System

As part of the DICE project, a design system for railway yards was developed. Inspired by this example, we show how Transaction Cells may be used in such an application. This yard design system was meant to support the designer by having the system check a number of relevant side conditions. For instance, when a train is supposed to traverse a part of the yard with some minimum speed, this has implications for the curves in that stretch. When curves are too sharp the train will not be able to reach that velocity. The designer must be notified when as a consequence of his decisions this condition is violated.

A yard consists of a number of tracks. The tracks in turn are described by a sequence of points. By linking the points we get a track profile. Tracks can be connected by switches to other tracks. A switch is merely a line from a point on one track to a point on another track.

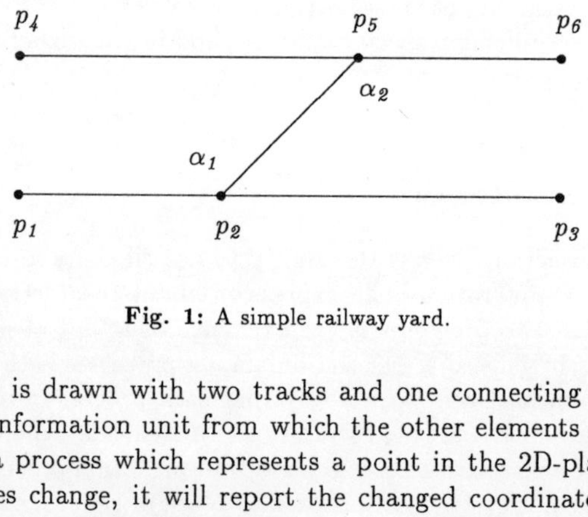

Fig. 1: A simple railway yard.

In Fig. 1 a yard is drawn with two tracks and one connecting switch. A point is the basic graphical information unit from which the other elements are derived. In our example a point is a process which represents a point in the 2D-plane. When for any reason its coordinates change, it will report the changed coordinates. It also draws a marker at the appropriate place on the screen.

The points p_1, p_2 and p_3 together form track t_1. The track process draws a connecting line between its points. It needs to know when a point has changed, so:

$$(p_1 \vee p_2 \vee p_3) \rightarrow t_1 \tag{1}$$

This means that when either p_1 *or* ($\vee$) p_2 *or* p_3 produces a result (i.e. changed coordinates) the information unit is transacted ($\rightarrow$) to process t_1. Likewise for switch s_1 the following holds:

$$(p_2 \vee p_5) \rightarrow s_1 \tag{2}$$

Now let us look at the angle formed by the points p_1, p_2 and p_5. The condition we want to check is whether a train can pass the switch with velocity v. This velocity is also represented by a process. The process which checks the sharpness for this particular angle is called α_1. Suppose that after it detects a violation of the condition, the system has to start blinking its comprising points. For α_1 we then write:

$$v \rightarrow \alpha_1 \tag{3}$$

$$(p_1 \vee p_2 \vee p_5) \rightarrow \alpha_1 \tag{4}$$

$$\alpha_1 \rightarrow (p_1 \wedge p_2 \wedge p_5) \tag{5}$$

v produces a information chunk when its value is changed. Thus the first of these expressions reflects the fact that the velocity is used in calculating the maximum angle. The second states that when any of the points are changed, the angle must be recalculated. The third says that when α_1 produces a chunk with an error status *true* or *false*, it is transacted to p_1 *and* ($\wedge$) p_2 *and* p_3. These points will then start or stop blinking in accordance with the information unit.

Now a change of the coordinates of point p_2 caused by the designer or even by another process causes the system to report to track t_1, switch s_1 and angle α_1. The processes t_1 and s_1 update their graphical representations on the screen and α_1 checks whether its condition is violated. Another scenario might be changing the velocity v. One could gradually let v grow until the points of a curve begin blinking to find out what the maximum speed is for a certain section.

The interpretation (or semantics) associated with these transaction rules are encoded in the processes. For instance the fact that rule 5 will have the effect of blinking on or off is encoded in the point processes upon recognition of a *false* or *true* sign produced by α_1. A different semantic encoding might have resulted in an adjustment of one of the points due to a change in α_1, causing subsequent adjustments of corresponding tracks. Hence the transaction rules give the natural dependencies. The processes themselves contain the interpretations of the dependencies, including the propagation of changes.

Rules do not have to be active all the time. Since (sets of) transaction rules are also represented by processes their enforcement can be deferred or discarded by making the process temporary inactive.

7 Conclusion

With the proposed Transaction Cells specification language complex user interfaces can be adequately modelled. It is possible to specify independently the individual process behaviour, the configuration rules and the activation periods and conditions of these rules. By having appropriate sets of transaction rules active at a given moment the desired behaviour of the user interface can be obtained. This provides great flexibility needed for both prototyping and for representing complicated user interfaces.

References

[1] H.R. Hartson and D. Hix. Human computer interface development: Concepts and systems for its management. *ACM Computing Surveys*, 21(1), 1989.

[2] C.A.R. Hoare. *Communicating Sequential Processes.* Pretence Hall International, 1985.

[3] G.E. Pfaff, editor. *User Interface Management Systems*. Springer Verlag, 1985.

[4] R. van Liere and P.J.H. ten Hagen. Introduction to dialogue cells. Technical Report CS-R8703, Centrum voor Wiskunde en Informatica (CWI), 1987.

Part III

Current Practice

Chapter 16

IUICE — An Interactive User Interface Construction Environment

Peter Sturm

Abstract: An interactive environment for the development of graphical user interfaces (IUICE) is presented. The environment provides an event-based language which allows an interactive and graphical specification of user interface applications. IUICE applications consist of *methods* which have event inputs and event outputs and are connected together by so-called *event streams*. Additional graphical support for event propagation and parent-child relations is provided for all methods that have graphical responses as side-effects to the receipt of events on one of their inputs. Methods which have been created or modified by the programmer, are compiled and linked dynamically to the IUICE environment at execution time. The IUICE system is intended for the development of prototypes as well as fully specified graphical applications. A first prototype implementation of IUICE and further applications which are planned to be developed within the environment are also discussed.

1. Introduction

Developing and implementing *human-computer interfaces* which strongly rely on computer graphics is becoming a time-consuming and complex task. Increasing demands and requirements are defined by the user community, psychological studies evaluate traditional human-computer interaction models and elaborate new models, and the scope to which human-computer interfaces are applied to is growing steadily, such as graphical development and animation of computer programs or visualization of scientific data. Because of improved computer equipment, graphics hardware, and bitmap displays, users expect adequate user interfaces that are capable to process textual as well as graphical user input and to represent program results by high-quality computer graphics.

Computer graphics are central to today's notion of user interfaces. Graphics—if used reasonably—are easier to understand and provide more expressive power than conventional textual representations because of additional dimensions such as shape, size, color, and texture. Since pictures are also reflections of the real world, they implicitly provide a large base of graphical metaphors that can make it easier to understand and think about represented informations (Raeder 1985). However, their possible use is also limited. The proverb "a picture is worth a thousand words" is true as well as "sometimes a few words

This project is funded by the Deutsche Forschungsgemeinschaft as part of the Research Institute SFB124 "VLSI-Design and Parallel Architectures", Kaiserslautern - Saarbrücken, Federal Republic of Germany

are worth a thousand pictures." But in general, a tendency towards graphics-oriented interaction and visualization techniques can be observed.

To relieve programmers of graphical applications from hardware dependencies and to provide a consistent and complete model of graphical interaction, *window systems* such as X Windows (Jones 1989) or NeWS (Gosling et al. 1989) have been developed. They are intended to cover a wide range of potential graphical applications. Their underlying concepts and interaction models consist of multiple layers (e.g. X Windows has at least three layers: the normal client to X server layer, the client to window manager layer, and the window manager to X server layer) and are complex in itself. The functionality of such graphics systems is made available to applications by a host of procedures and data structures. Their number is overwhelming: X for example provides about 330 different procedures and 76 different data structures. Novice users and very often also experienced X programmers are confused. Even very simple graphical applications such as the "Hello, World" problem (Rosenthal 1987) are complicated when implemented as X clients according to the rules prescribed by the X window system to get user-friendly and correct programs.

The experiences gained during the development of graphical applications on top of the window system itself resulted in additional and more abstract layers above the graphics systems. These layers (*toolkits*), such as the X Toolkit (McCormak and Asente 1988) and its derivations Open Look and Motif, the Macintosh Toolbox (Apple 1985), or *language dependent graphical toolkits* such as et++ (Weinand et al. 1988) and parts of Smalltalk (Goldberg and Robsin 1983; Goldberg 1984) encapsulate and hide specific graphical semantics within graphical entities or language entities. Toolkits provide objects such as editable or non-editable text items, bitmap images, different types of buttons, and compositions of toolkit primitives such as scroll bars, text windows, dialog boxes, alert boxes, and others. Applications using toolkits no longer consist of consecutive procedure calls; they are defined by a combination of toolkit entities together with user-defined code to control the interactive behavior. However, as stated in (Myers 1989), toolkits in general have several disadvantages. They provide only limited interaction styles and the creation of applications using toolkits remains relatively difficult —comparable to the programming on top of graphical window systems.

User-interface development systems (UIDS) try to overcome these difficulties. In most cases, these systems also rely on some specific graphical toolkit. The process of developing graphical applications, however, is simplified by several interactive and automatic mechanisms which provide more abstract concepts and try to free programmers from boring coding phases. User-interface development systems assist programmers—in some cases graphically—in the combination of graphical entities and provide techniques to specify interaction sequences and semantics. UIDS are based on special-purpose languages and can be classified whether they allow the graphical specification of user interfaces or not. A second classification criterion is defined by the type of the language used. It can be a language for the definition of menu hierachies or networks, but also state-transition diagrams, context-free grammars, declarative languages, object-oriented languages, and event-based languages have been used as specification languages (see Myers 1989 for further details).

The user interface development system IUICE (*Interactive User Interface Construction Environment)* presented in this paper is an interactive event-based environment for the development of graphical applications. In a first abstraction, IUICE provides interactive as well as graphical mechanisms to define, implement, and connect methods. *Methods* are code modules that have event inputs and may have event outputs. They are activated on the receipt of an event on one of their inputs and may issue other events. Additional graphical support is provided for all methods which have graphical responses as side-effects to the receipt of specific input events. The event-driven model for the development of graphical programs has proven to be a natural way for the description of graphical user interactions. The behavior of a method is only defined by a certain set of possible input and output events which simplifies program development, method reusage and extensions of methods. The graphical application—consisting of a set of methods and their interconnection—is embedded in the IUICE system itself. Methods that are changed by the programmer are compiled and linked dynamically to the executing system. Therefore, in any phase, the programmer is allowed to test his or her implementation immediately. This integration of the design and test phase enables *rapid prototyping* of graphical applications. However, the scope the IUICE system is intended for, ranges from such rapid prototypes up to fully specified graphical applications.

In the next section of this paper the IUICE model and its foundations are introduced. Section 3 sketches out additional mechanisms provided for graphical methods and in Section 4 some implementation issues are discussed. In Section 5, a first prototype implementation of the IUICE model is presented, together with a brief discussion of further applications that are planned to be developed with the IUICE system. The paper will close with a conclusion in Section 6.

2. The IUICE-Model

When studying the concepts and interaction models of existing graphics systems and the graphical applications built on top of them, often a common simple but powerful fundamental mechanism can be observed. Applications issue requests to the graphics system by calling procedures provided by a graphics library. These requests are executed directly (see figure 1a) or—in case of the X window system which supports a network-based approach—propagated by communication mechanisms to a graphics server in order to

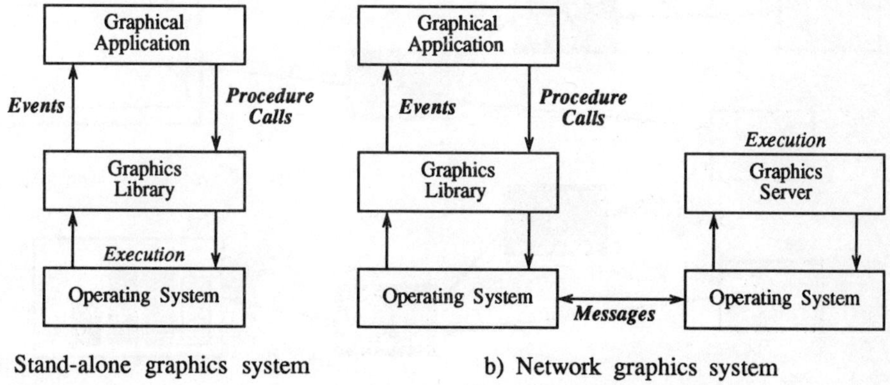

Fig. 1: Interaction mechanisms between application and graphics system

process them (see figure 1b). User inputs and other informations are delivered back to the graphical applications as short typed records or messages (*events*). Events cover user key strokes, pushed buttons, mouse motions, informations about status or changes in graphical objects, and in case of the X system notification to redraw uncovered windows. In most cases, graphical applications containing multiple graphical objects react, after some initializations, solely on the receipt of such events. The event-handling mechanisms are the most important parts in these programs, but receiving and processing events in such applications is often not well-structured. Typically, events are received within a single loop, the graphical object which is responsible for this event is determined, and the appropriate actions take place. The information "event e belongs to the graphical entity g" is lost in the context of the program source code. Using toolkits, at least the processing of events concerning toolkit entities is conceptually part of the encapsulating object and therefore hidden to the programmer.

The IUICE system is based on a uniform concept for receiving and processing events. Code sequences (so-called *methods*) representing a graphical entity are encapsulated and are responsible for the correct processing of events. All events are directly propagated to the entity to which they belong. Furthermore, IUICE provides interactive and graphical mechanisms for the specification of the propagation of events to methods. By extending the scope of graphical toolkits, IUICE can be classified as a user-interface development system which provides a graphically supported event language. The elements of the event language are *method types*, *instances of method types*, and *event streams* for method interconnections. In accordance to their input-output behavior, we distinguish three different classes of method types:

- Event sources
- Semantical methods
- Graphical methods

Event sources have no event inputs within the IUICE system, which means that the user is not allowed to connect event streams as inputs to these entities. They are

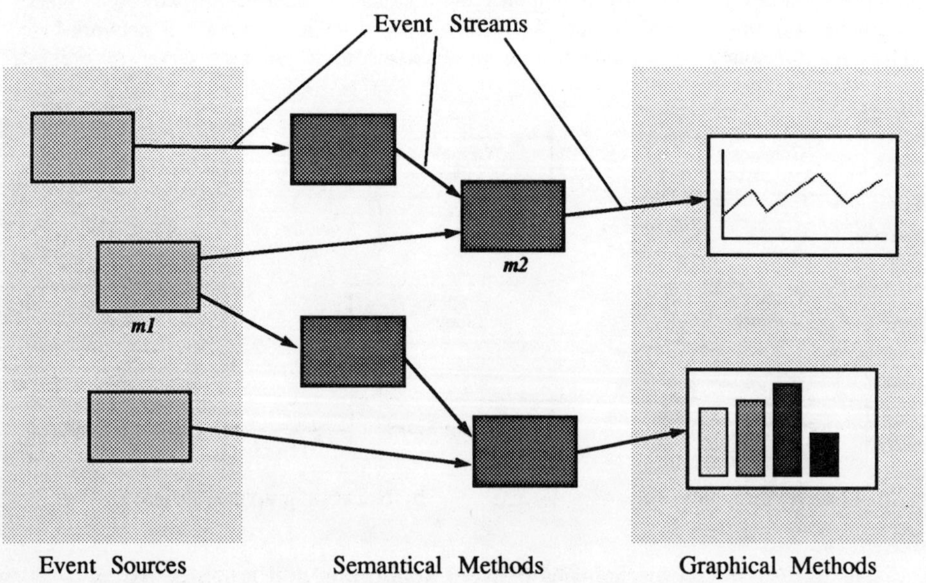

Fig. 2: Language elements of IUICE

methods that are responsible for the receipt of external events addressed to the IUICE system and to enable the user to access these events. *Semantical methods* represent intermediate states of event processing. These methods have no graphical representation outside the IUICE environment. *Graphical methods* on the other hand are usually event sinks. In most cases, they only have event inputs (but if needed they may have outputs as well) and transform incoming events into graphical outputs. From all the method types defined in an application—implemented by the user or stored in a method library of IUICE—an arbitrary number of instances can be created. The input and output channels of methods can be connected interactively by *event streams*. An event stream connecting one output channel of a method *m1* to one input channel of a method *m2* (see figure 2) signifies that every event issued by method *m1* is received by method *m2*. Methods and event streams can also be grouped to form more complex methods that can be manipulated by the user as one single entity. An IUICE application as a whole is defined by a collection of methods and their interconnections by event streams (see also figure 2).

The IUICE system provides all mechanisms needed to manipulate event methods and event streams. Methods are managed by a method library and can be created, duplicated, moved, and deleted interactively. Also program-driven creation and interconnection of methods is provided. Event streams between methods can be defined and deleted. The stream topology and the iconic representation of all the method types and instances used in the user interface application as well as the graphical representation of the application as defined solely by the graphical methods are offered to the programmer in two different windows.

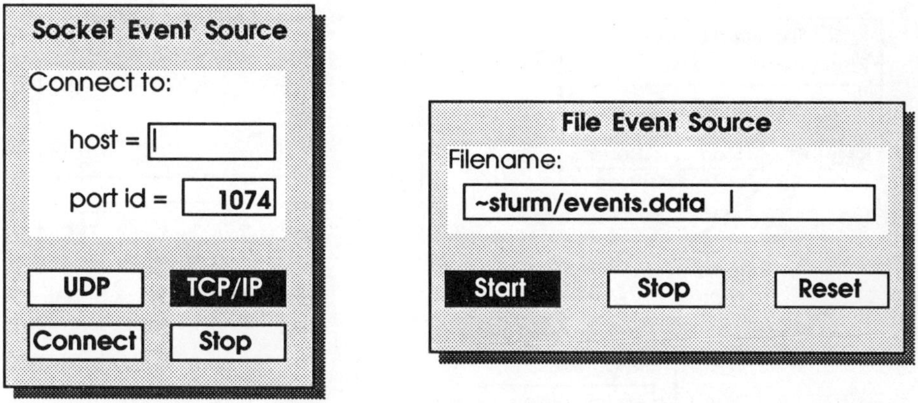

Fig. 3: Two types of event sources

Only one specific type of user input (for example the right mouse button) is dedicated to the IUICE system itself. All other kinds of user input sources are controlled by the application. This restriction is very important because the IUICE system does not only allow the specification of event methods and their interconnection. The method instances used by the application may be waiting for the input of user events concurrently to the design process. Thus, parts of the application may run while the programmer is implementing additional methods. The integration of two different software development phases, designing and implementing an application as well as software testing, is very useful for *rapid prototyping*. In this case, only the graphical representation of the application and the interactive behavior on user inputs is designed. By adding further semantics to the methods, the user can start from prototypes—validating the graphical outfit and the user interactions—and work towards fully implemented applications.

In addition to the processing of graphical events issued by the graphics system, IUICE enables the user to accept and process application-defined events from different sources such as datagrams, stream sockets, or files. By adding the availability of application-defined events to the functionality of IUICE, various kinds of graphical applications can be designed. For example, events may contain informations on status changes within processes of a distributed program that are propagated to the IUICE application by TCP/IP sockets. In this case, the IUICE system can be used to visualize and animate the behavior of the distributed program in a graphical way. This application which has already been implemented and several others which use the application-defined event mechanism are described in more detail in Section 5.

The externally generated events are available through specific event sources. Two types of event sources, *socket event sources* and *file event sources*, are provided when the IUICE system comes up and may be changed and extended to specific user requirements. The graphical representation of both types of event sources is shown in figure 3. The socket event source can be used by the programmer to establish an UDP or TCP/IP connection to some other process in the network environment which sends events as messages dedicated to the IUICE application. The event source waits for the receipt of such messages, transforms incoming messages into events of the appropriate type, and propagates these events to all subsequent connected methods. In case of the file event

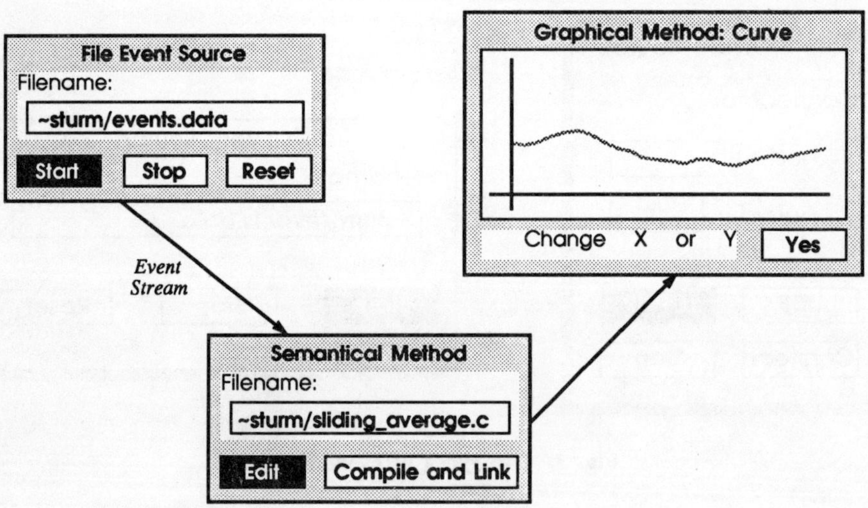

Fig. 4: Example of a graphical IUICE application

source, the user can specify a filename which contains events. Part of this event source is code which converts the file representation of events into instances of corresponding event types. The IUICE system provides a default conversion mechanism that can be changed to specific user requirements. Both types of event sources allow, among other things, to halt or continue the generation of events by simply clicking a stop and start button.

To understand the usage of event methods and event streams, the example represented in figure 4 is discussed in more detail. Assume that a text file with the pathname *~sturm/events.data* exists, which contains lines of floating point values. A file event source is connected to this event data file. For each value in the file, an event of the following type

```
typedef struct VALUE_EVENT {
    int type; /* contains unique identifier for this event */
    float val;
    }
```

is created and—because of the connecting event stream—propagated to the semantical method *sliding average.* Clicking the edit button in the iconic representation of *sliding average* creates an additional window containing the C code associated to this semantical method:

```
sliding_average ( EVENT ev ) {
    static float current_average = 0;
    static n = 0;

    switch (ev.type) {
        IS_VALUE_EVENT:
            current_average += ev.val;
            n++;
            ISSUE_VALUE_EVENT ( current_average / n );
            break;
        }
    }
```

The code should not be taken as fully specified, it only characterizes the behavior of the method. For each incoming event, the method is activated and executed. In case of an event of type VALUE_EVENT, the new sliding average is calculated and propagated to all the methods connected to *sliding average*. In this example, the *value events* are sent to the graphical method *curve. Curve* adds each value to the already represented polygon line

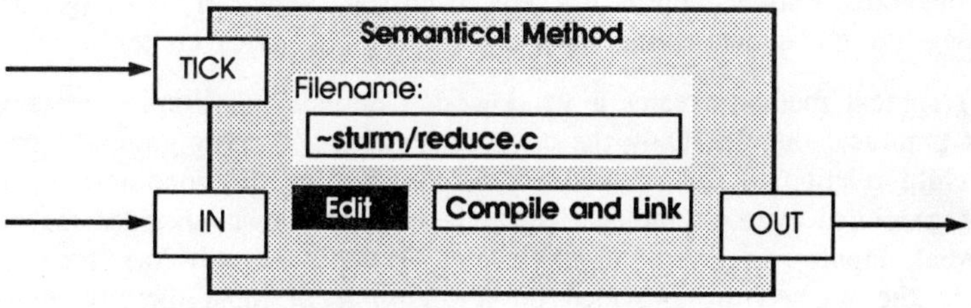

Fig. 5: A method with labeled input and outputs

by shifting the view to the left or by appropriate scaling of the x and y axes. The corresponding code belonging to the method *curve* can also be accessed by simply clicking the mouse button inside the window containing the method name. All semantical and graphical methods are subject to modifications and improvements. When requested by the user, the updated methods are compiled and dynamically linked to the IUICE environment.

The example discussed above is quite simple because all methods have at most one event input and output. No names identifying the channels are needed. In more complex applications, where methods have multiple input and output channels, it is sometimes necessary to address each channel individually. Consider for example the semantical method shown in figure 5. Its purpose is to reduce the amount of events that are transferred from the input channel *in* to the event output *out*. This can be done for example by maintaining an internal average variable. The current value of this variable will be propagated to all subsequent connected event methods only when a dedicated *tick event*, issued periodically by the IUICE system, arrives at the *tick* input. Tick events which may also arrive at the input *in* should not trigger the output of events. The code for this method must have access to the name of the input channel offering the event. Other examples are semantical methods acting as multiplexers, where the events arriving on one input are split and propagated to different event outputs. Thus, the IUICE system does not only propagate the arriving event to the method; the name of the input channel is also provided. When issuing output events, event methods can also select from a set of labeled output channels.

When the application fulfills the requirements defined by the designer, the IUICE system provides mechanisms to generate appropriate C source code files. All the semantics provided by IUICE the application depends on—especially in case of graphical methods as described in the next section—are automatically added to the output files. The structuring into methods and the method interconnection scheme remains visible. These source files can be a base for further developments, they can also be fully coded by the programmer and ready to use.

3. Additional Graphical Support in IUICE

The functionality of IUICE presented so far is sufficient for the implementation of semantical methods that have no graphical representation defined by the application. The development of graphical methods however, needs further assistance. Currently, graphical support in IUICE deals with two topics: enabling graphical methods to access events issued directly by the graphics system, and specification of parent-child relations between graphical methods. Further approaches are discussed, which try to give users direct access to long-living graphical entities such as pixel maps, graphical contexts, and others.

Each graphical method creates a window that defines the clipping rectangle for all subsequent graphical outputs. Only the creating method and other graphical methods that stay in a child relation to this method are responsible for the window content. For the delivery of graphical events, graphical methods implicitly own—besides the application-defined event inputs—an event input labeled *graphic_in*. All the graphical events addressed to the method are provided on the *graphic_in* input directly by the IUICE system. Only the semantical response to the receipt of a graphical event has to be done by the programmer.

The mechanism of event propagation of the underlying graphics system are retained in IUICE. The IUICE environment assumes that windows can be overlapped. In this case, the propagation of events to the method owning the window on top of the window hierarchie is in some situations not sufficient. Two classes of event types must be handled differently, whether the event is dedicated to one specific window (which corresponds to a specific graphical method) or whether it may—in case the first window does not need the event—be propagated to windows below. Graphical events such as *enter_window* or *leave_window* belong to the first class. When the corresponding graphical method accepts this event, it is consumed. In all other cases, the event is discarded. This situation arises in figure 6 (a) when the mouse pointer enters window *w_top*.

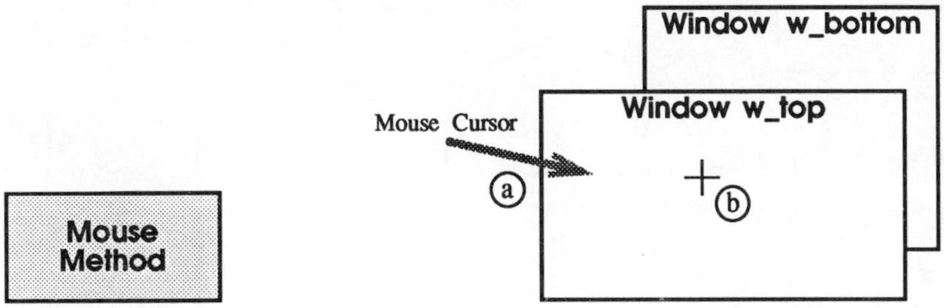

Fig. 6: Propagation of mouse events to graphical methods

Events of the second class may be needed by other windows, in case the window on top of the hierarchy is not soliciting them. Assume for example that in figure 6 the user pushes the left mouse button at the position of the cross near (b). Window *w_top* has not solicited events of type *button_pushed*. The *button_pushed* event is therefore delivered to the window *w_bottom*. If this window is also not concerned with these events, windows below *w_below* are taken into consideration. When no consumer can be found, the event is delivered to a specific IUICE event method *mouse* (see figure 6). All mouse and button events that are undeliverable are provided by this method. Normally, methods that act as window managers are clients of the mouse method and are allowed to accept and process these events. This mechanism, to make unconsumed events available by special event sources, is also used for user-defined window placement and other purposes that are normally handled by window managers. The additional mechanisms belonging to this type of graphical applications are also available by these event sources. Therefore, applications such as window managers can be designed using the IUICE system.

To simplify the development of the application, mechanisms for the specification of graphical parent-child relations are important. The first thing to be done is to define a graphical method as the child of another graphical method by dragging a line—indicating this relationship—from the child method to its parent. These lines are distinguished by the IUICE environment from lines identifying an event stream as described earlier. Such a relationship has some major consequences for the child, because its window is now clipped by the parent window.

All the windows of an application are subject to size changes. When the user reshapes the window of a parent, the child window must also be resized properly. Several approaches to this problem have been developed, among other things the stretching paradigm as presented in (Cardelli 1988). In this solution, *attachment points* are introduced for each edge of a window. These attachment points define the behavior of a child window in case the parent window is resized. An attachment point may or may not be connected by a *stretching line* to another attachment point. In the first case, the distance between the edge of the child window and the corresponding edge of an other window grows or shrinks proportionally to the resize request of the user. In case of two attachment points connected by a line, the distance defined by this line remains unchanged after resizing.

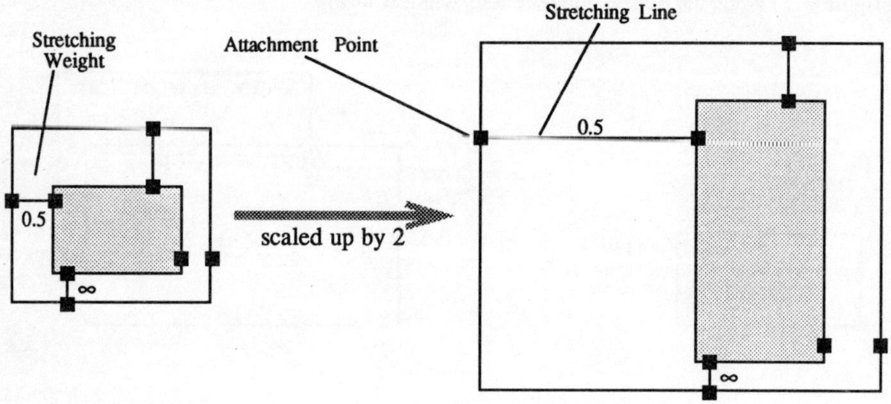

Fig. 7: Example of edge stretching

The resize mechanism used in IUICE is based on Cardellis stretching paradigm as described above. It has been extended by *stretching weights* that can be added by the programmer to the lines connecting two attachment points (as shown in figure 7). When l denotes the line length between two attachment points, $w>0$ the stretching weight associated to the line, and the main window is resized by a factor r, the resulting line length l'—after resizing—between the same two attachment points can be determined by the equation

$$l' = (1 + r / w) * l$$

For small w, the line length is increasing faster than the resize factor. By choosing a value for w near 1, approximately the same scaling behavior can be achieved as leaving the two attachment points unconnected. For $w = \infty$, the line length does not change (the same semantic is defined by dragging a line without weight). In the example of figure 7, the size of the outer window on the left side is doupled. The same window after resizing is shown on the right. The western edge distance is now 5 times longer than before because of the stretching weight 0.5, the northern and southern distances remain constant, and the eastern distance has been doupled.

Currently, a second approach is also taken into consideration. Here, the programmer is enabled to define the position and size constraints between several windows for two different situations: the relation between the windows when the parent window is normal sized and in case the parent window reaches its maximal extent. Intermediate size requests will be approximated by the IUICE system. As already mentioned in (Cardelli 1988), both mechanisms do not prevent from bad stretching behavior. After resizing, some windows may unintentionally overlap each other. But the advantages are predominant: stretching with such restricted constraints can be calculated efficiently, the stretching specification can be done graphically, and it is sufficient for a majority of applications.

4. Implementation Issues

It is essential for an interactive program such as the IUICE environment, that responses to user requests are fast. The time spent for the processing of graphical requests by the underlying graphics system cannot be improved, they are as fast (or slow) as they are. Also the code sequences implemented by the application programmer are no subject for speedups. Therefore, the overhead introduced by the additional mechanisms provided by the IUICE system has to be kept small. This strongly depends on the efficient implementation of two sensible code parts: scheduling methods with an event waiting on one of their inputs and dynamic linking of compiled methods.

Method instances which are ready for execution are stored in a *method queue*. To each entry of the queue a priority value can be associated that defines the queue position. When a method issues an event on a specified subset of its output channels, each method that is connected to one of these output channels is added to the queue. Method scheduling is non-preemptive, which means that only when the currently executed method terminates, the method located on the head of the queue is executed next. In contrast to a scheme where a method is executed immediately after its triggering event is generated, the asynchronous queuing mechanism is capable to process method interconnections containing cycles.

Event sources must be handled differently. File event sources, for example, may issue several hundred or more events until the end of file is reached and they are ready for termination. Therefore, standard file event sources provided by IUICE send an special *continuation event* to themselves each time after issuing a file event. This enables other methods to proceed between two activations of the file event source. Socket event sources are only activated when a message on the specified socket arrives. Before the method blocks again, all the events contained in the message are processed and propagated. When a new message arrives, the method is again inserted into the method queue.

It is possible to assign priority values to methods for the user-defined specification of currently more important methods. This dynamic priority scheme adapts to user requirements and is controlled by the position of the mouse pointer on the screen. The user moves the pointer inside the window of the graphical method he or she is currently interested in. The priority of every method that belongs to a sequence of interconnected methods which also contains the user-specified graphical method is increased.

A special *create event* is sent to each newly created instance of a method type to allow initializations. An initialization is very important, because method code has to be reentrant. Therefore, no global variables are allowed within a method. For many methods, this is no restriction. In case global data are needed, a new set of such variables used by the method must be allocated on the receipt of the create event. To simplify coding, IUICE provides a C code skeleton as the base for editing newly created method types. After defining and labeling the input and output channels of the method, the appropriate skeleton is created and provided to the user. As an example, consider a graphical method *abc* with two input channels labeled *control* and *data*. The excerpt of the corresponding C skeleton looks like:

```
/* Global Data used by abc */

typedef struct abc_data {
    ...;
    }

abc (   EVENT ev,
        SOURCE s,
        INSTANCE **inst,
        ENVIRON *environ ) {

    if (*inst == (INSTANCE *) 0)
        *inst = (INSTANCE *) malloc(sizeof(abc_data));

    if (ev.type == CREATE_EVENT) {
        /* Initialization */
        }
    else switch (SOURCE) {
        case GRAPHIC_IN:
            ...;
        case CONTROL:
            ...;
        case DATA:
            ...;
        }
    }
```

Each method type has four different input parameters: the event causing the activation, the name of the input channel, a pointer defining the global data of the method instance, and a pointer to some environment that contains, among other things, pointers to functions that may be called by the method (see below). In case of an empty instance pointer, the instance has been newly created and the appropriate amount of memory for global data must be allocated. For graphical methods, additional code fragments such as window creation or event soliciting are not shown but are also inserted. In a later version of IUICE it is intended to provide a preprocessor that enables the system to hide most of the implementation-specific details to the programmer.

The dynamic linking mechanism strongly depends on the provided operating system facilities, therefore this part of the IUICE system is only briefly sketched. In our case a BSD 4.3 UNIX derivative (SunOS) is used which enables the mapping of files into the virtual address space of a process. By this technique, compiled objectfiles are dynamically mapped into the address space of the environment. To skip a time-consuming binding phase, the methods are compiled into position independent code, and references back into the IUICE environment itself are resolved dynamically by the *environ* argument in the example above.

5. IUICE Applications

A first prototype version of the IUICE environment using the library of the X window system has been implemented and is ready for use since autumn 1989. The first goal was the development of a graphical tool for *monitoring and animating distributed evolutionary algorithms*. In this case, the IUICE system is not used for the design and implementation of user interfaces. It has been used as the user interface itself.

Evolutionary programs (Mühlenbein et al. 1988) belong to the class of probabilistic algorithms that are used to solve combinatorial optimization problems fast but not necessarily optimal. They imitate strategies such as gene recombination, mutation, and selection as observed in natural evolution. A distributed evolutionary program consists of multiple processes called *individuals*. During the evolutionary process, each individual executes several phases iteratively, communicates with other individuals in its neighborhood, and tries to improve its solution in every step by applying evolutionary strategies.

For the monitoring and animation of this class of applications, the prototype IUICE system has been applied for. Events that represent the different phases of each individual as well as events that describe the quality of the actual solution of each individual are inserted in the code of the evolutionary program. In the snapshot of the environment as shown in figure 8, the topology of the distributed evolutionary program is visualized by the IUICE prototype on the left side. Each rectangle corresponds to one specific individual. The neighborhood is represented as lines connecting the individuals.

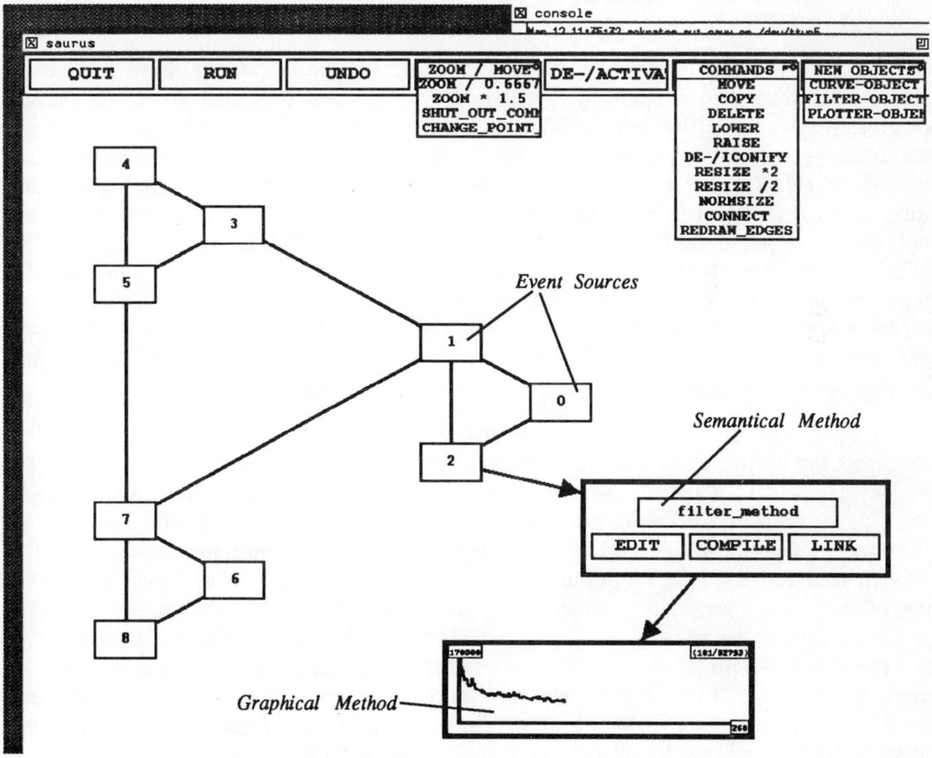

Fig. 8: Snapshot of the IUICE prototype

Technically, the graphical representation of individuals are event sources. They give users access to all the events issued by the corresponding process of the distributed program. These event sources are also capable to represent the different phases of the individuals by different colors. Each time a phase event arrives, the color is changed. This type of *program animation* can be implemented very efficiently and is used to get first insights into the program behavior. As shown in figure 8, semantical as well as graphical methods can be created and connected too. The graphical method on the right represents incoming floating point values as a polygon line and is therefore a possible implementation of the graphical method *curve* as described in the example of Section 2.

As part of an *integrated graphics-oriented programming environment for distributed systems* (Sturm et al. 1989a; Sturm et al. 1989b) the IUICE system will also be used as a tool for user-defined monitoring and animation of distributed systems in general. Each object of the distributed program is represented graphically by a corresponding event source as shown above. In contrast to the application area of evolutionary programs, the objects of the program can be created dynamically and the possible number of objects can be very large. Therefore, part of this IUICE application are methods that allow the definition and establishment of *program views*. A view is a subset of all the objects of the distributed program that defines the user's current point of interest. The filtering methods which cut out the events issued by non-selected objects are assisted by graphical methods that allow the graphical specification of objects the user is interested in. This filtering layer is located in front of the event sources which in this case only represent the objects the user has chosen.

Further semantical and graphical methods can be connected to the object representations of the distributed program by the user. A standard library of methods for monitoring distributed systems will be provided by the integrated programming environment. Program animation (Brown 1988) can be only partially supported by a method library because this type of graphical program visualization strongly depends on the specific application. But full support is provided for the development of such graphical tools. All the animation tools will also be stored in the IUICE library. Thus, for a given application the user may find an existing animation tool that has to be only slightly modified to fit the specific requirements. Each specific configuration of interconnected semantical and graphical methods forms—in the sense of the IUICE model—a graphical user interface of its own. We expect that monitoring and animating distributed systems as a whole becomes simpler and more structured when using such an interactive and graphics-oriented tool.

A third class of IUICE applications that are currently designed deals with graphical tools that support the programming of *transputer networks*. In this case, IUICE is used for the development of graphical user interfaces which is the main goal IUICE was designed for. Currently, two applications are considered: a prototype version of an *idle time monitor* for transputer systems and a *graphical specification tool for transputer topologies*. The first program forms a base for further investigations towards a general tool for the monitoring of transputer nets. Here, besides the graphical part of the application, several other problems have to be solved, among other things the propagation of events issued within the transputer system to the IUICE environment and an efficient implementation of the event issuing mechanism. The second application is needed for some transputer systems containing crossbar switches which allow the dynamical reconfiguration of the transputer network. The interconnection of links of a set of transputers should be described graphically and the corresponding source files controlling the crossbar switch configuration should be generated.

6. Conclusion

The realization of the first prototype version of IUICE as a monitoring and animation tool for evolutionary programs was an interesting project and many experiences have been gained concerning developing and interconnecting semantical as well as graphical methods. Most concepts and mechanisms provided by the IUICE model evolved from the usage of this prototype. The implementation of a functionally complete environment as described in the previous sections of this paper and its further evaluation is currently one of our major goals. It will also be implemented as an application client of the X window system, although the concepts of the IUICE model are mostly independent from a specific graphics system. The decision for using X resulted from the fact that it is a de facto standard for graphics systems and that it is available for a large number of different machine types.

Already with the prototype implementation we could show that the performance overhead introduced by facilities of the environment is negligible. More than 95% of the time has been spent during execution of graphics procedure calls of the X system. This was clearly observable while porting the IUICE prototype from X windows V11R3 to V11R4. In release 3, fine-tuning and performance improvement in the graphical X server was very poor especially in case of color applications. In release 4 of the X window system, the code parts belonging to black and white graphics and colored graphics have been strongly improved independently. Now, in the new version of the prototype no significant response delays can be observed by the user.

Besides the development of the complete IUICE environment, future work will concentrate on the development of a standard method library for monitoring and animating distributed programs as well as on the design and implementation of graphical methods that build up a complete collection of graphical entities as provided by graphical toolkits. In order to reduce the amount of re-implementation, tools which convert graphical entities realized as toolkit objects into IUICE methods are considered.

Acknowledgments

I would like to thank my colleagues Peter Buhler, Thomas Gauweiler, and Friedemann Mattern for many interesting discussions. Also many thanks to Martin Baade and Dirk Kohlbecher who succesfully implemented the first prototype version of the IUICE system.

References

Apple (1985), ***"Inside Macintosh,"*** Addison-Wesley

Brown, M.H. (1988), ***"Exploring Algorithms Using Balsa-II,"*** IEEE Computer, Vol. 21, No. 5, pp. 14-36

Cardelli, L. (1988), ***"Building User Interfaces by Direct Manipulation,"*** Proceedings of the ACM SIGGraph Symposium on User Interfaces, pp. 152-166

Goldberg, A., Robsin, D. (1983), ***"Smalltalk-80: The Language and its Implementation,"*** Addison-Wesley

Goldberg, A. (1984), ***"Smalltalk-80: The Interactive Programming Environment,"*** Addison-Wesley

Gosling, J., Rosenthal, D. S.H., Arden, M. (1989), ***"The NeWS Book,"*** Springer-Verlag

Jones, O. (1989), ***"Introduction to the X Window System,"*** Prentice Hall

McCormak, J., Asente, P. (1988), ***"An Overview of the X Toolkit,"*** Proceedings of the ACM SIGGraph Symposium User-Interface Software, ACM, pp. 46-55

Mühlenbein, H., Gorges-Schleuter, M., Krämer, O. (1988), ***"Evolution algorithms in combinatorial optimization,"*** Parallel Computing, North-Holland, No. 7, pp. 65-85

Myers, B.A. (1989), ***"User-Interface Tools: Introduction and Survey,"*** IEEE Software, Vol. 6, No. 1, pp. 15-23

Raeder, G. (1985), ***"A Survey of Current Graphical Programming Techniques,"*** IEEE Computer, Vol. 18, No. 8, pp. 11-25

Rosenthal, D. S.H. (1987), ***"A Simple X11 Client Program— or how hard can it really be to write 'Hello, World',"*** Sun Microsystems, (see also **Jones 1989**)

Sturm, P., Wybranietz, D., Mattern, F. (1989), ***"The INCAS Distributed Systems Project— Experiences and Current Topics,"*** Proceedings of the DEC Workshop "Distribution and Objects," pp. 97-114, DECUS Munich

Sturm, P., Buhler, P., Mattern, F., Wybranietz, D. (1989), ***"An Integrated Environment for Programming, Evaluating, and Visualizing Large Distributed Programs,"*** to appear in Proceedings of the Workshop on Parallel Computing in Practice, University of Jerusalem, Israel

Weinand, A., Gamma, E., Marty, R. (1988), ***"ET++ - An Object-Oriented Application Framework in C++,"*** in Proceedings of the OOPSLA '88 Conference, pp. 46-57

Chapter 17

Dialogue Specification for Knowledge Based Systems

Clive Hayball

17.1 Introduction

The computer science community has for a long time advocated the separation of the user interface from the application logic as an important principle in system development. This principle led to the birth of the Seeheim model [Pfaff, 1985] which splits interactive software into three components: the application interface, the dialogue controller and the presentation (display). Refer to figure 1 below for a diagrammatic representation of the Seeheim model. In this model, the notion of an explicit dialogue controller supports the top-down decomposition of the application task to the level of a detailed interaction specification which is independent of the detailed design of both the user interface and the application logic. Dialogue description languages based on state transition networks have been traditionally used to implement the dialogue component in the run-time system. The SET product from P.A. Consultants [Jeanes,1989] provides a good example of the use of this approach.

Figure 1 : The Seeheim Model

Although the Seeheim model provides an excellent separation of concerns, it has major limitations when applied to the modern generation of interactive systems. For example, it fails to support the interleaving of input and output which is required for feedback in direct manipulation interfaces and for multi-thread applications [Coutaz, 1989]. This paper outlines the special needs of Knowledge Based Systems (KBS) in respect of dialogue specification, and goes on to describe a rule-based dialogue description language which has been designed to support the Human Computer Interaction (HCI) for KBS. The language has been developed specifically for use within an object-oriented User Interface Management System (UIMS) and attempts to remedy the defects inherent in state transition dialogues and the Seeheim model.

17.2 Special Features of Knowledge Based Systems

Knowledge based systems support a number of features which impact on the nature and form of the desired user interfaces. These features should of course be seen as broad characteristics of such systems, rather than clear distinctions with conventional software :

- KBS code is usually non-sequential in nature. There is rarely a single thread of control running through a KBS program and the sequence of operations performed by the system is generally determined by a combination of user operations, data characteristics and the outcome of problem solving.

- KBS often employ interaction structures which reflect the nature of the underlying knowledge structures. Interactive Connection Diagrams [Dodson, 1988] are a good example of these. In addition, conventional display structures such as bar charts may be provided with interaction capability to support "what if" queries (sometimes known as "scenarios").
- In more advanced KBS there is a move away from user- or system- driven applications towards a mixed initiative approach, where user and system can solve problems cooperatively by volunteering information or adjusting the flow of control.
- KBS often provide several problem solving contexts, e.g. for global system control, information input, explanation, use of scenarios etc. The user is provided with the freedom to move between these contexts, each of which may need to retain a memory of its current state until control is eventually returned to that context.

The above features represent a move away from a task-based user interface towards a capability-based interface. The user is provided with a set of interaction objects which represent various system capabilities. The sequence in which these are used and the ordering of the display features which result are dictated by the whim of the user and the nature of the KBS application, rather than by some pre-defined and well structured task which the system is designed to support.

17.3 Dialogue Requirements for Knowledge Based Systems

Given the above features of KBS, there is a need to revisit the question of suitable dialogue description languages for this kind of system. Our research, which has involved the analysis of a variety of KBS application needs, has shown that the major requirements for such a language appear to be as follows:

(i) As with any dialogue description language, it must facilitate the specification of the user-system communication in an abstract but explicit form which is independent both of the display details and of the application logic.

(ii) The structure and expression of the dialogue description language should be "natural" in the way that it supports documentation of the designer's understanding and decomposition of the problem.

(iii) The language should be economic in expression, but sufficiently powerful to support the description of a wide range of applications.

(iv) The dialogue language must support mixed-initiative and multi-threading of control, as required by advanced KBS.

(v) Where possible the language should support consistency of interaction style across the features of an application interface.

(vi) In order to support the possibility of adaptive interfaces, the specification of dialogue for an application must be modifiable at run-time.

(vii) The dialogue should support control of exception conditions, to include the possibility of time-outs where user or system fails to react.

17.4 Review of Existing Dialogue Specification Techniques

A variety of dialogue description languages have been proposed in the literature, based on a range of techniques including state transition networks [Wasserman, 1985], extended context-free grammars [Olsen, 1984], event-response systems [Hill, 1987], Petri Nets [Pilote, 1983] and Communicating Sequential Processes [Alexander, 1987]. It has been argued [Cockton, 1988] that none of the above methods in isolation provides a sufficiently powerful and expressive approach to constitute a general method. Cockton himself proposes the notion of Generative Transition Networks (GTNs), which are an extension of state transition networks where the arcs between states are generated rather than described. The dialogue description language which is proposed in this paper combines the power and economy of expression of GTNs with mechanisms for dialogue decomposition and abstraction. The detailed description of the language below is followed with a discussion of the ways in which the language meets the requirements for the specification of KBS dialogues.

17.5 The Dialogue Language in Detail

17.5.1 Dialogue Scripts

The KBS Dialogue Language, which we term KDL, has been designed to operate in conjunction with an object oriented UIMS. The choice of an object-oriented approach to user interface design and implementation will not be addressed in this paper, but the reader is referred to [Knolle, 1989] for some reasons why this approach is preferred. A more detailed description of the development of the particular UIMS may be found in [Hayball, 1990]. Since the UIMS decomposes the user interface into a set of HCI objects which are organised at run-time into compositional hierarchies, KDL provides a corresponding decomposition of a dialogue into dialogue scripts, each of which is associated with an HCI object. In fact each script can be viewed as an extension of an HCI object, rather like a procedural attachment in frame-based languages [Bobrow et al, 1977]. Figure 2 below illustrates how the decomposition of a dialogue into scripts in this way represents a departure from the Seeheim model.

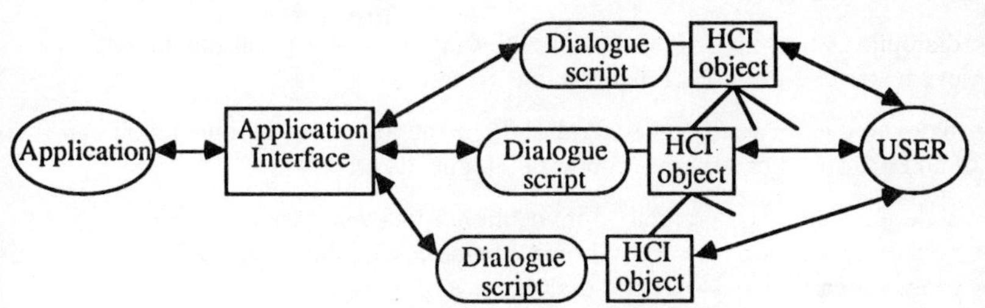

Figure 2 : The Object Oriented Dialogue Model

Figure 3 below illustrates the composition of the display of a 'house' object in terms of its component HCI objects and dialogue scripts. Note that not all HCI objects have dialogue attachments because some of the objects have no interactive behaviour of their own.

The example of the house composite will be used elsewhere in this paper to illustrate some of the characteristics of KDL. Each dialogue script in KDL is structured as a set of states with associated transition rules. The script is driven by dialogue events which may trigger state changes and/or dialogue actions. In line with the generative approach, states, events and actions need not be defined explicitly. They are specified in terms of patterns which may involve the use of variable parameters to be matched at execution time with specific state or event characteristics. Dialogue events may be generated by HCI objects in response to user actions or by the KBS application using a special method.

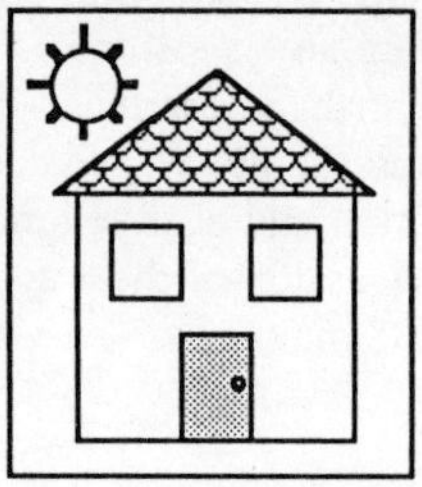

house_scene * :
  sky_frame
    sun *
  house_frame
    house *
      roof
      wall
        window_1 *
        window_2 *
        door *

* means 'has dialogue attachment'

Figure 3 : House Composite

17.5.2 Dialogue Syntax

A dialogue state in KDL is expressed as an atomic state name or as a term consisting of a state name plus one or more arguments. More formally:

< dialogue state > ::= < state name > | < state name > (< argument list >)
< argument list > ::= < argument > | < argument > , < argument list >

A dialogue event comprises an event source, an event name and optional event arguments. The event source must be an explicit HCI object name; however the keyword 'self' may be used within dialogue rules as a shorthand form of the name of the HCI object which is associated with the dialogue script.

< dialogue event > ::= (< event source > < event name > [< argument list >])
< event source > ::= < HCI object name > | self

A single dialogue event can trigger several dialogue actions. A dialogue action can invoke a method of an HCI object or generate another dialogue event:

< dialogue action > ::= < method invocation > | < event generation >
< method invocation > ::= < HCI object name > < method name > [< argument list >]
< event generation > ::= event < dialogue event >

A special method name called 'state' is defined for every HCI object to allow another HCI object or the application to force it into a specified state. Dialogue actions may also be triggered on entry to or exit from a dialogue state. The keywords 'entry' and 'exit' are used to introduce these actions. A dialogue script comprises a set of state transition rules. Each rule is triggered by pattern matching against a state-event pair and leads to a set of actions plus optionally a transition to a new state :

< dialogue script > ::= { < dialogue rule > }
< dialogue rule > ::= < event rule > | < entry rule > | < exit rule >
< entry rule > ::= < dialogue state > entry { < dialogue action > }
< exit rule > ::= < dialogue state > exit { < dialogue action > }
< event rule > ::= < state-event pair > [< state change >] { < dialogue action > }
< state-event pair > ::= < dialogue state> < dialogue event >
< state change > ::= --> < dialogue state >

If no state change is specified the dialogue remains in the same state. Dialogue states and dialogue events may be given variable fields in transition rules to allow for more general and concise specification of behaviour. A variable field is specified as $J<JnameJ> and acts as a "wild card" matching anything. If the same variable appears more than once in a pattern, all occurrences must match the same value. Occurrences of the same variable in actions are replaced by the matching value. Variables may also be used in rules to replace state names. Typically, a variable state name is used as a "catch-all" to intercept events which are processed identically in all states. However, rule firing always involves the most explicit pattern which matches with the current state-event pair, so "catch-all" rules are only fired if there is no match with a more explicit rule. This document will use an indented notation to represent dialogue scripts. Dialogue rules for the same state pattern are grouped together under the state pattern. Similarly, the actions for an event are listed under the pattern and optional state change for that event. A simple example of a dialogue script is provided by an object representing a window in a house, which alternates between the two states "light-on" and "light-off" on successive mouse clicks and generates a forwarding event giving the new window shading:

```
light(off)
        entry
                (self fill black)
                event(self shaded black)
        (self clicked) --> light(on)

light(on)
        entry
                (self fill white)
                event(self shaded white)
        (self clicked) --> light(off)
```

The use of variable arguments, together with a suitable renaming of the states, allows the two explicit states above to be replaced by a single implicit state pattern:

```
shading($current, $next)
        entry
                (self fill $current)
                event(self shaded $current)
        (self clicked) --> shading($next, $current)
```

Finally, the dialogue rule system in KDL allows more meaningful state names to be provided in terms of those already defined. The '==' keyword defines state name equivalence within a single dialogue script. For example, if for a window object the white and black shadings are in some way representative of night (light on) and day (light off) respectively, then:

```
day == shading(black,white)

night == shading(white,black).
```

The effect of the above equivalence relations is that all references to states 'day' and 'night' within the window dialogue are replaced by references to states 'shading(black,white)' and 'shading(white, black)' respectively.

The equivalence relation may also be used to define initial dialogue states. By default, a dialogue script starts in the state 'initial', which may be mapped onto any state pattern using an equivalence relation, e.g.

```
initial == shading(black,white).
```

The equivalence relation is a powerful construct because it facilitates the pre-definition of a dialogue rule in a form which can be tailored to match the semantics of an application.

17.6 Dialogue Inheritance and Delegation

The KBS dialogue requirement for consistency of interaction style across the features of an application interface, and indeed potentially across several applications, is met in KDL by inheritance of dialogue behaviour from HCI object classes. An important characteristic of the KDL approach, in its use of separate transition rules with variable fields and equivalence relations, is that complex HCI object behaviours may be constructed incrementally. For example, the "toggle" behaviour defined above for the window object can be inherited from a more general HCI object class. The initial state of the dialogue can be used to define the two fill colours to toggle between. So the window can be defined with initial state shading(black,white) and a door object can be defined in the same way but with initial state shading(brown, black) say, to provide the door with similar behaviour but with a different base colour. Equivalence relations can then be used to provide more meaningful state names, such as light(on) / light(off) or open / closed. Figure 4 provides an illustration of how this inheritance of dialogue behaviour operates.

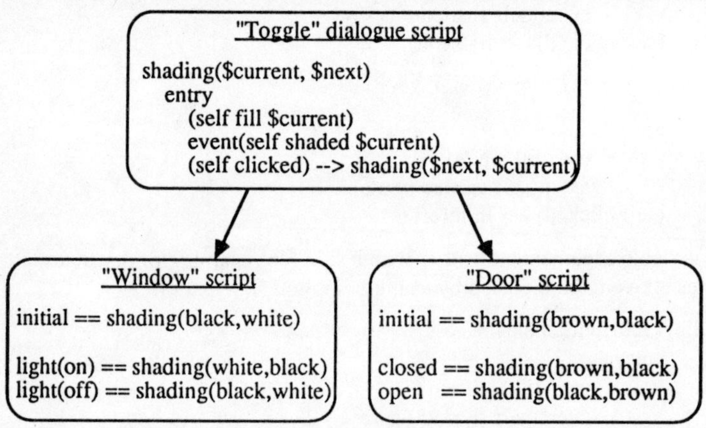

Figure 4 : Inheritance of Dialogue Behaviour

A dialogue script attached to an HCI object specifies behaviour relevant to that object and its embedded components. Thus, in the case of the house composite object introduced in section 5.1., the script at the house_scene level defines behaviour relevant to the composite as a whole. This is the level at which it is appropriate to specify the linkage of behaviours of the component parts of the house, i.e.. between the sky_frame and the house_frame (and thus between their components). Linkage of behaviours at the level of a composite is achieved by delegation of unmatched events up through the composition hierarchy. Events are passed up the composition hierarchy until they are matched within a dialogue script. Events unmatched by all scripts are passed back to the client application. Figure 5 illustrates the paths of delegation for the house composite.

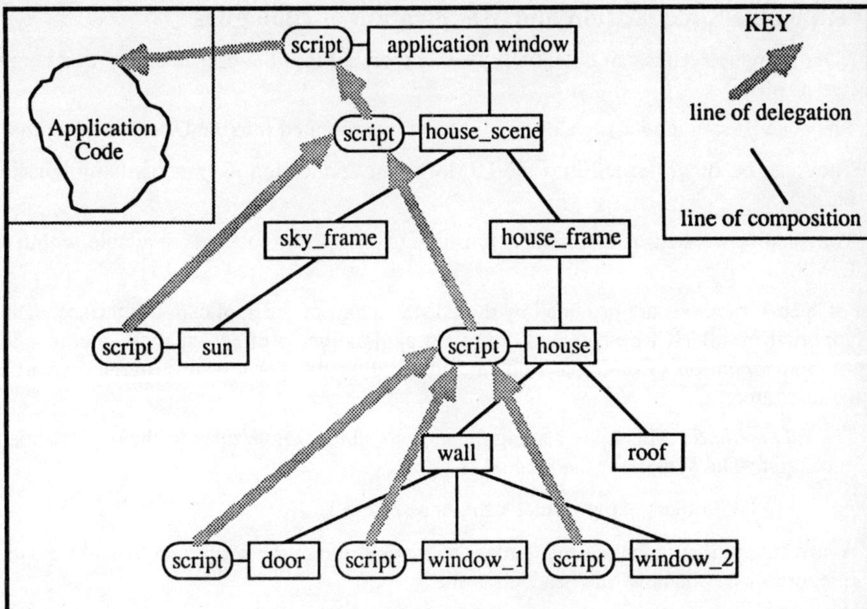

Figure 5 : Delegation Paths for House Composite

As an example of delegation, we might wish to specify that, when the ''sun'' object is clicked, the sun disappears, the lights are switched on in the house and the door is closed. This is best managed by defining ''day'' and ''night'' states within the house_scene dialogue script and trapping the (sun shaded $colour) events generated from the ''toggle'' behaviour on the sun object :

```
day
        entry
                (window_1, state,day)
                (window_2, state,day)
                (door, state,day )
                (sun reveal)
        (sun shaded blue) --> night

night
        entry
                (window_1, state,night)
                (window_2, state,night)
                (door, state,night )
                (sun hide)
        (sun shaded yellow) --> day.
```

Note that, with the above dialogue script, the application can force the house_scene into the day or night states independently of user actions simply by invoking the methods (house_scene,state,day) or (house_scene,state,night) respectively.

17.7 Run-time Specification and Modification of Dialogues

The KDL dialogue scripts can potentially be incorporated into the user interface in a number of different ways :

(i) They can be specified using a design tool and incorporated into the UIMS at load time

(ii) They can be down-loaded into the UIMS by an application as part of its initialisation phase

(iii) They can be created or modified at run-time using special methods available within the UIMS.

A set of special methods are provided by the UIMS as part of the application interface. These are supported by all HCI objects and allow an application to effect creation, modification, deletion and execution of dialogue rules at initialisation time or during program execution. The methods are:

(i) *The rule method*. This allows an application to add dialogue rules to the object's dialogue script. The syntax for the method is

(<HCI object name>, rule, < dialogue rule >)

A new rule with an identical pattern to an existing rule in the script redefines the existing rule, otherwise the new rule is added to the script.

(ii) *The event method*. This method generates a dialogue event. The event is processed by the object's dialogue script just as if the object itself had generated the event. Delegation applies in the case that the event is unmatched within the script.

(<HCI object name>, event, < dialogue event >)

(iii) *The norule method*. This method is also supported by all HCI objects and removes rules from the object's dialogue script. Any rule in the script with an identical pattern to that given as the argument to the norule method is removed from the script.

(<HCI object name>, norule, < dialogue rule >).

(iv) *The '==' method*. This method is used by an application to set up dialogue state equivalences.

(<HCI object name>, ==, <new name> <old name>).

(v) *The state method*. As mentioned in section 5.2. above, this method can be used to force a dialogue into a specified state:

(<HCI object name>, state, < dialogue state >).

17.8 Important Features of KDL

The KDL dialogue description language has been designed with the specific requirements of section 3. above in mind and meets these requirements in the following ways:

(i) KDL supports an abstract description of the communication aspects of a system. The dialogue scripts and rules are independent both of the display details (hidden in the implementation of the HCI objects) and of the application semantics (hidden within the application code).

(ii) The decomposition of KDL into dialogue scripts supports problem decomposition and description since, in a capability-based approach to KBS design, there is a close mapping between the composition of the user interface features and the system capabilities as presented to the user.

(iii) The use of inheritance, delegation, variables and equivalence relations in KDL supports compact but powerful expressions of behaviour.

(iv) KDL supports a high degree of parallelism, since each dialogue script can potentially provide a separate thread of control. The capability of dialogue rules to be triggered by either user- or application- generated events facilitates the construction of mixed initiative applications.

(v) The inheritance mechanism for dialogue rules supports consistency across interface features and, potentially, across applications, since HCI objects can inherit dialogue behaviour incrementally from higher-level classes. The dialogue scripts attached to basic HCI object classes can in fact be used to define a standard "look-and-feel" which is then inherited by lower-level classes and instances.

(vi) The application interface features of KDL support run-time creation, modification and deletion of dialogue rules.

(vii) KDL does not currently support explicit control of exception conditions. However the UIMS provides a timer object which can be used to generate time-out events when user or application has failed to react within a reasonable period. A dialogue script attached to the timer can be used to capture and process time-out events according to the needs of a particular application.

17.9 Conclusions

The UIMS architecture and dialogue description language presented in this paper overcome many of the problems which are traditionally associated with the Seeheim model. They also appear to offer good support for the design and implementation of KBS applications which offer a capability-based rather than task-based interface. The particular UIMS referenced earlier in this paper has been adopted as a standard HCI product within STC and is likely to be extended in future to incorporate the KDL dialogue language.

Acknowledgements

The author wishes to thank Dr. Paul Rautenbach (also of STC Technology Ltd) for his contribution to the results reported in this paper.

References

Alexander, H. (1987). Formally-based Techniques for Dialogue Description. In *People and Computers III*, eds. D. Diaper & R. Winder, Cambridge University Press, 1987, pp 201-214.

Bobrow, D. G., Kaplan, R. M., Kay, M., Norman, D. A., Thompson, H. and Winograd, T. GUS, a Frame-Driven Dialog System. Artificial Intelligence 8, 1977, pp 155-173. Cockton, G. (1988). Generative Transition Networks : A New Communication Control Abstraction. In *People and Computers IV*, eds. D. M. Jones & R. Winder, Cambridge University Press, 1988, pp 509-527.

Coutaz, J. (1989). UIMS: Promises, Failures and Trends. In *People and Computers V*, eds. A. Sutcliffe & L. Macaulay, Cambridge University Press, 1989, pp 71-84.

Dodson, D.C. (1988). Interaction with Knowledge Systems through Structure Diagrams : Where Next ? Proc. Human and Organisational Issues of Expert Systems. Stratford- upon-Avon, England, May 1988.

Jeanes, P. (1989). Software Engineering Toolkit (SET) Technical Overview. P.A. Consulting Group, Melbourn, Royston, Herts., U.K.

Hayball, C. (1990). KHS : A Run-Time Server for Knowledge Based Systems Applications. Submitted to Interact '90, Cambridge, U.K. 27th-31st August, 1990.

Hill, R. (1987). Event Response Systems - A Technique for Specifying Multi-Threaded Dialogues. Proceedings of CHI + GI 1987, pp 241-248.

Knolle, N, T. (1989). Why Object-Oriented User Interface Toolkits are Better. Journal of Object Oriented Programming, 2(4), Nov-Dec 1989, pp63-67.

Olsen, D.R. (1984). Pushdown Automata for User Interface Management. ACM Transactions on Graphics 3(3), 1984, pp 177-203.

Pllote, M. (1983). A Programming Language Framework for Designing User Interfaces. SIGPLAN Notices, 18(6), ACM, 1983, pp 118-136.

Pfaff, G.E. (1985). User Interface Management Systems. Proceedings of IFIP/EG Workshop on UIMS, Springer-Verlag, Seeheim, West Germany.

Wasserman, A.I. (1985). Extending State Transition Diagrams for the Specification of Human-Computer Interaction. IEEE Transactions on Software Engineering, SE- 11(8), August 1985, pp 699-713.

Chapter 18

SYSECA's Experience in UIMS for Industrial Applications

Jacqui Bangratz and Eric Le Thieis

Abstract

This paper describes our experience in the domain of graphical user interfaces (UI, GUI) in multiwindowing environment. This experience was gained on applied research projects and on product developments in the Computer Integrated Manufacturing (CIM) area. The results are a **UI development methodology** based on a UI specification model called the Linguistic Model, a **dialogue specification technique** extending ATNs to event driven GUI, and the **RAID system** composed of the **Navigator** and **Explorer tools**.

Keywords

User Interface Prototyping Tool, User Interface Development Methodology, User Interface Specification Technique, Graphical User Interface, User Interface Management System.

---

1. Introduction

During the last years, SYSECA's UI team had the opportunity to participate in several industrial and research projects, like ESPRIT-I VITAMIN [MORIN et al. 1989] or ESPRIT-II CIDAM[1] [NEELAMKAVIL 1989], covering the topic of graphical user interfaces in CIM (Computer Integrated Manufacturing). Our approach was to assess advanced methods and techniques, and if necessary to improve them, based on following requirements :

- General requirements :

  - End-user's & customer's feedback as early as possible;
  - UIMS (User Interface Management System) tools should run on target systems;
  - Gain in productivity for both end users and computer scientists;
  - Capability to adopt both standard and proprietary UI styles;

- Requirements concerning UI specification techniques :

  - Specification techniques should be usable by ergonomists, UI designers and hopefully customers[2];
  - Notation used as "formal" (in the sense of contractual, legal) definition of the UI;
  - Functional completeness : it should be possible to specify input, output, application interface;

- Requirements from industrial real time applications :

  - Multi-windowing;
  - Distributed architecture;
  - Multi-user;
  - Internal and external events;
  - Multi-threaded dialogues with multi-processing.

The selected methods and techniques were built on top of emerging standards like X Window System [SCHEIFLER 1988], Xt Toolkit [MACCORMACK 1988], OSF/Motif [ATLAS et al. 1989], OPEN LOOK [AT&T 1988]. These tools were later refined and validated in real industrial environment, obtaining a valuable feedback.

---

1 VITAMIN (1556) was an ESPRIT-I project, partly funded by the Commission of the European Communities (CEC);
CIDAM (2527) is an ESPRIT-II project, partly funded by the CEC.

2 We make a distinction between the **customer** and the **end-user**. The customer is the person who buys the system, whereas the end-user is the person who will use it.

This paper summarizes the experience we gained and expresses our point of view in the domain of U.I. realization methods (section III), U.I. dialogue specification techniques (section IV) and U.I.M.S. tools (section V). Section II recalls the most popular UI models encountered today, setting the stage for following sections.

2. Overview of Today's UI Models

As in every active research domain, many UI reference models have been proposed. Our experience taught us that it is very important to pick up the most appropriate model in a given situation, so as to benefit as much as possible from it. The models, reported in the following section, may be classified into four categories :

1) UIMS models, following the structure of a UIMS; a UIMS being "a program that automatically constructs an User Interface given a description of it." [GREEN 1985b]. Examples are the OSF/Motif layered Model [ATLAS et al. 1989] or the UIMS reference model proposed in [PRIME 1989];
2) UI models, structuring a UI or a UIMS instance. Examples are the X layered Model [SCHEIFLER 1986] or the PAC Model [COUTAZ 1987];
3) Logical models of UIMS. This kind of model does not represent how a UIMS should be structured or implemented, instead it presents the logical components that must appear in a UIMS" [GREEN 1985a]. The Seeheim Model [GREEN 1985a] is a well known logical model. To be effectively applied, the Seeheim Model must be conciliated with the implementation model. For example, it can be used as a guide in object oriented design of interactive object classes, where every object might be decomposed into three logical parts, corresponding to the three components of the Seeheim Model. Other logical models are described in [MYERS 1989]. One major drawback in applying these logical models is the natural tendency for most people to use them as a sheer UIMS implementation models;
4) UI specification models, which give a methodology for UI specification. The Linguistic Model belongs to this category. This model suggests that "the dialogue between the user and the machine is built upon two languages. With one the user communicates with the computer; with the other the computer communicates with the user" [FOLEY 1989]. Our experience in using the linguistic model was positive, despite its lacks (e.g. impossibility to specify a MOVE command [STRUBBE 1985]), provided a clear interface between dialogue and interaction is established. In our view, interaction is part of the Presentation Component of the Seeheim Model. Interaction is the part of dialogue included within the presentation objects. At the lexical level of the Linguistic Model, UI designers only have to specify the binding of the interaction with the dialogue

between the presentation objects. These presentation objects are instanciated from the classes provided by the underlying toolkit. On the other hand, when a new interactive object is required, existing toolkits offer appropriate specification techniques, e.g. the Translation Manager of Xt Toolkit.

3. UI Development Methodology

The proposed UI development methodology [MORIN et al. 1990] is based upon the Linguistic Model as used by Foley [FOLEY 1989]. Four main complements were made to the model as follows :

- C1 : a software system may be viewed as composed of a set of modules. Each of them in turn contains an application part, called *Application Module*, and, if necessary, a UI part, called *UI Module*. Every UI module communicates with the end user, with its associated Application Module, and possibly with other UI Modules. This structure is maintained through the whole *realization* process (design, implementation and integration). In the following the term "User Interface" (UI) designates the set of UI modules contained in the whole system.
- C2 : as a consequence of the previous point, since the UI is part of the entire system, its realization process must be integrated in the overall development process of the system. Therefore, links and constraints between realization methods of the UI part and of the application part were established. Examples of such "links and constraints" are design criteria common to UI and application part; constraints on functional and physical system architecture derived from either the application or the UI part; etc...
- C3 : skills and knowledge required to carry out each step of the method are scattered among different people : ergonomists, cognitive sciences experts, application domain experts, UI designers, developers, etc... The precise identification of the involved people and of the required techniques and tools clarifies the purpose of each stage of the method and helps the project management.
- C4 : window system and object oriented (OO) approach have been explicitly taken into account for each stage of the method. Every UI Module should be designed in an object oriented manner.

An excerpt of the SADT diagrams set modelling the resulting realization method is given at the end of the paper. The first one (A0 : TO REALIZE A SYSTEM) describes the cutting into UI and application parts (C1 and C2). Concepts borrowed to window systems and OO design (C4) can be found in the second diagram (A2 : TO DESIGN THE UI PART), which details the design of the UI part. In order not to clutter up the

Context	TITLE : A0 : TO REALIZE A SYSTEM	MEDOC / CIDAM		PAGE : REF : DATE : VERSION :

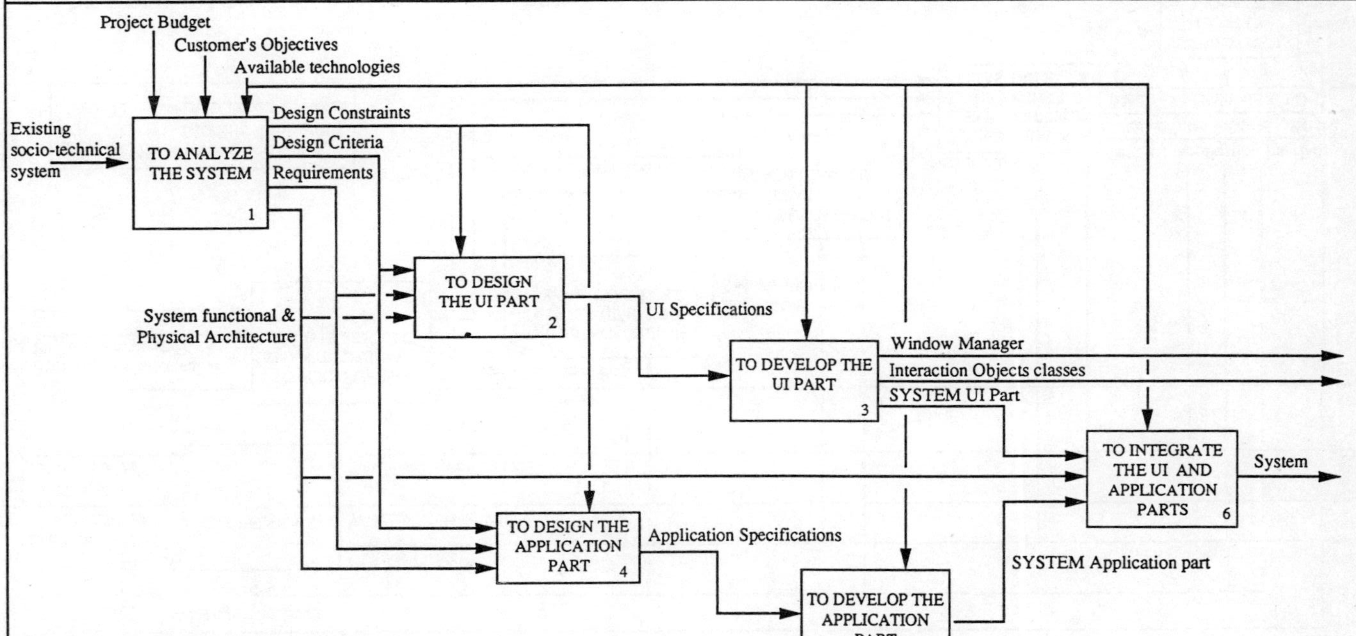

A0 : "TO REALIZE A SYSTEM"

AUTHOR : SYSECA TEMPS REEL	NOTES : 1 2 3 4 5 6 7 8 9			WORK	READER :
				RECOMMENDED	
DATE : 18/1/90	AUTHOR P.N°	KR P.N°	REPLACED BY :	PUBLISHED	DATE :

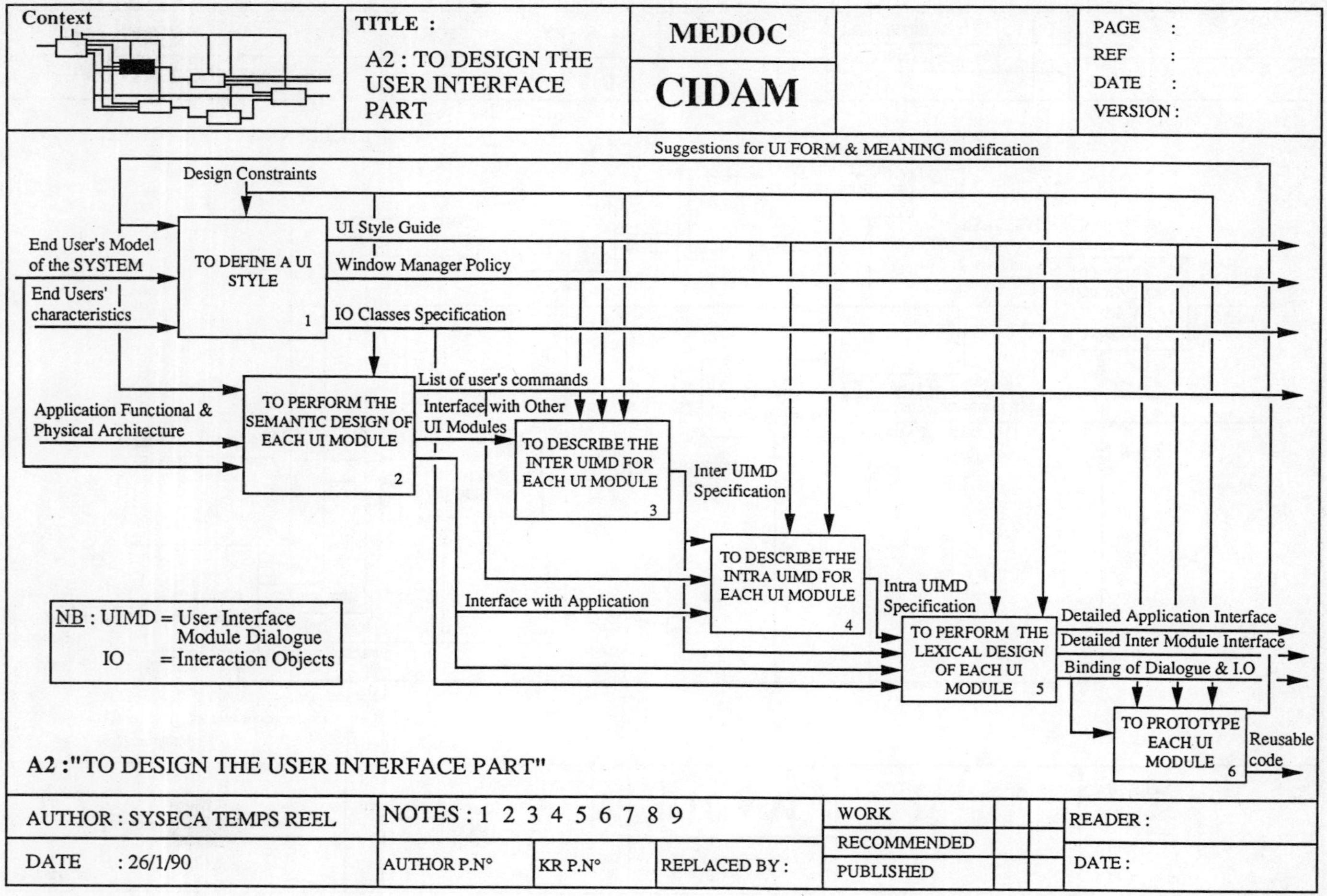
Context
TITLE :
A2 : TO DESIGN THE USER INTERFACE PART
MEDOC
CIDAM
PAGE :
REF :
DATE :
VERSION :
Suggestions for UI FORM & MEANING modification
Design Constraints
End User's Model of the SYSTEM
End Users' characteristics
TO DEFINE A UI STYLE 1
UI Style Guide
Window Manager Policy
IO Classes Specification
Application Functional & Physical Architecture
TO PERFORM THE SEMANTIC DESIGN OF EACH UI MODULE 2
List of user's commands
Interface with Other UI Modules
TO DESCRIBE THE INTER UIMD FOR EACH UI MODULE 3
Inter UIMD Specification
Interface with Application
TO DESCRIBE THE INTRA UIMD FOR EACH UI MODULE 4
Intra UIMD Specification
TO PERFORM THE LEXICAL DESIGN OF EACH UI MODULE 5
Detailed Application Interface
Detailed Inter Module Interface
Binding of Dialogue & I.O
TO PROTOTYPE EACH UI MODULE 6
Reusable code
NB : UIMD = User Interface Module Dialogue
IO = Interaction Objects
A2 :"TO DESIGN THE USER INTERFACE PART"
AUTHOR : SYSECA TEMPS REEL
DATE : 26/1/90
NOTES : 1 2 3 4 5 6 7 8 9
AUTHOR P.N°
KR P.N°
REPLACED BY :
WORK
RECOMMENDED
PUBLISHED
READER :
DATE :

diagrams, resources are not shown directly on the schemas, but listed in the associated text [MORIN et al. 1990].

Since methods and tools available today are not powerful enough, computer scientists are involved in all main phases of the methodology, namely the "Analysis", "Design", "Development" and "Integration" phases, but they complain in particular of the lack of integrated tools for UI design, especially for the specification of the syntactic and lexical levels of the UI design part. Therefore in the remainder of the paper, the focus will be on the dialogue specification techniques we selected and improved, and on resulting tools we integrated into the OSF/Motif environment.

4. Dialogue Specification Techniques

After having examined three classes of techniques commonly used for UI specification, namely *Transition Networks*, *Grammars*, and *Event Model* [GREEN 1986], we chose ATNs as the basis for our notation. The main reasons for this choice were :

- the superiority of ATNs diagrams in visual representation;
- their descriptive power of control flow;
- the relative ease of use for UI designers. Indeed, this is an immediate consequence of the two previous points;
- the general acceptance in their use, "either in read/write or read only mode", by non computer scientists like ergonomists and even customers. This is a practical consequence of the first point.

One major drawback of ATNs is the large size of resulting networks even when using the subdiagram facility. However, we found out that entangled diagrams mostly result from a wrong analysis. Anyway, due to the considered level of abstraction, a complex dialogue results in a complex specification and therefore in complex networks.

The Event Model, despite the fact that it fits well current window systems, in particular X, is too low level and too close to a programming language, like C language, to be readily understood by non computer scientists.

We combined together the power of the Event Model and the convenience of the ATN notation, by extending ATN concepts so that they can describe event driven interfaces. Furthermore, following requirements, corresponding to ATN lacks, were to be fulfilled :

- R1 : capability to specify either *External or Internal Events*, namely events produced either by an end user or by an application;
- R2 : capability to specify *multithreaded dialogues*, i.e. the capability to suspend temporarily a command or a sequence of commands, while performing one or more unrelated commands;

- R3 : capability to specify *context sensitive dialogues*, namely the capability for the UI to deal with event history;
- R4 : capability to specify *semantic constrained dialogues*, i.e. UI context to be dependent on application status;
- R5 : capability to specify *output* to the end user in terms of graphical and textual primitives;

The resulting notation was called Extended ATN (*E-ATN*);the semantic attached to the interpretation of E-ATN diagrams is defined by the *Context Model* [LETHIEIS 1988].

Basically the Context Model enhances the ATN's functionalities, for example as defined in [GREEN 1986], and can be described as follows.

The nodes represent the states of dialogue between user and computer system. The *Current Context* is defined by the Current Active States Set (*CASS*) and in turn for each state by the Current Active Transitions Set (*CATS*). The following definitions will actually show that the Context Model supports multiple states and that, in turn for each state, the availability of the associated transitions may be conditional. Each node is defined by the set of emanating transitions. The transitions determine how the dialogue moves from one state to another and therefore start from one node and end to another one, possibly the starting node. Each transition is typed and labelled by an Event Rule :

- The *transition type* specifies how the CASS is updated when the given transition is traversed. Several types were defined, including :
  - the *Simple Arc*, i.e. the origin state is replaced by the destination state in the CASS;
  - the *Plus Arc*, i.e. the destination state is added to the CASS;
  - the *Minus Arc*, i.e. the destination state is added to the CASS whereas the destination states of all other transitions emanating from the same origin state are removed from the CASS;

Thanks to transition typing, multithreaded dialogues requirement (R2) is fulfilled;

- An *Event Rule* is composed of a premiss part and an action part :
  - the *premiss part* is in turn composed of a Pre-Condition, an Event and an Object :
    - the *Event*, as defined previously in (R1) may be generated by an end user or an application operation. The Context Model defines external control UIs, i.e. UIs have full control on the events, but support a mixed source of events [BETTS et al. 1987], so as "to come into actions sometimes on behalf of the user, sometimes on behalf

of the application" [STRUBBE 1985]. Thus requirement R1 is fulfilled;

- the *Object* is always associated to the Event. In case of an External event, this object is the (abstract) UI object the end user interacted with. In case of an Internal Event, the object is the (abstract) application object the application dealt with;
- the *Pre-Conditions* related to the origin state defines the CATS, that is the context in which the operations are available to the end user or the application. Thus and although the Pre-Conditions are parts of the Event-Rules labelling the transition, the Context Model precises that, for a given state, the fireability of its transitions is determined by the evaluation of the associated Pre-Conditions prior to waiting for the next generated event. No other meaning is attached to the E-ATN nodes. This technique meets context sensitive requirement (R3).

- the *action part* may be composed of Application Calls, a Post-Condition and Output Calls :

  - the *Application Calls* invoke specific application functionalities;
  - the *Post-Condition* may use the application return values in order to update the Current Context. The Context Model enables a strong link between Dialogue and Application, by allowing the combination of Application Calls, Internal Events and Post-Conditions and therefore fulfils the semantic constrained dialogue requirement (R4);
  - the *Output Calls* provide the end user with the graphical and/or textual answer to the initial operation. Neither ATN nor E-ATN support specification of Output Calls. On the other hand object oriented design is the more natural way to specify interactive UI objects [LINTON et al. 1989]. But object oriented design lacks a representation of control flow [HARTSON 1989]. Consequently in practice we merge the two approaches so as to benefit from advantages of both.

With reference to the Seeheim Model, the following parallel can be made. The selected notation for the Presentation Component is Object Oriented, whereas the selected notation for the Dialogue Control Component is based on ATNs. Concerning the application, no formal notation has been selected yet. Nevertheless, two assumptions about the application are tied to the Context Model. First, the application is assumed to be modular so as to allow the UI to call it within Application Calls. Second, the application is assumed to be able to produce internal events if required. These assumptions are general enough to be acceptable for industrial systems.

The next section discusses the integration of these techniques into a standard multiwindowing environment, namely X Window System and OSF/Motif.

5. The RAID Approach

The UI development methodology as presented in section III was devised to support large industrial projects, generally composed of several functional and/or architectural modules. The associated UI Modules can be designed in parallel. Then integration phases are required. The *RAID* System (Rapid Advanced user Interface Design) is based on this approach [LETHIEIS 1990]. At present time it is composed of two tools :

- the *Explorer* tool assisting the UI module design team;
- the *Navigator* tool assisting the UI modules integration team;

The Explorer can be used without Navigator when dealing with a simple application. Again, our general policy was to use existing high level tools. Likewise we required from UIMS tools, especially for prototyping, to run on target system so as to be sure that the prototyped UI is as close as possible to the final UI, in particular from look & feel point of view. As a consequence of the previous requirement, UIMS tools implemented on target systems enable code reuse in the final UI. Thus the RAID system was integrated on UNIX workstations on top of X Window System and OSF/Motif, that is the Xm widget set, the UIL language [DEC 1988] and compiler and the mwm Motif Window Manager.

5.1. The Explorer Tool

The Explorer is a prototyping tool. We actually need a prototyping tool for the following main reasons :

- early customer's, ergonomist's and hopefully end-user's feedback;
- incremental refinement of the UI specification.

The Explorer supports the prototyping of the dialogue and presentation part of one UI Module. The flow of control (or sequencing) within one UI Module is called *Intra UIMD* (Intra User Interface Module Dialogue).

The UI Module specifications are described in *Extended UIL* (User Interface Language [DEC 1988]) files called *MAPs*. MAPs are compiled through UIL compiler and then interpreted by an Explorer.

UIL is a specification language for describing the static UI states. Using UIL, the UI designer can specify the hierarchy of objects (widgets) composing the UI, attributes of these objects, action functions related to an event occurrence on the objects (callback routines).

The Explorer also supports some aspects of application interface : it provides a skeleton of application process source code; it defines a communication protocol between the application process and the Explorer and provides the adequate communication functions. Calls to existing application functions can be specified in the MAP script. Likewise, the application functions can send requests to the Explorer so as to change the appearance of the UI objects. Simulation functions can also be triggered cyclically thanks to a timeout mechanism.

UIL needs extensions to support the description of the Intra UIMD and the binding with the application and the other UI modules. So as to be UIL compiler compliant, extensions are implemented as predefined callback routines provided by the Explorer. These extensions support all the functionalities of the E-ATNs.

Furthermore, the Explorer supports incremental design of the UI and of the application at Explorer's run time. The MAP and/or the application process source code can be edited and recompiled. Then the UI can be reset according to the MAP and/or the application modifications.

5.2. The Navigator Tool

The Navigator is a prototyping tool to integrate the UI Modules of a complex application. Such an application typically requires multi-windowing and multi-processing functionalities.

After each UI Module is prototyped, several UI Modules can be integrated together in one Explorer, depending on the run time architecture choices. Depending on the application, several run time UI architectures are possible [BANGRATZ 1989], [ENDERLE 1985]. For instance, applications requiring several commands to be executed simultaneously may need multi-threaded dialogue with multi-programming. This is specified by defining the first arc of each corresponding dialogue thread as a "Plus" arc.

The Navigator supports the _Inter UIMD_ (Inter UI Modules Dialogue). Inter UIMD describes the flow of control (or sequencing) and communication between the UI Modules. This means that the Navigator is able to chain the execution of several Explorers.

The use of the Navigator is closely related to the Window Management policy (tiling, overlapping...). However, in X Window System environment, Window Management is carried out by a specific X client called *Window Manager*. Therefore it is the union of services offered by the Navigator and the Window Manager that will enable the complete integration of the different UI Modules (e.g. cut & paste, dialogue freezing, mouse grabbing). Likewise, one single UI Module, prototyped by one Explorer, can have several top level windows, and therefore may require some services from the Window Manager.

The Inter-UIMD described through E-ATN are stored in ASCII files called _CHARTs._ CHARTs are interpreted by the Navigator [LETHIEIS 1990].

5.3. Miscellaneous RAID Functionalities

Since the Navigator and the Explorer manage a memory image of the Extended ATN, they can provide the UI designer with very interesting additional functionalities :

- *Context Sensitive Help* : For each state of the CASS, each possible transition of the CATS can be listed in a help window.
- *Macro* : The access path to a state can be memorised as a new command so as to automatically access this state later on. This is helpful to extend the command set, to support different user's skill levels, and to prepare demonstrations.
- *Undo, Redo* : The memorization of the access path to a state, can also be used to support undo and/or redo commands, provided that it is allowed by the application.

UIs look very simple, as observed from the end-user's point of view. End users do not usually realize the complexity of implementing them, neither are they prepared to accept slow development cycles. There is a strong requirement for tools enabling major UI changes to be carried out in a very short time. One important aim of our prototyping tools was therefore to reduce the effort of UI implementation.

The RAID system addresses following four levels of hierarchy :

- Inter UIMD states created and managed by the Navigator.
- UNIX process created and managed by the Navigator.
- Top level X windows created by Explorers and managed by the Window Manager.
- Widgets created and managed by the Explorer.

Mastering these four hierarchies for the UI designer is not easy since they are very specific and yet strongly interrelated.

RAID tools help the customer, the ergonomist and the UI designer to quickly match the required functionalities with the ones provided by the underlying toolkit. Thus, the typical OO design issue of reusing the available tools (widget classes, Window Manager), or developing new ones, can be resolved for the best.

6. Conclusion

We have applied methods and techniques found in the literature with some extensions to industrial applications in currently available environments like OSF/Motif and X Window System. The methods, techniques and tools presented in this paper have been validated in industrial projects related to production planning, supervision & control in process technology and system control & data acquisition. For example, ORDO MANAGER™ provides a GUI to an existing real time short term scheduler, SYSECA's ORDO™ product. We believe this way to be a valuable means of experimentation for our approach. Our objective is now to refine these concepts and to further enhance or develop tools supporting them. New tools likely to be usable in industrial applications, are announced by software suppliers. These include Xcessory, ExoCODE, OpenWindows Developer's GUIDE, UIMX,... They could be integrated in our approach, whenever possible.

As opposed to other research projects [FOLEY 1987], [GREEN 1987], covering high level specification languages which integrate a data model, we still stick to a "classical" approach in which the UI designer starts designing the UI after the task model, application model and user characteristics are collected. We do this because, in a company, skills are distributed among different people, because existing environments provide low level tools and because at present time no widely accepted standard exists for data management in industrial applications. We therefore prefer to enhance available techniques, so that they become powerful enough for industrial UI specification, to integrate them into the overall system realization method and to bind them to existing environments. We intend to pay attention to data modelling problems so as to improve the integration of the UI design and the application design. High level specification languages could also become means to meet the requirement expressed in the introduction : they could be used first as a common communication means for all people involved in the system development and hopefully as a contractual definition of UI, upon which customers and designers can discuss and agree.

Acknowledgments

We are grateful to the Commission of the European Community and to SYSECA for their support in VITAMIN (1556) and CIDAM (2527) ESPRIT projects. We are most appreciative of Dominique Morin, SYSECA's leader for these two projects, for the valuable suggestions he made. We also thank our colleagues and partners in the VITAMIN and CIDAM projects.
Special thanks to Dr. G. Mauri, from Mannesman Kienzle, and to Dr. F. Neelamkavil, from Trinity College Dublin, for their detailed and advisable comments.

References

[ATLAS et al. 1989]
A. Atlas, A. Burton, E. Cohen, E. Connolly, K. Flowers, H. Hersh, K. Hinckley, J. Paul, R. Stich, T. Wilson, T. Yamaura : OSF User Environment Component. Decision Rationale Document, Open Software Foundation, January 1989

[AT&T 1988]
AT&T: OPEN LOOK Graphical User Interface. A Product Overview, AT&T 1988

[BANGRATZ 1989]
J. Bangratz: Study of some UI architecture problems in the X11.3 toolkit environment
CIDAM paper T5.3.1-STR-TR6#1-SEP89

[BANGRATZ et al. 1988]
J. Bangratz, E. Le Thieis, H. Moalic: Wlib library User's Guide. VITAMIN Project Deliverable (May 1988)

[BETTS et al. 1987]
B. Betts, D. Burlingame, G. Fisher, J. Foley, M. Green, D. Kasik, T. Kerr, D. Olsen, J. Thomas : Goals and Objectives for User Interface Software Computer Graphics. Volume 21. Number 2. April 1987.

[COUTAZ 1987]
J. Coutaz: The Construction of User Interfaces and the Object Paradigm. European Conference on Object-Oriented Programming. June 15-17 1987 Paris, France (organized by AFCET.Special issue of BIGRE No 54 p135-144

[DEC 1988]
Digital Equipment Corporation: ULTRIX Worksystem Software, Version 2.0 (DECwindows, XUI, UIL...). 1988.

[ENDERLE 1985]
G. Enderle: Report on the Interface of the UIMS to the Application. Proceedings of the Workshop on UIMS held in Seeheim, FRG, November 1-3 1983.Edited by Gunther E. Pfaff, Springer-Verlag, 1985

[FOLEY 1987]
J. Foley: Transformation on a Formal Specification of User-Computer Interfaces Computer Graphics. Volume 21. Number 2. April 1987.

[FOLEY 1989]
J. Foley: Summer School on User Interfaces. Tampere, Finland 1989

[GREEN 1985a]
M. Green: Report on Dialogue Specification Tools. Proceedings of the Workshop on UIMS held in Seeheim, FRG, November 1-3 1983.Edited by Gunther E. Pfaff, Springer-Verlag, 1985

[GREEN 1985b]
M. Green: Design Notations and User Interface Management System. Proceedings of the Workshop on UIMS held in Seeheim, FRG, November 1-3 1983. Edited by Gunther E. Pfaff, Springer-Verlag, 1985

[GREEN 1986]
M. Green: A Survey of Three Dialogue Models.
ACM Transactions on Graphics, Vol. 5, No3, July 1986

[GREEN 1987]
M. Green: Directions for User Interface Management Systems Research.
Computer Graphics. Volume 21. Number 2. April 1987.

[HARTSON 1989]
R. Hartson: User-Interface Management Control and Communication.
IEEE Software January 1989

[LETHIEIS 1988]
E. Le Thieis: Dialogue Control (From Specification to Implementation).
VITAMIN project internal document WD(SBt2)/STR13/V2.January 1988

[LETHIEIS 1990]
E. Le Thieis: RAID (Rapid Advanced user Interface Design):
Overview & Terminology Definition.
CIDAM project document T5.1.2- STR- TR7#2- JAN90

[LINTON et al. 1989]
M. A. Linton, J. M. Vlissides, P. R. Calder: Composing User Interfaces with InterViews. IEEE Software February 1989

[MACCORMACK 1988]
J. McCormack, P. Asente: Using the X Toolkit or How to Write a Widget Summer USENIX '88

[MORIN & MAURI 1988]
D. Morin, G.A. Mauri : VITAMIN Toolkit: a UIMS for CIM Applications.
Esprit Conference 1988

[MORIN et al. 1989]
D. Morin: VITAMIN Final Report October 1989.

[MORIN et al. 1990]
D. Morin, J. Bangratz, E. Le Thieis, F. Mauclin, S. Mondie: Ideal Scenario for User Interface Design.CIDAM internal document

[MYERS 1989]
B. A. Myers: User-Interface Tools: Introduction and Survey.
IEEE Software January 1989

[NEELAMKAVIL 1989]
Dr. F. Neelamkavil: CIDAM. ESPRIT Conference 1989

[PRIME 1989]
M. Prime: User Interface Management Systems - A Current Product Review.Eurographics '89, Hamburg, Germany

[SCHEIFLER 1986]
R.W. Scheifler, J. Gettys: The X Window System.
ACM Transactions on Graphics, Vol. 63, 1986

[STRUBBE 1985]
H.J. Strubbe: Report on Role, Model, Structure and Construction of a UIMS.
Proceedings of the Workshop on UIMS held in Seeheim, FRG,
November 1-3 1983 edited by Gunther E. Pfaff, Springer-Verlag, 1985

Authors' Address

Post: Syseca, 315 bureaux de la Colline, 92213 St Cloud Cedex, France
Tel.: 33-1-49-11-74-40 or 33-1-60-79-81-93
Fax: 33-1-47-71-16-00
E-mail: bangratz@syseca.uucp

Chapter 19

The Growth of a MOSAIC

Dag Svanæs and Asbjørn Thomassen

Abstract

MOSAIC is an object oriented UIMS and design environment for MS-DOS PCs. It has been in use for about five years, mostly in Scandinavia. In this paper we try to sum up the user feedback and draw some conclusions. We found that most PASCAL/C programmers initially had great problems seeing a design as a collection of interacting objects. It made them feel less "in control". We consequently recommend to teach the programmers object oriented design before letting them implement large systems. The non-programmers often used the MOSAIC user interface editor to its limits, and in ways unintended by the tool designers. An easy-to-use, closed and consistent world of simple building blocks seems to give user interface designers the necessary security to be able to be creative and productive.

1. Introduction

User Interface Management Systems have already been around for about 10 years, but few empirical studies are available on their use. The available literature is mostly focused on the technical aspects of the systems and on the *shoulds* and *musts* of user interface design [6,7]. These issues are of course important, but to be able to design good second generation UIMS we need a sound empirical foundation concerning todays UIMS users. What is going on in the design process and how is it affected by the tools?

It is tempting to use a Darwinian metaphor to describe the evolution of artifacts. Every change can be fully explained by the mechanisms of mutation and selection. The software mutations occur in the heads of creative programmers and the selections are done by the market. Darwin´s contemporary Lamarc had a different, but probably wrong, view on evolution. He claimed that the giraffes gave birth to offsprings with longer necks because the parents had to stretch their necks. The difference lies in the unit of selection. Nature select individuals, not details. Empirical field studies and prototypes allow software designers to make "unnatural" shortcuts directly from the market place back to the design process. Design details thus become the unit of selection and not total systems. The tighter we make the loop of software evolution, the more monster artifacts can be avoided. These "Lamarcian tricks" change the mechanisms of software evolution and Darwin does no longer fully apply.

We present in this paper a UIMS case study, the MOSAIC project. There is no single revolutionary technical breakthrough in the MOSAIC design tool, but the complexity of the system and the number of users hopefully make it worthwhile to sum up our experiences.

We first present the background of the MOSAIC project. This is followed by a technical description. We thereafter sum up the user feedback and draw some possible conclusions. The paper ends with some ideas for the next version of MOSAIC.

2. Background

In 1984 the Norwegian Ministry of Education initiated a programme for the introduction of computers in the school system [1]. The Ministry initiated software design courses and workshops for ordinary teachers. American and Canadian lecturers were invited. They brought with them the "open" software approach of SMALLTALK-80 and the Apple Macintosh. The teachers consequently came up with highly interactive designs making heavy use of the graphics capacities of the hardware. As the target machines were not Macintoshes, there emerged a need for a powerful toolbox, a good prototyping tool and a user friendly design environment. The MOSAIC project [9,10,13] was initiated to help solve these problems.

The resulting design tool has been used in teacher courses and by software design groups (about 1000 user). By 1987 we had given teacher courses all over Scandinavia and felt that very few new design ideas came up. As an experiment we spent one week with 43 ordinary 9th grade (14-15 years old) students, letting them do educational software design. They mastered the tools and methods after two days and were surprisingly creative [8].

New versions of MOSAIC have been produced, but the basic idea and structure of the tool has been unchanged. At present (spring 1990) a MS-WINDOWS 3.0 version is being released and a totally new Display PostScript version is being designed. To date about 10 man-year has been invested in the MOSAIC project.

3. Technical Details

The MOSAIC system consists of an interactive user-interface editor and a graphics toolbox/interpreter. The software designer can build and test his user interface without doing any programming. User-interface descriptions made with the editor can be interpreted by the toolbox. Connection to application-specific PASCAL/C code is made easy. MOSAIC is strongly inspired by SMALLTALK [2,4]. It runs on any IBM PC in CGA, EGA, VGA or Hercules mode.

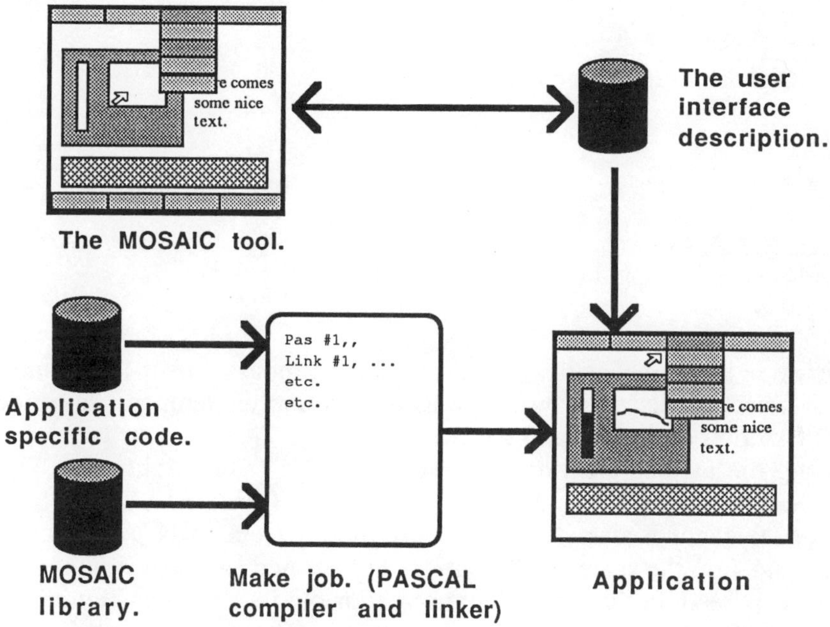

Figure 1. MOSAIC

A MOSAIC user interface description consists of a number of hierarchically ordered graphic objects. The object classes include screens, menus, boxes, texts, icons and rasters. The object hierarchy reflects the layout of the objects. The frame of an object is always inside the frame of its super-object. When objects are created, changed or deleted in the editor, the hierarchy is updated automatically. Objects can be popup (have their "patch property" on). When an object is shown, all its non-popup sub-objects are shown automatically. When a popup object is shown, its background ("shadow") is saved for later use by screen refresh operations.

Every object can have a set of user-event handles, each with a corresponding sequence of actions. The user events include keyboard events and mouse events.

The six mouse-related events with corresponding semantics are:

- Click in X ⇔
  ((Mouse is in X) and (Button is pressed) and (Button was not pressed))
  or
  ((Mouse is in X) and (Button is pressed) and (Mouse was not in X)).

- Up in X ⇔
  (Mouse is in X) and (Button was pressed) and (Button is not pressed).

- Enter X ⇔
  (Mouse is in X) and (Mouse was not in X).

- Leave X ⇔
  (Mouse is not in X) and (Mouse was in X).

- Is in X ⇔
  (Mouse is in X).

- Is down in X ⇔
  (Mouse is in X) and (Button is pressed).

"Mouse is in X" means that the hotspot of the mouse cursor is within the frame of object X. "Is" and "was" are used to define the temporal semantics of the interaction (at times **t** and **t-Δt**).

Among the available actions are "show", "hide", "highlight" and "send message". The action sequences may include IF-THEN-ELSE structures. When a user event is detected by the run-time system, it is passed to the topmost object on the screen. If no actions are defined for this event and this object, it is passed up the object hierarchy. For obvious reasons "Enter" and "Leave" events are not passed up the hierarchy. The topmost object in every MOSAIC design is a design object. All non-processed events end up in this non-visible object.

Each time a "send message" is executed by the MOSAIC library in the final application, the control is transferred to a corresponding application specific PASCAL/C procedure. When testing a user interface in the MOSAIC editor, the execution of a "send message" action is simulated. A user interface can thus be designed and tested before its "kernel" software is written.

A copy facility is included in the editor and as a toolbox function. When an object is copied, copies are also made of all its sub-objects with corresponding handles/actions. Actions referring to objects below the copied object in the hierarchy are renumbered to make complex objects functionally equivalent to their originals. The copy facility is MOSAIC´s substitute for a class concept. It is simpler in use, but we can not do simultaneous changes to whole classes of objects as in SMALLTALK-80.

The MOSAIC editor is itself an ordinary MOSAIC design, allowing advanced user groups to change the behaviour of the editor to suit their specific needs.

The very first version of MOSAIC emerged during a one week workshop in 1985. It was purely a prototype and was written in an early PROLOG version Svanæs had just ported to an 16 bit "school micro". It is interesting to note that this 3 day (and night) PROLOG prototype inspired 5-10 man years of programming and a lot of blood, sweat and tears during the next 5 years.

The current implementation consists of some 30.000 lines of TURBO PASCAL 4.0. Libraries with corresponding MOSAIC messages have been developed for Video Disc Control, Dynamic Simulation (STELLA), Database Management and Speech.

4. MOSAIC in Use

Teachers with no prior programming background normally learn to master MOSAIC in one to two days. Prior experience with MacDraw, SuperPaint or equivalent normally lead to a decreased learning time. The design of "open" user friendly software has been strongly emphasised during the teacher courses.

During its first two years (1985-86), MOSAIC was mainly used as a prototyping tool by teachers and designers (non-programmers). The resulting prototypes were analysed by programmers and reprogrammed from scratch. The reason for this was mainly that the target machines did not allow room for an (at that time) expensive 40 KByte MOSAIC library.

The programmers allocated to the projects also felt a certain discomfort not being "in control" of the programs. Being reduced to just filling in the PASCAL code for complex "methods" was very unsatisfactory for most of them. We made the error of not giving enough attention to the problems most PASCAL/C programmers have in adjusting to the object oriented way of thinking. This was also found by [6]: *"Software developers typically stress improved UIMS performance and more direct mechanisms for applications to manipulate the user interface"*. We also made the error of not making the source code of the toolbox "public domain". A well documented, totally open toolbox would probably have made the programmers feel much more at home with the system.

As time passed by and new versions were made available for larger PCs, more of the projects were taken all the way to products using MOSAIC. It has so far been used in prototyping some 1000 designs of which a little less than 100 have survived as products of some sort. A lot of the designs were very much larger than what MOSAIC had originally been designed to deal with. It seems to be an universal law that "every tool will be used in ways different from what was intended, and often such that all available resources will be exhausted". The current limit of 2000 objects seems to be accepted by most designers as sufficient to express most of their ideas.

The feedback from most users seems to indicate that MOSAIC has been especially useful in group work to clarify the design ideas. Most designers though make the initial error of trying to do "stream of consciousness" design in MOSAIC without having made sketches on paper. We also found that most non-programmers had problems structuring large designs on their own. It seems that the idea of building up a design graphically from a set of simple building blocks is very powerful. The event/action way of specifying interaction also seems to be close to the intuitive way of describing interaction.

It was interesting to observe how 15 years old students with no prior programming background used the MOSAIC editor. They accepted it as the most natural thing and used it to try out a lot of exiting design ideas. In contrast to most other computer-related activities we found no gender differences. We suspected that the aesthetic aspects of user interface design might be important to explain this. The need to explain lack of gender differences shows our male prejudges in these matters. As no biological differences have been found, it is of course gender differences that need to be explained, not the other way around.

5. Open Questions

We made the choice of not extending the MOSAIC actions towards a full programming language. This decision was based on the assumption that the system would then have been too complex for the content domain designers and too simple and limiting for the programmers. We consequently ended up with a very simple set of actions and an easy-to-use connection to PASCAL/C. Was this decision correct? How is HyperCard [3] used? Who is doing the HyperTalk programming? Does *"if it is three then put one into it"* make programming more easy?

We feel a need to be able to let objects be "reflections" of other objects (prototype objects). A "reflection" will in contrast to a copy keep track of its "original". The changes made to the original will be "reflected" in the "reflections". What is the experience with interactive systems using dynamic binding? Are there any other solutions to the problem of making a design tool both very simple and very flexible without introducing the class concept.

Some of the designs being prototyped are themselves tools. One good example is a graphic adventure game generator. These designs often work on complex data structures, and we feel a strong need for good visual metaphors for these data constructors (arrays, dictionaries etc.). MOSAIC and other systems have given the basic classes of SMALLTALK-80 a visual "gestalt", but no systems have to our knowledge tried to visualise the other built-in classes of SMALLTALK-80.

We have found the Model-View-Controller paradigm very useful as a design guideline. We have to admit that we actually reinvented the MVC idea when we tried to make some dynamic-modelling extensions to MOSAIC [10,11]. This was partly due to the lack of easy-to-understand literature on

MVC a couple of years ago and partly due to our ignorance. We find it significant that most of our attempts at extending MOSAIC have ended up in ideas that are already present in SMALLTALK-80 or ThingLab. It seems to us that SMALLTALK-80 (and SIMULA) was such an immense breakthrough that the use of the term paradigm in Thomas Kuhn´s sense actually can be justified. Its impact has been enormous, but it is being exhausted. Where do we find the inspiration for the 90s. What will be to the 90s what SMALLTALK-80 was to the 80s?

References

1. Bork A., Crapper S.A., Hebenstreit J.: The introduction of computers in schools: The Norwegian experience. OECD, Paris, 1987.
2. Goldberg A.: SMALLTALK-80. Addison-Wesley. Menlo Park, Cal., 1984.
3. Goodman D.: The complete HyperCard Handbook. Bantam Books, New York, 1987.
4. Kay A., Goldberg A.: Personal Dynamic Media. Computer, March 1977:10; 31-41.
5. Minken, I., Stenseth, B., Vavik, L.: Pedagogisk Programvare. Ultimagruppen, Norway, 1987.
6. Manheimer J.M., Burnett R.C., Wallers J.A.: A case study of user interface management system development and application. CHI´89 Proceedings. ACM Press, 1989.
7. Singh G., Green M.: A high-level user interface management system. CHI´89 Proceedings. ACM Press, 1989.
8. Stenseth B., Minken I, Tingstad D., Svanæs D.: Rapport fra Selbu kurset. Report from Norwegian Ministry of Edudcation, Oslo 1988.
9. Svanæs, D.: Verktøyutvikling i Datasekretariatet, MOSAIKK. Datatid, 1986.
10. Svanæs, D.: MOSAIC user´s guide. K.U.D. Datasekretariatet/ SimSim 1988.
11. Svanæs D., Cyvin J.: The use of system dynamics in ecology education. (in Norwegian) Report from NAVF, Oslo 1989.
12. Svanæs D.: The confessions of a tool maker. (in Norw.) Scandinavian Educational Software Conference NTH, Norway 1989.
13. Svanæs D.: Simulation Models + User Interfaces = Interactive Applications. To appear in: Computers and Education, An International Journal, Pergamon Press, 1990 .

[illegible]

References

[illegible]

Chapter 20

A Framework for Integrating UIMS and User Task Models in the Design of User Interfaces

Peter Johnson, Kieron Drake and Stephanie Wilson

Abstract

This paper describes work towards the development of a framework for relating User Interface Management System (UIMS) architectural models and User Task Models (UTMs). The aim of the framework is to enable us to position features of user interface models and features of user task models in a common space. As a preliminary to the framework, we review recent work in both fields and identify the elements of user tasks and user interfaces (as reflected by UIMS architectures). We then propose an initial version of a framework to integrate the two forms of model.

1. Introduction

The development of user interfaces requires input from both software engineering and human factors methods. Much work has been done to develop software engineering methodologies and tools and human factors methods for user interface design, for example (van Harmelen and Wilson 1987) and (Johnson and Johnson 1990a). However, (Johnson and Johnson 1990b) amongst others have identified that interface designers require tools and methods that may be used in conjunction with each other. Tools and methods that are not integrated are often unused (Rossen et al. 1988).

This paper describes a framework we are developing to integrate tools and methods for use in user interface design. We are interested in integrating User Interface Management System (UIMS) architectural models and User Task Models (UTMs). Our eventual goal is the development of a new generation of user interface design tools. These tools will support models of both the components of the user interface, as embodied in a UIMS architecture, and components of the user interaction, as embodied in a UTM, and will encourage development of such models with reference to each other.

In contrast to this unified view of user interface design, current user interface design environments provide some support for the design and development of the user interface but do not cater in any way for the design and development of the user interaction. User interaction design involves designing and developing a model of the user task (amongst other things). A user task model identifies the purposes and structure of any interaction a user might be expected to engage in.

The two classes of models, UIMS and UTM, serve different purposes in the development of a user interface and have different forms. UIMS architectural models are of the designed interface and are there to help the designer reason about the properties of the design and to ease the process of implementation. In contrast, models of users and tasks (e.g. Waddington and Johnson 1989a,b) are used to understand the properties of the user and the tasks that are performed in a given domain. Because of these differences of purpose and form, the two classes of models are not well integrated and are therefore not used to their fullest extent in the design of user interfaces. The consequences of this are that user interfaces are often sub-optimum in terms of their performance and acceptability with respect to the users and their tasks, and fail to exploit the available technology in an efficient manner. We argue that a new generation of design tools supporting both UIMS models and UTMs should help address these deficiencies.

Our framework is developed from an existing classification of UIMSs (Cook et al. 1988) and a classification of task models (Johnson 1987). Both of these classification schemes were developed as a result of the authors' experiences in designing and implementing user interfaces to support a range of tasks in a number of domains. The basis for this current framework is discussed with reference to these earlier experiences. The scope of this framework is broad enough to cover existing UIMS architectures and to be applicable to a defined range of domains and a wide range of tasks.

2. User Interface Management Systems

The GIIT (Thomas and Hamlin 1983) and Seeheim (Pfaff 1985) workshops proposed models for the architecture of interactive systems whereby the user interface software of the run-time system would be separate from the application software. These models included a software component known as a "User Interface Management System" (UIMS) which was responsible for managing the interaction between a user and an application. An interface designer used the tools of the UIMS design environment to create a description of the user interface in some suitable notation. This description covered both presentation and dialogue control aspects of the interface. The description was then submitted to the run-time part of the UIMS which mediated the interaction between user and application accordingly. The arguments in favour of this scheme were such things as consistency of interfaces, ability to prototype rapidly, hardware independence for applications, etc.

More recently, there has been a proliferation of different environments providing support for user interface design and management, based on a variety of architectures. This has given rise to the question of what is meant by the term UIMS? (Myers 1989) offers a useful categorisation of these systems: he divides them into user-interface toolkits and user-interface development systems (UIDSs). Toolkits provide libraries of interaction techniques for the interface designer but offer little support for sequencing or dialogue control, whereas UIDSs are integrated sets of tools for the creation and management of user interfaces. UIDSs help the interface designer to combine and sequence interaction techniques: they handle all aspects of the user interface. Myers uses the term UIDS rather than UIMS because he views the system as providing design support as well as the run-time management functions of the early UIMSs. Within the class of systems that he calls UIDSs, Myers makes further subdivisions:

- Language based — the designer describes the user interface in a special language.
- Graphical specification — visual programming techniques are used to create the interface.
- Automatic generation — the UIDS generates an interface automatically from a specification of the semantics of the system.

An alternative viewpoint is that the term UIMS should encompass the design environment as well as the run-time environment. We follow this school of thought for the purposes of this paper.

In this section we review some of the models that have been proposed for the architecture of a UIMS and look at recent examples of UIMS technology.

2.1 UIMS Architectures

The Seeheim model of UIMS architecture is given in Figure 1. It is based on the concept of separability of the user interface and the functionality of an interactive system. A UIMS is considered to be comprised of three major components: a presentation component, a dialogue control component and an application interface component. These components communicate via tokens. This is sometimes referred to as the "linguistic model" of a UIMS. Drawing on traditional programming language and compiler terminology, the presentation component is the lexical layer of a linguistic model, the dialogue control represents the syntactic level, and the application is considered to embody the semantics of the system.

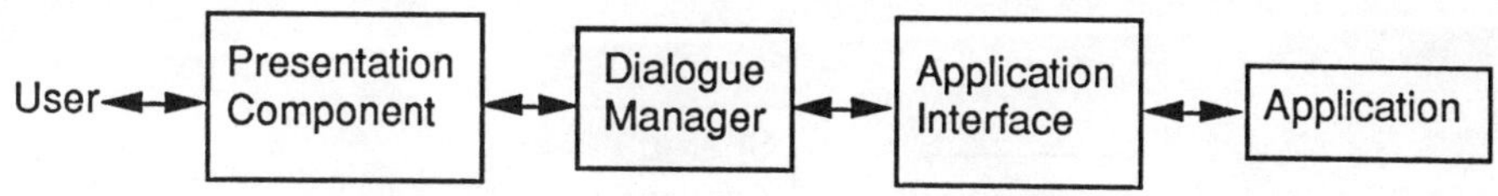

Figure 1: The Seeheim Model

Many early UIMSs were based on this model, for example Viz (van Harmelen and Wilson 1987), RAPID (Wasserman and Shewmake 1982). Such UIMSs differ in the nature of their dialogue control language (BNF, transition diagrams, event languages, etc), their model of control (internal, external, or mixed), and their ability to handle multiple threads of interaction.

The appeal of such a model lies in the complete separation of interface from application. However, there are drawbacks with this arrangement which provides for only a narrow channel of communication between UIMS and application. Most notably, the goal of separability conflicts with the need to support semantic feedback as Dance (Dance et al. 1987) and others have indicated. Sophisticated direct manipulation interfaces must provide the user with fine-grain semantic feedback (Hudson 1987).

Recently developed UIMSs which have attempted to address the semantic feedback problem are not easily represented by the Seeheim model. A number of alternatives have been proposed. (Dance et al. 1987) discuss the beginnings of a model which provides for tighter coupling of the application and the dialogue manager through what they term the "Semantic Support Component".

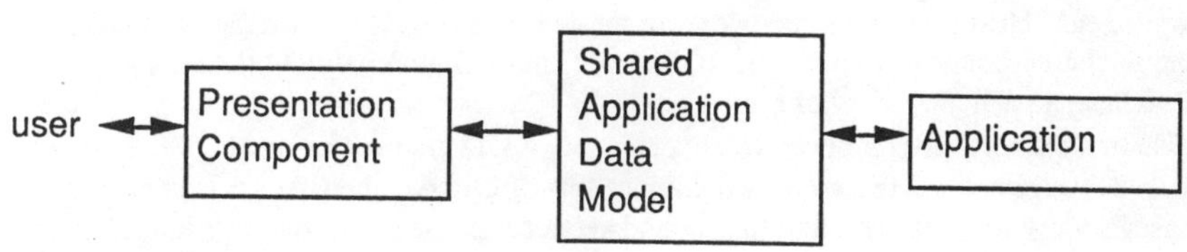

Figure 2: Hudson's Model

Hudson (Hudson 1987) is particularly concerned with architectures for supporting direct manipulation interfaces (Schneiderman 1983). He argues that syntactic concepts should be minimised and replaced by more physical actions such as pointing and dragging. For this reason, he presents an architecture without any explicit dialogue control component. The application interface component is replaced by the Shared Application Data Model (Figure 2). This component consists of a set of shared data objects. These are active objects rather than passive data: they react to changes in ways that reflect the semantics of the application, facilitating fine-grained semantic feedback.

(Cook et al. 1988) suggest that Hudson's model is rather restrictive in limiting the shared data to "active values". They propose that it should consist of objects (in the object-oriented sense) instead (Figure 3). This model gives better encapsulation and abstraction and represents more of the existing UIMS architectures successfully.

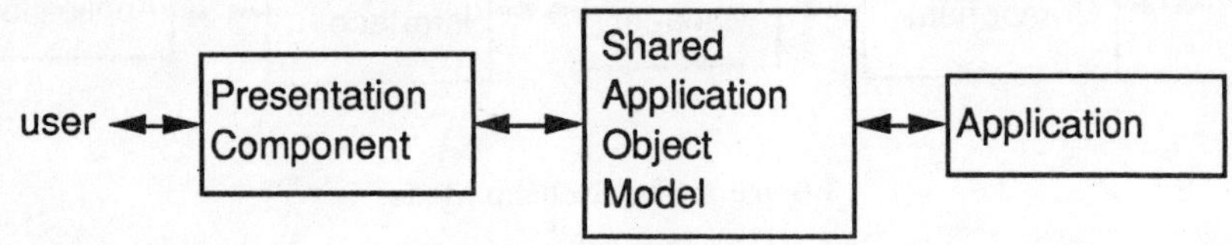

Figure 3: Modified Version of Hudson's Model

2.2 Examples of Recent UIMS Work

Models of software or abstractions of software designs are used to model such things as the presentation design, the dialogue design and the application functionality. Architectural models for UIMSs have tried to compartmentalise these features as separate elements that can be developed and designed independently. The problem these models then try to solve is how to provide appropriate links or "hooks" between the various components. This is where the models tend to break down: there is not a clean separation between the components and the links become complex.

We prefer to think of models such as the Seeheim one not as constraining architectures for design and development, but as ways of viewing the various functional attributes of a system. We regard the presentation, dialogue and application functionality as different functional views of the complete interactive software system. By taking a functional view, we mean to say that there is not necessarily any specific component or module of the software that is the presentation or the dialogue, etc. However, when considering the features of UIMSs, we can still talk of the presentation characteristics, the dialogue, or the application functionality of the system whenever we want to have a particular view of it.

There are many criteria upon which a critique of UIMSs may be based. For example, (Betts et al. 1987) suggest that there are two distinct sets of criteria: the first set is concerned with the end user's view of the UIMS and the second set is concerned with the user interface designer's view of a UIMS.

PAC

PAC (Coutaz 1987) falls into Myers' category of language-based UIMSs: it is based on the object-oriented paradigm. The PAC model of an interactive system structures it into three parts:

presentation, abstraction and *control.* These basic divisions are similar to those of the Seeheim model. The presentation displays information to the user and receives input from the user, the abstraction contains application functionality and the control maintains consistency between the presentation and the abstraction. The presentation is itself composed of a set of PACs (called interactors) each of which may be built up from a further set of PACs. Thus, the whole of an interactive application may be built up recursively as a set of PAC objects. This framework gives pluggable interactors which can provide semantic feedback because they can contain a semantic component in the form of an abstraction. PAC provides the user with the ability to switch between interactions: the control part of each PAC object retains the state of the interaction at a local level to facilitate this. This gives some degree of multi-threading of interactions, though not full concurrency as PAC does not support objects as separate processes. PAC has an external model of control with some hooks for mixed control. Systems which are structured in this manner present the designer with the problem of how to partition the system into its various components. It is not obvious how to structure a design in terms of PACs. Extra support is required to facilitate design and programming.

Tube

Tube (Hill and Herrmann 1989) is similar to PAC in that it is based on an object-oriented paradigm and also uses the notion of building user interfaces by composing objects. A Tube interactive system consists of an application and a user interface constructed from User Interface Objects (UIOs). Each UIO contains both display (presentation) and behaviour (dialogue). The behaviours of objects are described in a rule-based language which is a variation of the Event-Response-Language (ERL) designed for the Sassafras UIMS (Hill 1986). All objects are implemented as very light weight processes, providing concurrency (or multi-threading). They communicate via an asynchronous message passing mechanism based on the Local Event Broadcast Mechanism (LEBM) from Sassafras. At present, the UIOs are constrained to be composed in a tree-structured fashion and may communicate only with their neighbours. Finally, Tube incorporates an attribute system: objects may have associated attributes. The attributes can be used to specify relationships between objects and to describe the display properties of objects. The system automatically maintains any such constraints. It is possible to incorporate some of the semantics of the application in the user interface via the attribute scheme — simplifying the problem of semantic feedback. Alternatively, semantics may be included in each UIO by writing methods in the underlying object-oriented language (Common Loops).

IDL

Some recent work has focussed on describing an interactive system at a higher level of abstraction than is supported by traditional UIMSs. These are the systems that Myers terms "UIDSs involving automatic creation". The aim is to create an interface automatically from a specification of the semantics of the system. (Foley 1987; Foley et al. 1989) use the idea of specifying the user interface at the semantic and conceptual level. At the heart of their User-Interface Design Environment (UIDE) is a knowledge base containing the specification written in terms of objects, actions, relations, attributes, and pre- and post- conditions associated with the actions. They have built an interactive system using a frame-based expert system shell to help the designer create the specification for an intended interface. The specification does not describe the syntactic or lexical aspects of the user interface so, for example, a number of user interfaces with different dialogue structures may be created to meet any given specification. Having constructed a formal specification of this sort, it is possible to check it for completeness and consistency, to evaluate the interface, to transform it into functionally equivalent specifications each of which has a slightly different user interface, and to prototype it using an appropriate UIMS. Foley et al. include a "Simple UIMS" (SUIMS) in their system for prototyping purposes.

2.3 Implications for Future Work

UIMS research has tended to focus on architectures and methodologies for implementing user interfaces and existing systems support only a limited part of the complete interface design process. This is a reflection of one of the original goals of UIMS research: that of assisting a designer who has formulated a design to produce a prototype or working system. As (Rhyne et al. 1987) point out, UIMSs fail to support other phases of design such as requirements analysis, conceptual design, or evaluation.

Work such as that of (Foley et al. 1989) is of interest as it signals a move away from concerns with the architecture of run-time systems towards supporting user interface design at a higher level of abstraction. In their system the designer produces an abstract specification of the user interface. However, there is no notion of including a model of the user or the user's tasks in the specification and no way of ascertaining whether the specified interface meets the requirements of the users' tasks.

In our view, a major deficiency of existing UIMSs is that there is no provision for ensuring that the delivered system embodies any task or requirements analysis that may have been carried out. We propose a framework for integrating UIMS models and UTMs and hope to develop an interface design environment that will offer more comprehensive support for the complete process of user interface design.

Apart from any limitations arising from their architecture, builders of UIMSs have discovered that their systems are not easy to use. The language based nature of many UIMSs is largely oriented towards programmers rather than human factors experts and the tools or environments available to support the design process are inadequate. These issues must also be addressed by a new generation of interface design tools.

2.4 A Characterisation of UIMSs

A problem with models such as Hudson's (Figure 2) or Cook et al.'s (Figure 3) is that they are not much use for predicting behaviour nor for deciding which portions of the application semantics need to be known by the UIMS components. The model is too general and does not allow for useful characterisation of UIMSs. To mitigate this problem, (Cook et al. 1988) propose a framework for characterising UIMSs that may be represented by the model of Figure 3.

The framework characterises UIMSs in terms of two criteria: *vocabulary* and *connectivity*. The vocabulary refers to the set of messages that given objects need to understand. Such messages may originate from within the object pool or external to it. The connectivity refers to which objects can send/receive messages to/from other objects within the pool and to/from the presentation component and the application. Particular paradigms may impose constraints upon the connectivity, for example MVC (Krasner and Pope 1984), PAC (Coutaz 1987). As the two criteria are independent, a given UIMS may be characterised in these terms as a point in 2D space. Figure 4 gives an overview of this characterisation for a number of UIMSs; (Cook et al. 1988) give a justification and more details of this characterisation.

(Cook et al. 1988) also make a tentative attempt to correlate regions within this 2D space with attributes such as flexibility, ease of construction, etc., as shown in Figure 5. This is of interest as it suggests the applicability of a given UIMS to a particular task.

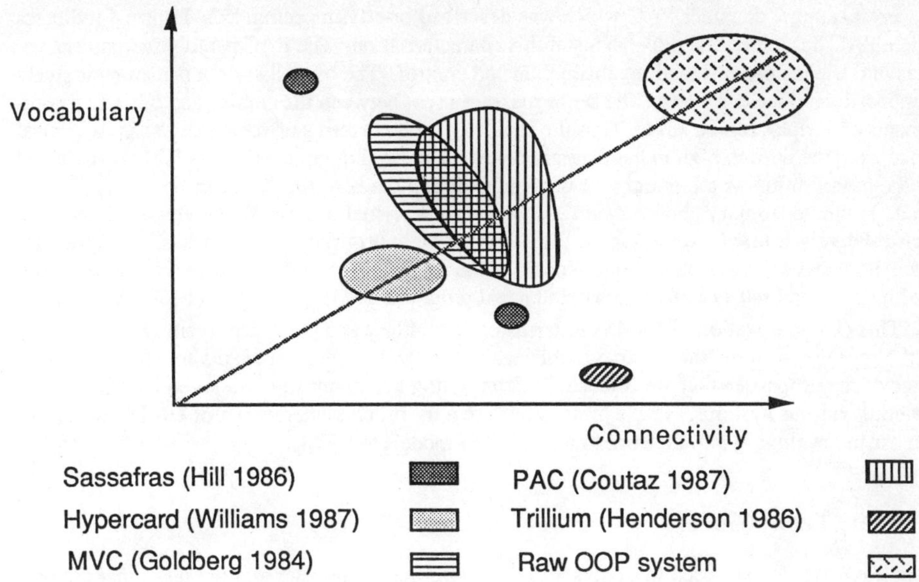

Figure 4: UIMS Characterisations

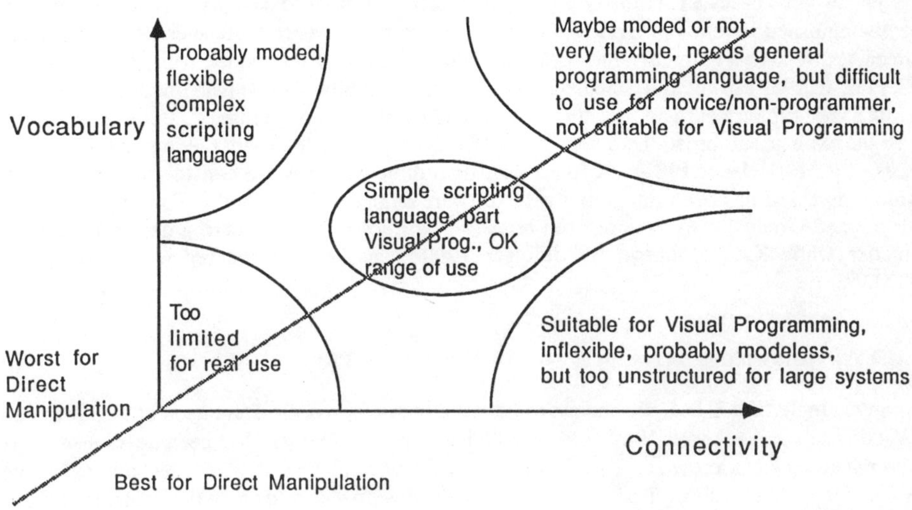

Figure 5: Assignment of Attributes to Regions of the Framework

For example, consider PAC which was described briefly in section 2.2. Figure 4 indicates where PAC lies within the dimensions of this characterisation. The PAC paradigm organises objects into triplets of presentation, abstraction and control. The overall system is then recursively composed from these triplets. The set of messages sent between the control and other two components of a triplet can be large. Thus the characterisation in terms of vocabulary spans a vertical range from medium to high in the diagram below. The level of connectivity is fairly constrained by the organisation as a hierarchy of triplets, although the resulting tree can be as large as desired. If the vocabulary chosen is at the low end, then visual programming techniques — with their relatively limited expressive power — might be appropriate. Systems built this way are often modeless and restricted to one screen. If the maximum expressive power is required, then the limits on the final system are fewer but a real programming language is probably required.

This characterisation of UIMSs in terms of vocabulary and connectivity allows more to be said about the systems than was possible with Hudson's model. It seems to capture at least some of the properties that are relevant in determining the suitability of a given UIMS for constructing various systems. These dimensions are a useful characterisation of UIMSs which we can use in developing a framework to relate UIMS models to UTMs.

3. User Task Models

User Task Models are used to understand the properties of the user and the tasks that are performed in a given domain. The models can be of the current properties of users and tasks, and provide a basis for identifying the requirements of the design. They can also be used to reflect the consequences of the design on the users and tasks, by identifying new or changed tasks and where user training is appropriate.

Current work on UTMs can be categorised according to a number of dimensions. First, we can consider whether the UTM provides an evaluation or a requirement definition input to the design (in some cases a UTM may provide both forms of input to design). Second, UTMs can be distinguished in terms of their formality, in that some UTMs (e.g. Reisner 1981; Payne and Green 1986) have a defined syntax describing the structure of the model, while others such as (Card et al. 1983) have no defined syntax. A third distinction can be made between UTMs in terms of the explicitness and breadth of psychological theory they embrace. For example, contrast the explicit and broad theoretical basis of ICS (Barnard 1987) with the implicit theoretical basis of TAL (Reisner 1981). A fourth and final dimension we can consider is the extent to which the UTM has been integrated with software engineering methods. For example, TAG (Payne and Green 1986) has not been related to any software engineering design method or practice while KAT (Johnson and Johnson 1990b) has been considered in the context of SSADM.

3.1 Task Knowledge Structures — An Example UTM

As an example of a UTM, we choose to describe previous work by (Johnson et al. 1988) and (Waddington and Johnson 1989a,b) in which a theory of user tasks has been developed. The theoretical model is known as Task Knowledge Structures (TKS). Analysis techniques known as Knowledge Analysis of Tasks (KAT) have been developed to identify the contents of these TKSs. TKS theory is task independent and applicable to all domains. It is a theory based on psychological principles of human knowledge and problem solving.

TKS theory assumes that people represent their knowledge about a task in terms of a universal set of structures. A TKS is comprised of the following elements: a goal structure which models the user's goals and sub-goals, and is the product of any planning activity that the user has to engage in; a procedure set which defines the executable actions and their control structures which satisfy each sub-goal; an object (or taxonomic) substructure which identifies the objects, their class membership, their properties and attributes and their relations to other objects and actions.

More recently, we have been able to show that it is possible to construct a formal mapping between a UTM and a formal specification of an interactive software system (Gikas et al. in press). This work uses formal notations to specify TKSs in a precise and complete way. We use a propositional temporal logic to formalise the relationship between goals and subgoals and between these and procedures. We also use a modal action logic to define the semantics of procedures in terms of the objects that they perform computations on and to define the pre- and post-conditions that form the relations between procedures. Finally, we have used an equational specification language to define objects.

In terms of the dimensions mentioned in the previous section, KAT is characterised as having requirements and evaluation input, little formality, a well developed psychological theory, and some integration with a top-down design method. This UTM has been applied to modelling user tasks in the context of user interface design and is intended to provide an input to system design. The theory has been mapped onto the design of interfaces by showing how elements of the UTM can be used to predict good and bad features of design (Waddington and Johnson 1989a,b) and by showing how design recommendations can arise from a UTM (Johnson and Johnson 1990a; Johnson and Nicolosi 1990).

4. A Framework for Integrating UIMSs and UTMs

The aim of the framework is to enable us to position features of UIMSs models and features of UTMs in a common space. This will enable us to relate and compare different UIMSs and UTMs, such that a particular UIMS when paired with an appropriate UTM can be used to predict some aspect(s) of user task performance on a particular interactive software system, and this performance can be related to particular features of the interactive software system through the UIMS. For example, we might expect to be able to take a software system that has been designed for use in a particular domain and characterise features of its design in terms of a given UIMS model and its usability in terms of a particular UTM. The two models would be expressed in a common language and each would be related to enable the designer to identify what usability performance on given tasks would be expected and what particular features of the design were likely to have given rise to that performance prediction. Thus the framework could be used to evaluate designs for their usability. An alternative scenario we would envisage is that the designer could use the framework to choose between alternative designs. For example, it should be possible for a designer to make predictions about the effects on usability of changing one aspect of the design while holding others constant.

Leading on from this, a second purpose of the framework is to enable us to develop a single, integrated user interface design environment involving modelling techniques derived from mappings between UIMS and UTM.

4.2 A Framework for Integrating UIMS Models and UTMs

Our aim is to model both UIMSs and UTMs in a common framework. The UIMS architectural model and characterisation developed by (Cook et al. 1988) are seen as useful starting points.

However, we feel that the concept of a shared object pool is too general for our purposes and we propose describing both UIMS architectures and UTMs in terms of three elements:

- Activity — any behaviour that is explicitly represented and may give rise to state changes.
- State — any explicit representation of state in the course of an interaction.
- Object — any objects used during the interaction.

We are not suggesting that a given system will necessarily have components that are referred to in these terms. We regard this as a functional view which we believe may be applied to UIMSs and UTMs alike, in the same way as we regard the Seeheim model as a functional view of UIMSs. Figure 6 shows how the TKS UTM and the Tube UIMS could be modelled using this scheme.

	State	Activity	Objects
TKS	Goals and sub-goals. Properties (attributes) of objects.	Procedures (expressed as executable behaviours of actions on objects).	Objects (informative, conceptual or physical).
Tube	Flags in ERL (for dialogue state). Attributes associated with UIOs.	ERL rules to describe dialogue control. Attribute evaluation. Methods written in the underlying OO language.	User interface objects.

Figure 6: Modelling TKS and Tube

Positioning a UTM and a UIMS in the same framework allows us to compare and contrast them more readily and to speculate upon their potential compatibility. For example, we can observe that both TKS and Tube represent interaction objects and that they associate state with these objects through an attribute mechanism.

	Connectivity	Vocabulary
TKS	Not constrained by TKS.	Determined by the actions that may be applied to objects, hence may be large.
Tube	Restricted by the tree structure of composed UIOs.	Can be large (determined by set of events accepted by an ERL module and the methods implemented in a UIO).

Figure 7: A Characterisation of Objects in TKS and Tube

Having positioned UIMSs and UTMs in the same model space, we can extend the framework by applying various characterisations. One possible characterisation is that proposed by (Cook et al. 1988) for UIMSs. Figure 7 shows how we might characterise the object elements of TKS and Tube in terms of vocabulary and connectivity.

To apply this framework in an integrated UTM/UIMS interface design environment would require us to be able to ignore those parts of each model that have no correspondence and to utilise commonalities. A further application of the framework would be to use it to identify where to extend one model so that it would bear a closer relationship to the other.

5. Towards an Integrated User Interface Design Environment

The framework outlined above for relating UTMs and UIMS architectural models is a first step towards the development of an integrated user interface design environment. Our goal is that such an environment will support both forms of model, encourage their development with reference to each other and incorporate both in the delivered system. It will address observed deficiencies in existing interface design environments by providing better support for the design process as a whole, by ensuring that the delivered system meets the users task requirements and by increasing the usability of the tools. We have already identified a number of high and low level criteria that must be satisfied to enable a UTM to be used alongside a UIMS in this way:

1. A well developed mapping relation

A mapping relation must be established between particular UIMS and UTM, presumably between the components of each form of model. For example, since UIMSs address the design and construction of user interfaces from a software engineering perspective they have a programming language or some other formal system underlying them. For example, Sassafras and later Tube use ERL to manage the control of the interactive dialogue (Hill 1986). From this we might conclude that there should be some mapping between the language or representation of the UTM and that of the UIMS, and vice versa. We believe that work on formal notations for UTMs and on more abstract descriptions of the user interface for the UIMS will be of value in this context.

2. A defined input to features of system design

While we have identified that UTMs may provide an evaluative and/or requirement definition input to design, it is not always clear exactly which aspects of the interactive system the UTM output should be related to. For example, evaluating an interactive software system against a UTM may show that the user can only perform particular tasks or that particular tasks may be prone to errorful performance. Such information is less useful than is required as it fails to diagnose which features of the system needed to be changed. For example, it would be necessary to identify if the functionality was inadequate, if the dialogue were too complex, or if the presentation characteristics made the dialogue and the available functionality too opaque. Consequently, the UTM should provide input that can be related to the functional views of an interactive system, in terms of presentation, dialogue and application features.

3. Theoretical and methodological support

The form of a model in UTM and UIMS are often quite different. For example, a UTM model may be derived from a sound theory but have a poorly defined modelling framework. In contrast, a UIMS may have a well defined modelling framework but have a poorly defined theoretical basis. To this end, it should be clear to the user of the UTM and the UIMS that the modelling is based on a theory of known strength and scope and that there is a well designed modelling framework.

4. Support for model users

Many UTMs have little support for users. This appears also to be true of many UIMSs. The user of the UIMS and the UTM is likely to have a strong background in at best only one area of interface design (either as a software engineer or from a human factors background). Consequently it is necessary that the UTM and the UIMS should provide adequate support for users of each background.

4.4 Comparison with Foley's Work

As described earlier, (Foley et al. 1989) have done interesting work on the development of a common environment for designing and evaluating user interfaces based upon the integration of a UIMS model with appropriate human factors methods. They utilise an Interface Design Language (IDL) and the notion of different schemata concerned with modelling aspects of the interface design such as the attributes and the objects of the interface. This interface design environment is implemented in ART (a software environment for developing knowledge based systems). While the overall objective of Foley et al.'s work is entirely in line with our goal of an integrated user interface design environment, our ideas differ in a number of ways.

First, we are not proposing to construct an interface design environment around a UIMS. Instead, we intend to construct a integrated design environment that enables alternative types of UIMS to be related to alternative types of UTM. Consequently, our view of an integrated design environment is more like that of a shell in which a designer can develop interactive software using whichever UIMS or UTM best suit the type of application and the designer.

Second, we see no reason why it should not be possible for the designer to be able to develop alternative (new) UIMSs or UTMs as weaknesses and shortcomings of existing UIMSs/UTMs become more obvious. Thus, the environment would allow the designer to create new and more powerful modelling tools.

Third, we are starting from a more theoretical position by first developing a framework for integrating UIMSs and UTMs. In this way we are less likely to develop one part of the environment, such as the UIMS capability, while neglecting the UTM capability. We feel that it is unwise to assume that a UTM tool can be mapped on to a UIMS environment without invoking changes to the UIMS part of the environment, or vice versa. For example, we believe that one important requirement is that the UIMS and the UTM are capable of being mapped on to each other through a common formal system. Consequently, the common formal system will be influenced by both the UTM and the UIMS.

Fourth, even at this early stage in our development of an environment we have explicit UTMs which we have developed and have used in the context of designing highly graphical interactive software systems (Johnson and Nicolosi 1990). Also, we have experimented with developing an integrated UTM/UIMS design environment using KEE (an Intellicorp product similar to ART) and have reported this early work in (Johnson 1989). The results of these experiments lead us to believe that developing design environments inside extant design environments such as ART and KEE overly constrains the form of representations and languages we wish to use for the various models.

7. Summary

In this paper we have reviewed recent work on UIMSs and user tasks. The different models and characterisations proposed for these have been combined and augmented to produce a initial version of a framework for relating UIMS architectural models and UTMs. The framework is effective in allowing us to relate a human factors based UTM to the software engineering requirements for a UIMS. We have given some review of our ideas for an integrated design environment that would be based around such a framework and have made a speculative comparison between our intended use of this framework and similar intentions arising in the work of Foley and his colleagues. We see this as a first and major step towards the construction of a truly integrated UIMS/UTM based software design environment.

Acknowledgements

This work was supported by the IED (grant 4/1/1573) as part of the ADEPT project, in collaboration with British Maritime Technology and British Aerospace.

We would like to acknowledge the contribution of the London HCI Centre, and in particular Peter Rosner, for their survey of UIMSs and prototyping systems which provided background to the UIMS section of this paper.

References

Barnard, P. (1987) Cognitive resources and the learning of human-computer dialogues. In: J.M. Carroll (ed.) Interfacing thought: Cognitive aspects of human computer interaction. MIT Press, Cambridge, Mass.

Betts, B., Burlingame, D., Fischer, G., Foley, J., Green, M., Kasik, D., Kerr, S.T., Olsen, D., Thomas, J. (1987) Goals and Objectives for User Interface Software. Computer Graphics 21 (2), pp. 73-78.

Card, S.K., Moran, T.P., Newell, A. (1983) The Psychology of Human-Computer Interaction. Lawrence-Erlbaum, Hillsdale, NJ.

Cook, S., Drake, K., Hyde, C., Rosner, P., Slater, M. (1988) Report of Prototyping Stream, London HCI Centre, Year 1 Deliverables, Chapter 2.

Coutaz, J. (1987) PAC, An Object Oriented Model for Implementing User Interfaces. Laboratoire de Genie Informatique (University of Grenoble), BP 68.

Dance, J.R., Tamar, G.E., Hill, R.D., Hudson, S.E., Meads, J., Myers, B.A., Schulert, A. (1987) The Run-Time Structure of UIMS-Supported Applications. Computer Graphics 21 (2), pp. 97-101.

Foley, J. (1987) Transformations on a Formal Specification of User-Computer Interfaces. Computer Graphics 21 (2), pp. 109-113.

Foley, J., Kim, W., Kovavevic, S., Murray, K. (1989) Defining Interfaces at a High Level of Abstraction. IEEE Software 6 (1), pp. 25-32.

Gikas, S., Johnson, P., Reeves, S. (1990) Formal Framework for Task Oriented Modelling of Devices. Technical Report, Dept. of Computer Science, Queen Mary and Westfield College.

Goldberg, A. (1984) Smalltalk-80: The Interactive Programming Environment, Addison-Wesley.

Henderson, D.A. (1986) The Trillium User Interface Design Environment. In: Human Factors in Computer Systems. Proceedings SIGCHI '86.

Hill, R.D. (1986) Supporting Concurrency, Communication and Synchronisation in Human-Computer Interaction — The Sassafras UIMS, ACM Transactions on Graphics 5 (3) , pp. 179-210.

Hill, R.D., Herrmann, M. (1989) The Structure of Tube — A Tool for Implementing Advanced User Interfaces. In: Eurographics '89, North-Holland.

Hudson, S.E. (1987) UIMS Support for Direct Manipulation Interfaces. Computer Graphics 21 (2).

Jakob, R.J.K. (1986) A Specification for Direct-Manipulation User Interfaces. ACM Trans. on Graphics 5 (4).

Johnson, P. (1987) Task Models in HCI. Presented to Alvey Conference, Sussex University, Brighton.

Johnson, P. (1989) HCI Models in Software Design: Task Oriented Models of Interactive Software Systems. In: K.H. Bennett (ed.) Software Engineering Environments, Ellis Horwood, pp. 111-140.

Johnson, P., Nicolosi, E. (1990) Task-Based User Interface Development Tools. Submitted to Interact '90.

Johnson, P., Johnson, H., Waddington, R., Shouls, A. (1988) Task Related Knowledge Structures: Analysis, Modelling and Application. In: D.M. Jones and R. Winder (eds.), People and Computers: From Research to Implementation, HCI '88, Cambridge University Press, pp. 137-155.

Johnson, H., Johnson, P. (1990a) Integrating Task Analysis into System Design: Surveying Designers' Needs. Ergonomics Special Issue.

Johnson, P., Johnson H. (1990b) Knowledge Analysis of Tasks: Task Analysis and Specification for Human-Computer systems. In A. Downton (ed), Engineering the Human-Computer Interface. McGraw-Hill.

Krasner, G., Pope, S. (1988) A Cookbook for Using the Model-View-Controller User Interface Paradigm in Smalltalk-80. Journal of Object-Oriented Programming 1 (3), pp. 26-49, Aug/Sept 88.

Myers, B.A. (1989) User Interface Tools: Introduction and Survey. IEEE Software 6 (1), pp. 15-23.

Payne, S.J., Green, T.R.G. (1986) Task Action Grammars. Human-Computer Interaction 2, pp. 93-133.

Pfaff, G.E., ed. (1985) User Interface Management Systems, Springer-Verlag.

Reisner, P. (1981) Formal Grammar and Design of an Interactive System. IEEE Transactions on Software Engineering, SE-3, pp. 218-229.

Rhyne, J., Ehrich, R., Bennett, J., Hewett, T., Sibert, J., Bleser, T. (1987) Tools and Methodology for User Interface Development. Computer Graphics 21 (2), pp. 78-87.

Rossen, M.B., Maass, S., Kellogg, W.A. (1988) The Designer as User: Building Requirements for Design Tools from Design Practice. Communications of the ACM 31 (11), pp. 1288-1298.

Schneiderman, B. (1983) Direct Manipulation: A Step Beyond Programming Languages. IEEE Computer 16 (8).

Thomas, J.J., Hamlin, G. (1983) Graphical Input Interaction Technique (GIIT) Workshop Summary, Computer Graphics 17 (1), pp. 5-30.

van Harmelen, M., Wilson, S.M. (1987) Viz: A Production System Based User Interface Management System. Proc. Eurographics '87, North-Holland.

Waddington, R., Johnson, P. (1989a) Designing and Evaluating Interfaces Using Task Models. In: G.X. Ritter (ed.) 11th World Computer Congress (IFIP Congress 1989), North-Holland.

Waddington, R., Johnson, P. (1989b) A Family of Task Models for Interface Design. In: A. Sutcliffe and L. Macaulay (eds.), HCI '89, Cambridge University Press.

Wasserman, A.I., Shewmake, D.T. (1982) Rapid Prototyping of Interactive Information Systems. ACM Sigsoft Engineering Notes, 7 (5), pp. 171-180.

Williams, G. (1987) Review of Hypercard. In: BYTE, December 1987.

Chapter 21

PROMETHEUS: A System for Programming Graphical User Interfaces

Dierk Ehmke

ABSTRACT

This paper describes PROMETHEUS, a system for programming graphical user interfaces. It starts with the description of the projects and their goals, which resulted in PROMETHEUS predecessors. Experiences with them and reasons for combining them to PROMETHEUS are reported. The PROMETHEUS concepts windows, frames, frame contents, control and dialogue management are described.

Key Words: User Interface, Window Manager, Dialogue Programming, Graphics Systems.

Introduction: PROMETHEUS Predecessors, History and Goals

During the last years the Zentrum für Graphische Datenverarbeitung (ZGDV) has conducted research and development work in the area of graphical user interfaces. As a result of the two nationally joint projects UniBase and PROSYT the systems THESEUS and PRODIA exist.

The participants of both projects were composed of industrial partners and research institutions.

Until the beginning of the year 1990 the work (maintenance, extension and adaptation to different dialogue styles) has been continued in several projects. So far an amount of about 30 person years has been spent.

The most important design criteria in both groups - the THESEUS and the PRODIA developers - were to offer user interfaces with standardized interaction techniques for graphical interactive applications in general and for software engineering environment systems in particular.

On the one hand, techniques for graphic, window and dialogue programming should be integrated in one tool. On the other hand, the expense of programming graphical user interfaces should be reduced in comparison to user interface toolkits, user interface management systems (UIMS) and graphical systems.

Other - different - design criteria justified two conceptual designs and implementations. The requirement in the PROSYT project to integrate already existing tools and personal preferences in both groups resulted in two different systems.

The request to offer highly interactive graphics was realized in THESEUS' graphic windows. Requirements to integrate already existing tools (without changing them) resulted in the PRODIA frame-window-concept. This concept allows the integration of GKS based applications. Frames are virtual displays. They represent workstations in GKS. Terminal emulations enabled PRODIA to integrate already existing tools using alphanumerical input and output into a window environment. That is why the use of **X** was proposed at an early stage of the PRODIA development. In addition comfortable output functions for text and raster were provided in PRODIA.

The specifications of THESEUS [HÜB-87] and PRODIA [EHM-89] are available within the ZGDV book series *Beiträge zur graphischen Datenverarbeitung.*

Author's address: Zentrum für Graphische Datenverarbeitung e.V., Wilhelminenstraße 7, W-6100 Darmstadt, Telefon 06151/100014

Experiences with Both Systems

Both systems are used not only for software engineering environment systems. Besides software development tools, application programs exist like a syntax and structure driven SGML editor, a process control system, a database object editor and a word processing program, all of them making use of the graphical interactive user interface.

Minimizing the cost of dialogue programming of graphical interactive programs was a main goal. By separating lexical and - as far as possible - syntactical dialogue tasks and creating a high level application interface this goal was achieved. Thus, the application need not to take care of detailed properties of the user interface. Its code is reduced and the time to develop an application is shortened. The reasons are, that the concepts are unified and the set of the necessary functions is small. Tasks like converting physical input events, prompt, echo, feedback, input verification, rejection of and reaction to input errors, coordinate transformation and management of all window interactions including screen update are realized within THESEUS and PRODIA.

Providing broad capabilities was another main goal. Meanwhile the applications make use of it. Both groups noticed, that it's easy to integrate graphics into user interface tools. We wonder, why this isn't done more often.

The interaction techniques allow solving many dialogue tasks. There are quite common interaction techniques like text input, menu input, mask input, position input and object identification. Beyond that THESEUS provides interaction techniques for object dragging (direct manipulation). The model of abstract input classes simplifies the programming of all interaction techniques.

PROMETHEUS' Starting Situation

Because of further requirements a possible integration of both systems was examined. One experience was, that the maintenance of both systems was very expensive. Often application programmers wanted to add concepts to one system, which already existed in the other one. A revision of concepts, application program interface and implementation was desirable. For example, THESEUS was implemented under DOS with GEM and later ported to Unix with **X** and Athena widgets. The rolltext concept was added. PRODIA was implemented on **X** Version 10 with the Sx Toolkit and later ported to **X** Version 11 with Athena widgets. Regardless of the fact that a lot of work was spent for the implementation, both systems are prototypes which should be reimplemented.

Nevertheless, it is possible to combine PRODIA and THESEUS into a common system because

- the concepts are compatible with each other
- both were written in **C**
- meanwhile both systems are based on OSF/Motif widgets.

This new system is called PROMETHEUS (PRODIA meets THESEUS). THESEUS' graphic windows, the biggest part of its extensive dialogue handler and PRODIA's frames, windows, text and raster modules will be used.

PROMETHEUS Concepts

Frames are virtual screens of arbitrary size. Tools direct their output to frames. Tools may create frames and destroy them.

According to the different kinds of information in documents PROMETHEUS provides the following frame types: mask, graphic, text and raster. Functions exist for the manipulation of each frame type.

Frame contents may be saved into and be loaded from the file system . Three update modes enable tools to control the screen updating process, which helps to prevent flickering. Frames can be cleared. Usually tools only take care of the frames and not of the windows.

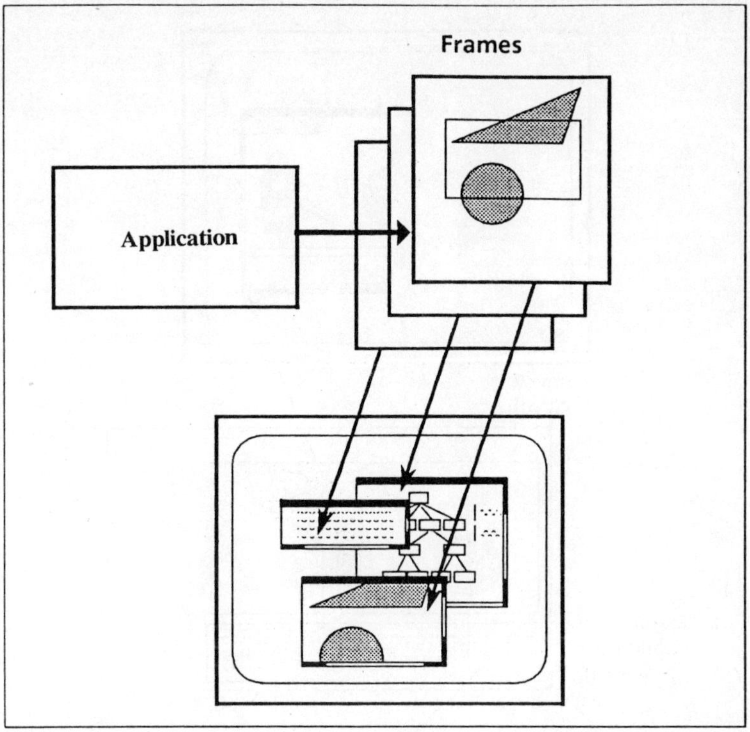

An Application uses a Frame and Frames are displayed in Windows

PROMETHEUS Windows

Frame sections are displayed within windows. There is one very powerful function for opening windows, named *win_openInteractive*. It only has four parameters:

title - a string, which will be written into the window's title bar.

parent_frame- PROMETHEUS supports a hierarchical window concept. The window will be only visible within the parent frames' window. In most cases the parent frame will be the screen itself (called Root-Frame), but it may also be any other frame. The text/graphic/raster integration is achieved by mixing frame sections within windows.

child_frame- this is the frame, which will be displayed in the window.

attributes- this is parameter controls the creation of the window attributes: scrollbars, titlebar, menubar and a buttonbox.

win_openInteractive is user centered: it prompts the user to position and size the window. The user manipulates a so called rubber-rectangle and determines the window's size and position. The tool need not to know the window's location and extent. Afterwards the windowing and the mapping from frames to windows is done by PROMETHEUS.

Usually the tool is involved only once more: before termination it closes the window.

Several other operations on windows exist. They are provided for the unusual case, when tools need to control windows.

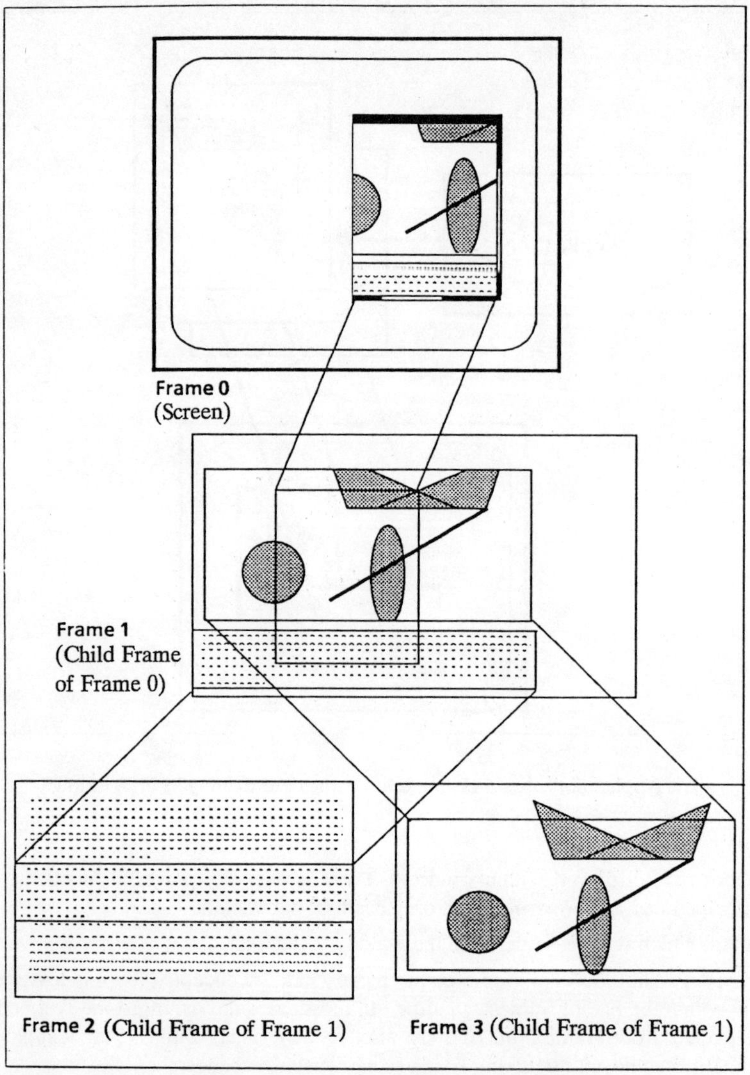

Parent Frame and Child Frame

Prometheus Frame Contents

From the application programmer's point of view, it is not necessary to know how Prometheus maps frame contents into a window. For him or her it is more important to get sufficient support for complex output tasks. E.g. in graphics programming, segments and transformations are concepts, which provide the possibility of structuring, storing and modifying graphical elements. Prometheus supplies applications with high level interfaces for frames. Prometheus distinguishes four frame types: mask, graphic, text and raster. Functions reflecting the structure of each type of information can be used on frames. For text frames we created a new interface, which provides text output with proportionally spaced font. Functions for raster frames include moving or copying rectangular areas and setting color values.

PROMETHEUS Mask Frames

Application programs often handle forms. PROMETHEUS mask frames provide a simple text output, menus, buttons and masks inside frames. Besides text raster can be used as button content. Input of mask frames is combined with the dialogue concept.

PROMETHEUS Graphic Frames

A high application-oriented level of abstraction is important especially in the area of graphics output. The critical point in conventional graphics systems is, that they include a bulk of concepts and details which must be considered by an application programmer, even though many of them are unnecessary in this working context. Usually graphics output of software engineering tools deals with structured objects like networks, trees or diagrams. Therefore PROMETHEUS uses an object-oriented approach to represent the graphical entities as viewed by the application program[3].

There are two kinds of objects: basic objects and complex objects. Basic objects are the smallest graphical units used by the application to built up larger graphical structures. Such a structure is called complex object and can, in turn, be manipulated like any other object. Basic objects are simple geometric types like polygons, boxes, circles, text, or other specific symbols typically used in the software engineering business.

Each object is connected to exactly one window. At run-time the application uses an object identifier to create, manipulate and delete objects of the different types.

The objects are positioned in a two-dimensional world coordinate system that is defined by the application program. Only the application program controls the position of the objects and may change them at any time.

Each graphic frame incorporates one world coordinate system whose objects are mapped into this window. The transformation of world coordinates to frame or window coordinates (the scaling factor) is defined at the time the frame is created. The window represents the visible area of the world coordinate system. The objects whose positions fall within the window's working area can be seen on the screen. All objects or object parts outside the window's boundary are automatically clipped. The position of the visible area within the world coordinate system is determined only by the user by means of window panning functions.

Visual characteristics of objects like geometry, size, line type or fill interior style are divided into three groups:

- the first group of characteristics describes the object types, e.g. the shape and orientation of a diamond. These characteristics are fixed and determine the layout of the object type.
- other characteristics like size or radius describe how a single occurrence of a specific object is to be drawn on the screen. These attributes are defined before drawing the object.
- the third group of attributes can be changed dynamically; e.g., line type, color or visibility. Such dynamic changes to graphics attributes may either be deferred or are immediately put into effect. They will be visible on the screen at once.

The set of basic object types cannot comprise all graphical objects needed in software engineering tools. Therefore the user interface provides facilities to create hierarchically complex objects. A complex object consists of basic objects and/or other complex objects and can be seen as a logical tree with basic objects as leaves. A complex object describes a new object type identified by an object name. From then on it is treated like a basic object.

An inheritance mechanism is used for binding complex object attributes to child objects. Each child object is annotated whether it inherits the attributes of the parent object or not. In the first case the attribute values of the parent object are evaluated; otherwise, the child attributes are valid. If the child object itself is a complex object, the mechanism is applied also to its subtree.

PROMETHEUS Text Frames

The objectives for the design of text functions were

- to simplify text output with proportionally spaced fonts
- the functions should be powerful enough, so that applications like editors or document systems can be implemented
- the functions should supply enough flexibility for the construction of any underlying text model of the application. Using the text functions should not restrict the scope of applications
- an internal data structure permitting storage of text together with its attributes should be accessible to the application.

The model of a text frame as it is presented to the application is that of a text buffer with columns and rows. One entry in the buffer is called a text cell. Attributes like font, typeface, typeweight or character spacing may be assigned to each text cell. A text cursor indicates the current position in the frame. Text strings can be inserted or deleted at the cursor position, lines are created or deleted.

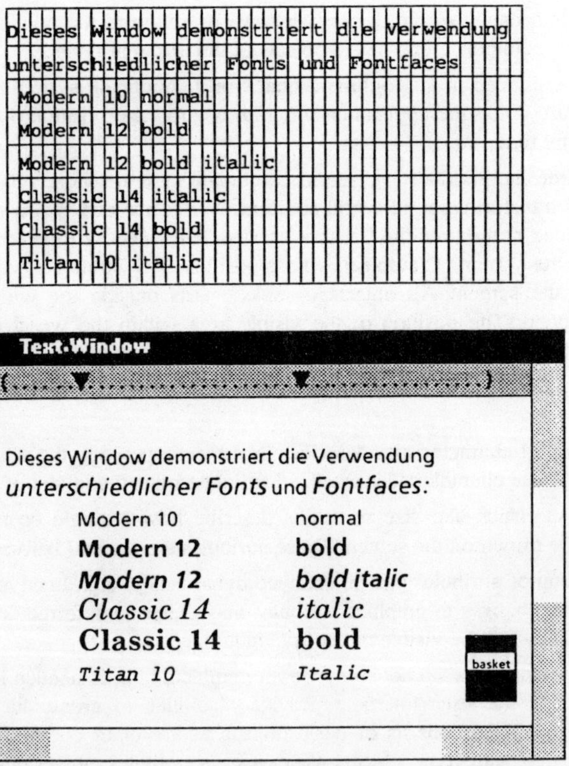

Text Model and Text Window

The structure of a textframe will be modified by editing functions, e.g. inserting and deleting strings. A text frame grows at the bottom, when lines are inserted, that do not fit in the current frame rectangle.

For more sophisticated applications, e.g. text or document systems, functions for formatting and line breaking are provided. Another group of functions sets the current values of the text attributes. Other functions determine the page layout. Margins and tabulators can be set. One function aligns the text in the current line to the left or right margin, centers it or justifies the text between the margins.

A special mechanism controls the breaking of lines. If an application wants to handle line breaking, it has to specify a function for that task. PROMETHEUS will call the linebreak function whenever text exceeds the right margin of the current line.

Other features of PROMETHEUS text frames which are especially provided for interactive applications are:

- operations on text blocks, like highlighting, copying or deleting blocks
- a waste paper basket that stores deleted text may be displayed in the window. The user may open the content of the basket and copy text back into the frame
- a tabulator line for the current tabulator stops may be displayed. The user can adjust the tabulator positions interactively.

PROMETHEUS Raster Frames

The interface to raster frames contains typical raster operations like moving and copying rectangular areas and also functions for converting frames of different type into raster frames. Storing and reloading images is also provided. According to the available raster types, raster frames offer the four raster types (*bitmap, greyscale, direct color* and *mapped color*). Functions for the manipulation of colors are device independent.

Associated with raster functions is the dragging plane which may control the echo for the drag event. In future it may use special hardware, so that very fast object movement will be achieved. Applications copy the objects to the dragging plane if they receive an event, that signals the start of an object drag.

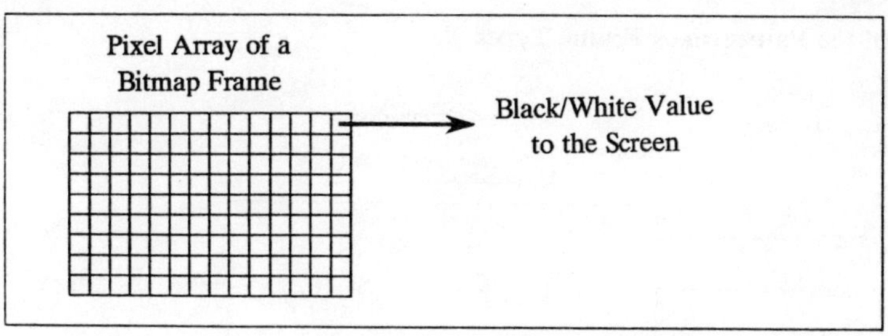

Raster Type Bitmap

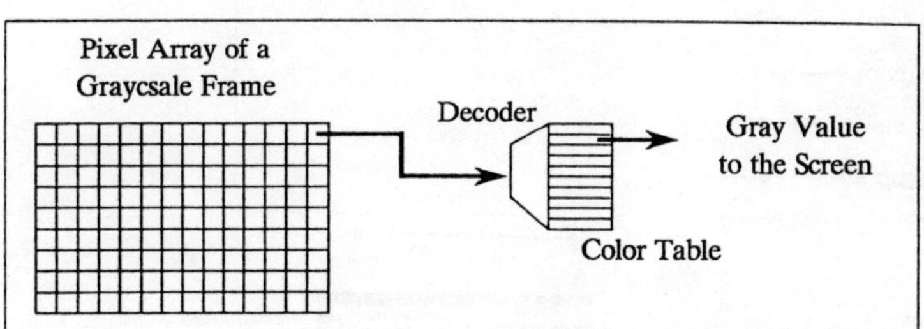

Raster Type Greyscale

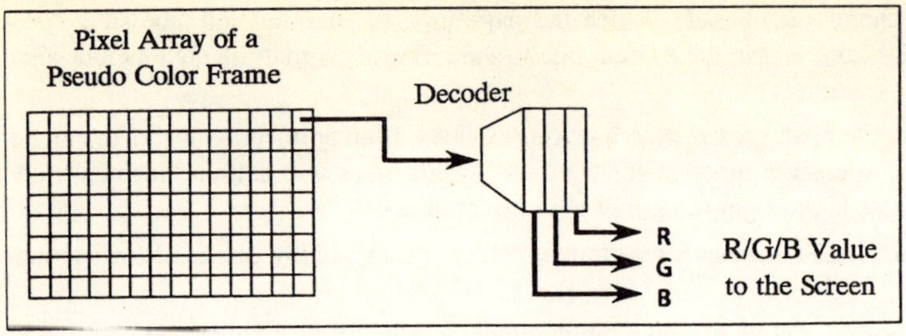

Raster Type Pseudo Color

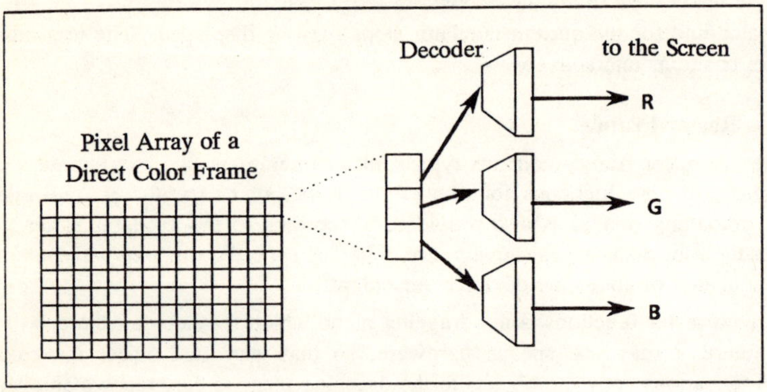

Raster Type Direct Color

Extension of the Prometheus Frame Types

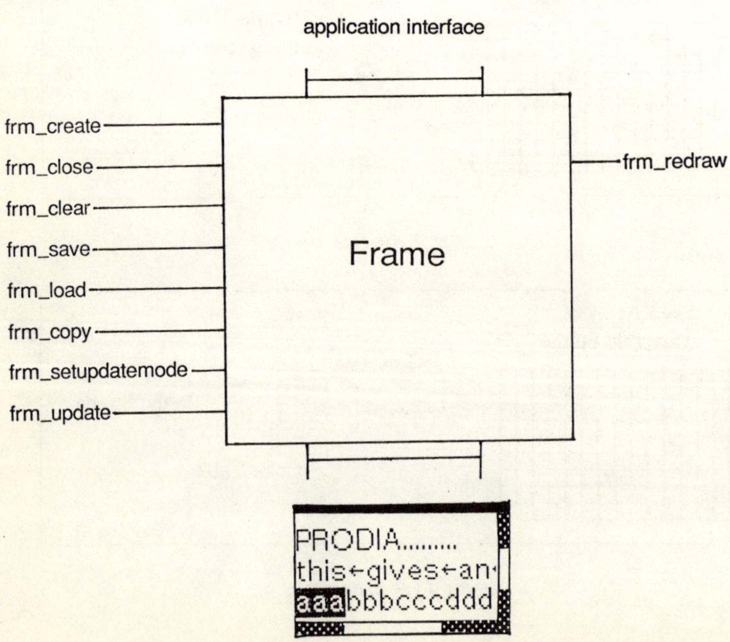

Interfaces of a Frame Module

From PROMETHEUS's point of view a frame is a virtual screen that stores output. The internal interface to the PROMETHEUS window handler consists of one function that initiates redraw events to the window. The frame satisfies this demand by calling output functions of the underlying window system. In addition to this internal interface, the general control functions for frames have to be implemented. All other functionality (the tool interface) depends of the frame type.

Currently a new frame type is added. It provides three-dimensional line graphics. As a further improvement a frame type for interactive video will be added.

Division of Control

The PROMETHEUS application interface architecture is based on a modified external control model. External control means dividing applications into small packages, each processing one dialogue unit. Initiated by predefined user input sequences, the user interface calls an application function to give semantic feedback and to carry out application-specific processing. External control ensures a clean separation of application-specific functionality and I/O responsibilities. Controlling the context of all possible interactions, the user interface is able to respond appropriately to any context switching the user performs.

As opposed to internal control, where dialogue sequences are implicitly defined by the control flow of the application, external control needs an explicit specification of every dialogue step.

The PROMETHEUS description of dialogues is based on an event model. The dialogue is defined as a set of events representing user actions. They are triggered by user interactions with physical devices. Some events are processed autonomously by the user interface, (e.g. all events referring to windows like move, size or scroll). Other events requiring application specific processing start an application routine.

The PROMETHEUS dialogue control model specifies and modifies events at run-time to reach a higher level of flexibility using powerful mechanisms of high-level programming languages. That is why it offers functions to create, delete and modify input events, to connect them to application units and to specify and change the sequence of events. PROMETHEUS provides this functionality, as well as all output and window control capabilities, as services similar to internal control.

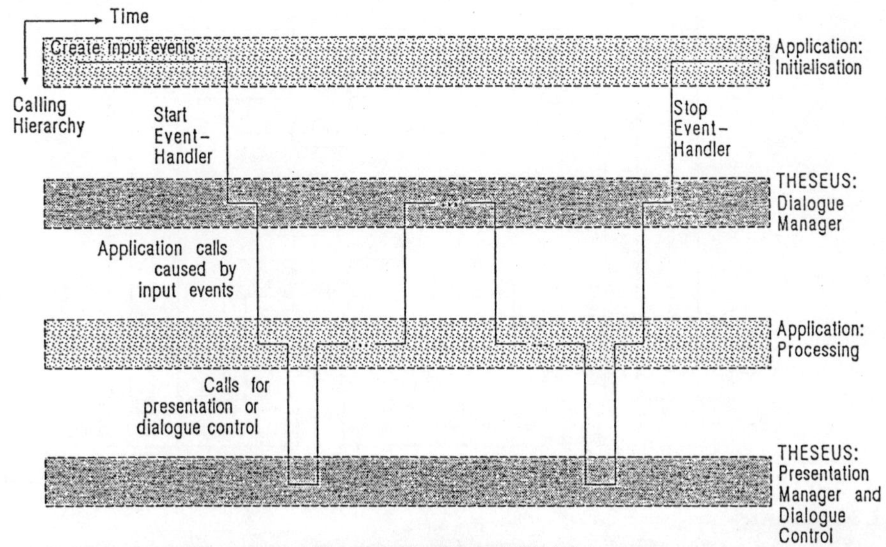

PROMETHEUS Control Model

After the initialization input events, the event handler, as part of the dialogue manager, is started. It awaits and collects user input, checks its permission, performs lexical, syntactical and in some case semantic feedback and activates the application, if necessary. Those applications use PROMETHEUS' facilities for output and window control, as part of their semantic feedback, and dialogue control components for specifying the next dialogue step.

Dialogue Management and Control

Physical user input like keyboard input, pressing or releasing the mouse button or moving the mouse are collected and assigns to one of the following input classes:

1. Menu Selection:
   One menu item is selected from a restricted number of alternatives.
2. Object Identification:
   An visible object within a window is picked.

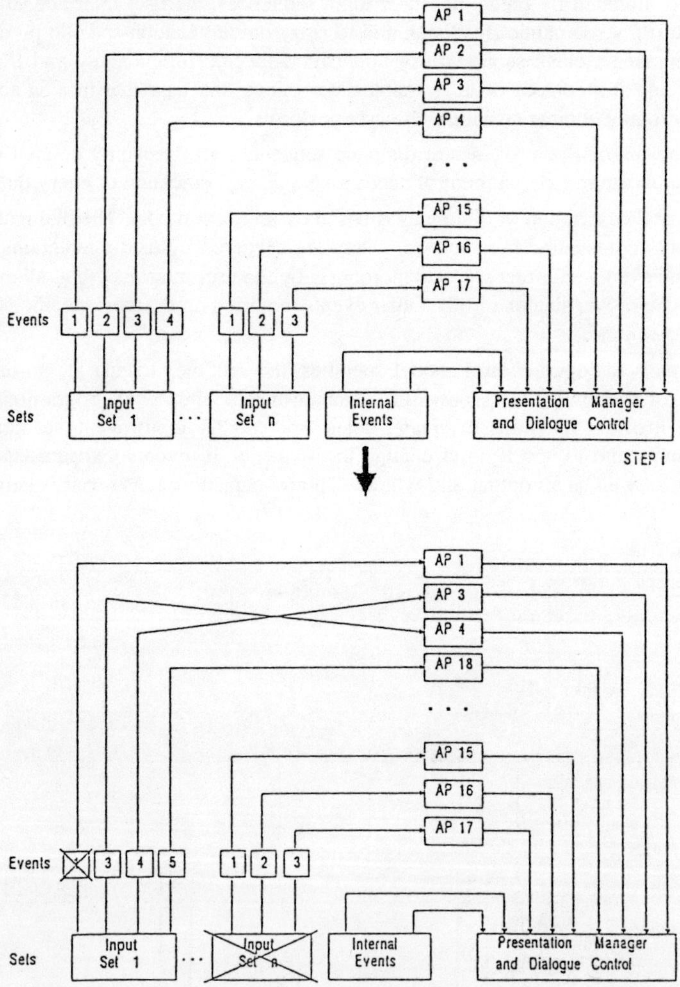

Dialogue Specification

3. Position Area:
   A position in frame coordinates (or world coordinates in a graphic frame) is entered within predefined areas. Overlapped areas are attributed by priorities.

4. Keyboard Input:
   A key (including function keys) is pressed.
5. Object Dragging:
   An object is moved within a window.

Events of the input classes are grouped into input sets. Input sets consist of elements or other input classes. One predefined input set - named rootset - includes all of them. Thus, the application creates a dialogue tree. The tree's structure reflects application requirements. PROMETHEUS provides functions to add and remove input sets from other sets (including the rootset). Sets may be enabled or disabled and their attributes may be set or inquire. Not only the input sets but also their elements may be changed dynamically. New events are added to or deleted from a set, each event is disabled or enabled and its attributes are inquired and changed. Finally the relation between events and application functions is established.

Conclusions

PROMETHEUS combines the meanwhile well working concepts of THESEUS and PRODIA. Nevertheless the development will continue:

At the moment PROMETHEUS contains a fixed set of interaction techniques like dragging, object picking and window functions. Also the set of graphical objects is fixed. Some new basic objects and input classes and attributes will be useful. Additional techniques or alternatives to existing techniques could be predefined and presented in a library of options to provide a set of interaction styles. New frame types will be added. The final goal is to create a comfortable User Interface Management System which is able to support large applications for professional users.

Acknowledgements:

The author thanks E. Berkhan, A. Bolloni, C. Braun, D. Eckardt, M. Kreiter, G. Lux-Mülders, M. Muth, C. Sänger and D. Siepmann for their valuable help supporting this paper.

References

[EHM-89] D. Ehmke, W. Hinderer, M. Kreiter, D. Krömker
PRODIA - Das PROSYT-Dialogsystem,
In: D. Krömker, H. Steusloff, H.-P. Subel (eds.),
PRODIA und PRODAT, Dialog- und Datenbankschnittstellen für Systementwurfswerkzeuge,
Springer Verlag, Berlin Heidelberg 1989.

[HÜB-87a] W. Hübner, G. Lux-Mülders, M. Muth,
Designing a System to Provide Graphical User Interfaces: The THESEUS Approach.
In: Marechal, G. (ed.): EUROGRAPHICS'87, proceedings, pp. 309-322.
Amsterdam, New York, Oxford, Tokyo: North-Holland 1987.

[HÜB-87b] W. Hübner, G. Lux-Mülders, M. Muth,
THESEUS, die Benutzungsoberfläche der UniBase-Softwareentwicklungsumgebung,
Springer Verlag, Berlin Heidelberg 1987.

[HÜB-89] W. Hübner, G. Lux-Mülders, M. Muth,
THESEUS - Ein System zur Programmierung graphischer Benutzerschnittstellen
Informatik Forschung und Entwicklung 4: 205-222

[FWC-84] J. D. Foley, V. L. Wallace, P. Chan,
The Human Factors of Computer Graphics Interaction Techniques,
Computer Graphics & Applications, pp. 13-48, IEEE, November 1984

[SIK-82] D. C. Smith, C. Irby, R. Kimball, B. Verplank, E. Harslem,
Designing the Star User Interface,
Byte Magazine, Vol. 7, No. 4, April 1982

[ScG-86] R. W. Scheifler, J. Gettys, *The X-Window System*,
ACM Transactions on Graphics, Vol. 5, pp. 79-109

The THESEUS development has been carried out since the beginning of the year 1985 within the UniBase project, partially sponsored by the Federal Ministry for Research and Technology (BMFT), grant number ITS 8308.

The PRODIA development has been carried out since October 1986 within the PROSYT project, partially sponsored by the Federal Ministry for Research and Technology (BMFT), grant number ITS 8306.

Part IV

Visual Programming, Multi-Media and UI Generators

Chapter 22

An Environment for User Interface Development Based on the ATN and Petri Nets Notations

M. Bordegoni, U. Cugini, M. Motta and C. Rizzi

ABSTRACT

This paper presents two UIMS prototypes: GIGA (Generatore di Interfacce Grafico ed Automatico) and GIGA+ which provide an environment for defining and handling different types of man-machine dialogue.
Both tools are based on the user interface Seeheim model and the System Builder approach which splits user interface construction in two phases: specification and automatic code generation. In order to support the user interface designer during these activities graphic and easy-to-use modules have been developed.
Main emphasis has been put on the Dialogue Control component. Different notations have been adopted: ATN (Augmented Transition Network) notation to support sequential dialogue in GIGA and Petri Nets notation to support multi-threaded dialogues in GIGA+.
Even if either GIGA or GIGA+ are based on the same philosophy, different architectural solutions have been adopted: at source code generation level (interpreter vs compiler) and at run time execution level (single process vs multi-processes).
The tools have been implemented in Unix and X-Window environment.

Keywords: Seeheim model, System Builder, sequential and multi-threaded dialogue, ATN, Petri Nets, multi-processes.

INTRODUCTION

This paper presents two UIMS prototypes developed at CAD Group of IMU-CNR, Milan: GIGA (Generatore di Interfacce Grafico ed Automatico) and GIGA+.
Our aim is to provide an environment in which different types of man-machine dialogue can be defined and handled.
For this purpose we focused on the problems concerning design, implementation, rapid prototyping, execution, evaluation and maintenance of user interfaces.
First of all we analysed the structural models of the user interface. In fact they represent an important feature for the user interface designer since they allow the user interface developer to understand the elements of an interface and they guide and help him in the user interface construction activity. In general these models split the man-machine interaction in more tasks or components.
Some of the studied models not only describe the human-computer interaction but also represent an architectural description of the system by a specification activity and a run-time execution viewpoint.

Authors' addresses: IMU - CNR - Gruppo CAD - Via Ampere, 56 - 20131 Milano - Italy
Cugini also: Università degli Studi di Parma - Viale delle Scienze - 43100 Parma - Italy

In the following phase of our work we analysed some models to describe the man-machine interaction. We pointed out two general types of dialogue: sequential and multi-threaded&multi-programming.
In the first case the system provides a predefined manner in which to move from one status of the dialogue to another and the end-user can perform one task at a time.
The second is an asynchronous dialogue model in which many tasks (threads) are available to the end user at one time and the system can execute these tasks simultaneously. Obviously the user interface descriptive power of this last is higher than the first one. Among the models presented in literature we took into consideration the Transition Networks (in particular Augmented Transition Network), the free-context grammar, the Event notation and the Petri Nets.
In our approach, named System Builder, the construction of an user interface is performed in two phases: user interface specification through high level languages and automatic generation of the specific source code.
During the design phase of the system architecture we had to deal particularly with two problems.
The first concerns the format of the output produced in the user interface specification phase: we analysed if it would be better to produce a source code to be compiled and linked in the user interface generation phase or to produce a structural file to be interpreted during the run-time execution of the user interface.
The second refers to the opportunity to implement the whole system with only one process or with multi-processes, one for each component of the adopted user interface model.
Both tools described in this paper are based on the System Builder approach, but different techniques have been adopted to solve previous mentioned problems.
The prototypes have been implemented in Unix and X-Window environment, and coded in C language. These technical choices led to an easy portability of two systems on different hardware platforms.

1. DESCRIPTION OF GIGA

1.1 Theoretical background

In the following the theoretical choices representing the basis of GIGA prototype design will be described.
The structure of a UIMS is heavily dependent on the underlying user interface model. In our tool the Seeheim model [1] was adopted. It splits a user interface into three components: *Presentation Techniques* component (*lexical* level), *Dialogue Control* component (*syntactic* level), and *Application Interface* component (*semantic* level).
In our system main emphasis has been put on the Dialogue Control component. An analysis of notations commonly used to describe the man-machine dialogue has been carried out. In literature several notation can be found: Transition Networks [2][3][4], Context-free grammar [2][3], Event model [2][3][5].
For the choice of the notation following parameters have been taken into account:

- ease of use;
- ease of learning;
- descriptive power.

The Augmented Transition Networks - ATN [3][4] notation, that is a particular kind of transition network, has been chosen, because it is sufficiently well known, easily understandable by non-programmers and provides an immediate global view of the dialogue structure. Moreover the dialogue model can be graphically represented.
This notation is based on the concept of user interface state and consists of a set of states and transitions from one state to another, where:

state is a static situation in the dialogue between the end-user and the application package (e.g. when the system is waiting for a user action);
transition describes how the dialogue moves from one state to another;
square state represents a state reachable from any other state [2].

In order to give a complete dialogue description a set of specific information [6] has been associated to each elements of the ATN notation.
The information associated to the state is:

- *state name* (unambiguous identifier);
- *screen layout*, set of objects defining the graphical appearance of the user interface corresponding to the state.

Information associated to a transition refers to the corresponding rules and action performed at user and application level; these actions represent links towards Presentation Techniques and Application Interface components.
These information are:

- *transition name* (unambiguous identifier);
- *event rule*: 3-tuple of values which identifies the expected event (action at user level), the logical identifier associated to the graphical object on which must occur the event, and the name of interface routine corresponding to specific application routine (action at application level);
- *conditional function*, is a function attached to each transition which determines if the transition can be performed; this allows the definition of context-sensitive dialogues.
- *output rule* : couple of values which identifies the logical identifier associated to the object where the output data will be displayed, and the function to display output data.

The information associated to the square state comprises both state and transition information.

1.2 Architecture

GIGA architecture is based on the System Builder concept [6][7], which splits the construction of the user interface in two phases:

1. *specification of the user interface.* In this phase the user interface designer can describe the behaviour of the user interface through high level languages and a user friendly interaction style.
2. *generation of the user interface.* This phase is automatically performed by the system, which exploits the logical level information given by the user interface designer, and generates the executable control code for the specific user interface.

These activities are supported by a set of interactive graphic tools (Figure 1):

- *Logical Model Builder - LMB* . This tool supports the specification of the user interface. The result of the design description is stored in a *Description File*, available for further control, analysis and maintenance. According to the Seeheim model, LMB consists of three modules, one for each user interface components;
- *User Interface Monitor Builder - UIMB* This module, on the basis of the user interface description given by the user interface designer, and adopting automatic code generation techniques, is able to generate an 'ad hoc' *User Interface Monitor - UIM* that is automatically linked to the specific application.

From the user interface designer's point of view most emphasis is put on the logical descriptions [8]. The user interface designer has not to deal with coding activity : the source code is automatically generated by the UIMB. For this reason GIGA and GIGA+ can be considered "CASE" instruments supporting the design and implementation of a user interface for an application package in a fully automatic way.
Another important feature of the system is the possibility to create and manage Description Files libraries, containing different user interfaces, that can be reused and fitted for other application packages. This allows a rapid prototyping of the user interface.
In the following sections the user interface development phases and corresponding tools will be illustrated in more detail.

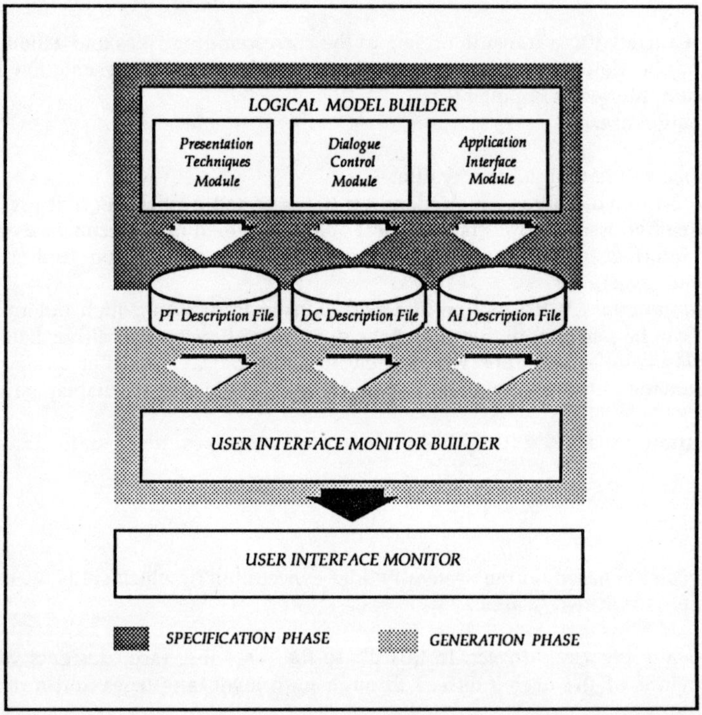

Figure 1 - General system architecture

2. SPECIFICATION PHASE

During this phase the user interface designer provides a logical description of the user interface to be constructed by means of the three LMB modules.
In order to provide the user interface designer with easy-to-use tools, graphic editors (where possible) which don't require specific computer science background have been developed.
Moreover, they are integrated with a common text editor (i.e. "vi" editor of Unix environment) to allow a more expert user interface programmer to introduce the user interface logical description through a specification language.

2.1 Presentation Technique Module

This module permits the definition of the user interface graphical appearance which the end-user interacts with.
A graphic and interactive module, named *Layout Editor* [7] has been implemented. The system provides a predefined set of graphic objects the user can manage and combine in order to create the screen layouts (set of graphic objects) for his own personal user interface. Following types of objects are available:

- horizontal and vertical menu (textual and/or iconic)
- pop-up menu
- graphical area
- alphanumeric area
- form
- icon

The objects are automatically given an identifier which is used as a reference by the other LMB modules. Graphic attributes (e.g. background, foreground color, etc.) are then associated to each object.
Common editing functionalities for the manipulation of the objects and their attributes have been implemented.
The main advantage of this tool is due to the fact that in every moment the user has an immediate feedback of what he is doing. For example the user can simply place or move a menu picking its position on the screen by the pointer. The user does not have to calculate the coordinates of point position since the system itself determines them.

2.2 Dialogue Control Module

An ATN graphic Editor has been implemented [6]. By this tool the user interface designer describes the interaction model in terms of states and transitions organized in a main network and sub-networks hierarchically structured. Either main network or sub-networks are specified in the same way.
The objects which can be defined and handled by the user are:

- *states* graphically represented by *circles*
- *transitions* graphically represented by *directed arcs*
- *square states* graphically represented by *square*

including the definition of all information that must be associated to each object.
The system offers a complete set of editing functionalities: object creation, modification, deletion, storage, etc. A consistency check facility is also provided in order to verify the syntactic correctness of the ATN.

2.3 Application Interface Module

This tool allows the designer to create the interface between user interface and application routines.
The user has only to enter the name of the Description File containing the logical model of interaction. The system retrieves from it the names of application routines and automatically generates the source code (in our case written in C language) for routines calls.
The direct call technique [7] has been adopted for routine calls. The source code will be later used by the UIMB in order to build up the user interface program.

3. GENERATION PHASE

During this phase, the logical descriptions produced in the previous one, are processed by the UIMB in order to build up the executable user interface. The UIMB tool is based on the skeleton technique. The skeleton is a predefined standard User Interface Monitor (C source code) which has to be adapted to the specific application package. The UIMB is in charge to complete the Skeleton source code. The UIM has been implemented as a single process that is at run time the subdivision of the user interface into three components is only at logical level. The executable UIM manages the man-machine interaction interpreting the information stored in the Description Files.
The main activities of the UIMB are to:

- build up automatically the source code of the UIM. It generates the lacking source code, retrieving necessary information from the Description files and inserts it in predefined location into the skeleton (Figure 2);
- compile the source code;
- link it with the application modules.

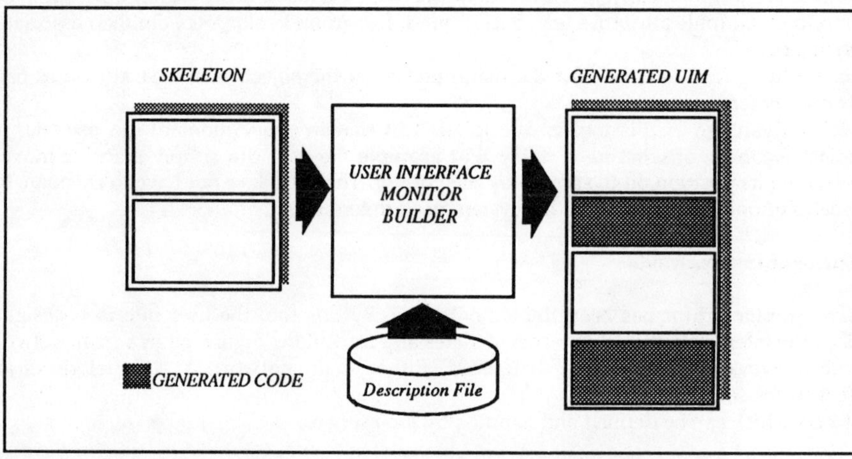

Figure 2 - User Interface Monitor Builder

All these operations are handled automatically by the tool, but last two activities can be manually performed by the user interface designer.
The input to the UIMB consists of:

- Dialogue Control Description File which contains the specification of the dialogue;
- conditional functions file (C-code) defined at LMB level using the ATN Graphic Editor and associated to each transition of the ATN;
- Skeleton program.

The tasks performed by the UIMB can be subdivided into three phases (Figure 3):

Phase 1:

- insert into the skeleton the name of the dialogue Description File;
- recover from the Description File the names of the conditional functions associated to the transitions;
- generate source code for conditional functions calls and insert them into the skeleton.

Phase 2:
compile source code generated in the previous step and file containing the application routines calls.

Phase 3:
Link binary files produced in the Phase 2 with those of the ones of application routines.

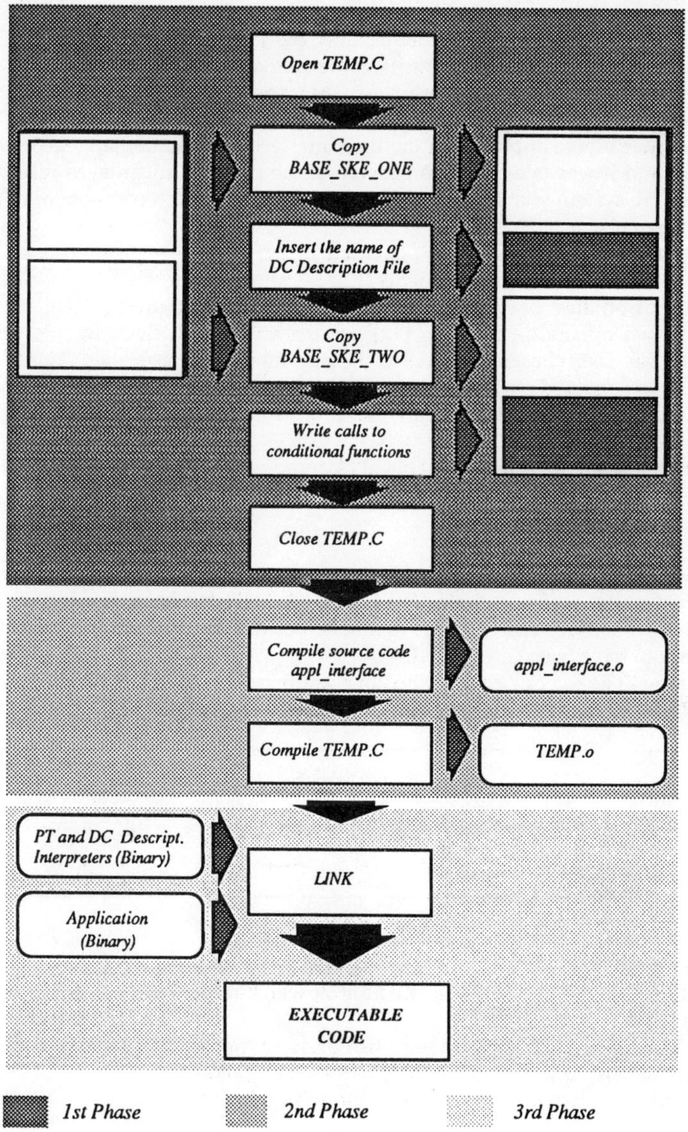

where:

TEMP.C	temporary file used to create UIM source code 'ad hoc';
BASE_SKE_ONE:	file containing variables declarations, structures and system initialization;
BASE_SKE_TWO:	file for interaction management.

Figure 3 - User Interface Monitor Builder tasks

4. DESCRIPTION OF THE NEW PROTOTYPE : GIGA+

In order to evaluate the capabilities and the validity of the approach adopted in GIGA, the system was given to non-expert programmer users to construct user interfaces for some application packages. These tests have risen positive judgments for what concerns the System Builder approach, the Skeleton Technique and the graphical tools implemented for the definition of the three components of the user interface model.
On the other side some problems rose since the prototype doesn't give the possibility to describe multi-threaded dialogues while it is required by some applications.
Moreover the interpretive approach of the user interface specification appeared slow and not much efficient and it was taken into consideration the possible advantages resulting from an architecture of the system which uses more processes, one for each component of the adopted user interface model.
Consequently these considerations, we decided to design a new prototype, called GIGA+, which could satisfy these new requirements.
Particular attention has been put on multi-threaded dialogues [9][10][11]and a new architecture based on multi-processes [12] has been defined. Even in this prototype the Seeheim model has been chosen as model of the user interface.
As our interest was focused on the Dialogue Control component, in the following we are going to describe in particular the adopted notation and the specification and generation phase of this component.
The other components represent a subset of GIGA ones.

4.1 Theoretical background

In order to describe multi-threaded dialogues a notation, called DPN (Dialogue Petri Nets) [13], based on Condition/Event Petri Nets [14][15][16] [17] has been developed. To make the Petri Nets design activity easier, other symbols, besides the typical ones of the Petri Nets classical notation, have been introduced.
The model of the dialogue can be described in a graphic way using a set of graphic objects and transitions. The objects and their graphical appearance are as follows [17]:

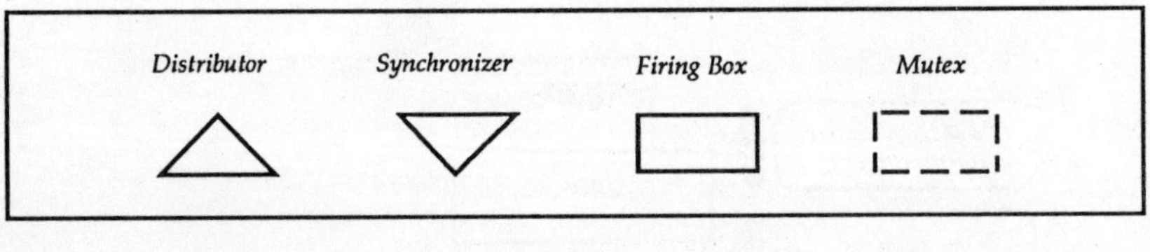

where:

distributor allows the description of a situation in which more than one dialogue threads can be activated;
synchronizer allows the synchronization of two or more concurrent dialogue threads;
firing box activates the application routines requested by the user;
mutex allows to make two or more dialogue threads exclusive.

Each object implicitly contains the basic Petri Nets elements.
The transition is that entity which graphically joins the DPN objects. Its meaning is similar to the ATN one: it permits the information exchange among different DPN objects by means of an abstraction of an event called *event token*.
The information associated to the token is:

- a logical identifier of the event;
- an identifier of the graphic object where the event occurs;
- parameters associated to the event.

The dialogue moves from one object of the DPN to another one if and only if the information associated to the transition matches the one associated to the token.
It is possible to associate conditional functions to each transition. They allow the modification of both local variables and some values contained in the tokens.

4.2 Specification phase of the Dialogue Control Component

At the moment the DPN describing the user interface dialogue is specified in a textual way using the 'vi' editor of the Unix operating system.
The user has to define the following entities: *box, branch* and *sync* which corresponds respectively to the DPN objects *firing box, distributor,* and *synchronizer.*
Specific information is associated to each entity.
The information associated to the box is:

- name of the box;
- input and output tokens;
- identifier of the object where the event occurs;
- identifier of the object where the output must be visualized;
- application routine name,
- name of the next object to be executed.

The information associated to the branch is:

- name of the distributor;
- list of the possible tokens and the corresponding name of the next object to process;
- list of the exclusive and concurrent threads.

The information associated to the sync is:

- name of the synchronizer;
- list of the threads and their priority;
- name of the next object to be processed.

The specified entities are stored in a proper Description File in order to be processed during the generation phase.
Figure 4 visualizes a piece of a DPN Description file.

```
#
#
Box_id = View;
InputToken = BUTTONPRESS;
OutputToken = VIEWOBJECT;
InputInstance = scenario;
OutputInstance = res_wind;
Application = NULL;
Next = Sel_input;
#
#
```

Figure 4 - Example of a Box entity definition

4.3 Generation phase of the Dialogue Control Component

In this phase a module, called *DCC Builder*, generates in an automatic way the executable code of the dialogue control.
This module performs the following tasks:

- translate into an intermediate data structure and then in a 'C' source code the dialogue specification retrieven from the Description file;
- insert the generated code within the skeletons (adopting the Skeleton technique like in GIGA) in order to generate the 'ad hoc' source code of the DCC.
- compile and link the code with to the system libraries obtaining the executable code of the dialogue component.

In this approach the description file is directly processed in order to generate the source code, instead of being interpreted at run-time level like in GIGA. This approach optimizes the response time of the system.

4.4 A new architecture for the User Interface Monitor

The user interface monitor has been subdivided into three components both at logical and physical levels.
The three user interface components cooperate through a message-passing mechanism using three FIFO queues which allow the token passing among the components (Figure 5).

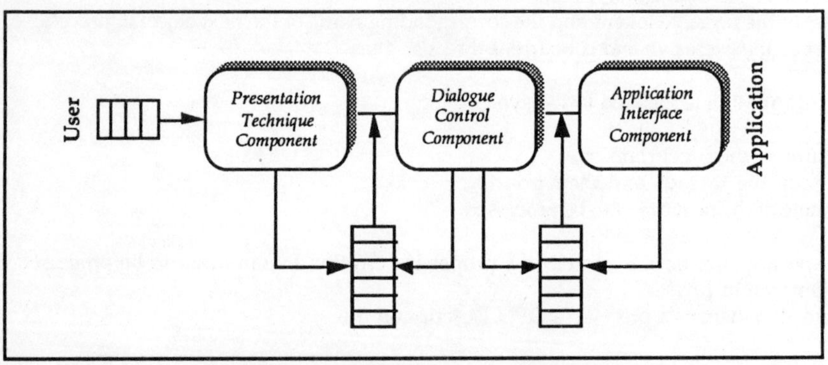

Figure 5 - User Interface Monitor at run time

Each component analyses simultaneously two bi-directional queues [12].
The adopted architecture based on three parallel processes allows the optimization of execution times and performances of the system.

5. EXAMPLE

In order to allow an evaluation of GIGA and GIGA+ two examples will be shown.
The first one illustrates the construction of a user interface for the Unix operating system by means of GIGA, so that also a non-expert user can interact with the system without having to learn the syntax of Unix commands. A set of functions for directory and file management (e.g. change directory, list directory, copy file) was chosen. The user interface constructed allows the user to log in the system and interact with it through iconic menu, providing an iconic representation of directories and files Macintosh-like.

Figure 6 and 7 show the main ATN network and sub-network defined using the ATN Editor and describing the dialogue for Unix functions management.

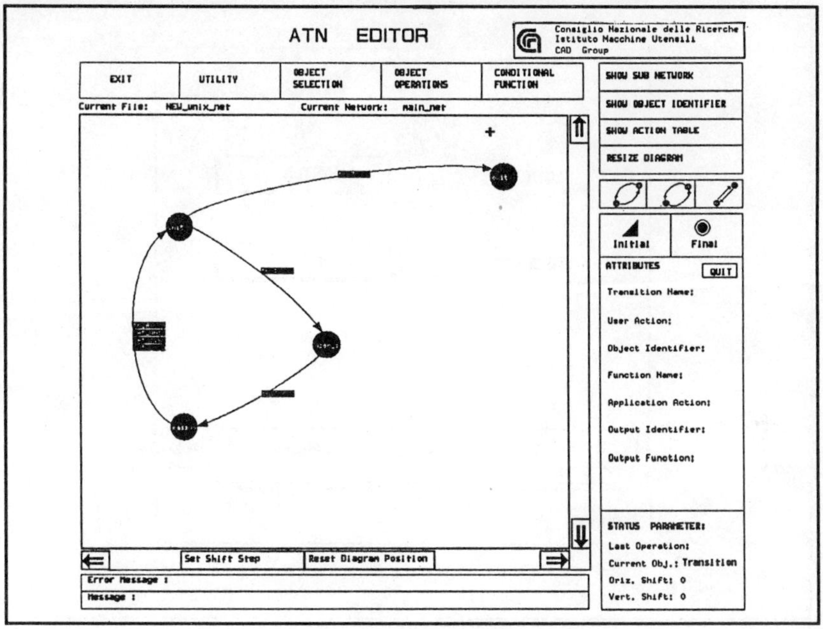

Figure 6- Main ATN network

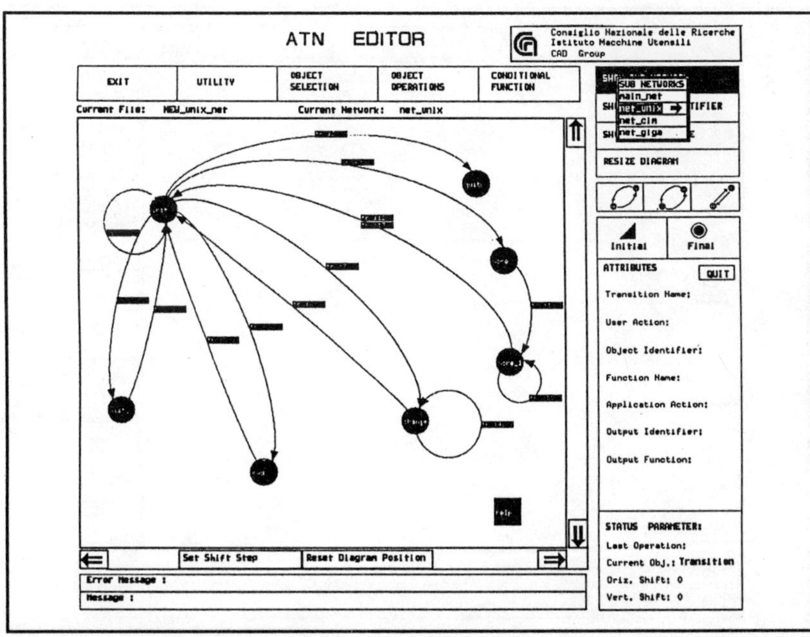

Figure 7 - sub-network

Figure 8 and 9 show two states of the user interface run time execution.

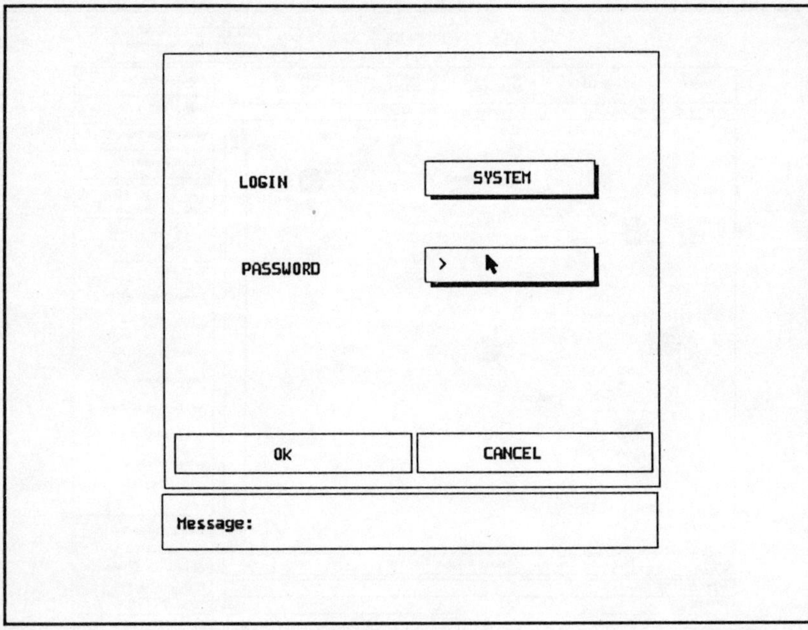

Figure 8 - Log in

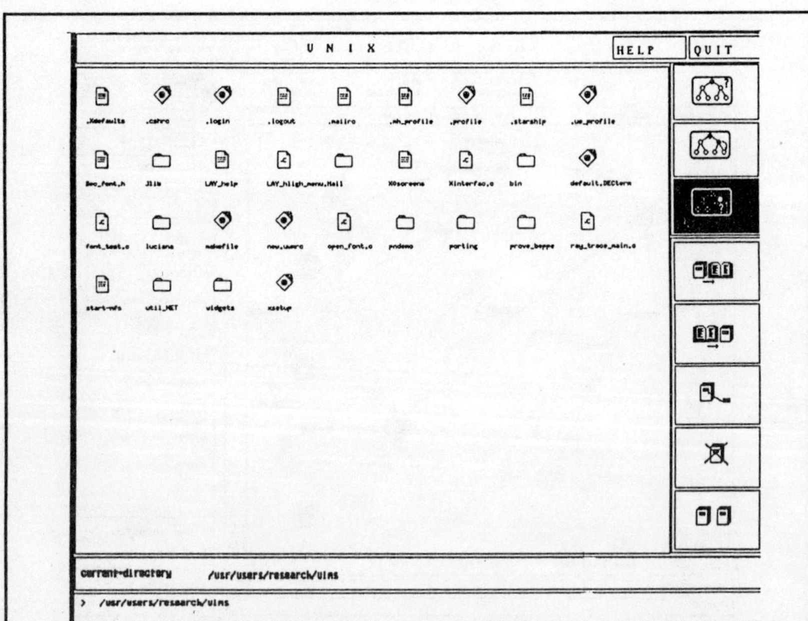

Figure 9 - Directory list

The second benchmark simulates a manufacturing environment. The context of the benchmark refers to the resources monitoring and scheduling activities. It represents a shop floor environment in which mechanical parts are produced, and it is subdivided into working sections. Each section has its own resources (drills, mills, lathe machines) that must be organized and controlled by the operator. He can choose among different monitoring policies, depending on the specified field he is dealing with. Moreover, he is allowed to directly modify parameters that determine the working schedule of the machines.
A first version of the user interface was constructed by means of GIGA within the framework of the Esprit I project n. 1556 - VITAMIN [18]. As it was not possible to describe parallel activities using the ATN notation because it sequential nature, another user interface for this example was built up using GIGA+.
The main difference between the two user interfaces is that while GIGA allows to manage only one dialogue at a time, GIGA+ can manage more than one activity, corresponding to more threads of the DPN dialogue, at the same time. It means that the end user can perform the monitoring and scheduling activity simultaneously because the system is able to maintain the context of each parallel activity.
A part of DPN describing the dialogue is shown in Figure 10.

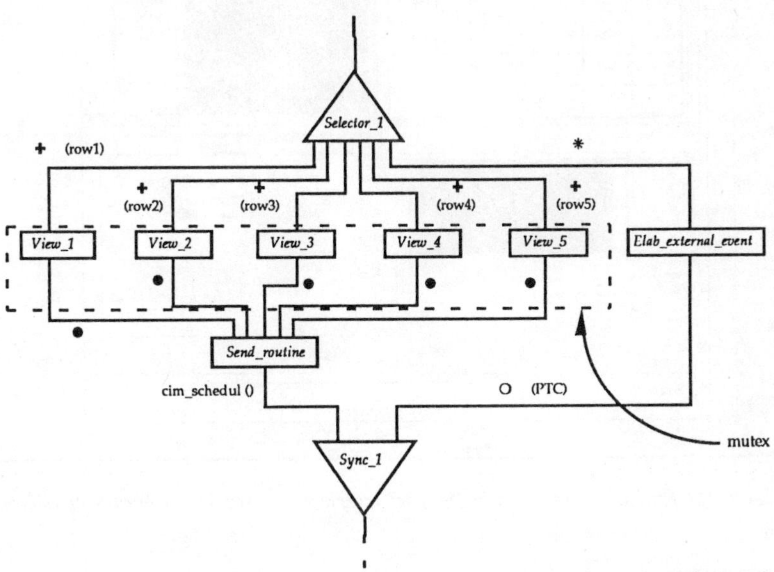

where:

- ✚ textual token (String)
- ✳ Asynchronous token (External Event)
- ● Application call request (Application)
- O Visualization request (Output)
- (..) graphical object in which occurs the event associated to the token

Figure 10- Sketch of the DPN

The dialogue description is translated by the DCC Builder into a 'C' source code which is then compiled and linked to the system binary code in order to produce the DCC run time module. The same tasks are performed to generate the AIC run time module.
During the run time execution PTC, DCC and AIC, and application package run in parallel.

The PTC reads the user input actions from the queue controlled by the application package (X in our case) and then sends the information through a queue to the DCC.
The main characteristic of the notation is that the users can perform the monitoring activity controlling and inquiring the state of a resource in the monitoring window and simultaneously modify some resource parameters (for example the number of working pieces) in the scheduling window as a concurrent thread of the DPN is associated to each task.
On the other side the AI reads the information concerning the state of the resources in the queue shared with the application and manages and sends it to the DCC through another queue.
Figure 11 visualizes a frame appearing during the run-time execution. In this case the operator can modify resources schedule in a window while the system simultaneously goes on updating the resources status on another window .

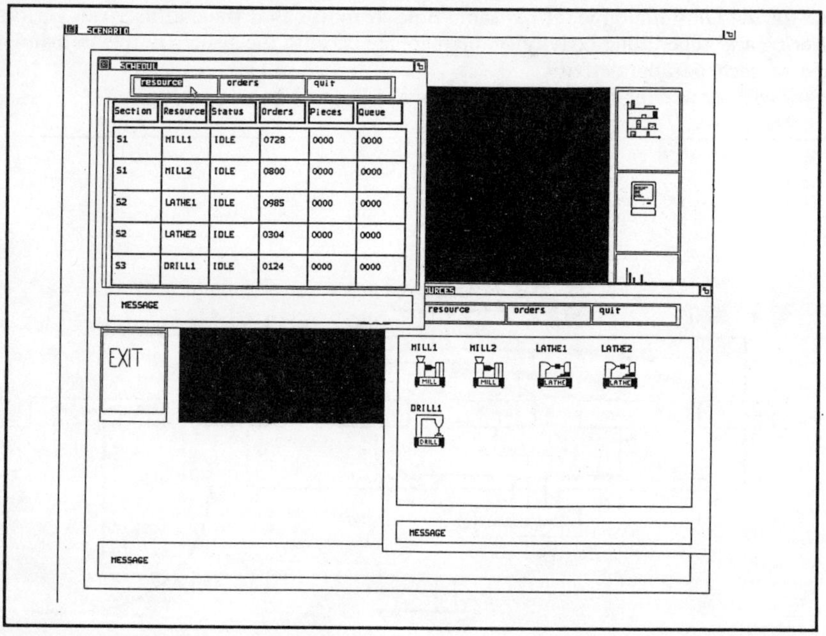

Figure 11- Run time execution of the user interface constructed by means of GIGA+.

CONCLUSIONS

In order to evaluate the performances of the two systems and possible future improvements, user interfaces for applications in different areas are being developed.
According to the criteria mentioned in [8], [10] a table of toolkit characteristics has been produced.
The evolution trends already pointed out are the following:

- bring the implementation of GIGA+ to an end developing the Presentation Technique component and a graphic and interactive editor to define the Dialogue Petri Net;
- integrate the two systems in a more general one in which the user interface designer can switch between the two notations according with his application requirements. For this purpose it has been though to implement a module which translates an ATN in the corresponding DPN one.

Moreover it has been planned to evaluate OSF/Motif and to align the two prototypes to it.

REFERENCES

[1] Pfaff Ed., G.E., *User Interface Management System*, (Springer Verlag, Berlin 1985).

[2] Foley J.D., *Models and Tools for Designers of User Computer Interfaces*, in Theoretical Foundations of Computer Graphics and CAD, NATO ASI Series, Series F, Vol. 20 (Springer Verlag,1988), pp. 1121-1151.

[3] Green M., *A survey of three Dialogue models*, ACM Transactions on Graphics, 4, 3, pp. 244-275, July 1986.

[4] Jacob Robert J.K., *A specification language for Direct-Manipulation User Interface*, ACM Vol. 5, N. 4, October 1986, pp. 283-317.

[5] Green M., *The University of Alberta User Interface Management System*, Proceeding SIGGRAPH 1985, published as Computer Graphics, 19, 3 , pp. 205-213, July 1985.

[6] Barzaghi G., *Sviluppo di un sistema per la definizione e gestione dell'interazione uomo-macchina nell'implementazione di uno UIMS*, Diploma Thesis, A.A. 87/88, Facoltà di Scienze dell'Informazione, Università di Milano.

[7] Bordegoni M., *Sviluppo di un sistema per la definizione e gestione delle tecniche di interazione e presentazione nella realizzazione di un prototipo di UIMS*, Diploma Thesis, A.A. 87/88, Facoltà di Scienze dell'Informazione, Università di Milano.

[8] Prime M., *User Interface Management Systems - A Current Product Review*, Computer Graphics Forum, Vol. 9, N.1, March 1990.

[9] Hill R.D., *Event-Responses Systems - A technique for Specifying Multi-threaded dialogues*, CHI+GI, pp. 241-247, 1987.

[10] Hartson H.R., Hix D., *Human-Computer Interface Development: Concepts and Systems for its Management*, ACM Computing Surveys, Vol. 21, N. 1, March 1989.

[11] Tanner P., *Multi-threaded Input*, published on ACM, Vol. 21, N. 2, April 1987.

[12] Moalic H., *UIM Builder Requirements*, Vitamin Document WD(SBt4.2)/STR23/V1, October 1988.

[13] Motta M., *Strumenti per la generazione di interfacce utente: sviluppo di un sistema per la descrizione e la gestione di dialoghi concorrenti basato sulle reti di Petri*, Diploma Thesis, A.A. 88/89, Facoltà di Scienze dell'Informazione, Università di Milano.

[14] Reisig W., *Reti di Petri*, Arnoldo Mondadori Editore, 1979.

[15] Bruno G., Baldassari M., *PROTOB: a case tool for modelling and prototyping production systems*, Dipartimento di Automatica e Informatica, Politecnico di Torino, 1987.

[16] Yaohan Chu, *Petri Net Design Language*, IEEE Computer Graphics, September 88.

[17] Stotts P. D., Cai Z. N., *Hierarchical Graph Models of Concurrent CIM Systems*, IEEE Computer Graphics , September 88.

[18] Allari S., Rizzi C., *LMB integration and UIM functionality based on ACD benchmark scenario*, Vitamin Document WD(SBt3.4-4.2)/R&PDM/V3, January 1989.

Chapter 23

Creating Interaction Primitives

Leif Larsson

During the use of our User Interface Management System (UIMS) TeleUSE[1] we have recognized a strong need for creating new interaction objects. We want to avoid requiring general-purpose programming skill of the designer, which is done today. If the designer can use a direct manipulative editor most of the time, and sometimes supply relations textually, we have reached that goal. A constraint solver with an intuitive interface is proposed as the solution to this problem.

1. INTRODUCTION

Since 1987 we have been developing the commercial UIMS TeleUSE and are now about to release the second version. It is based on the Seeheim model [8] developed at the original Eurographics workshop on UIMSs at Seeheim in 1983, and is at the moment built on top of the X Window System[2] and the OSF/Motif[3] toolkit.

During our customers and our own use of this system a strong need for making new interaction primitives has emerged. This is at the moment a difficult task requiring C programming skill and extensive knowledge about the toolkit. It is undesirable to require these skills of the designer.

In this paper I will first present the TeleUSE system as a framework for later discussion. The discussion then proposes a solution, based on the constraint concept, to the problem of creating new interaction primitives.

2. The TeleUSE UIMS

The TeleUSE system is based on the Seeheim model with some extensions. An overview of the system is shown in Fig. 1, where the three components of the Seeheim model are easily recognized.

Central to this system is the concept of event broadcasting. This is an extension to the Seeheim model based on the Local Event Broadcast Method (LEBM) which Hill defines in [9]. The broadcasting is done on the D-Event Bus, which thus constitutes the communication channel between the modules of the UI. In contrast to the Seeheim model, where the Application Interface Model (AIM) and the Presentation components are connected through the Dialog component, this bus connects all three components.

---

1 TeleUSE is a trademark of TELESOFT AB

2 X Window System is a trademark of the Massachusetts Institute of Technology

3 OSF, OSF/Motif and Motif are trademarks of The Open Software Foundation, Inc.

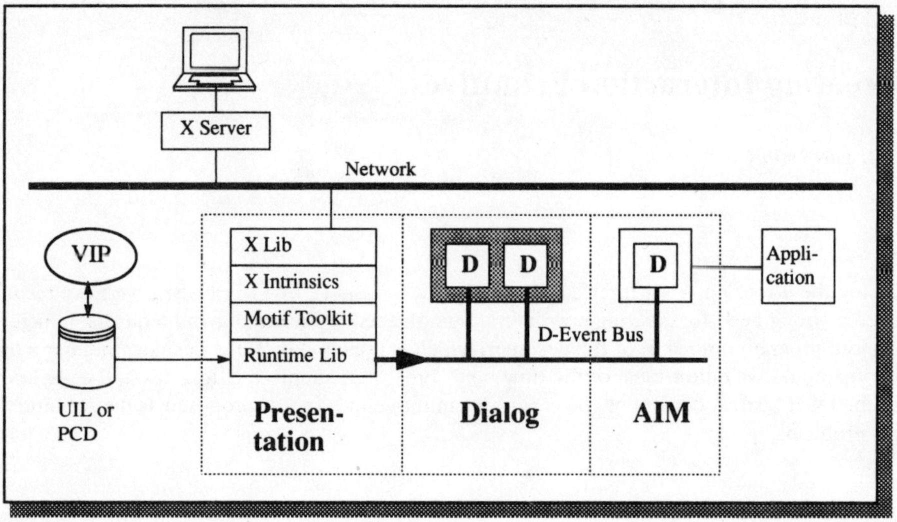

Fig. 1 The TeleUSE system

The Dialog Control component is built up by several modules, called D-Modules. These are written in a rule-based language, called D, specially designed to handle events on the bus and direct the presentation. Each rule corresponds to an event, and is fired whenever that event appears on the bus. Attached to each rule there can be a number of flags, each of which must be raised for the rule to take effect. These flags are automatically cleared when the rule is fired. The language is based on the event language ideas of LEBM, and among the advantages of it is the possibility to have multiple interactive systems running simultaneously.

The code of the rules are written in a Pascal-like syntax, extended with the possibility to raise and clear flags, and generate new events. Procedures and functions written in other languages, like C and Ada, can be called. The modules are actually compiled into C code, but they can also be interpreted when debugging.

The AIM component is formed by D-Modules which use the above calling mechanism for calling procedures and functions of the application.

The Presentation component is built up by the X-Window system, the OSF/Motif and other toolkits, and the Runtime Library. In the toolkits, interaction primitives are called widgets. These widgets use callbacks, that is call registered functions, when they want to notify the application. The Runtime Library uses this to generate D-Events on the event bus, while the reverse communication goes through a procedural interface. This is because the amount of data needed to be transferred to the toolkit is not conveniently transferred through the bus.

The Runtime Library fetches presentation objects from one or several files, each of which can be of either PCD- or UIL-format. The PCD-format is a proprietary format for defining presentation objects, both the initial state of the UI as well as dynamically instantiated objects. The UIL-format is OSF's format and does the same thing, except it only handles the initial state. The toolkit primarily handled is the OSF/Motif toolkit, but the Athena toolkit and user defined widgets, which are based on the same toolkit intrinsics, are handled as well.

The specification files can be generated by a direct manipulation editor, the VIP. With this the designer builds templates for presentation objects instantiating primitive widgets or other already defined templates. An instance inherits the attributes and their values from the template, thus if the template later is changed the instance will change accordingly. However, attributes of an instance can be set through the editor, either by direct manipulation as with position and size, or by giving values in an attribute window, and these attributes are no longer affected by inheritance. The attribute window lists some or all attributes of an instance, and the designer can set explicit values, or set that values should be inherited, for any attributes. After the designer has made his changes the result is immediately shown in all affected templates.

The use of the UIMS clearly reduces the time effort, by 50% to 90%, and cost of designing UIs. However, we have seen that the UI-designer is quite often not satisfied with the widgets available. He is then forced to construct a new widget, which is done in C language. This requires knowledge, not only about general programming, but also about the toolkit intrinsics, which is not trivial. This knowledge requirement is partly what we wanted to avoid by introducing the UIMS.

3. Constraint Programming Alternatives

To achieve the goal of not requiring general-purpose programming skill of the designer we want him to be able, as much as possible, to construct new primitives through direct manipulation. This implies there has to be a way to specify not only appearance, but also behavior, through direct manipulation. Specifying behavior in this way is actually visual programming, which Shu discusses rather thoroughly in [11]. This is very difficult when it comes to general purpose programming.

However when this technique fails we do not have to drop down to general purpose programming languages immediately. The concept of declarative programming has proven to be rather easy to understand. Spreadsheets, for example, are programmed declaratively and are normally used by non-programmers. When programming a spreadsheet the user declares a number of dependencies between objects of the spreadsheet. These dependencies are special cases of the general concept constraints.

A constraint is a relation that should be satisfied at all times. It can be any type of relation between any number of objects, but normally it is a mathematical relation, as with spreadsheets. The relations can be either one-way or multidirectional. The one-way constraint `a = b + c` means that `a` should at all times be equal to `b` plus `c` and it should not be possible to change `a`'s value to anything else, which also means that there can be no other constraint connected to `a`. The multidirectional constraint `a = b + c` means that this relation should always be satisfied, but any variable can change its value in order to satisfy the relation. For example, if `c` is given a new value, then either `a` or `b`, or both `a` and `b` change their values. This ability to redirect the constraints makes it possible to have any number of constraints connected to a variable.

In both cases the constraints can be interrelated, so when satisfying one constraint others can become not satisfied. To handle such a net of constraints we introduce a constraint solver. This powerful tool can be used directly by the designer, that is, he can textually declare relations between objects in his design, or he can instantiate templates of constraints through direct manipulation. An example of the second technique is given in Fig. 2. Here we have a toolbox with a set of icons corresponding to four constraint templates. These operates on marked objects in the Edit Window. The clothespin operates on any number of objects and constrains them to having the same position. In this case it would attach the two marked lines producing the same behavior as the attach constraint in the OSF/Motif toolkit. The distance icon operates on two objects and constrains them to maintain their current separation. The line

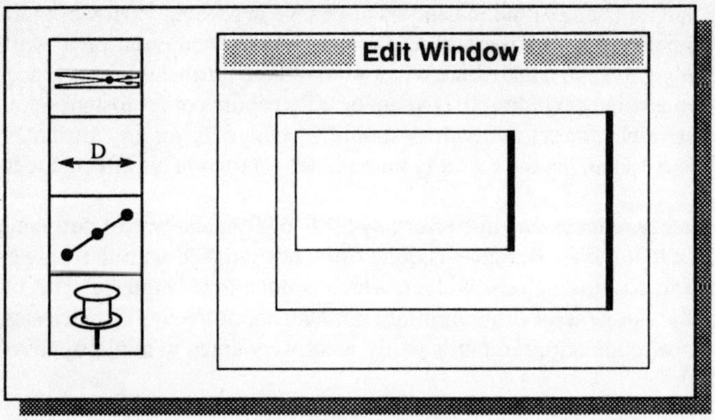

Fig. 2 Constraints through direct manipulation

with the three dots operates on three objects and constrains one of them to be in the middle of the two others. The last icon, the thumbtack, constrains one object to keep its position.

Already with this limited set of constraints we can define rather potent behaviors for our primitives. How many constraint templates we can provide the designer with is governed by our ability to construct meaningful icons when using the toolbox approach, or meaningful words or short phrases when using the menu approach. In any case, we have a limited set of constraints which probably satisfies most of the designers requirements, but not all. This is where the designer proceeds to the textual declaration of the constraints.

The textual interface could look something like Fig. 3. The sides of the two rectangles

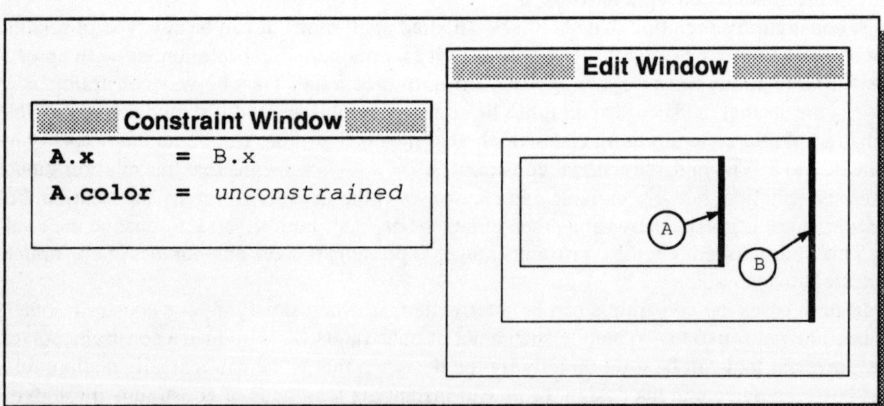

Fig. 3 Textually declared constraints

have been selected by the designer and the system has temporarily assigned them the names `A` and `B` respectively, and listed the properties of `A`. The designer has also written a constraint for the `x` property, which will have the same effect as the clothespin above. If we have a one-way constraint solver this declaration states that A.x must be equal to B.x, but it says nothing about the value of B.x. Thus the position of B can be set freely, but the position of A can only be set by setting the position of B.

If, on the other hand, we have a multidirectional constraint solver, both objects' positions may be freely set. Furthermore, if side B now is to be selected so that its properties are listed, then the x property will have the same constraint as the one defined earlier for A, but reversely defined this time.

Now the designer can declare constraints using continuous mathematical functions and operators. With a one-way constraint solver this is handled in a straight-forward manner, but with a multidirectional solver we have the problem of constructing the complementary expressions to be able to propagate values in any direction. A possible solution is to require that the designer gives these expressions too, which unfortunately impairs the declarative properties rather seriously, too much in fact for this application, as we want an intuitive tool. Thus we want either the automatic multidirectional solver or the one-way solver.

There are a number of problems which make the multidirectional solver a difficult task to implement. One was described above. Another is that the designer can very easily define an equation. If he gives the following expression:

$$A.x = (B.x)^2 + 2 \cdot (B.x) + 5$$

we have got an equation of the second degree when reversing it. This can be solved by using some iterative algorithm, but this will be slow and it adds complexity to the solver.

The semantics of the two solvers are clearly different. The multidirectional is the more powerful one, but there are situations where the semantics of the one-way solver are wanted. For example, we want to restrain the slider of a scrollbar from going outside the slider frame. If we use the multidirectional solver the frame might be enlarged when we try to drag the slider outside the boundary. The behavior we expect is that of the one-way solver. Of course we could introduce one-way constraints into the multidirectional solver, but again at the cost of a more complex system.

We believe that the power of the multidirectional solver is not of such great value in this application that it justifies the complexity involved. The one-way constraints have proven to be both powerful and easy to understand and use. Spreadsheets, for example, use one-way constraints.

We have not yet implemented the ideas presented in this paper, but in a subproject we have made a widget capable of drawing pictures from a textual definition. The properties of the objects in such a picture can have one-way constraints connected to them. Despite the lack of a direct manipulation editor for making these pictures, and a poor syntax for the constraints, the users of the widget have found it very easy to define the behavior they want through these constraints.

4. Related Work

Extensive research has been done on constraints, starting in the early 1960s with Sutherland's Sketchpad system [12]. This system, truly years ahead of its time, supplies its user with a limited set of hard-coded constraints, such as make lines vertical, horizontal, parallel or perpendicular, and a limited set of graphical primitives consisting of points, lines and circular arcs. The constraints are both displayed and manipulated graphically. Unfortunately the computers of the time was not powerful enough to support this functionality.

About fifteen years later economical personal graphics workstations, powerful enough, started to show, and in the late 1970s Borning made another milestone with ThingLab[1, 2]. This system is built as an extension of Smalltalk, combining the ideas in Sketchpad with the extensibility and object-oriented techniques of this language.

A group of Ph.D. students at the University of Washington, along with Alan Borning and Robert Duisberg, have further developed the ThingLab system and the concepts of it. This work has presented a major result, the constraint hierarchy concept. It introduces strengths for the constraints ordering them into a hierachy. At the top of the hierachy are the constraints that must be satisfied, otherwise an error condition will be raised. The constraints of the lower levels does not have to be satisfied, but the solver tries to find the best solution where the higher levels has priority over the lower ones.

This technique could actually solve the problem in the above scrollbar example. If we introduce a constraint on the size of the slider frame, with precedence over the constraint on the slider to stay within the boundary, we will get the expected behavior.

In [7] Freeman-Benson, Maloney and Borning presents an algorithm for fast solving of constraint hierachies, the DeltaBlue algorithm. It is incremental, exploiting its knowledge about the last solution to find a new. This relies on the fact that in interactive applications, which is the algorithms intended area of use, the constraint hierachy evolves gradually. They have also implemented this algorithm in ThingLab II, and this system shows the algorithm's potential for interactive use, as it is quite fast.

As a part of the article they also summarize the research on constraints, which span over many areas of computer science. They group the work done on constraint-based languages and systems into five areas: geometric layout; simulations; design, analysis, and reasoning support; user interface support; and general-purpose programming languages. The system proposed in this paper fits into both geometric layout, and user interface support, as does the above mentioned systems.

A similar system to ours, but more ambitious, is Myers' Peridot [10] with which the designer specifies the whole UI by demonstrating its appearance and behavior. It uses a one-way constraint solver for maintaining relations between objects of the UI. The system infers (guesses) what the designer means by his actions, and asks if the guesses are correct. This method actually expands the number of constraints possible to instantiate, that the system reasonably can provide, by suggesting one of them instead of listing them for selection. Thus, this could be an alternative to the iconic or menu approach. There are, however, some situations where it will generate a lot of suggestion. For example, if we have put a rectangle inside another rectangle, as in Fig. 3, the system may suggest that it should be centered; aligned left, right, down or up, with or without the current offset; hold the same relative size, horizontally or vertically; etc. The designer may actually want no constraint, or one of or a combination of the suggested constraints. This is similar to the menu approach, but the constraints available are governed by the inference system.

Other work on constraint systems for UIMSs has been done by Carter and LaLonde [3], using constraints in implementing a syntax-based program editor; Szekely and Myers with Coral [13], which is related to Peridot; vander Zanden [14], combining constraints with attribute grammars; Ege [4, 5], building a UI construction system that uses a filter metaphor; and Epstein and LaLonde [6], using constraint hierachies in controlling the layout of Smalltalk windows.

5. CONCLUSION

Constraint solvers are powerful tools which are highly suitable for the area of UIs, where much of the behavior of interaction objects is easily expressed through constraints. When limiting ourselves to the area of making new interaction primitives, it is also possible to identify a small set of constraints which handles the most common behaviors. This small set can be instantiated by means of direct manipulation, taking us very near our goal of not requiring general-purpose programming skill of the designer. As the designer gains more experience he can move on to the more difficult levels of textually defining powerful constraints. This is actually the major advantage of this system; as the designer's experience increases he gains more power!

This model should be highly applicable to the dialog component. The set of constraints handling the most common behaviors though will probably be larger, and thus less suitable for direct manipulation.

REFERENCES

1. Borning A.: ThingLab—A constraint-oriented simulation laboratory. Ph.D. dissertation, Dept. of Computer Science, Stanford Univ., Stanford, Calif., Mars 1979.
2. Borning A.: The programming language aspects of ThingLab, a constraint-oriented simulation laboratory. ACM Trans. Prog. Lang. Syst. 3, October 1981, pp. 353-387.
3. Carter C. A., and LaLonde W. R.: The design of a program editor based on constraints. Tech. Rep. CS TR 50, Carleton University, May 1984.
4. Ege R. K.: Automatic Generation of Interactive Displays Using Constraints. Ph.D. dissertation, Department of Computer Science and Engineering, Oregon Graduate Center, August 1987.
5. Ege R. K., Maier D., and Borning A.: The filter browser—Defining interfaces graphically. Proceedings of the European Conference on Object-Oriented Programming, Paris, June 1987, pp. 155-165.
6. Epstein D., and LaLonde W.: A smalltalk window system based on constraints. Proceedings of the 1988 ACM Conference on Object-Oriented Programming Systems, Languages and Applications, San Diego, September 1988, pp. 83-94.
7. Freeman-Benson B.N., Maloney J., and Borning A.: An Incremental Constraint Solver. Communications of the ACM 1, January 1990, *pp. 54-63*.
8. Green M.: Report on Dialogue Specification Tools. In: Günther E.Pfaff (ed.) User Interface Management Systems. Springer-Verlag, 1985, *pp. 9-20*.
9. Hill R.D.: Supporting Concurrency, Communication and Synchronization in Human-Computer Interaction. Ph.D. dissertation, Computer Science Department, University of Toronto, 1987.
10. Myers B.: Creating user interfaces by demonstration. Ph.D. dissertation, Computer Science Department, University of Toronto, 1987.
11. Shu N. C.: Visual programming: Perspectives and approaches. IBM Systems Journal, vol. 28, no. 4, 1989, pp. 525-547.
12. Sutherland I.: Sketchpad: A man-machine graphical communication system. Proc. Spring Joint Computer Conference, IFIPS, 1963, *pp. 329-345*.
13. Szekely P., and Myers B. A.: A user-interface toolkit based on graphical objects and constraints. Proceedings of the 1988 ACM Conference on Object-Oriented Programming Systems, Languages and Applications, San Diego, September 1988, pp. 36-45.
14. vander Zanden B. T.: An Incremental Planning Algorithm for Ordering Equations in a Multilinear System of Constraints. Ph.D. dissertation, Department of Computer Science, Cornell University, April 1988.

Part V

Toolkits, Environments and the OO Paradigm

Chapter 24

The Composite Object User Interface Architecture

Ralph D. Hill and Marc Herrmann

1 Abstract

In order to provide effective support for the development of direct manipulation interfaces, the Tube project proposes an alternative to the widely discussed linguistic and Seeheim models. The alternative structure, called the Composite Object Architecture (COA), is based on the concept of User Interface Object.

The architecture of the Tube environment has been described in (*Hill and Herrmann 89*), the methodological basis of the Composite Object Architecture is discussed in (*Herrmann and Hill 89.b*) and as reported in (*Kuntz and Melchert 89 a, b and c*) the implementation of a graphical direct manipulation interface to a KBMS has been based on the COA.

The purpose of this paper is to describe the principles of the COA, to illustrate it on a non trivial example and to make its advantages explicit.

Keywords: User interface architecture, user interface development and prototyping tools, interactive software structure.

2 Introduction — The Problem

Historically, User Interface Management Systems and the design of user interfaces has been based on a layered linguistic model first proposed by Foley and Wallace (*Foley and Wallace 74*), and reinforced in (*Foley and van Dam 82*), and the Seeheim model of UIMSs (*Green 85*). This model decomposes an interface into lexical, syntactical and semantic layers, following standard practice in linguistics and in compiler construction.

This decomposition works well for small interfaces with static displays and for interfaces that fit the linguistic model well, but this does not include modern graphical direct manipulation interfaces. In these interfaces, there is a large, frequently changed set of objects visible to the end-user. Most of these objects can change and interact with the end-user at virtually any time. Because of the dynamic nature of these dialogues, they are difficult to encode as single language specification, suggesting that a linguistic structured UIMS is not appropriate.

Four main limitations of the linguistic model in the context of modern direct manipulation interfaces (DM) are:

Modularity
: For a large DM interface, each layer becomes very large, but there are no guidelines for decomposing each layer. In particular, it is impractical to explicitly represent all the options that are available to a user in a single syntax specification.

Levels of Abstraction
: To a powerful character oriented text editor, every key stroke (even the shift and control keys) should be seen at the syntactic level. A spreadsheet program, however, may only want to get complete words, commands or lines at the syntactic level. Now,

if the text editor is used by the spreadsheet to collect user input for each cell, where does the lexical-syntactic boundary go?

The lexical-syntactic and syntactic-semantic boundaries can be more or less abstract, depending on the context and the application. The model does not say how to establish boundaries on the different levels, or how to address problems arising from the different levels of abstraction at the boundaries between the layers.

Feedback and Output

The Seeheim model tries to provide for feedback and output, but the problem of providing rapid feedback that depends on the state of the application (and hence tells the user what is really happening) remains. Input must go through all the layers before application dependent feedback can be generated. This is computationally expensive and requires writing code at each level to establish the connection. Minor changes in feedback may require a lot of coding to access the required information and to transfer it through each layer.

Dynamics

The linguistic model does not offer any help when dealing with interfaces where objects can be added and deleted dynamically, as is common in many DM interfaces such those based on the desktop metaphore. These changes to the set of objects change the set of commands accepted and the way they can be applied. Using the linguistic model, this is supported by statically coding all possible options into the interface.

Despite the success of the linguistic and Seeheim models in dealing with some types of interfaces, these problems render them unusable for modern interfaces. The problem is that the origin of the linguistic model lies in the processing of static sequential languages. DM interfaces can be represented as static sequential languages, but the transformation requires tremendous effort, and results in an implementation structure that is far removed from the conceptual structure. As concluded in (*Olsen, et al. 87*), what is needed is a new approach to structuring the implementation of the user interface that addresses the needs of DM interfaces and lets the implementation structure match the conceptual structure.

3 The Composite Object Architecture and Tube

The goal of the Composite Object Architecture (COA), the architectural basis of Tube, is to support advanced graphical direct manipulation interfaces, and be extensible to support future user interface styles. It does this by providing object definition and composition tools that match the dynamic, object-oriented conceptual models of DM interfaces.

Using the COA, interfaces are built by composing the appearance, behaviour, and (sometimes) semantics of objects, into more complex objects. A user interface as a whole is simply an object that is the composition of other objects. These compositions can be changed at run-time (adding, deleting or modifying component objects of objects), thus providing a mechanism for supporting dynamic changes to object appearance and behaviour, and hence user interface appearance and behaviour.

3.1 User Interface Objects

User Interface Objects (UIOs) are the basic building blocks of the Composite Object Architecture. In general, a UIO is anything a user can see or manipulate.

This implies that there are three aspects of a UIO that must be defined: display, behaviour and, when required, semantics or the connection to the application.

These aspects are orthogonal to the linguistic model's layers.

Tube provides a basic set of primitive UIOs. These are simple graphical classes such as line, rectangle and text. All UIOs are built by composing or specializing these objects into more complex objects, and extending them with behaviour and semantics. Tube also provides a library of commonly used User Interface Objects such as text box, button and radio button set — these were built with Tube from the primitives. Application domain specialized libraries can be obtained in a similar way.

3.2 Compositions of Objects

To build an interface from UIOs, it is necessary to select or construct UIOs that are specific to the needs of the interface or application and assemble them into an interface.

Ultimately, a user interface is just a large, application specific UIO made by composing or specializing simpler UIOs. Thus, most aspects of user interface construction are thus reduced to selection and composition of UIOs.

The result of these compositions is a tree of UIOs. For example, a menu could be constructed as follows:

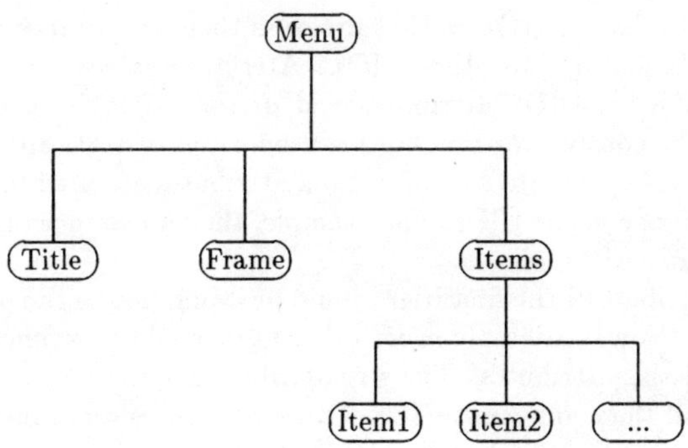

Figure 3.1: Structure of the *menu* UIO

This menu is a composition of a *title* UIO, a *frame* UIO, and a collection of *item* UIOs. The specification of the menu UIO would say that the title appears *above* the items, and the frame goes *around* everything. There would also be some specification of the behaviour of the menu in terms of the behaviour of the items.

The *items* UIO is a composition of several *items*. Its specification would say how to organize these items on the display. The *items* would be constructed from the basic UIOs *text* and *rectangle*:

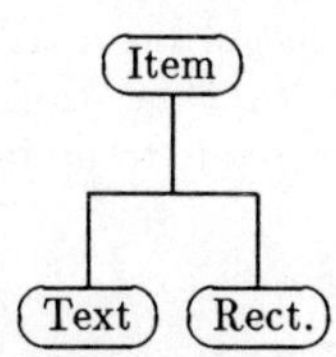

Figure 3.2: Structure of the *item* UIO

The specification of the item class would say how to arrange the text and rectangle (text *inside* the rectangle), and how to react to the mouse (highlighting, de-highlighting, signalling the *menu* UIO when they are selected). The *text* and *rectangle* UIO classes are not likely to have useful default behaviours, so the behaviour for the items would have to be a new behaviour associated with the *item* class.

The UIOs are retained in an explicit tree used as the basis of the run-time system. Hence, no single UIO has a large or complex specification or implementation, but the overall behaviour can be arbitrarily complex by making the tree of UIOs arbitrarily large. Also, making the UIOs explicit in the run-time structure makes it easy to add and delete objects in the interface at run-time by extending and pruning the tree, thus supporting dynamic aspects of the interface.

Note that having an explicit structure of UIOs is necessary, but not sufficient. There must be suitable tools for manipulating the structure, maintaining consistency between the tree and the display, and creating the UIOs.

3.3 The Composition *Glue*

Composing Presentation

In Tube, all UIOs have *attributes* that describe their appearance (e.g., position, size, font, colour) or relationships to other UIOs. Attribute values are often constants but can be *functions* of other UIOs' attributes and/or the display structure. The values of attributes (either the constant or function) can be assigned statically or at run-time.

When UIOs are collected into a composition, attributes are used to control the composition of the appearance of the UIOs. For example, the appearance of a vertically aligned menu could be composed as follows:

The position attribute of the first item would be a function of the position of the menu as a whole. The position attribute of every other item would be a function of the previous item's position and size attributes. The size attribute for the menu would be a function of the the sizes of all the component UIOs. Other attributes and functions could be used to ensure consistency of fonts, colours and sizes.

(Tube includes a library of common attribute functions, so most, or all of these functions would be selected from a library rather than written anew.)

These attribute functions would be assigned when the composition is defined, or at run-time when the composition is changed (say, setting the position attribute of a new menu item as it is added to the menu, or changing the functions to switch from a horizontal menu to a vertical menu). Once the functions are in place, the attribute system automatically maintains their values, so the appearance of the composite object is maintained. For example, moving the menu would cause the positions of all the the items in the menu to be updated, so they all move with it.

The attributes are automatically and efficiently updated by an attribute evaluator which is based on attribute grammar techniques (*Reps 82*). Because the complete description of the appearance of the UIOs is stored in attribute values and the display structure, it is easy to monitor the state of the attributes and display structure, and update the display whenever necessary. In Tube, this is handled automatically – the user interface implementor never writes any code to update the display.

Composing Behaviour

In Tube, the behaviour of each UIO is expressed in a short program written in an extension of Event-Response Language (ERL) (*Hill 87*). ERL is a rule based language that was designed to simplify the implementation of complex behaviour in user interfaces.

ERL provides a very light weight process mechanism that uses non-blocking message passing for communication and synchronization. This process mechanism is used to run the rules for each UIO as a separate process.

Each ERL rule has three components: input, condition and actions. When the input is received, and condition is true, the actions are carried out. Typically, the input is an indication of a user action, but could be a message from another UIO. At the lowest level, the input is a message from the mouse indicating mouse motion or a button press. The actions can change attribute values in the UIO, and can send messages to other UIOs.

Behaviour is explicitly composed by passing messages up and down the tree. For example, a menu item will accept input from the mouse, and detect that the user has selected the item. The item would then send a message up the tree to the menu indicating that the item was selected. The menu then may send a more abstract message further up the tree of UIOs, indicating that a specific command or option has been selected. Similarly, control messages coming from higher in the tree can be broadcast to component UIOs.

Note that this approach to composition leaves control in the hands of every UIO. Each UIO gets to choose what to do. This ensures that interacts that are directly with a UIO (such as simple highlighting for feedback) are handled locally. Other objects only become involved when necessary. As a result, behaviour specifications remain small and response is usually very quick.

Composition of Semantics

Some UIOs must be connected to the application, to notify the application of updates the user has requested, and to notify the user interface of new or changed data that must be displayed to the user. The connections between the UIOs and the application are orthogonal to the tree of UIOs. In particular, the application structure need not be analogous to the structure of the tree of UIOs.

Currently, in Tube, we use both the attribute system and ERL's message passing to communicate between the UIOs and the application. Attributes and functions are convenient for communicating stateful information, while message passing is convenient for event oriented information.

Since user interface designers and implementors, and the COA, have little impact on the structure of the application, it is difficult to provide elegant techniques to compose semantics that are beyond object oriented programming. In practice, UIOs that must access the application, access those parts that they have to. This may mean that some UIOs may communicate with several parts of the application, or that one part of the application must communicate with several UIOs. Composition is a consequence of this ad hoc, non-one-to-one communication.

3.4 Interface Dynamics in Tube

The display the user sees is altered at run-time by changing attributes of UIOs, or the structure of the display tree (adding, deleting, and moving UIOs in the tree). Both of these are done from ERL rules in response to user input, or by the application program. Note that changing the structure of the tree changes more than the appearance. It changes the composition of composite objects, implying great flexibility. Also, it can add or delete UIOs that the user can manipulate, thus changing the behaviour of the interface as a whole. These dynamic aspects of the interface would be difficult to support in a system based on the linguistic or Seeheim models, but is trivial in Tube because the COA makes the objects and their composition explicit. Making the composition explicit makes it a manipulable aspect of the interface design and implementation.

4 Structuring Interactive Software

The purpose if this section is to show:

- that, using the COA, the interface implementation structure matches the application's conceptual structure;
- how the COA helps to design user interfaces that are on the application level of abstraction;
- how to implement these UIs using Tube.

For illustrating the COA applied to a realistic task, we will sketch the development of a syntax directed editor.

Syntax-directed editors allow the end-user, who is a programmer, to concentrate on the programming tasks by providing:

syntactic assistance in that the system has explicit knowledge of the language's syntax and lets the end-user build a program by manipulating[1] so called *templates*. Each *template* represents a syntactic construct, e.g. an **if** statement, which makes explicit, the information the programmer has to provide. From this point of view, creating a program using a syntax-directed editor is a kind of form filling operation, in which the form itself is evolving through interaction with the user.

static semantics assistance in that the system also has the knowledge of the language's static semantics. It is therefore able to provide immediate feedback when an error of this nature occurs, e.g. the reference to the non-declared variable **m** in function **fact** (see figure 4.1).

```
program prog-name ( file-name, file-name )
   const const-name = value ;
   type type-name = type-definition ;
   var i : integer ;
       j : type ;
       var-name : type ;

   function fact (n : integer) : integer ;
   begin
       if boolean-expression
       then fact := 1
       else [fact := [m] * fact( n - 1 )] ;
   end ;

   begin (* MAIN *)
       writeln( "fact( "; n ; ") = ", fact( read (input)));
   end .
```

Figure 4.1: Syntax directed editing

During the specification and the development of interactive software, we will have to consider it from four different points of view:

[1]Manipulating: inserting, deleting, modifying, moving around, etc.

The abstract point of view (section 4.1) tells how the software will meet its requirements from a functional point of view, e.g. which are the concepts, how are they represented and manipulated. This is done by taking interactiveness into account from the start[2].

The concrete point of view (section 4.2) defines how the concepts are presented, i.e. how the output devices are used, and how the user will interact with the presented concepts using the input devices, e.g. keyboard, mouse, etc.

The relation between the abstract and concrete points of view (section 4.3) which leads to choose the type control, e.g. internal, external or mixed control, knowing and making sure that the abstract and concrete points of view must be kept consistent.

The implementation point of view (section 4.4).

4.1 The Abstract Point of View

In syntax directed editors, programs are represented internally as decorated *abstract-syntax trees* (*Reps 82*). These are used by the system for both syntax and incremental static semantics checking. An abstract-syntax tree is built up by nodes — each node class corresponding to a template.

In the abstract syntax tree an *if* statement, for example, is represented as a node of arity two or three, i.e.:

- *if*(Condition, ThenPart), where *ThenPart* is a statement;
- *if*(Condition, ThenPart, ElsePart), *ElsePart* also being a statement.

The operations the end-user can perform are represented by tree-operators, i.e. operations defined on the corresponding class (or type) of nodes. For *if* nodes, the following set can be defined:

Accessors	Modifiers
Condition(if) ⇒ expr	SetCondition(if, expr) ⇒ if
ThenPart(if) ⇒ stmt	SetThenPart(if, stmt) ⇒ if
ElsePart(if) ⇒ stmt	SetElsePart(if, stmt) ⇒ if

Figure 4.2: Operations defined on the *if* template

Each template is then considered as an abstraction which is characterized by:

the parameters , e.g. the *if*'s condition, ThenPart and ElsePart;

the accessors and modifiers which are defining the operations the end-user can perform.

4.2 The Concrete Point of View - The Interface with the User

Depending on the targeted end-users and/or program layout style preferences, abstract syntax trees can be presented in many different ways, as show in figure 4.3 representing if templates.

[2]This last statement is particularly obvious for syntax-directed editors: incremental evaluation techniques are only justified by the software's interactive use.

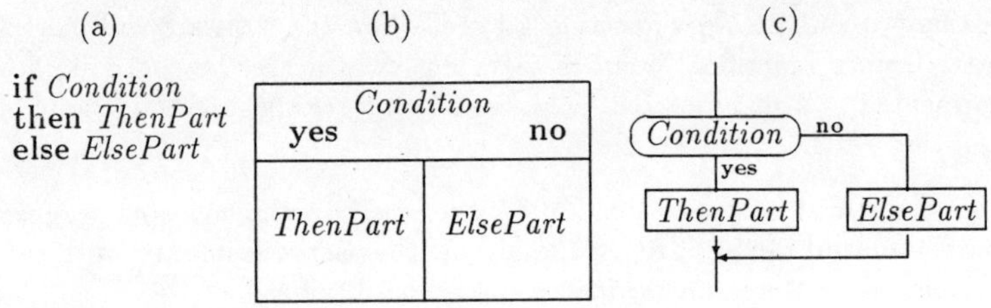

Figure 4.3: Different representations of the same information.

Ignoring the ergonomic properties of each representation, we will focus on the fact that these different representations have fundamentally different geometric and interaction properties — never the less, they will have to be considered by the application implementor as having the same *characteristics* since:

- they are representing the same abstraction and,
- this aspect of the software is subject to improvements and therefore to changes. In effect, (rapid) prototyping is well known to be the best method for designing good (acceptable ?) user-interfaces.

Therefore, these *characteristics* have to be choosen so that they are:

1. device independent;
2. look and feel independent, since it is what we want to be able to prototype and to change at low cost;
3. relevant to the user and user-interface designer's concepts.

Rather than trying to define these *characteristics* artificially, we are choosing the simplest way to go which is to delegate inside the interface as much semantics as necessary so that both parts, i.e. application and user-interface, are talking the same "language" — with the ultimate goal of maintaining both views consistent.

4.3 The Relation Between the Abstract and Concrete Points of View

The protocol which implements the relation between application and UI is based on the application's abstractions. The parameters, accessors and modifiers defined for the abstract syntax tree-nodes are therefore also defined for the UIOs which are representing them.

This entails that the *if* UIO is a parameterized object taking up to three arguments, the first one being the representation of the *Condition*, the second one the *ThenPart*'s representation, etc and its accessors and modifiers will be those defined in section 4.1.

More formally, if $\mathcal{U}(x)$ represents the operation that transforms the abstraction x into its concrete representation x_{uio} and $\mathcal{P}(x_{uio})$ being the reverse operation, then the abstraction and its corresponding representation are linked by the constraint:

The purpose of the application-UI protocol is the incremental maintenance of the just described constraint. It can be implemented either by announcement/recognition (*Szekely*

$$\mathcal{U}(if(Condition, ThenPart, ElsePart))$$
$$=$$
$$if_{uio}(\mathcal{U}(Condition), \mathcal{U}(ThenPart), \mathcal{U}(ElsePart)) \ (1)$$
and
$$\mathcal{P}(if_{uio}(Condition_{uio}, ThenPart_{uio}, ElsePart_{uio}))$$
$$=$$
$$if(\mathcal{P}(Condition_{uio}), \mathcal{P}(ThenPart_{uio}), \mathcal{P}(ElsePart_{uio}))(2)$$

Figure 4.4:

88), or by using a constraint system (*Ege 86*) — the point here is that the maintenance must take place at the application abstraction level. In our example, this is done by implementing the following protocol:

$$SetCondition(if, new - condition) \leadsto SetCondition(if_{uio}, \mathcal{U}(new - condition)) \ (1)$$
and
$$SetCondition(if_{uio}, new - condition_{uio}) \leadsto SetCondition(if, \mathcal{P}(new - condition_{uio})) \ (2)$$

Figure 4.5:

Where $X \leadsto Y$ has the meaning: Y is a consequence of X.

The scheme defined in figure 4.5 also holds for the *then* and *else* parts. More generally, it applies for all application modifiers having a consequence on the user-interface and/or to all UIO modifiers having a consequence on the application data.

Depending on where the control resides, the just defined relation scheme can be simplified. When internal control is used, the protocol is defined by the parts marked (1) in figures 4.4 and 4.5. When external control is used, part (1) of figure 4.5 is not required and part (1) of figure 4.4 is only used during the application's initialization phase; mixed control requires the full protocol.

The implementation of the user interface, as it is shown in section 4.4, consists in the implemention of this protocol, i.e. defining new classes of objects using pre-existing ones (specialization) and defining on the resulting UIOs the required access-methods. This is done by expressing the mapping between the abstract point of view and the UIO's real representation.

4.4 Implementing the Interface Between User and Application

The following UIO definition implements figure 4.3 (a). It is obtained by specializing the VBox UIO, which arranges vertically a collection of UIOs (here three HBoxes), and its behaviour is defined by the *if-behaviour* rule set (included below). An HBox arranges horizontally a collection of UIOs. The three HBoxes containt the three parts of the if statement, i.e. *Condition*, *ThenPart* and *ElsePart*. The *if* UIO class is thus defined as:

```
(def-uio if (Condition ThenPart &OPTIONAL (ElsePart placeholder) )
;;;
;;; An IF object is parameterized by its Condition, ThenStmt and ElseStm
;;; which already are UIOs. What is expressed herein is how to obtain the
;;; class of IF objects by using some more general class of objects,
;;; VBOX in this case.
;;;
   (%include   VBox)              ; if is a specialization of VBox.
   (%behaviour if-behaviour)      ; behaviour defined by if-behaviour rule set.
   (%presentation
       (%part HBox (%part SelectableText ''if'') Condition)
       (%part HBox (%part SelectableText ''then'') ThenPart)
       (%part HBox (%part SelectableText ''else'') ElsePart)
) )
```

Let us now sketch the *if*'s behaviour by showing an example of dialogue combination: the *if* will react differently when the *ThenPart* and *ElsePart* are, or are not, both filled-in. This is implemented as follows: when the ThenPart is filled in, it sends the event ThenFilledIn to the if UIO, similarly, the ElsePart sends the event ElseFilledIn. These two events carry a boolean value which is T when the UIOs have been filled-in and nil if the value is the PlaceHolder. This is implemented by:

```
(erl-module if-behaviour

   (%context (ThenIsFilledIn  ())    ; the if's module local variables.
             (ElseIsFilledIn  ()))

   (ThenFilledIn T     ; the <ThenFilledIn> comes in and the associated
                       ; condition is T. Keep the value carried by the event.
             (setq ThenIsFilledIn (value ThenFilledIn)))
   (ElseFilledIn T     ; ditto
             (setq ElseIsFilledIn (value ElseFilledIn)))
   (Selected (and ThenIsFilledIn ElseIsFilledIn)
             ;
             ; The <Selected> event comes in and both parts are filled in.
             ; => Use the menu allowing the swap.
             ;
   )
   (Selected (not (and ThenIsFilledIn ElseIsFilledIn))
             ; The <Selected> event comes in and both parts are not filled in.
             ; => Use the menu which does not allow the swap.
             ;
   )
   ...)
```

The presentation and the behaviour being defined, we now have to implement the relations defined in figure 4.5, i.e. the *if*'s accessors and modifiers.

Remark: in a polished system, these accessors and modifiers could be generated more or less automatically. This aspect of Tube is currently under development.

```
(defmethod Condition ((object if) &optional (new-value 'NoNewValue))
;;;
;;; Returns: The <if>'s Condition of <object>if one argument is provided.
;;;          <object> and Sets the <if>'s Condition to <new-value> otherwise.
;;;
  (if (eq new-value 'NoNewValue)
      ;;;
      ;;;  It is the rightmost part of <if>'s first part. No doubt, the tree
      ;;; structure is not transparent to the UI implementor... Return
      ;;; the <condition> UIO.
      ;;;
      (right-most-part (ith-part object 1))
      ;;;
      ;;;  Modify the <if>'s Condition.
      ;;;
      (progn (right-most-part (ith-part object 1) new-value))
             object))
```

The other accessors of the if UIO, *ThenPart* and *ElsePart*, are defined similarly.

Continuing with the implementation of the presentation facet, we will now show how to implement "boxes" as described in (*Coutaz 84*), (*Ceugniet, et al. 87*) or in a slightly different way in (*Linton, et al. 89*).

As previously stated, a VBox is a compound object that arranges all its components vertically by setting the components' position attribute with the right function, i.e. the *below-previous* equation. The VBox class can thus be defined as:

```
(def-uio VBox (&REST list-of-components)
;;;
;;;  VBox's parts are those contained in the list <list-of-components>. Since
;;; these parts are positioned vertically, the value of their <position>
;;; attribute will be defined by an equation: the one named <below-previous>.
;;;
  (%include  tree)              ; VBox is a specialization of <tree>
  (%attributes                  ; New attributes to be defined.
      (VSpacement   0)
      (HSpacement  10))
  (%presentation                ; How to transform and initialize the items
      (%append-parts            ; contained in <list-of-components> so that
          (%init-attributes     ; the result matches the parameters required
                                ; by the <tree> UIO.
              (position (equation-named 'below-previous))
          )
          list-of-components)))
```

In order to be able to manipulate *VBoxes*, one has to define two methods. These simply tell what to do when an object is inserted or extracted from the context defined by the compound object. These are:

```
(defmethod insert-in-context ((context VBox) component)
;;;
;;;  What to do when <component> is inserted in a VBox... set the
;;; position attribute with the right equation !!!
;;;
   (position component (equation-named 'below-previous))
   component)


(defmethod extract-from-context ((context VBox) component)
;;;
;;;  What to do when <component> is extracted from a VBox... remove the
;;; position attribute's equation !!!
;;;
   (rema component 'position)
   component)
```

We must now define the equation which computes the position of a VBox's components, i.e. below the previous one if any. The form *(dynamic (previous component))* which is used in this equation simply tells the attribute system that any attribute whose value is defined by this equation must be re-evaluated when an object is added or removed in the local neighborhood.

```
(def-equation below-previous (component)
;;;
;;;  This equation computes the position of <component> so that it appears
;;; below its predecessor.
;;;
  (let ((object-box (geta component 'bounding-box)))
    (build-point
      (- (geta component 'HSpacement) (region-x object-box))   ; The X
      (+ (geta component 'VSpacement)                          ; The Y
         (- (region-y component))
         (if (previous component)
             (+ (point-y  (geta (dynamic (previous component)) 'position))
                (region-y (geta (dynamic (previous component))
                                'bounding-box))
                (region-height (geta (dynamic (previous component))
                                       'bounding-box))
                (geta (part-of component) 'VSpacement))
             0)))))
```

The *def-uio* expression, the two methods and this last equation completely describe the implementation of the VBox class; the HBox can be implemented in a similar way.

5 Advantages of the Composite Object Architecture

Section 1 describes four limitations of the linguistic model of interaction: here they are discussed as advantages of the composite object architecture.

Modularity

The composite object architecture leads naturally to a decomposition into components that are small enough to be easily created and modified. Also, each UIO class is a class in the object-oriented programming sense. Hence, the UIO class definitions can be freely modified as long as the interface to the application and the other UIOs remains unchanged by virtue of abstraction (*[Herrmann and Hill 89.a]*). This allows the implementation of the UIO or the interface to the user to be changed without affecting the rest of the interface — a common goal of modularity.

Levels of Abstraction

The various levels in the tree can be viewed as different levels of abstraction. The UIOs near the leaves of the tree are concerned with low-level input and feedback. Higher levels in the tree deal with more abstract events such as complete commands. If a user interface designer is concerned with details of interaction, such as the exact meaning of button clicks in a powerful text editor, then the designer can work with the lowest level of the tree. Someone building a spread sheet could take the whole editor, and use it like any other UIO, (possibly using one editor per spread sheet cell), concentrating not on how the information is input, edited and presented, but what it means in the context of the spread sheet.

Feedback and Output

The COA bring together, in each UIO, all the elements needed to provide useful feedback for that node, quickly. As well, the declarative nature of the display specification and the display manager significantly simplify the generation of graphical output and the maintenance of display consistency.

Dynamics

The composite object architecture encourages interfaces whose behaviour is linked to the visible objects, and whose appearance can be easily and quickly changed at run-time. By simply changing the display structure or some attributes, both the appearance and global behaviour of the interface are changed.

6 Other Advantages of COA

Relation to the User Model

The UIOs have a natural relation with user's concepts. Thus, the COA allows interfaces to be designed, implemented and managed in terms of concepts that are relevant to the user and the user interface designer, not artificially designed to meet the needs of the implementation structure. This greatly simplifies the implementation and the modification of user interfaces.

Simple Decomposition

It is easy to argue for modularity and structured programming, but often difficult to provide good tools and guidelines for decomposition. In our experience, it is easy to decompose an interface into UIOs because the COA matches the natural structure of the interface.

7 Conclusion

The traditional UIMS structures work well for some classes of interfaces, but are not appropriate for modern graphical DM interfaces. Object-oriented programming has been proposed as an alternative, but it lacks the structure and the task specific support required (*Dance, et al. 87*). We have developed the Composite Object Architecture to explicitly address the needs of modern interfaces. It goes beyond object-oriented programming by having an appropriate structure and supporting composition of behaviour and presentation using a well founded methodology (*Herrmann and Hill 89.b*).

To test the COA, we built the Tube user interface development environment, built several interfaces with it, including Pasta an advanced DM interface to a KBMS (*Kuntz and Melchert 89 a, b c*). We have found that Tube and the COA overcome the major limitations of the Seeheim and linguistic models, and makes it very easy to implement and modify graphical direct manipulation interfaces.

Authors' Addresses

- Marc Herrmann, ECRC, Arabellastrasse 17, 8000 München 81, Germany.
- Ralph, D. Hill, Bell Communication Research, 445 South Street, Room 2D-295, Morristown, NJ 07960 - 1910, USA.

Bibliography

Ceugniet, et al. 87 (1987) X. Ceugniet, B. Chabrier, L. Chauvin, J.M. Deniau, T. Graf, V. Lextrait
Prototypage d'un générateur d'éditeurs syntaxiques graphiques
DESS ISI - Cerisi, Université de Nice, Sophia-Antipolis, May 1987.

Coutaz 84 (1984) J. Coutaz, M. Herrmann
Adele and the Compositor-Mediator or how to make an interactive application program independant of the user interface
in Proceedings of the second software engineering conference, Nice 1984, pp. 78-86.

Dance, et al. 87 (1987) J.R. Dance, T.E. Granor, R.D. Hill, S.E. Hudson, J. Meads, B.A. Myers and A. Schulert.
The Run-Time Structure of UIMS-Supported Applications
Computer-Graphics 21.2: pp. 97-101.

Ege 86 (1986) Raimund K. Ege
The Filter - A Paradigm for Interfaces
Technical Report No. CSE-86-011, Oregon State University, September 1986.

Foley and van Dam (1982) J.D. Foley and A. van Dam
Fundamentals of Interactive Computer Graphics
Reading, Massachusetts: Addison-Wesley.

Foley and Wallace 74 (1974) J.D. Foley and V.L. Wallace
The Art of Natural Graphics Man-Machine Conversation
Proc. IEEE 62: pp. 462-471.

Green 85 (1985) M. Green
Report on Dialogue Specification Tools.
In G. Pfaff (Ed.), User Interface Management Systems. Berlin: Springer-Verlag, pp 9-20.

Herrmann and Hill 89.a (1989) M. Herrmann, R.D. Hill
Some Conclusions about UIMS design based on the Tube Experience
Colloque sur l'ingénierie des interfaces Homme-Machine, Sophia-Antipolis, 24-26 Mai 1989.

Herrmann and Hill 89.b (1989) M. Herrmann, R.D. Hill
Abstraction and Declarativeness in User Interface Development — The Methodological Basis of the Composite Object Architecture
Information Processing 89, G.X. Ritter (Ed.), North-Holland, Elsevier Science Publisher, pp. 253-258.

Hill 87 (1987) R.D. Hill
Event-Response Systems - A Technique for Specifying Multi-Threaded Dialogues
Proc. of CHI+GI 1987: pp. 241-248.

Hill and Herrmann 89 (1989) R.D. Hill, M. Herrmann
The Structure of Tube — A Tool for Implementing Advanced User Interfaces
Proc. Eurographics'89, pp. 15-25.

Kuntz and Melchert 89.a (1989) M. Kuntz, R. Melchert
Pasta-3: a Complete, Integrated Graphical Direct Manipulation Interface for Knowledge Base Management Systems. Information Processing 89, G.X. Ritter (Ed.), North-Holland, Elsevier Science Publisher, pp. 547-552.

Kuntz and Melchert 89.b (1989) M. Kuntz, R. Melchert
Pasta-3's Graphical Query Language: Direct Manipulation, Cooperative Queries, Full Expressive Power.
Proc. VLDB '89, VLDB Endowment, August 1989.

Kuntz and Melchert 89.c (1989) M. Kuntz, R. Melchert
Pasta-3's Requirements, Design and Implementation: A Case Study in Building a Large, Complex Direct Manipulation Interface. in Proc. IFIP WG2.7 Working Conference on Engineering for Human-Computer Interaction, August 1989.

Linton, et al. 89 (1989) M.A. Linton, J.M. Vlissides, P.R. Colder
Composing User Interfaces with Interviews
in IEEE Computer, February 1989, pp 8-22.

Olsen, et al. 87 (1987) D.R. Olsen, Jr, D. Kasik, P. Tanner, B. Myers and J. Rhyne.
Software Tools For User Interface Management
Proc. of SIGGRAPH'87. See especially the section by B. Myers.

Reps 82 (1982) T.W. Reps
Generating Language-Based Environments
Cambridge, Mass.: MIT Press. (PhD. Thesis, Cornell University, August 1982).

Szekely 88 (1988) Pedro Szekely
Separating the User Interface from the Functionality of Application Programs
PhD. Thesis. CMU-CS-88-101, January 1988

Chapter 25

An Overview of GINA — the Generic Interactive Application

Michael Spenke and Christian Beilken

Abstract

GINA is an object-oriented application framework written in CommonLisp and CLOS. It is based on an interface between CommonLisp and the OSF/Motif software. The generic interactive application is executable and has a complete graphical user interface, but lacks any application-specific behaviour. New applications are created by defining subclasses of GINA classes and adding or overriding methods. The standard functionality of a typical application is already implemented in GINA. Only the differences to the standard application have to be coded. For example, commands for opening, closing, saving and creating new documents are already available in GINA. The programmer only has to write a method to translate the document contents into a stream of characters and vice versa.

Motif widgets are encapsulated in CLOS objects. Instantiating an object implicitly creates a widget within OSF/Motif. Graphic output and direct manipulation with individual graphical feedback are also supported.

The combination of framework concepts, the flexible Motif toolkit, and the interactive Lisp environment leads to an extremely powerful user interface development environment (UIDE). There is already a dozen demo applications including a Finder to start applications and documents, a simple text editor and a simple graphic editor, each consisting of only a few pages of code. Even the first version of an interface builder, which treats Motif widgets like MacDraw objects, could be completed within a few days. The interface builder is not just a demo, but an important component of our UIDE: The resources of each widget can be modified by a dialog box, and Lisp code to be used in connection with GINA can be generated.

A version of GINA for C++ is currently under development.

1. Introduction

GINA (the Generic INteractive Application) has been developed as part of GMD's long term project *Assisting Computer* (AC) started in 1989. From our point of view, the AC will be a set of integrated AI-based applications — the so called *assistants* — with a graphical user interface, which will cooperate to assist the knowledge worker in the context of office tasks. The assistants will be implemented in CommonLisp and its object-oriented extension CLOS [Keene89], or alternatively in C++. OSF/Motif [OSF89] was chosen as the user interface toolkit.

Using a graphical, direct-manipulation interface makes life easier for the user, but much more difficult for the programmer. Therefore, the object oriented application framework GINA was designed and implemented. It contains code which is identical for all assistants. Because a uniform user interface and behaviour of the assistants is one of the design goals of the AC, a large part of the functionality has to be implemented only once, namely within GINA. The common code is mainly concerned with user interface issues, but other aspects like loading and saving documents are also handled. New applications are created by defining subclasses of GINA classes and adding or overriding methods. Only the application-specific differences to the standard application have to be coded.

The power of a generic application can be explained by a metaphor: Using an interface toolkit is like building a house from scratch, whereby a lot of guidelines have to be followed. Using a generic application is like starting with a complete standard house, already following the guidelines, and adding some specific modifications.

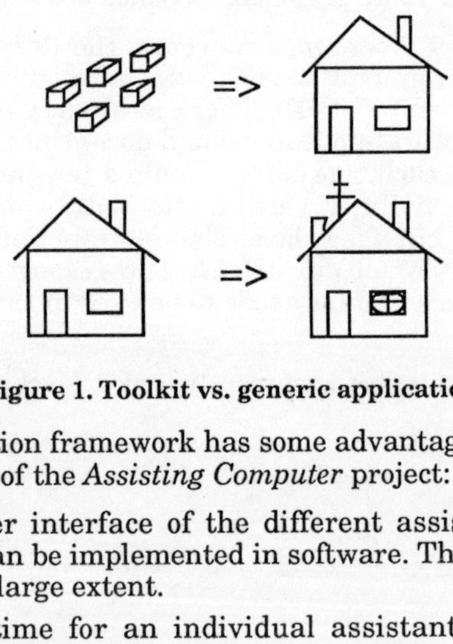

Figure 1. Toolkit vs. generic application

The concept of an application framework has some advantages which are of special importance in the context of the *Assisting Computer* project:

- Guidelines for the user interface of the different assistants cannot only be written on paper, but can be implemented in software. Thus, a uniform interface can be guaranteed to a large extent.
- The implementation time for an individual assistant can be considerably reduced.
- Because there is a common layer of software for all assistants, better integration and cooperation among the components of the AC is possible.
- Further development of the AC user interface can be done in a central project group. Future extensions and new interface features can be incorporated into existing assistants with the release of a new GINA version. This is very

important because research in the user interface area and in artificial intelligence is conducted in parallel.

GINA is based on concepts known from MacApp [Schm86] and ET++ [WGM88] and the resulting applications have a lot of similarities to typical Macintosh applications. Because the OSF/Motif toolkit is very powerful and flexible, and because CLOS (the Common Lisp Object System) is very well suited for the implementation of generic code, the scope of MacApp was reached quite fast. We are now working on extensions like animation of user actions, a more flexible menu system, constraint-based techniques to couple user interface and application objects, better integration of different (small) applications, and last not least an interface builder for the graphical construction of user interfaces.

2. Interface Between Lisp and OSF/Motif

OSF/Motif is based on the X Window System and the X toolkit. It consists of a special *window manager* and a set of interface objects (widgets) such as e.g. push-buttons and scrollbars. The widgets are implemented in C and therefore cannot be used in connection with CLX and CLUE [KO88], the Lisp counterparts of the X library and the X toolkit [ASP89].

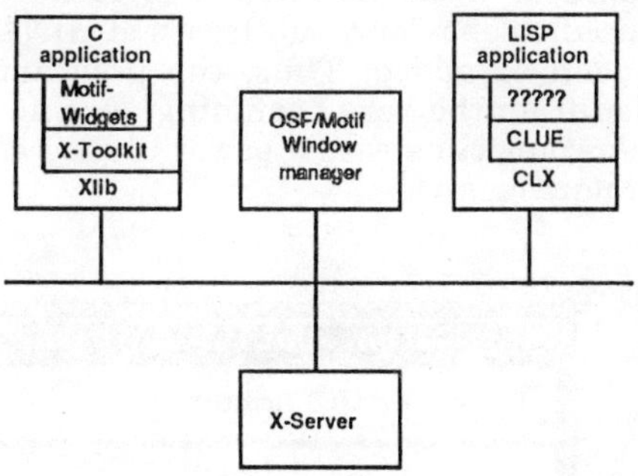

Figure 2. Architecture of X and Motif

Therefore, it is necessary to run the Motif software in an extra *Motif server* process implemented in C [Bäcker89]. From the point of view of the Lisp application, this is a second server similar to the X server. From the point of view of the X server, the Motif server is just another client creating windows and receiving events.

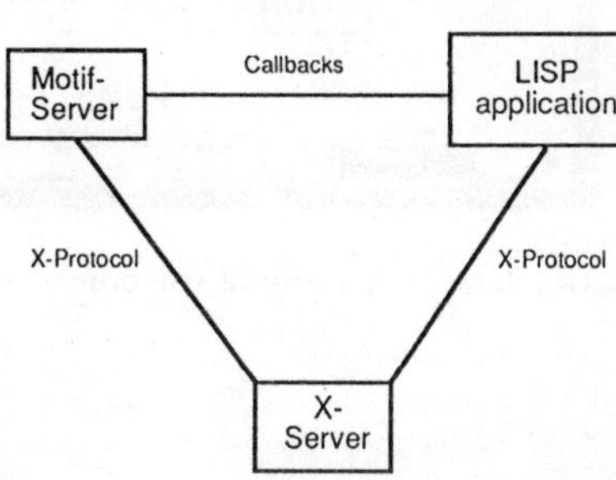

Figure 3. Running Motif as a separate server

The Lisp application communicates with the Motif server using a special protocol, similar to the X protocol, but at a higher semantic level: The application tells the server to create or modify widgets, and the server informs the application when *callbacks* are to be executed, i.e. a Lisp function has to be called as a result of a user action. Low level interactions can be handled by the Motif server, without the need to run any Lisp code, which results in good performance at the user interface level.

The Lisp application can also directly contact the X server in order to perform graphic output into drawing areas or to receive low level events. For example, dragging operations with semantic feedback cannot be handled by Motif, and therefore are implemented using this direct connection.

The three components can be arbitrarily distributed in the local net, so that e.g. our Lispmachines can be used for application development. Furthermore, this solution is highly portable because the Lisp side is completely implemented in pure CommonLisp and no foreign-function interface from Lisp to C is used.

3. The Empty Application

New applications are developed starting with the (empty) generic application. It has a complete graphical user interface, but lacks any application-specific behaviour. To add specific behaviour, subclasses of GINA classes are defined and methods are overridden or added. Thus, the programmer can work with an executable application from the very beginning, and new features added can be immediately tested. In connection with a powerful Lisp environment, this leads to an incremental programming style.

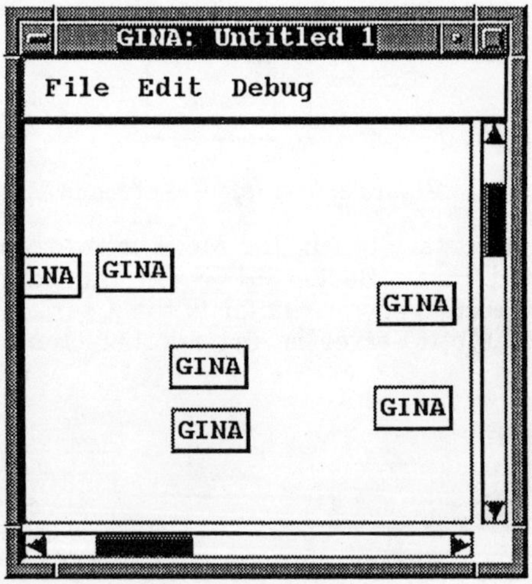

Figure 4. Screen dump of the empty application

The empty application already contains a lot of functionality that is inherited by other applications:

- A main window (shell) representing a document is displayed. It contains the names of the application and the document as a title and can be resized, moved, zoomed, and turned into an icon.
- The menu bar already contains the standard commands `new`, `open`, `close`, `save`, `save as`, `revert`, `print`, and `quit`.
- The window can be scrolled using the two scrollbars.
- Multiple documents, each with its own window, can be created (`new`).
- Documents can be saved in a file and existing documents can be opened again, using predefined dialogs to select a file. The current size of the window is automatically stored.
- Documents can be started from the Finder (see below), because they know which application can handle them.
- The document contents can be printed according to WYSIWYG paradigm.
- The debug menu contains entries to inspect the current state of the most important CLOS objects, making up the empty application. The slots of each object are shown in a scrollable list. Following the pointers to further objects, the complete internal state of an application can be inspected. Each widget shown at the surface can be inspected by a special mouse click (control-right, the "inspect click").
- Finally, the window contains some buttons labeled "GINA", which will beep when they are pressed. This behavior will be overridden by every application.

The functionality of the empty application reveals a certain common model on which all applications are based. It is closely related to the Macintosh application model. As the Macintosh shows, the model is sufficiently general to cover nearly all types of applications.

4. Hello-World Using GINA

The first experiment with a new programming environment is always the implementation of the hello-world program. The traditional version just prints out "Hello world!" on standard output. Of course, this is too simple in the context of graphical user interfaces.

Our version of hello-world is somewhat more complex: The user can click the mouse within the main area of our window and at this position the string "Hi!" will appear. An entry in the menu bar allows the user to clear all strings again. Hello-world documents can be saved in a file and remember the position of each string.

Additionally, all the features of the empty application described above are inherited by hello-world.

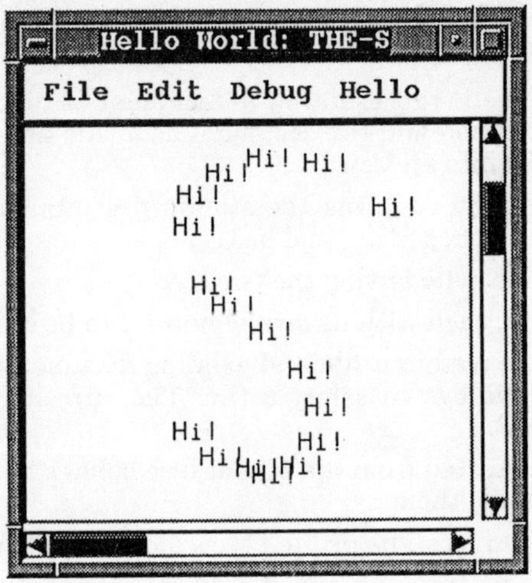

Figure 5. The hello-world application

We will show the implementation of the hello-world application and thereby explain the most important classes of GINA.

First of all, we have to define a subclass of the GINA class `application`. At run-time, exactly one instance of this class will exist. It contains the main event loop and transforms incoming events or callbacks into messages to other objects.

```
(defclass hello-world-application (application)
  ((name          :initform "Hello World")
   (document-type      :initform 'hello-world-document)
   (signature     :initform "hello")
   (file-type     :initform "hello")))

(defun make-hello-world-application  (display-host &key (document-pathname nil))
  "start the hello-world-application"
  (make-application :display-host display-host
                    :document-pathname document-pathname
                    :class 'hello-world-application))
```

Figure 6. Defining a subclass of class `application`

The *initial values* for some slots of the superclass are overridden. The slot `name` is used e.g. in the title of each document window. `Document-type` denotes the type of document to be created when the `new`-command is executed. `Hello-world-document` is a subclass of the GINA class `document` explained below. The `file-type` implies that the document shown in Figure 5 will be stored in the file named `"THE-S.hello"` when saved. The `signature` will be stored inside that file and will be later used to find the application which can handle the document.

Besides the definition of the new class, a *constructor function* is defined, that can be used to create instances of the new class. This is an elegant way to document required and optional parameters and their defaults. The constructor function of the subclass calls the constructor of the superclass.

Next, a subclass of the GINA class `document` is defined. An instance of this class will represent an open document at run-time. It contains the internal representation of the document contents and has methods to transform the contents into a stream of characters and vice versa.

```
(defclass hello-world-document (document)
  ((hi-list  :initform nil  :accessor hi-list :documentation "List of coordinates of HIs")))

(defmethod write-to-stream ((doc hello-world-document) stream)
  "write the document to the specified stream"
  (print (hi-list doc) stream))

(defmethod read-from-stream ((doc hello-world-document) stream)
  "read the document from the specified stream"
  (setf (hi-list doc) (read stream)))

(defmethod create-windows ((doc hello-world-document)  &aux scroller)
  "create the windows belonging to this document"
  (with-slots (main-shell main-view) doc
    (setq main-shell (make-document-shell doc))
    (setq scroller    (make-scroller main-shell))
    (setq main-view (make-hello-world-view scroller doc))

    ;; add an application specific command
    (add-menu-command (main-menu main-shell) "Hello"
     "Clear all" (make-callback #'clear-all doc))))

(defmethod clear-all ((doc hello-world-document))
  "reset hi-list and redraw"
  (with-slots (hi-list modified main-view) doc
    (setq hi-list  nil)
    (force-redraw main-view)
    (setq modified t)))
```

Figure 7. Defining a subclass of class document

The class `hello-world-document` contains a slot to hold the list of mouse click positions. `Read-from-stream` and `write-to-stream` are called by GINA whenever a documented is opened or saved. The document defines its own representation on the screen by overriding the method `create-windows`. In this case a shell containing a scrollable view is created. The menu bar is implicitly created as part of the `document-shell`. The actual display of the Hi-strings and the reaction to mouse clicks is handled by the class `hello-world-view`. Finally, an application-specific command "Clear all" is added to the menu bar. When the menu item is chosen, the method `clear-all` will be called, which clears the `hi-list` and redisplays. Marking the document as modified tells GINA to ask the user whether he wants to save the document first, if it is closed.

Finally, a subclass of the GINA class `view` has to be defined. Views are drawing areas, often larger than the screen and therefore scrollable, where documents display their contents. The contents of a view are normally not drawn by Motif, but by the Lisp application itself, using graphic primitives of the X library. Also, mouse clicks in the view are directly reported to the Lisp application.

```
(defclass hello-world-view (view)
  ())

(defun make-hello-world-view (parent doc)
  "create a new hello-world-view"
  (make-view parent        :document doc
                           :class 'hello-world-view))

(defmethod draw ((view hello-world-view)  count x y width height)
  "draw window contents"
  (when (zerop count)
    ;; Ignore all but the last exposure event
    (loop for (x  y) in (hi-list (document view))
          do (draw-glyphs view x y "Hi!")))))

(defmethod button-press ((view hello-world-view)  code x y root-x root-y)
  "react to button-press event in the window"
  (with-slots (hi-list modified) (document view)
    (push (list x y) hi-list)
    (force-redraw view)
    (setq modified t)))
```

Figure 8. Defining a subclass of class view

The class `hello-world-view` overrides the method `draw`, which is called by GINA whenever the view or some part of it is exposed. It uses the method `draw-glyphs`, which directly corresponds to the CLX function `draw-glyphs` to draw the Hi-strings. The `button-press` method is called whenever the mouse button goes down in the view. It adds a new pair of coordinates to the document contents and redisplays.

The main program which starts the hello-world application is quite simple: We just create an instance of class `hello-world-application` using the constructor function. This creates a separate Lisp process executing the main event loop.

```
(make-hello-world-application *default-display-host*)
```

Figure 9. The main program

GINA also contains an *application-independent undo/redo mechanism* with unlimited history. However, in order to exploit this facility, we need a slight extension of the code shown so far. Instead of directly modifying the `hi-list` when the user presses the mouse button, we have to define a subclass of the GINA class `command`, and create a new instance of it each time the user clicks the mouse. The command object contains all the necessary information to execute and later undo the command. In this case, the coordinates of the mouse click are sufficient. GINA calls the method `doit` to execute the command and then pushes it onto a stack of commands already executed. Later, when the user calls the undo facility, GINA executes the method `undoit`. If the command is repeated in a redo operation, `doit` is called again. If repeating a command is different from executing it for the first time, the programmer can also override the method `redoit`.

```
(defmethod button-press ((view hello-world-view) code x y root-x root-y)
  "react to button-press event in the window"
  (make-add-hi-command (document view) x y))

(defclass add-hi-command (command)
  ((name   :initform "Add Hi")
   (hi     :accessor hi   :initarg :hi)))

(defun make-add-hi-command (document x y)
  "store coordinates in a command object "
  (make-command document   :class 'add-hi-command
                           :initargs (list :hi (list x y))))


(defmethod doit ((cmd add-hi-command))
  "add a new pair to hi-list"
  (with-slots (document hi) cmd
    (push hi (hi-list document))
    (force-redraw (main-view document))))

(defmethod undoit ((cmd add-hi-command))
  "pop hi-list"
  (with-slots (document) cmd
    (pop (hi-list document))
    (force-redraw (main-view document))))
```

Figure 10. Extension for undoable commands

The method `button-press` creates an `add-hi-command` object. The method `doit` pushes the new coordinates on the `hi-list`, `undoit` pops it. A similar extension is necessary to make the `clear-all` command undoable.

The user can call undo and redo operations using the menu entries `undo` and `redo` in the `edit` menu. However, the history can become quite long and it may be necessary to go back a long way. Therefore, GINA also offers a *history scroller* as an alternative user interface.

Figure 11. The history scroller

Using this device, the user can replay a sequence of commands like a video movie, or jump back and forth in the history. Single steps are activated by the two buttons at the bottom labeled with the command names.

We are planning to use the animation of user actions as a base for help components and tutorials for applications. Storing commands as objects will also constitute the base for context-sensitive help and adaptive systems. Furthermore, it seems to be possible to define macros using a programming-by-example technique.

5. Object-Oriented Toolkit

Windows on the screen are constructed as a tree of Motif widgets. Conceptually, widgets are objects, and widget classes are arranged in an inheritance hierarchy, even though Motif is implemented in pure C and not in any object-oriented programming language. Therefore, it is a straightforward idea to encapsulate Motif widgets in CLOS objects on the Lisp side. Instantiating such an object implicitly creates a widget within the Motif server. So, for each Motif widget class there is a corresponding CLOS class and a constructor function. For example,

```
(make-push-button parent " Beep"  :activate-callback '(lambda () (xlib:bell *display*)))
```

creates a CLOS object of type `push-button` and a widget of class `XmPushButton` in the Motif server. The first parameter of the constructor is always the parent object within the tree of widgets. Shells (main windows) do not have a parent, they represent the root of a widget tree. Inner nodes are composite widgets such as `row-column` or `form` which are not visible, but layout their children according to a certain scheme. The leaves of the tree are primitive widgets like `push-button`, `label`, `scrollbar` and `text`.

The remaining positional and keyword parameters of a constructor function document the most important *Motif resources* and their defaults. (Resources are the attributes of the widgets which determine their appearance and behaviour.) There is also a bulk of resources for each widget class, which are modified in very rare cases only. These resources can be specified in the keyword parameter `:motif-resources` as in the following example:

```
(make-push-button parent  "Doit"
                          :motif-resources (list  :shadow-thickness 5  :margin-height 4))
```

A widget class also defines some *callbacks*. Callbacks are linked to Lisp functions which are called whenever the user produces certain input events. For example, an `activate-callback` is executed when a push-button is pressed and a `value-changed-callback` is executed when the user has dragged the slider of a `scale`-widget. Each callback defines certain parameters passed to the Lisp function. For example, when a push-button is pressed, a function with no parameters is called. When a scale is dragged, the new value is passed as a parameter to the `value-changed-callback`. The programmer can determine which Lisp function should be called by specifying a lambda-expression, the name of a compiled function, or a *callback object*. Callback objects are CLOS objects storing the name of a function plus additional parameters to be passed to the function each time the callback is executed. In this way it can be specified e.g. that a method of a certain object is called in response to a user action:

```
(make-scale parent :value-changed-callback (make-callback #'set-volume speaker))
```

A scale is created which calls the method `set-volume` of the object `speaker` each time the user drags the elevator. Besides the reference to the speaker object, the method `set-volume` must have a second parameter `new-value`.

For each Motif widget class there is one corresponding CLOS class. However, there are also predefined CLOS classes in GINA which have no direct counterpart in Motif. For example, there is a CLOS class `radio-button-group`. When an instance of this class is created, not only a single Motif widget but a whole subtree is created.

```
(make-radio-button-group
    parent '(("Red" :r) ("Green" :g) ("Blue" :b))
    :label-string "Color"
    :initial-value :b
    :value-changed-callback
    '(lambda (new-value old-value) ... ))
```

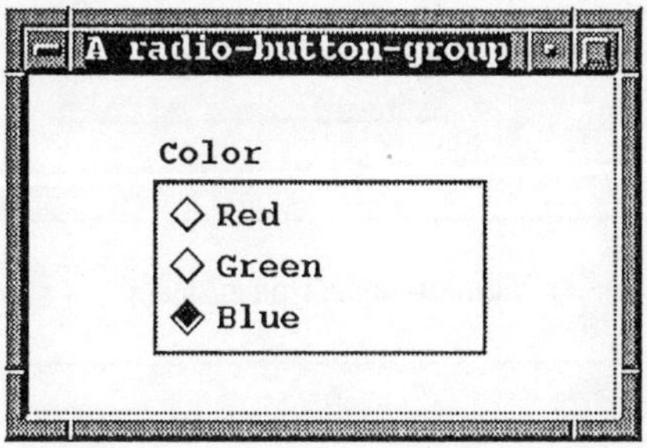

Figure 12. Lisp code to create a radio-button-group

The radio-button-group consists of a `label` ("Color") and a `frame` organized in a column (`row-column` widget). The frame contains a column of `toggle-button` widgets. The programmer need not know the detailed structure of this subtree, but can treat the `radio-button-group` as a single object. For example, he can specify a `value-changed-callback` for the whole group, whereas at the Motif level there are callbacks for each single toggle-button.

New subclasses representing widgets with a special appearance or behaviour can easily be defined.

We give an overview of the most important widgets and how they are created from Lisp:

```
(make-toggle-button
    parent "Print page numbers"
    :value-changed-callback
    '(lambda (set) (when set (xlib:bell *display*))))
```

```
(make-push-button parent " Beep "
        :activate-callback '(lambda () (xlib:bell *display*)))
```

```
(make-push-button parent "woman" :label-type :pixmap)
```

```
(make-scale
        parent
        :title-string "Pressure"
        :maximum 250
        :value-changed-callback
        '(lambda (new-value)  (format t "New Pressure ~d~%" new-value)))
```

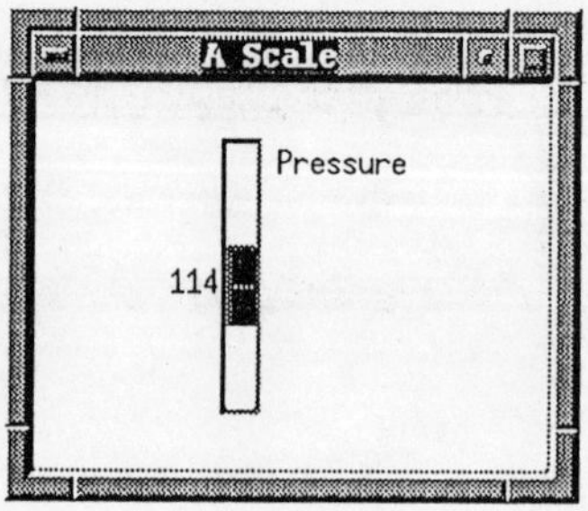

```
(make-scrollbar
        parent
        :orientation :horizontal
        :maximum 100
        :page-increment 20
        :value-changed-callback
        '(lambda (new-value)  (format t "New Value ~d~%" new-value)))
```

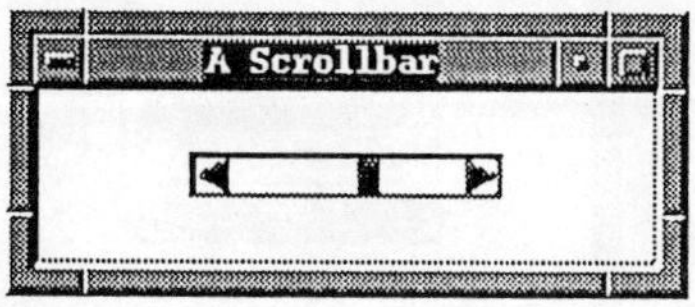


```
(make-label (make-frame parent)
            "A text with a frame around it")
```

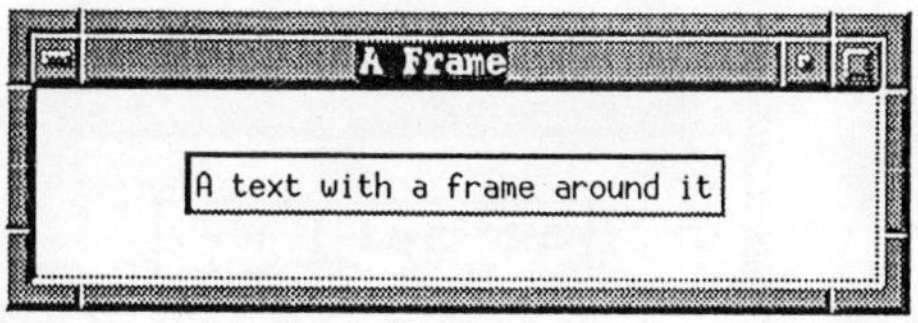


```
(setq rc (make-row-column parent :orientation :vertical))
(make-label rc "One")   (make-label rc "Two")
(make-separator rc)
(make-label rc "Three")   (make-label rc "Four")
```

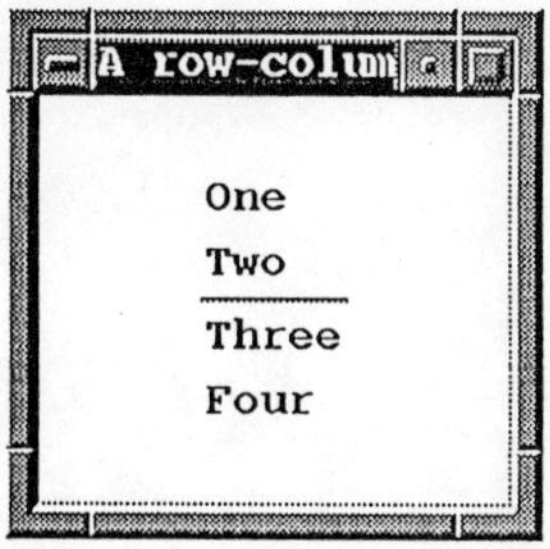

```
(make-scrollable-selection-list
     parent
     '("Red" "Green" "Blue" "Yellow" "Black" "White")
     :visible-item-count 4)
```

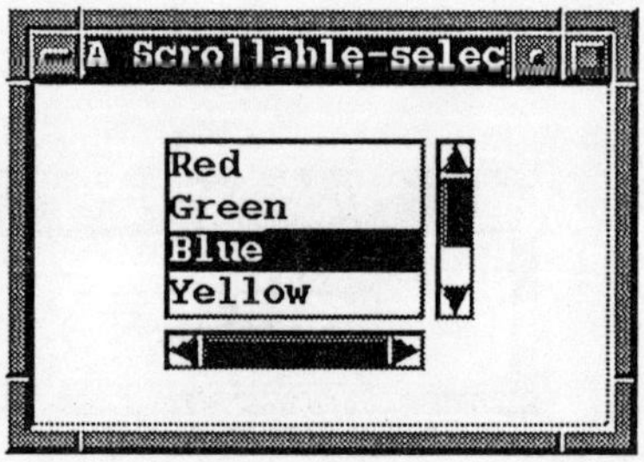


```
(make-text  parent  :value "Untitled 1" :columns 15)
```

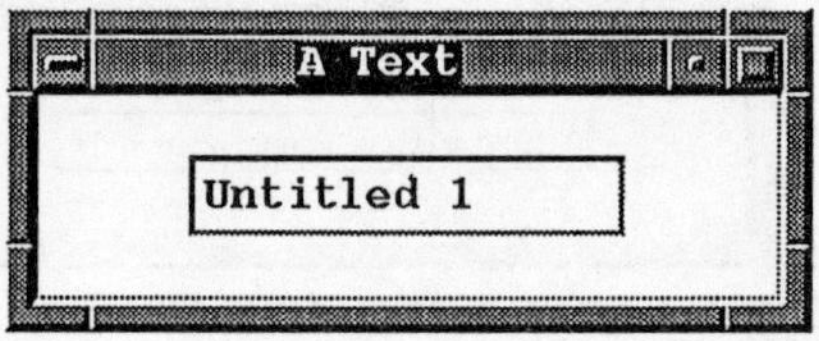

6. Graphic Output in Views

In general, the Motif widgets are not suited to represent the complete contents of a document. For example, the objects manipulated by a graphic editor cannot be implemented as Motif widgets.

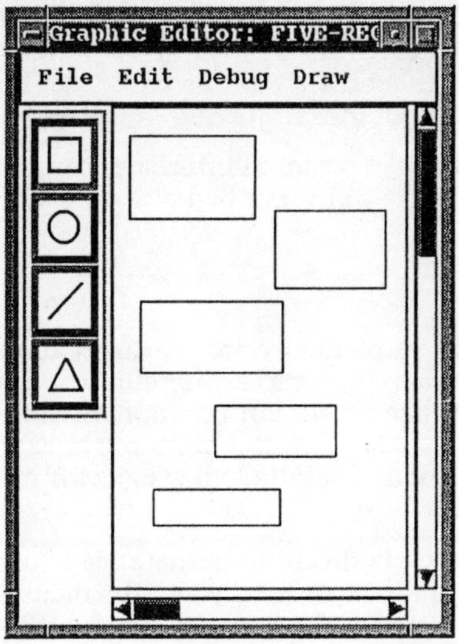

Figure 13. A simple graphic editor

Instead, the central drawing area where the graphical objects are shown is represented by a CLOS object of class `view`. The contents of the view are displayed using the graphic primitives of the X Window System like e.g. `draw-rectangle`.

The programmer can choose between a *procedural* and an *object-oriented interface* for graphic output.

Using the *procedural* interface, the programmer overrides the `draw`-method of his view as in the hello-world example. In this method he can call the CLX primitives which are available as methods of class view. GINA calls the `draw`-method in response to expose events. Each view has an associated *X graphics context* containing attributes like font, line width and clipping area and a reference to the underlying X window.

Encapsulating the CLX primitives in methods of class `view` makes it possible to hardcopy views according to the WYSIWYG paradigm. GINA simply switches to hardcopy mode and calls `draw` for the whole view. In hardcopy mode, methods of class `view`, such as `draw-rectangle`, do not call the corresponding CLX function but generate *Postscript* calls. The programmer need not write a single line of code to enable printing. However, this feature is not yet implemented in the current version of GINA.

The *object-oriented interface* to graphic output is implemented on top of the procedural one. A view can store a list of so called *view-objects*. The class `view-object` is the superclass of graphical objects like `circle`, `rectangle`, and `line`. View objects can be *installed* at a certain position in a view and later be moved or resized. They remember their own size and position. The view makes sure that an installed view-object will be redisplayed whenever the corresponding part of the view is redrawn. This is done by calling the method `draw` of each view-object.

Each view-object knows how to display itself, i.e. has a method `draw`. The predefined view-objects correspond to the CLX graphic functions: Their `draw-`

method contains a single call to a CLX function. More complex application-dependent subclasses can be easily implemented. For example, in the implementation of a spreadsheet a subclass `grid` could be defined, which draws a lot of horizontal and vertical lines in its `draw`-method.

The procedural and object-oriented interfaces can be both used in a single view. It is possible to override the `draw`-method of a view and additionally install some objects.

7. Mouse Input

GINA also supports the implementation of direct manipulation commands with graphical feedback like moving or resizing objects in a graphic editor. A special reaction of a view to mouse input can be implemented by overriding the method `button-press` of class `view` as in the hello-world example. A view also calls the method `button-press` of an installed view-object if it is hit. This is another hook to react to a mouse click.

If a graphical feedback is desired, an instance of a subclass of the GINA class `mouse-down-command` must be created when the mouse button goes down. `Mouse-down-command` is a subclass of `command`. The methods `doit` and `undoit` are inherited. However, `doit` is not called before the mouse button is released. As long as the mouse button remains pressed and the mouse is moved around, the feedback is drawn and additional parameters for the command can be collected (e.g. all intermediate mouse positions). The feedback is defined by overriding the method `draw-feedback` of class `mouse-down-command`. The default feedback is a rubberband line from the place where the mouse went down to its current position.

Furthermore, it is possible to modify the coordinates reported to `draw-feedback` by overriding the method `constrain-mouse`. For example, forcing the y-coordinate to the y-value of the point where the mouse was pressed, results in a horizontal feedback line.

Autoscrolling is completely implemented in GINA: Moving the mouse outside the view while the button is pressed, causes the view to be automatically scrolled.

The class `mouse-down-command` represents a special but very frequent type of mouse command: The feedback is shown as long as the button is held down. When the button comes up, the command is executed. Other types of mouse commands, e.g. with multiple mouse clicks, are possible. We expect, however, that a finite set of types is sufficient in practice, which is also confirmed by Myers [Myers89].

As an extension, we are planning to implement subclasses of view-objects which are already coupled with undoable mouse commands for selecting, moving, and resizing them.

8. Demo Applications

Up to now, we have implemented a dozen demo applications demonstrating different aspects of GINA. Each of these applications consists of only a few pages of code. So, even though they are quite different, at least 95% of the code executed is part of GINA. We will give a short overview of some of these applications.

The *Micky application* was heavily influenced by Schmucker's demo for MacApp [Schm86]. Our version, however, allows the user to stretch the width and height of Micky's head using the two scales. The size is stored as the document contents on disk.

Figure 14. The Micky application

We also have implemented a simple *Finder* to start applications and documents in a hierarchical file system. Its function is similar to the Macintosh Finder. Double-clicking a file name opens a document and starts the corresponding application if necessary. The contents of a Finder document (a folder) are stored as a directory. Extra information like the size of the window for a folder is stored in a file within the directory.

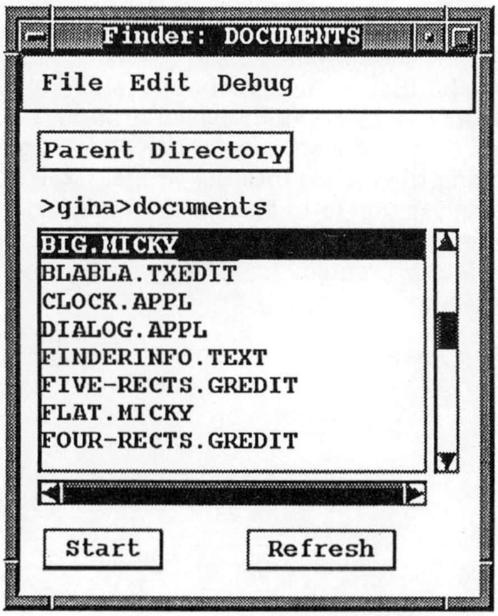

Figure 15. A simple Finder

The *text editor* demo shows, how with a few lines of code the Motif text-widget can be turned into a complete and useful application.

Figure 16. The text editor

The *graphic editor* shown in Section 6 demonstrates the use of object-oriented graphics and mouse commands with feedback. It can be used to draw and move rectangles.

9. Interface Builder

Starting with the code for the graphic editor, it was quite easy to implement a first version of an interface builder, which treats widgets like MacDraw objects (Figure 17). All kinds of widgets can be created, moved around, resized, and deleted. Each Motif widget is placed on top of a so called *widget-plate*, a special view-object with dashed borders. Clicking the mouse into the widget itself activates it: The elevator of a scrollbar is moved, a toggle button is selected, and so on. If the mouse is pressed near the dashed line, the widget-plate is notified and a mouse command to move or resize the widget is created.

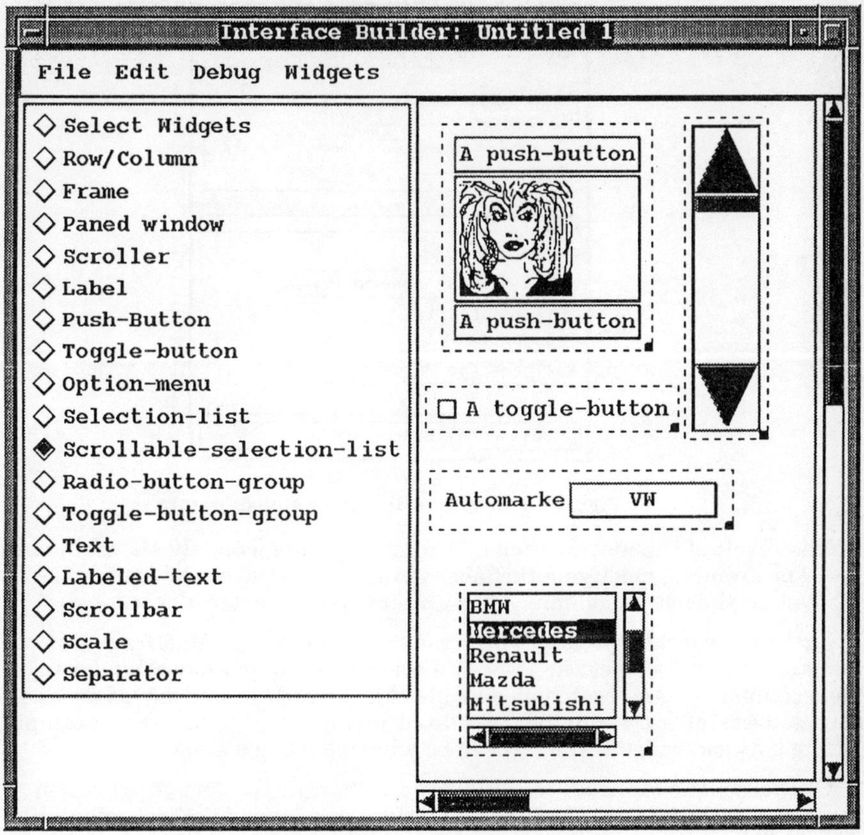

Figure 17: The Interface Builder

Double clicking a widget-plate pops up a modeless dialog box to modify the resources of a widget.

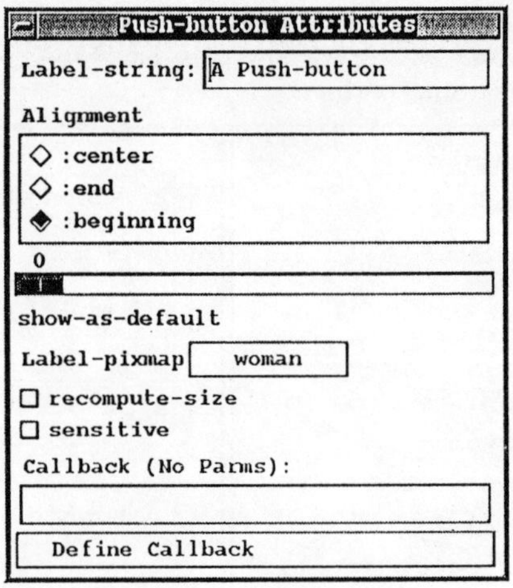

Figure 18: Resource dialog for a push-button

The result of the modification of a resource is immediately shown in the main view. For example, modifying the label-string causes the push-button to be resized and to show the new label immediately after each character is typed.

Just like several objects can be arranged in a group in MacDraw, it is possible to arrange several widgets in a row or a column creating a row-column widget. The whole column is then treated as a single object which can be moved around. Also, the resources of a column can be edited using a dialog box. For example, the spacing between widgets in a row can be adjusted using a scale.

Of course, the interface builder is more than just a demo application. It will soon be an essential part of our user interface development environment. For each shell or dialog box of an application there will be a corresponding interface builder document defining its layout. The Lisp code generated will consist of one new subclass of class `shell` or `dialog-box`, together with a constructor function defining the layout. The programmer can create an instance of this class using the constructor. Components of the dialog box, such as push-buttons, can be accessed as slots of the new class. In this way, callback functions can be set or the items of a selection-list can be modified. As a result, the interface code is clearly separated from the semantics of the application. It is even possible to change the layout of a dialog box with the interface builder while the program is running. The resulting Lisp code can be compiled and produces a new version of the constructor function which will be used as soon as the next instance of the dialog box is created. It will also be possible to generate C++ code.

10. Conclusions

Our experience has shown that an object-oriented application framework is very well suited to simplify the construction of applications with a graphical user interfaces. An interface builder, which allows to define interfaces by drawing them, is not an alternative but an important supplement for the framework. It is an excellent tool to define the *layout* of windows, but there is much more about a user interface. Using an application framework, it is also possible to predefine the *behaviour* of the interface. For example, the algorithms and dialogs for opening and closing documents are completely defined in GINA. Also, an application-independent framework for undo/redo means much more than defining two menu entries.

An application framework is an excellent vehicle to define a common basic model for a set of applications and to propagate user interface guidelines. This is very important in the context of our Assisting Computer project. Because research in the user interface area and in artificial intelligence is conducted in parallel, it is a great advantage that new interface features can be incorporated into existing assistants with the release of a new GINA version.

11. References

[Apple88] Apple Computer: Human Interface Guidelines: The Apple Desktop Interface, Addison Wesley (1988).

[ASP89] ASP Inc.: X Manual Set, Addison Wesley Publishing Company, 1989.

[Bäcker89] Andreas Bäcker, CLM: An Interface from CommonLisp to OSF/Motif, Manual, GMD Report, March 1990.

[HSC86] D. Austin Henderson, Jr., Stuart K. Card: Rooms: The Use of Multiple Virtual Workspaces to Reduce Space Contention in a Window-Based Graphical User Interface, ACM Transactions on Graphics, Vol 5, No 3, pp 211-243, July 1986.

[HH89] Rex Hartson, Deborah Hix: Human-Computer Interface Development: Concepts and Systems for its Management, ACM Computing Surveys, Vol. 2, No. 1, March 1989, pp 5-92.

[Keene89] Sonya E. Keene: Object-Oriented Programming in COMMON LISP - A Programmer's Guide to CLOS, Addison-Wesley Publishing Company, 1989.

[KO88] Kerry Kimbrough, LaMott Oren: Common Lisp User Interface Environment, Version 1.15, Texas Instruments, 1. Sept. 1988.

[Myers89] Brad A. Myers: Encapsulating Interactive Behaviors, CHI '89 Conference, 30.4-4.5.89, Austin, Texas, ACM, pp 319-324.

[OSF89] Open Software Foundation: Motif Toolkit Programmers's Guide, Prentice Hall, 1989.

[SG86] Robert W. Scheifler, Jim Gettys: The X Window System, Transactions on Graphics, Vol 5, No 2, pp 79-109, April 1986.

[Schm86] Kurt J. Schmucker: Object-Oriented Programming for the Macintosh, Hayden Book Company, New Jersey 1986.

[SM88] Pedro A. Szekely, Brad A. Myers: A User Interface Toolkit Based on Graphical Objects and Constraints, OOPSLA '88 Proceedings, pp 36-45,ACM, 25-30. Sept. 88.

[WGM88] André Weinand, Erich Gamma, Rudolf Marty: ET++ - An Object-Oriented Application Framework in C++, OOPSLA '88 Proceedings, pp 46-57, ACM, 25-30. Sept. 88.

[Will84] G. Williams: Software Frameworks, Byte, Vol. 9, No. 13 (1984).

Chapter 26

The Use of OPEN LOOK/Motif GUI Standards for Applications in Control System Design

H.A. Barker, M. Chen, P. W. Grant, C.P. Jobling, A. Parkman and P. Townsend

Abstract

The emergence of powerful graphics workstations has brought about the possibility of implementing sophisticated graphics based user interfaces (GUI's). In this paper we discuss aspects of the design and specification of a generic graphical user interface for control systems design and the emerging standards for user interface implementation that underlie it, with special reference to the OPEN LOOK and Motif standards. The use of these interface standards in future design environments should enable the rapid development of novel design methods and at the same time enforce a consistent 'look and feel' across applications. We discuss the problems faced by the implementor in developing applications for different interface standards and also comment on the effects these different GUI standards have on the user's view. [1]

1. Introduction

The development of the Xerox Star in the early eighties [Smith 82] brought about a major change in thinking in relation to the provision of user interfaces for application programs. Until that time users were in general restricted to relatively unsophisticated input/output hardware which was usually capable of supporting only text dialogue. The decision by Xerox to base their office system on high powered graphics workstations connected by a local area network resulted in very significant improvements to the lot of the inexpert user. In particular the emergence of the earliest forms of 'WIMP' interface together with the use of familiar visual metaphors - graphical images of documents, file drawers, in/out trays and so on, enabled users to develop intuitive methods of interacting with application software. Users became familiar with the so-called 'look and feel' of a particular interface and were able to transfer with minimal effort to a new package having the same look and feel. The spread of this new technology was hampered initially by the high cost of the graphics hardware but the introduction of first the Apple Lisa and subsequently the Apple Macintosh, firmly established this methodology of interaction between user and computer. All modern workstations make use of graphical user interfaces GUI's but as has happened so many times in the past, each manufacturer has followed a different development path so that the look and feel of one workstation may resemble another apparently quite closely but then differ in some significant and, for the user, irritating way.

The awareness of these problems has led more recently to the emergence of de-facto standards in graphical interface development. These standards include not only the underlying software technology i.e. the window system, but also 'standards' that have emerged for the look and feel of a GUI. A whole host of proprietory window systems have appeared at one time or another but for

[1] **Acknowledgement:** this work is supported by the United Kingdom Science and Engineering Research Council

a number of reasons, (to be discussed briefly later), the X window system developed as part of the Athena project at MIT [Scheifler 88] has become the most widely adopted. As far as the look and feel of a GUI is concerned, again most proprietory systems have their own. For a number of years now for example, reference has been made to a Macintosh-like interface. In some cases there has even been legal action taken by one manufacturer against another over copying of a look and feel. Currently, two de-facto standards would appear to have emerged, namely OPEN LOOK [SUN 88] and Motif [OSF 89]. Both of these give detailed specifications on precisely how their respective interfaces - the windows, menus, scroll bars, and so on, should appear on the display and also exactly how they should function. Both specifications have been implemented as toolkits for the X-window system.

In this paper we consider the implications of having two specification standards both from the user's and the implementor's point of view. The conclusion is drawn that if one is careful about the particular type of X-toolkit employed, it is possible to provide an application with a choice of either interface without the need for a complete duplication of programming effort. We discuss some of our experiences in the Control and Computer-Aided Engineering Research Group at Swansea University in trying to adopt standards in the development of a GUI for computer aided control system design (CACSD). In particular we will look at the needs of the control engineer and show how the facilities offered by OPEN LOOK can be best used to give such an engineer an interface which mimics the familiar operations that he or she might have otherwise performed with pen and paper together with an assortment of command driven computational tools. We highlight some of the differences in the interface design if we were to adopt Motif as an alternative standard. Before we consider any of the above issues however, we shall first discuss some of the background to the development of standards in GUI development.

2.0 Background

In the 1980's as part of Project Athena [Balkovich 85] researchers at the Massachussetts Institute of Technology developed a protocol for networked windowed graphics which would enable a wide variety of bit-mapped graphics devices to support WIMP interfaces across a network. The current version of this protocol called X11 has already established itself as a standard for workstations.

X11 is essentially a windowing system but differs from many other such systems in that it provides only those facilities required in order that it can be used as a starting point on top of which more sophisticated facilities can be built. The system is network transparent and is based on a *client-server* model consisting of a set of nodes, each node equipped with processor, display, keyboard and mouse. These facilities are managed by a server which provides windowing facilities on the display in response to requests made of it from client processes running on any node in the network. A client and server may be connected over the network, or, where they both reside on the same processor, by local interprocess communication.

To the implementor of a GUI, apart from providing basic windowing facilities, the X Window system has a number of advantages. Not least of these is that X overcomes the portability problem, a major reason why it has already been adopted by most of the major workstation manufacturers. This portability results from the modular structure of X whereby to add a new display architecture to the network requires only the addition of a server implementation for that architecture, and where one employs a device independent layer implemented on top of a device dependent layer, so that only a small portion of the server needs to be rewritten. Other advantages of X11 include the public domain status of X as well as its lack of a fully prescribed user interface. The latter might seem to be a drawback but does offer a manufacturer the possibility of imposing a proprietory look and feel to products implemented with X. One of the major disadvantages of X to the GUI implementor is the very low level of facilities, Xlib, provided for software development. To overcome these difficulties a number of higher level toolkits have emerged, implemented on top of Xlib. We shall discuss some of the relative merits of these later.

In a separate, but essentially linked development, some considerable attention has been recently focussed on attempts to standardise the look and feel of GUI's. A number of X toolkits have already imposed their own proprietory look and feel without standardisation. However, two separate groups - a SUN/AT&T/Xerox consortium and the OSF (Open Software Foundation) have tried to lay down specifications for standards for look and feel, namely the OPEN LOOK and Motif standards, respectively. These standards try to avoid some of the consistency problems which have been, and are still, prevalent, in user interfaces. For example, movement of a scroll bar in one direction might scroll text up in one package and down in another; clicking mouse buttons on one system may initiate operations totally different from those on another. For a casual user such as a control engineer, who might use several totally different simulation packages on a relatively infrequent basis, the effort required to memorise the mode of operation of one specific interface is considerable. To move to yet another look and feel requires an extensive learning period. The OPEN LOOK and Motif specifications would minimise this expensive waste of effort by imposing the same look and feel on all applications so that a user picking up a new package would already be familiar with the basic overall operational structure from experience gained with other like packages which use the same look and feel. Many of the features would be intuitively obvious, particularly where visual metaphors are used to aid familiarisation.

Motif grew out of already existing GUIs and as a result can be considered a super-set of the proprietary look and feels on a number of hardware platforms. It offers users the benefit of familiarity and it is likely that it will become the dominant interface on these platforms.

OPEN LOOK on the other hand, has been designed from scratch, avoiding mixing features from existing look and feels. By so doing, OPEN LOOK promises to address existing deficiencies in interaction and yield a look and feel which is more consistent overall. Of the two, OPEN LOOK is both richer and more well defined.

Out of these look and feel specifications have come X-based tookits which implement the facilities laid down. There are a number of these, which, although they may provide the same look and feel from the user's point of view, provide different application programmer interfaces (API). The API determines how the programmer sees the implementation of a GUI and clearly one wishes to preserve the flavour of tools used in the past. For example, a programmer who has used SUN's SUNVIEW toolkit would adapt well to an OPEN LOOK X-toolkit which presented a similar API to that of SUNVIEW.

It is unfortunate that, as has happened so often in the past in other areas of computing, two separate incompatible 'standards' have emerged. It is not clear yet just which of these will eventually dominate (if any). For a research group such as our own, implementing a very large graphical user interface package, the obvious question which arises is which standard should one choose? Although one can compare their relative merits, as we shall in the next two sections, the answer to this question is not clear. At the present time it may well be best to back both horses and try to implement both OPEN LOOK and Motif interfaces. There are resource implications for this of course and we shall address this point later.

3.0 User's View

Both OPEN LOOK and Motif provide the user with the opportunity to customise the appearance of the GUI in such factors as colours and fonts, and also control functions such as keyboard focus policy and mouse button functions. The user is allowed to select the best mechanism for operating a function according to:

level of experience	a totally new user may wish to interact through menus; an expert may prefer command 'short-cuts'
personal preference	a left-handed user prefers a different assignment of mouse button functions
special requirement	with a non-standard keyboard one has to modify default function keys for copy, undo, help and so on
familiarity	one may have a strong background of previous experience with another GUI, and would like the new working environment to be as familiar as possible.

The above increases the flexibility and extensibility of the application and enhances the user's sense of control over the application. This feature rarely exists in non-X-based window systems such as the Macintosh, MSWindows or Andrew.

Both OPEN LOOK and Motif GUI's have similar operational models based on direct manipulation. Instead of using a command language or traditional menu system, the user interacts directly with visual objects, following a simple rule — select-then-operate. The result of the action is immediately visible (for example, clicking on a scrollbar immediately scrolls the window).

In Table 1 we list the main components of the two specifications, where similar features are paired with each other. We note that although there may be differences of visual appearance, the functionality provided by the features of both OPEN LOOK and Motif is essentially the same.

OPEN LOOK	Motif
base window	primary window
window menu button	window menu button
	maximize button
	minimize button
header	title bar
resize corner	resize border
control area	menu bar
	control panel
pane	window pane
footer	
pull-down menu	pull-down menu
pull-right menu	cascading menu
pop-up menu	pop-up menu option menu
scroll bar	scroll bar
exclusive setting	radio button
non-exclusive settings check box	check button
scrolling list	list box
slider	scale
gauge	
numeric field	stepper button
text field	entry box
read only message	
push pin	
pop-up window	dialog box
command window	command window
property window	selection window
notice window	message window
help key	help menu

Table 1

Despite the large number of similarities between OPEN LOOK and Motif, they are basically two competitive products and each tries to lay down a diverse spectrum of guidelines for GUIs. Some, it should be noted, are due to political rather than technical reasons.

One of the major differences between OPEN LOOK and Motif is in their visual design. OPEN LOOK does not try to mimic any previous GUI but takes features from many popular systems. Components such as the scrollbars and gauges have a simple but well-designed appearance, suitable for both colour and monochrome display.

Motif, on the other hand, would seem to be an attempt to achieve consistency with Microsoft's Presentation Manager. It has a realistic 3D appearance which is very appealing and intuitive to users, particularly with high resolution colour display monitors. Buttons, for example, actually appear to push in when selected.

Table 1 shows that there are several features provided in one GUI but not another. For example, pushpins in OPEN LOOK enable the user to pin menus or pop-up windows (except Notice windows) onto the screen for repeated operations. However, in Motif, there is no straightforward alternative, this will be discussed further in section 5. Motif has clear guidelines for a variety of help facilities including: Help Index, Help Tutorial, Help on Context, Help on Windows, Help on Keys, Help on Versions and Help on Help. Although OPEN LOOK provides for Help on Context and defines the appearance of the Help window, there are few guidelines for other Help facilities.

What may confuse users most is probably the occurrence of components which appear similar yet which represent different functions in the two GUIs. One obvious example is the window border that is used for resizing a window in Motif but for moving a window in OPEN LOOK. Another is the different use of mouse buttons. It is these types of inconsistency which are most annoying for users who have to use applications conforming to the two GUIs.

There may be a number of valid reasons for preferring one look and feel to another: familiarity, functionality or just personal taste. However, the main goal for the end user is consistency of interaction across the different applications used.

Although this latter consideration is by far the most important, it should not be the factor dictating which look and feel a user has to adopt. From the user perspective, it is desirable to select a look and feel specification and to have all applications then interact through the conventions of this specification. Thus a user need never suffer a loss of productivity when moving across different applications or hardware implementations.

4.0 Implementation Issues

The X window system provides the developer with basic facilities for windowing and two-dimensional graphics. However, the graphics primitives provided by X are at a very low level and using them to build each component of the user interface (menus, scrollbars, valuators etc.) would be both difficult and time consuming. In order to reduce the time necessary to get a product to market, the developer requires the use of a toolkit, a set of pre-built user interface components. Toolkits having the X window system as their underlying platform offer developers a significantly higher level at which to work whilst maintaining the same degree of portability as the lower level X graphic primitives. Such toolkits are normally implemented as C libraries with which the application programmer can interface the application specific code. Two features distinguish between the different toolkits

- The Look and Feel
- The API

Currently, applications built with a specific toolkit will support only one look and feel. The API essentially defines the manner in which a programmer would use the toolkit to build up the user interface for an application and attach application specific functionality to it.

To the implementor, issues concerning the API have the greatest impact in choosing which toolkit to adopt. The existence of a product built from a toolkit with a similar API may make adoption of a toolkit attractive as a migration route to a new look and feel or to best utilise the existing experience of programmers. One such example of this is Sun's XView toolkit providing the look and feel of OPEN LOOK whilst offering an API very similar to SunView.

Another factor worthy of consideration is the increased productivity which may be obtained through the use of higher level tools. Tools such as ExoCODE (Expert Object Corp.) and DevGuide (Sun), both for XView, are able to generate user interface code interactively, thereby dramatically reducing the time spent writing code.

The adoption of a toolkit involves considerable investment in time for programmer familiarisation with the API it provides. The longevity of the toolkit, the generality of its API and its likely future development are therefore important considerations when adopting a toolkit.

So far much consideration has been given to the portability of an application across hardware platforms but little discussion has been made of the portability of an application between the two proposed look and feel standards. It is to this issue we now turn. We shall detail the course taken in our own work in deciding how best to construct software to run under a X-based windowing system.

The first and most difficult implementation issue that had to be addressed was which toolkit would be adopted. Initial work had been carried out using Xt+ the OPEN LOOK toolkit provided by AT&T based on the standard toolkit (Xt) for user interface construction within the X community. With the emergence of XView from Sun, the adoption of this toolkit became attractive because of the increased support and maintainence gained by using a toolkit pioneered on the same hardware platform with which the team was already familiar. The availability of higher level tools such as ExoCODE again added to the attractiveness of XView.

However, given the current state of the look and feel it was difficult to justify total commitment to XView because of it's unique API. In the event that Motif became the dominant look and feel we realized that it would be very difficult to transfer our investment in XView to the only toolkit available for Motif which is based on Xt.

Adopting Xt as the API for our software development has offered the project far greater flexibility than would have been possible using XView because of the availability of Xt based toolkits for both OPEN LOOK and Motif.

Xt toolkits allow user interface components to be specified as a set of modules (widgets) accessible through a common API. The degree of portability between any two Xt toolkits is directly proportional to the common functionality between the two sets of widgets. As we saw in section 3 there is a high degree of common functionality between the OPEN LOOK widget set of AT&T's Xt+ widget set and that of OSF's Motif widget set so this implies that the support of both should be fairly straight-forward.

For any differences that remain, a small amount of effort would be required to implement them in a different fashion. For example Motif lacks a push pin facility. This is used in Fig. 2 for the drawing tools, which in the OPEN LOOK implementation is simply a pinnable menu of bitmaps. This has to be implemented within a sub-window under Motif. Similarly the Motif help facility, which provides menu access to help messages in addition to the context sensitive help facilities provided by OPEN LOOK, would have to be implemented separately as a menu under OPEN LOOK.

In many cases, the two standards offer different, sometimes conflicting, guidelines to developers. For example, in OPEN LOOK, controls (such as settings and text fields) in property window should always be arranged according to the following formula: one property per line, with the label on the left followed by the controls on the right. On the contrary, in a Motif dialog box, controls of a property is normally arranged in vertical order, and surrounded by a simple framebox above which is displayed the label. That is just what OPEN LOOK does not recommend. This problem is illustrated in Fig. 4 and Fig. 5.

Clearly, at present a degree of portability is available but only at the expense of a small amount of programmer effort. In addition this portability is only available for the API of one particular toolkit. In the same way that the user should be free to choose the style of interaction that best suites his needs so to the application programmer should be free to select his API. If the current players in the GUI market are truly comitted toward Open Systems then one day we could perhaps hope to see toolkits offering many different API's, each toolkit able to generate applications in a variety of look and feels without any additional programmer effort.

5.0 Specification and Design of the *EXCES* Interface

The Control and Computer Aided Engineering Research Group at Swansea has been developing a software system CES, (Control Engineering workStation), to provide sophisticated graphical interfaces for the modelling of dynamic systems together with links to foreign numerical simulation, analysis and controller implementation tools. CES contains several graphical editors and an operation editor for defining mathematical relationships represented by the blocks in a block diagram. In addition, rule-based tools for the automatic transformation and aesthetic layout of diagrams [Barker 88], the symbolic manipulation of signal flow graphs [Jobling 88] and the translation of discrete event systems have been added to the system. At the moment, CES has links to several simulation languages and to the computer algebra system MACSYMA. Further description of the user interface can be found in [Barker 87b] and the philosophy of the system is described in [Barker-89].

In the early stages of the project the two-dimensional graphics standard GKS was adopted but that did not support any windowing facilities. At that time there were no accepted standards for window management or interface design and software support for these was not readily available.

With the advent of the windowing and interface standards, described earlier, a of review the current status of CES was made and a very detailed specification was written to define the successor to CES, eXCeS (Extended X-based Control Engineering workStation) [CCAE 89]. This is now currently being implemented. eXCeS followed the OPENLOOK user interface specification [SUN 88]. It is a general purpose computer-aided engineering environment for the design, manipulation, analysis and simulation of dynamic systems and for the support of control implementation.

The system is to provide:

- a working environment associated with a set of software tools,
- a data environment for system descriptions and
- a software environment into which foreign software packages may easily be integrated. The architecture of eXCeS is illustrated in Fig. 1.

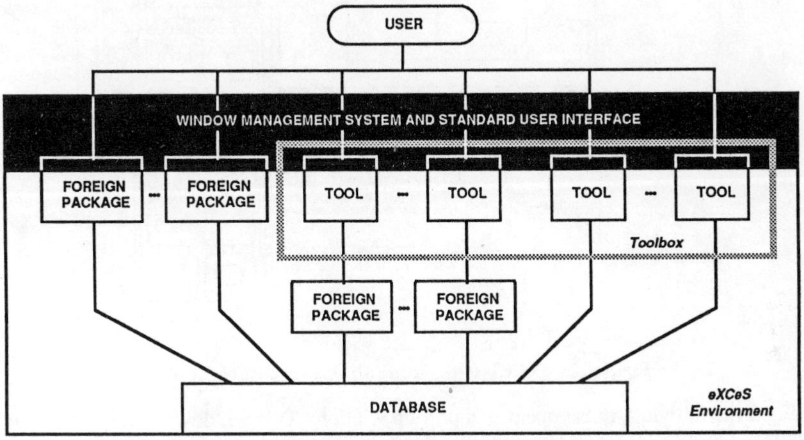

Figure 1 The Architecture of eXCeS

eXCeS will offer a very much larger selection of tools than CES, but we concentrate here only on the differences in the interface. The system is to make full use of the X Window system and our original aim was to conform solely to the OPEN LOOK interface specification. However, it is at present not clear, as stated in section 2, whether this will be the de facto standard for GUI's. For this reason we have decided to take a broader view of things and produce in addition a system conforming to Motif interface.

The two GUI standards are in fact not that dissimilar and so it is not too difficult a task to extend the specification so that it can be used for constructing eXCeS for both and this we are now doing. The new system will be easier to use as it will have all the advantages of a window based system as outlined in section 3. The learning phase will be simpler and faster for users familiar with other OPEN LOOK or Motif applications.

In section 3 the differences that the user might perceive in the two interfaces were outlined and in section 4 we considered the problems faced by the implementor in trying to produce a software system for both standards. We will illustrate in the rest of this section, the differences between OPEN LOOK and Motif specifications of eXCeS, by comparing the features offered by one of the basic tools – the icon editor IconEdit. This is an application for constructing and editing icons, the small pictorial representations used throughout eXCeS to identify the various type of objects. The user can see at a glance what kind of entity it represents, e.g. a special icon would be used to denote a non-linear block. IconEdit is thus fundamental to all other tools in eXCeS.

Fig. 2 shows a view of eXCeS with the IconEdit tool in use using the OPEN LOOK GUI and Fig 3 using Motif. The main features, as they relate to the two interface standards, will now be described and contrasted.

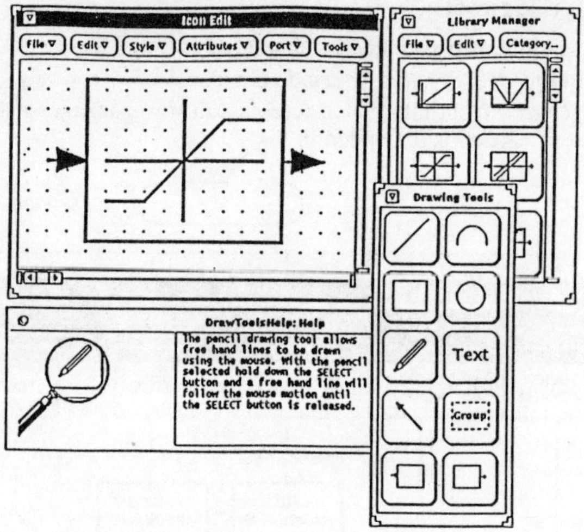

Figure 2. eXCeS with IconEdit using OPEN LOOK

In Fig 2 the drawing tools appear in a pop-up window. This window contains all the tools for constructing the icon in the main IconEdit window. The diagram shows that the pen has been selected. A push-pin can be seen at the top right of the drawing tools window. This is an OPEN LOOK metaphor which means that the window remains visible until the user specifically removes it. It can also be moved to any part of the screen which is convenient. Two options in the drawing tools window are for adding input or output ports to an icon. This can be done by one click of the mouse in eXCeS.

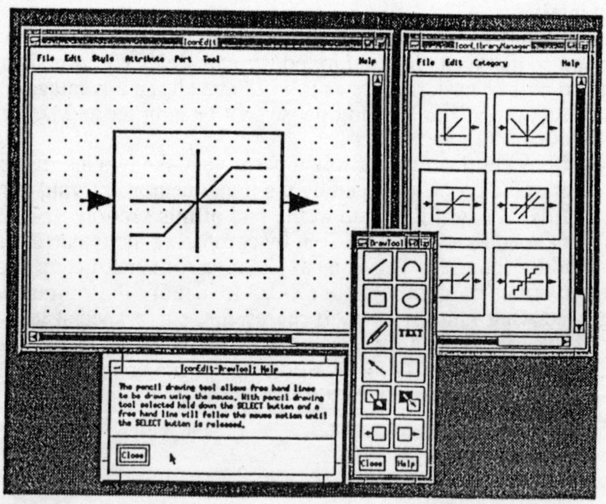

Figure 3. eXCeS with IconEdit using Motif

Fig 3 shows the Motif view. Functionally, of course, IconEdit is the same as before. The differences only relate to the use of the push-pin and the access to help.

In Motif there is no concept of the push-pin but it is desirable for the user that this feature be carried over into this specification. To obtain a similar effect to OPEN LOOK there are two alternatives. The first solution is to implement the push-pin menu as a Motif modeless dialog box which can mimic an OPEN LOOK menu. Unlike Motif menus, dialog boxes can remain visible until explicitly removed and this is the style of operation required here.

The second solution, is to have the drawing tools as a control panel fixed in the application's main window. This is not as desirable in this context as the interaction of a user with the static drawing tool palette is rather different from the interaction with OPEN LOOK's moveable menu. Fig. 3 show the drawing tool specified by a Motif dialog box.

As mentioned in section 4, the help facilities in the two GUIs are different. In Fig 2 the OPENLOOK help window shown gives information on the pen icon in the drawing tools window. Notice the icon of the pen in the magnifier glass giving a visual indication of the object selected for which help is required. This has been activated as described in section 4 and is context sensitive only. An OPEN LOOK toolkit will provide the help tool and so relieve the programmer from reprogramming this useful feature.

In Fig 3 we see the help window giving help on the selected object. This is invoked a mentioned in section 3 and as indicated in Motif we are also able to request help on other items besides the selected one.

The BlockLibrary Manager, which can be seen on the right in Fig 2 and Fig 3. This allows large numbers of icons to be organised in the form of a library so that they are easier for the user to access and maintain. This tool is invoked automatically by some tools such as the block diagram editor and IconEdit when required. Browsing through the icons in the chosen library is achieved by a scroll bar indicated in the figure. In eXCeS, BlockLibrary Manager has its own window and so can be positioned anywhere on the screen. The are only essentially cosmetic differences between OPEN LOOK and Motif for this window.

Another feature of IconEdit, is the attribute button stack. On selection a property window is produced as shown in Fig 4 and Fig 5 where icon attributes can then be set by either pointing to a text insertion point and typing an input string or by selecting an appropriate button.

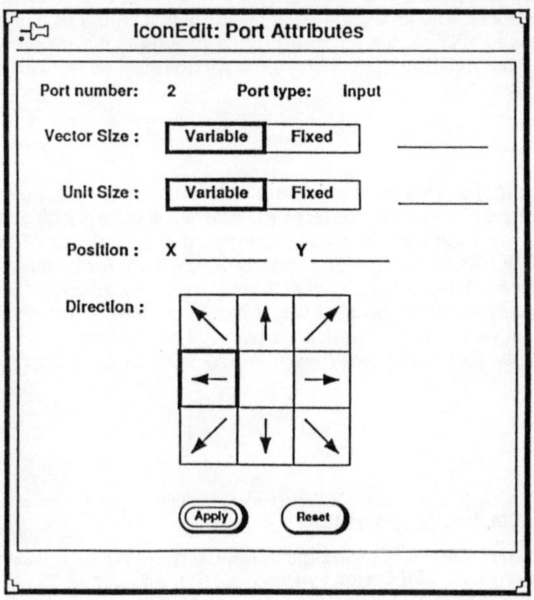

Figure 4. The Attribute Property Window of eXCeS using OPEN LOOK

Fig. 4 conforms to the OPEN LOOK style where one property should appear per line and sets of properties laid out vertically. Contrast this with the Motif attribute property window, Fig 5.

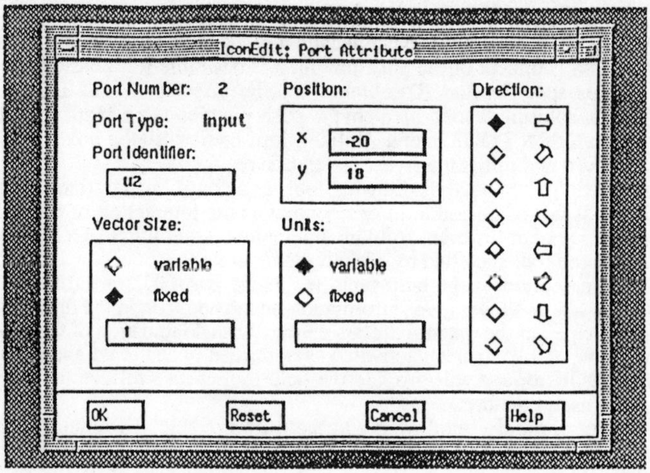

Figure 5. The Attribute Property Window of eXCeS using Motif

To select from a set of alternative values, Motif style guide suggests the use of exclusive radio buttons (the diamond shaped symbols in Fig. 5). In addition properties should be grouped together and enclosed in boxes.

This style of layout is in fact explicitly rejected in the OPEN LOOK guidelines! It is these types of cosmetic differences which add to the problem of specifying for two standards. However it is important to follow the style guides, as otherwise one would obtain improper implementations which destroy the whole concept of look and feel. One can imagine for example translating the attribute layout of OPEN LOOK exhibited in Fig. 3 in a naive and direct manner into Motif and thus imposing an OPEN LOOK look and feel on Motif which would be a disaster.

The two features of eXCeS we have discussed highlight the problems of writing for two specification standards and illustrate the typical difficulties which can arise and have to be addressed.

6.0 Conclusions

In this paper we have looked closely at the recent technological developments which have enabled an implementation of graphical user interfaces to impose a standard look and feel across a number of different application packages. We have compared the facilities offered by the two main contenders, OPEN LOOK and Motif, in the context of graphical user interfaces for computer aided control system design and have concluded that there is little fundamental difference in the facilities offered by either. We have also concluded that it would be desirable to be able to offer a user the choice of look and feel for a specific application package and, provided one takes care of particular implementation details, this choice may be provided without excessive programming resource implications.

References

[Balkovich 85] E. Balkovich, S. Lerman and R.P. Parmalee, *"Computing in higher education: The Athena experience,"* in CACM, Vol. 28, pp 12i4-1224.

[Barker 87a] H.A. Barker, M. Chen, C.P. Jobling and P. Townsend, *"Interactive graphics for the computer aided design of dynamic systems"*, IEEE Control Systems Magazine, vol. 7, pp 19-25.

[Barker 88] H.A. Barker, M. Chen and P. Townsend, *"Algorithms for transformations between block diagrams and signal flow graphs"*, in Preprints of 4th IFAC Symposium on Computer Aided Design in Control Systems – CADCS '88, Beijing, P.R. China, 23-25 August 1988,pp 231-236.

[Barker 88b] H.A. Barker, P. Townsend, C.P. Jobling, P.W. Grant, M. Chen, D.A. Simon and I.T. Harvey, *"A Human-Computer Interface for control system design"*, People and Computers III, Cambridge University Press, Cambridge, UK,

[Barker 89] H.A. Barker, M. Chen, P.W. Grant, C.P. Jobling and P. Townsend, *"Development of an Intelligent Man-Machine Interface for Computer-Aided Control System Design and Simulation"*, *to appear in* Automatica, vol. 25.

[CCAE 89] *"The Specification of eXCeS"*, Tech. Report, Control and Computer-Aided Engineering Research Group, University of Swansea,
#(CCAE|TR-1989|002)

[Gregg 84] W. Gregg, *"The Apple Macintosh computer,"* in Byte, Vol 9. No 2. pp 30-54.

[Jobling 88] C.P. Jobling and P.W. Grant, *"A rule-based program for signal flow graph reduction"*, Engineering Applications of Artificial Intelligence, Vol. 1, pp 22-23.

[OSF 89] OSF/Motif Style Guide, Revision 1.0, Open Software Foundation, Cambridge, Ma, USA.

[Scheifler 88] R. Scheifler, J. Gettys, *"The X-Window System"*, ACM Trans on Graphics, vol 15, pp 75-109.

[Smith 82] Smith, Irby, Kimball, Verplank and Harslem, *"Designing the Star User Interface,"* in Byte, Vol 7. No 4 .pp 242-282.

[SUN 88] The OPEN LOOK Graphical User Interface Functional Specification, Pre-Release, July 1988, Sun Microsystems, Inc.

[Williams 83] G. Williams, *"The Lisa Computer system,"* in Byte, Vol 8, No 2, pp 33-50

Authors' Address

Control and Computer Aided Engineering Research Group
Departments of Electrical and Electronic Engineering
and
Mathematics and Computer Science
University College of Swansea
Singleton Park
Swansea SA2 8PP
UK

Telephone: +44-792-205678
Telex: 48358
Fax: +44-792-295532

Chapter 27

The OO-AGES Model — An Overview

Mário Rui Gomes and João Carlos Lourenço Fernandes

The Object Oriented Paradigm is proving to be the best approach for the creation of Interactive Graphical Applications. Up to now several Object Oriented Interactive Graphic Applications were developed but no global Model has been presented.

The Design of OO-AGES, Object Oriented Architecture of Graphic EditorS, is based on the Client/Server concept and the Responsibility Driven Approach. The Model supports both Direct Manipulation at the Interface and at the Application level.

A decentralized extension to the, 10 years old, GKS Input Model is described. The separation between Dialogue Managers and Geometric Managers is also proposed.

The OO-AGES Model can deal, in a homogeneous framework, with so different issues as the implementation of a 3D pipeline in different Workstations and the broadcast of high-level information generated by user's actions.

Authors' address: IST/INESC, Projecto CAD/CAM, Rua Alves Redol 9 2º, 1000 Lisboa, Portugal, (01)-528163, mrg@inesc.inesc.pt, mcsun!inesc!mrg

1. Introduction

1.1 Main Issue

The development of Graphical Direct Manipulation Applications based on Object Oriented Models is a challenge to system programmers due to the lack of well defined Models and Architectures for that family of Applications.

Most of the OO programs are a collection of objects that encapsulate both behavior and structure, interact with each other, through messages, and are organized to perform the application dependent job.

The OO paradigm has introduced a new view to the problem of programming an Interactive Application. To define what is and what is not semantics does not make sense any more. Nowadays an application is implemented, in a decentralized, way as a set of objects. Even so it is possible to define the semantic part of an Application as the objects of a set of classes that must be developed and linked to other objects of already programmed classes.

The challenge nowadays is to define Models and Architecture for families of applications and to find the best way to insert new objects, the so called "semantic objects".

1.2 History

Two main approaches for the implementation of Interactive Graphic Applications were followed during the last decade:

-Most of the Applications are based on Graphic Kernel ISO Standards, like GKS or PHIGS that have a common Input Model [Rosenthal82] according to which the application can consume instances of predefined (input) types. The gathering of the information is done by implementation dependent Interaction Techniques. This approach gives a good support to the development of Graphic Applications but has several drawbacks: the Interaction Techniques are coded; no tools are given to parametrize an Interaction Technique (only placement is available); no support is given to create higher level (input) types.

-With the introduction of Window Managers, Object Oriented toolkits (XToolkit [McCormack88]) and frameworks (MacApp [Schmucker86]) are becoming very popular. They enable the placement and parametrization of Interaction Techniques but the predefined (input) types are of lower level then those supported by the first approach. The creation of an User Interface on top of a Window Manager can be done with a specific programming language, like Open Dialogue [Apollo88] or with Interactive Tools like the Cardelli's [Cardelli87] or the NeXT Interface Builder [Webster89].

The definition of an Input Model was the main contribution of the first approach. Unfortunately it is a centralized Model where it is very difficult to parametrize any Interaction Technique.

Decentralizing the implementation of the user-Interface was the best contribution of the second approach. Each object is responsible for a part of the User Interface, both the dialogue control and the prompt/feedback is implemented by each object.

According to Brad Myers [Myers89] approaches like MacApp or XToolkit, are giving support only to the creation of User Interfaces but not to Interactive Graphic Application. Our experience, teaching Computer Graphics at the Technical University of Lisbon to final year undergraduated students, has shown that it is easier to specify the architecture of a Graphic Application than to use a XToolkit architecture.

1.3 Requirements

None of the described approaches is suitable for the creation of Graphical Direct Manipulation Editors using also Graphical Direct Manipulation Interactions [Shneiderman 83] because there should exist a common architecture for Generic User Interface, GUI, and for Application Dependent User Interface, ADUI.

A GUI implementation is composed by generic Interaction Techniques like buttons, menus, dialogue boxes that are used by the User, to control the application.

ADUI objects are the Interaction Techniques used to manipulate the application dependent objects like a "bus" or a "pin" on a Schematic Electric Editor.

Some of the common requirements of a GUI and an ADUI are:

-sophisticated graphics

-any command given at any time

-different ways to give the same command

-multiple input and output devices

-complex dialogues

-non static interfaces

-fast and continuous prompt/feedback

1.4 Related Work

The OO-AGES is a Model for Graphical Direct Manipulation Applications integrating in one conceptual framework the manipulation of both GUI objects and ADUI objects. An implementation based on the OO-AGES Model is under implementation at INESC, Instituto de Engenharia de Sistemas e Computadores.

The OO-AGES Model was strongly influenced by Peridot [Myers86], Sassafras [Hill87] and Grow [Barth 86] and good synergism with Hubner [Hubner89]. The influence of Graphic Standards and "de facto" Window Manager Standards were also very important.

Like OO-AGES, recent works including Garnet [Myers 88] and Tube [Hill89] are aimed to build Graphical, Highly Interactive, Direct Manipulation Applications. Both Garnet and Tube are implemented on top of Object Oriented extensions to Lisp, the former in CommonLisp [Steele84] and the later in CommonLoops [Bobrow86]. The OO-AGES, written in C++ [Stroustrup86], is an integration of the principles use in the MAGOO Model [Gomes89a] only with graphic output, and in the OOI Model [Hubner89] that allows the definition of Dialogues.

1.5 Paper Organization

In this paper a Model for Graphical Direct Manipulation Applications, the OO-AGES is presented. The main concepts of the Model are presented in section 2. Their application to the case of Graphical Direct Manipulation Editors is dealt in section 3. In section 4 some of the details of the Model are presented. The actual implementation and future work are presented in the final sections.

2. The 00-AGES Model

2.1 The Responsibility Driven Approach

There are two main approaches to the organization of Object Oriented Applications, the Data Driven Approach and the Responsibility Driven Approach [Brock89].

Following a Data Driven approach an object, like a 3D polyline, should know how to set/get each of its internal attributes and also know how to rotate, translate, draw and so on.

The Responsibility Driven approach is based on a Client/Server Model where any object can be a Server or a Client at any given time. To implement the Client/Server relationship the Client must know what actions the Server is responsible for and what information should it share with the Server. A 3D Polyline becomes a passive object that only knows out to get/set its internal attributes. Specialized Objects will have the knowledge to rotate, translate or draw any 3D Graphic Object.

2.2 Main Principles

Usually objects encapsulate both behavior and structure. In our approach there are two families of objects, the **Data Objects,** that encapsulate only structure and the **Transformer Objects,** that encapsulate any kind of behavior and knowledge. The Responsibility Driven approach is followed. The **Application** and the **Human Operator**, are examples of **Transformers.**

Objects communicate between them using a trigger mechanism. Actually a trigger is a message that is sent by an object to another object.

A **Data Object,** is always created, destroyed, inquired and modified by **Transformer Objects.** It is an obvious extension of the procedural base data variables. The control is always returned to the transformer that send the trigger.

Data objects are always slaves and they are organized in two main families, the **Exclusive Data Objects** family and the **Shared Data Objects** family. Objects of the former family are always slaves of only one Transformer object, and the ones of the later family can be slaves of several Transformer objects.

A **Transformer Object,** is responsible for the creation of a data representation from another data representation or for the management of a specific data representation. For example a 3D output pipeline is a Transformer that creates a 2D Object from a 3D Object.

A Transformer Object and a set of Data Objects managed him can be predefined, forming **Sub-Societies**.

The **Sub-Society** concept is fundamental in the OO-AGES Model. A Sub-Society is a set of Transformers linked together forming a DAG, Directed Acycle Graph. A Sub-Society is dynamic, in the sense that those links can be changed in Run Time. The organization of a Sub-Society as a DAG is also suitable for the implementation of the Model on multitasks and multiprocessing environments.

The **Human Operator** is a Sub-Society that manages input devices which are sources of DO's, and gets information contained in visualization surfaces. This special Sub-Society is not dynamic because is dependant on the hardware architecture of the system.

The **Application** is a society that creates **Transformers and Shared Data Objects**, links them together, forming also a **DAG**, Direct Acycle Graph, and, eventually, gives away the control to the **Human Operator** (external control).

3. Interactive Graphic Applications

In this section we will apply the concepts presented above to the Interactive Graphic Applications.

The two most important tasks of a Graphic Editor are the computation of screen views of entities and the gathering of information sent by the operator and used to define and change those entities.

For a Graphic Editor implemented on top of an Window Management environment it is also necessary to impose placement restrictions between screen views, like the tiles and overlapping windows policies.

This family of applications requires specialized Transformers and Sata Objects, like **Output Transformers, Interactors, Geometric Managers** and **Graphic Data Objects**.

The computation of screen views of a graphical entity is carried out by an **Output Sub-Society, OSS** which is modeled by a **DAG** of **Output Transformer Objects**. The conversion of a 3D graphic Data object into several 2D graphic Data object is carried out by an OSS which can be implemented by concurrent sequential pipelines. In the example views of a 3D Graphic Data Object will be seen in two X11 Windows, a Display PostScript Window and a Pex [Pex88] Window (fig 1).

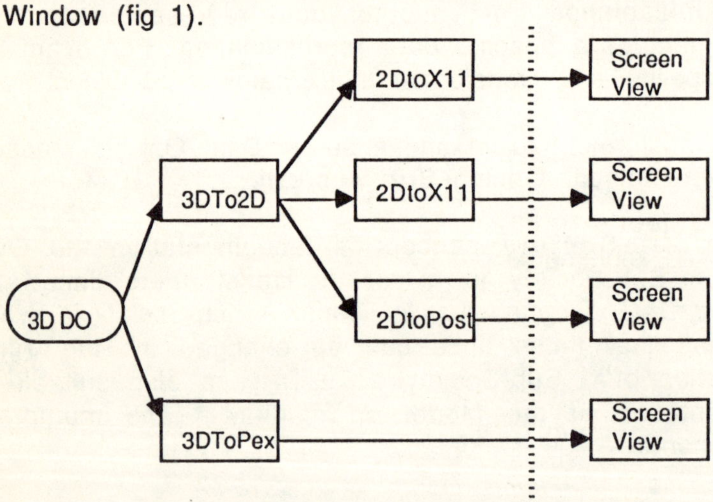

Fig 1 - An Output Sub-Society

The gathering of information sent by the operator is carried out by a **DAG** of **Interactor Transformer Objects,** forming an **Interactors Sub-Society, ISS**. An Interactor can trigger others Transformers, performing both the dialogue composition and the graphic feedback. The modelling of the Dialogue as a Sub-Society connected with an Output Sub-Society assure both a strong coupling of input and output needed for continuous prompt/feedback and the creation of complex dialogues.

An example of a ISS is a converter of a temporal sequence of two locators into both a Polyline and a Polymarker. For the Polymarker it is needed additional information about its type. This information is measured from object "C" (fig 2).

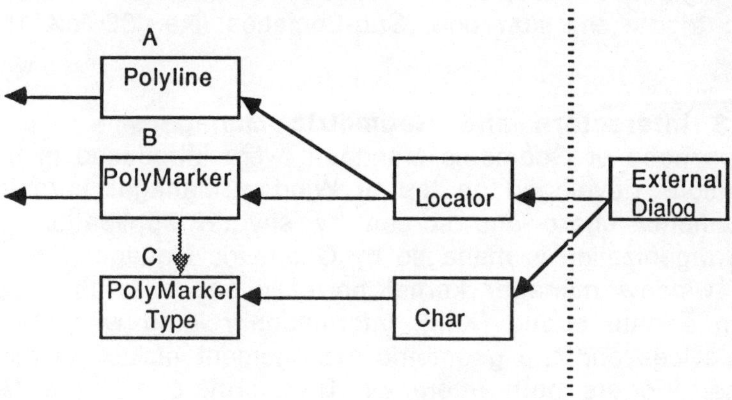

Figure 2 - An Input Sub-Society

The functionality of a Graphical Direct Manipulation Applications based on the OO-AGES Model is quite powerful because it can accommodate, in the same framework, dynamic dialogues and dynamic pipelines, just by changing the links between Transformer Objects.

4. Object's Internal Control

For the implementation of an application based on the OO-AGES Model it is necessary to define the internal behavior of the main Transformer and Data classes.

4.1 Data Objects

The Data Objects are very easy to define because they encapsulate only structure. Each internal element of a Data Object can be defined and inquired. For example a 3D polyline is composed by a geometric part, (list of 3D points, bounding box and matrix) and an aspect part (line style, colour, visibility, detectability between others).

4.2 Output Transformers

The Output Transformer Objects are responsible for the transformation of Graphic Data Objects between different stages of a conventional output pipeline. The internal control of this family of Transformer objects is very simple. When they are triggered they immediately compute the transformation between Data Objects and trigger all their servers. One way to trigger an Output Transformer is to send a message with a reference to a Shared Graphic Data Object.

The Screen View Data Objects correspond to the final Graphic Data Object created after the execution of an Output Pipeline. So, to generate a Screen View Data object it is just necessary to link, in the right sequence, all the needed Output Transformer Objects and to trigger the first one. Sub-Societies like "3DToX11" can be used.

4.3 Interactors and Geometric Managers

The need of Geometric Managers were introduced in Interactive Applications developed on top of Window Manager kernels. Those environments share one screen by several applications and the screen organization is managed by Geometric Managers.

A window manager kernel normally sends to the application, through a data queue [X88], information related with the physical input devices and the geometric management tasks. So the window manager triggers both Interactor Transformers and the Geometric Managers Transformers.

Each Geometric Manager Transformer objects maintains a predefined policy, e.g. no Screen View can overlap another Screen View.

Although the information, used by objects of both the Interactor and the Geometric Manager families, is received through the same queue, their internal control and architecture are quite different. Data Objects of the first family use temporal operators to control the dialogue sequence and those of the second family use geometric operators to control and to guarantee the geometric coherence.

The tasks carried out by Interactors and the Geometric Managers were already identified by other authors. For example Myers [Myers86] call them the *interaction or behavior* and the *presentation or layout* .

It is now important to describe the internal control structure of these special transformers.

4.3.1 Interactors

The internal architecture of an Interactor Transformer object is based on the GKS/PHIGS input Model. This Model describes the interaction between the application program with physical input devices in terms of a class, an operation mode and attributes [Rosenthal82]. Conceptually, the dynamic of the Model is explained in terms of two processes, the measure process and the trigger process. The former determines how the user controls the input data value and the later determines how the user indicates that the current value is significant.

An improvement of this Model was proposed recently by Duce and others [Duce89]. Using CSP, the Hoare´s language for specification of dynamic systems [Hoare85], the Model was defined in terms of five processes (measure, trigger, echo, logical input device and storage) that are mediators between the Operator and the Application. The Operator is also modeled as the "operator process" that can change the values of the device's measure process and that can fire the trigger process.

As soon as the value of the device's measure is changed the information is sent to the echo process. As soon as a trigger is fired the information is sent to the application.

This new Model has still several drawbacks. First, the information about the trigger firing is shared by four processes, the operator, the measure, the logical input device and the trigger. Second, the Model is only used at the lowest input level and no support is given for the composition of interactions. Third, the modelling of a single input operation is done by 5 processes. Fourth, and last, there is no reason to support only a 1:1 relation between the trigger process and the measure process. One trigger process should be able to trigger several measure processes (1:n) and a measure process should be triggered by different trigger processes (n:1).

These problems are overcame in the OO-AGES Model where a decentralized approach suitable for interactions composition is used. The same object can be triggered and measured by other TO's.

Internally any Interactor object maintains a Data object and an internal state transition network. When the Interactor is fired and his internal final state is reached it will perform the feedback - trigger - prompt cycle.

The feedback and prompt operations are done through an Output Sub-Society. The trigger operation is a broadcast operation composed by individual triggers send by the server to their clients.

Many alternative proposals to defined dialogues were presented by Anson [Anson82] and van den Bos [Bos88] among others but the use of normal programming control structures (temporal logic based constructors) seems to be the easiest approach for an Application Designer.

In the OO-AGES Model, temporal logic based operators, like "seq", "and", "or", "if" are used to define the internal control of each Interactor Transformer objects.

A "seq" ITO is triggered when the last server sends a trigger.

An "and" ITO is triggered when all the servers have already send a trigger, whatever sequence was followed.

An "or" ITO is a "switch" like object. It is triggered when any of its server sends a trigger.

An "if a then b else c" ITO is triggered when the servers a sends b trigger after server a or when the server c sends a trigger before any trigger send by the server a.

An Interactor class, to be useful, must be derived according to the information it is supposed to gather. For example the implementation of alternative ways to consume an Integer Object can be implemented by an Object of a class derived from "or" where its servers are also Interaction Objects that know how to produce Integer Data Objects.

This gathering mechanism enables the programmer to handle information coming from the user at the right level of abstraction. For example a Schematic Electric Editor Programmer does not want to know about menus, points, scroll bars or polylines but only about "nets", "components", "pins", "vias" and "buses".

4.2.2 Geometric Managers

A Geometric Manager Transformer object, is responsible for the maintenance of geometric restrictions between a set of managed Screen View Data Objects.

When any Transformer object attempts to change the geometry of a Screen View his Geometric Manager is triggered in order to compute the geometry for that Screen View. This operation is performed in two steps. First the proposed geometry is received and then the negotiation with all the managed Screen View Data objects is carried out based on the predefined policy. Once the negotiation is finished the Geometric Manager will change the Screen View Data objects using the output pipeline.

5. Implementation

5.1 Implementation Environment

An implementation of an environment based on the OO-AGES Model is under development. The system, called MAGOO, is implemented in the Free Software Foundation version of C++, the g++ and is based on the existence of a Virtual Window Manager [Gomes88] supporting both the X11 [Scheifler86] and the PostScript Graphic Pipeline.

The nowadays most popular toolkit family, the XToolkit is also integrated. A new C++ encapsulation where each widget is a Sub-Society composed by two TO's, an Output Transformer, called Driver and an Input Transformer, called Dialogue and a DO, the Display (the pixelmap inside the window of the widget) was developed [Gomes88] (Fig 3).

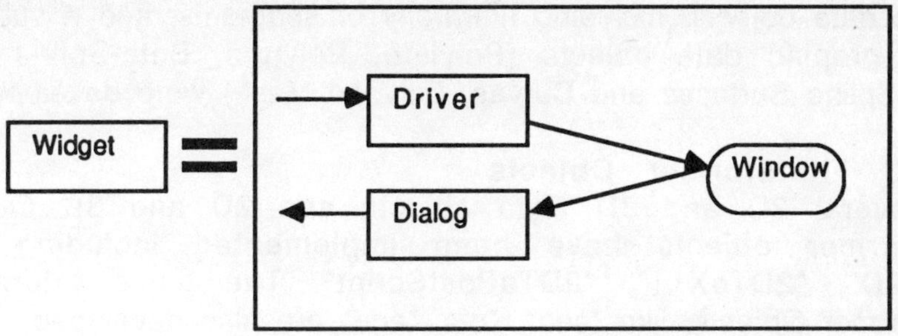

Figure 3 - An Widget = 2 TO and a DO

With this integration it is possible to use already programmed Interaction Techniques and to extend their functionality using the internal "event handler" mechanism. It is possible to mix the functionality of any widget, including the internal state transitions, prompts and feedbacks, with the draw and managing of retained graphics. This part of the implementation has been successfully experimented with Athenas Widgets, Motif Widgets and INESC Widgets.

In the example of fig 4 the information generated by a Widget is send to several Interaction Objects. The feedback of B is done, through an Output Sub-Society on the windows of two other widgets.

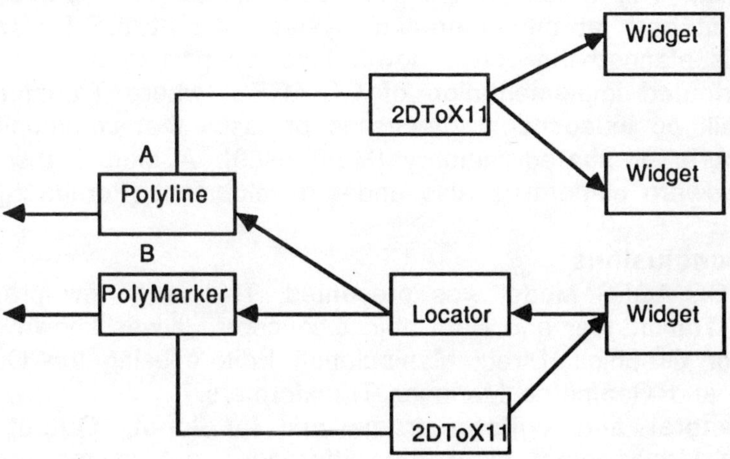

Figure 4 - Transformers and Widgets

5.2 Data Objects

The main primitive programming language based data objects are supported (boolean, integer, float,..). The most popular 2D graphic data objects, including hierarchy of segments, and a sub set of 3D graphic data objects (Polyline, Polygon, Beta-Spline and Bezier-Spline Surfaces and Curves, Polygon Mesh) were developed.

5.3 Transformer Objects

Several 2D and 3D Data objects and 2D and 3D Output Transformer objects have been implemented including the "3DTo2D", "2DToX11", "2DToPostScript". The basic Interactor Transformer Objects, like "seq", "or", "and" are also developed.

The Geometric Manager task has been fulfilled only by Composite and Constraint Widgets.

6. Future Work

Future work will proceed in two main directions. First the enrichment of the OO-AGES Model (new TO's and DO's) and second the implementation of applications using MAGOO.

Parametric Data Objects and 4D Data Objects will be developed as well as specialized TO´s for Pex and GL from Silicon Graphics.

The most important applications using the OO-AGES will be the Gear++, an integration of the Gear Animation System [Casteleiro89] and the development of an application to be used in the class room for teaching Computer Graphics and CAD/CAM technologies (splines surfaces and curves).

A third, long term, research direction, will proceed in close collaboration with other groups at INESC aimed to improve the environment both at the Operation System and at the Hardware Level. It is planned the use of lower level support to the creation of a distributed implementation of OO-AGES, where Transformer Objects will be independent processes or tasks that communicate through ports or shared memory [Marques89]. A Multi-Transputer based hardware platform is also under development [Pereira88].

7. Conclusions

The OO-AGES Model was presented. This is a new proposal based on Transformer and Data object concepts. It was shown to be suitable for Graphical Direct Manipulation Editors using the Output, Interactor and Geometric Manager Transformers.

A general and uniform framework for Input, Output and Geometric Management were the differences are at the internal control of Transformer Objects was proposed. The implementation of the Model allows the definition of dynamic dialogues and dynamic output pipelines, simply by changing the links between Transformer Objects.

A new decentralized Input Model where each Interactor Transformer Object can be both trigger and measured is also described.

The C++ language has proved, so far, to be an adequate language for its implementation.

Acknowledgement

The authors wish to express their thanks to Rui Casteleiro and Fernando Vasconcelos for the development of Magoo kernel, to Alfons Spiegelhauer for the specification and implementation of the XToolkit encapsulation and to Manuel Lancastre for the development of the first version of the OOI kernel.

References

[Anson82] E. K. Anson, "The device model of interaction", Computer Graphics, 16(3), pp 107-114, 1982.

[Apollo88], Apollo Computer Inc, "Open Dialogue Reference", April 1988.

[Barth 86] Paul S. Barth, "An Object-Oriented Approach to Graphical Interfaces", ACM Transactions on Graphics, 5(2) pp 142-172, April 1986.

[Bobrow86] D. G. Bobrow, K. Kann, G. Kiczales, L. Masinter, M. Stefik and R. Zdyble, "CommonLoops: Merging Lisp and Object-Oriented Programming" in OOPSLA'86 Proceedings, pp 17-29, Special Issue of SIGPLAN Notices, Vol 21 (11), October 1986.

[Bos88] Jan Van Den Bos, "Abstract Interaction Tools: A Language for User Interface Management Systems", ACM Transactions on Programming Languages and Systems, 10(2), pp 215-247, April 1988.

[Brock89] Rebecca Wirfs-Brock and Brian Wilkerson, "Object-Oriented Design: A Responsibility-Driven Approach", in OOPSLA'89 Proceedings, Norman Meyrowit (Editor), pp 71-75, Special Issue of SIGPLAN Notices, Vol 24 (10), October 1989.

[Cardelli87] Luca Cardelli, "Building User Interfaces by Direct Manipulation", Digital SRC Research Report 22, October 1987.

[Casteleiro89] Rui P. Casteleiro, Pedro Diniz and Pedro Domingos, "GEAR - A 3D Computer Animation System for CAD and Simulation", IEEE Student papers 1989, to be published.

[Duce89] D. A. Duce, P. J. W. ten Hagen and R. van Liere, "Components, Frameworks and GKS input", in Eurographics'89 Proceedings, W. Hansmann, F. R. A. Hopgood and W. Strasser (Editors), pp 87-103, Elsevier Science Publishers B. V. (North-Holland), September 1989.

[Gomes88] Mário R. Gomes and João L. Fernandes, "VWM - Sistema Virtual de Gestão de Janelas",1º Encontro Português de Computação Gráfica, pp 2-17, Julho 1988.

[Gomes89a] Mário R. Gomes and Rui P. Casteleiro, "MAGOO - Modelação de Aplicações Gráficas Orientadas para Objectos", 2º Encontro Português de Computação Gráfica, Porto, Outubro de 1989.

[Gomes89b] Mário R. Gomes and João Filipe Silva, "SisPerTI, Um SIStema PERito em Técnicas de Interacção", 2º Encontro Português de Computação Gráfica, Porto, Outubro de 1989.

[Green85] M. Green, "Report on Dialogue-Specification Tools", in User Interface Management Systems, Gunther E. Pfaff (editor), pp 9-20, Springer-Verlag, 1985.

[Hill87] Ralph D. Hill, "Event-Response Systems - A Technique for Specifying Multi-Threaded Dialogues", Proceedings of CHI + GI 1987, pp 241-248, 1987.

[Hill89] Ralph D. Hill and Marc Herrmann, "The Structure of Tube - A Tool for Implementing Advanced User Interfaces", in in Eurographics'89 Proceedings, W. Hansmann, F. R. A. Hopgood and W. Strasser (Editors), pp 15-25, Elsevier Science Publishers B. V. (North-Holland), September 1989.

[Hoare85], C. A. R. Hoare, "Communicating Sequence Processes", Prentice-Hall International, 1985.

[Hubner89] Wolfgang Hubner and Mario Rui Gomes, "Two Object-Oriented Models to Design Graphical User Interfaces", in Eurographics'89 Proceedings, W. Hansmann, F. R. A. Hopgood and W. Strasser (Editors), pp 63-74, Elsevier Science Publishers B. V. (North-Holland), September 1989.

[Marques89] José Alves Marques and Paulo Guedes, "Extending the Operating System to Support an Object-Oriented Environment", in OOPSLA'89 Proceedings, Norman Meyrowit (Editor), pp 113-122, Special Issue of SIGPLAN Notices, Vol 24 (10), October 1989.

[McCormack88] J. McCormack, P. Asente, "X11 Toolkit for the X Window Manager: An Overview of the X Toolkit", Symposium on User Interface Software", ACM, 1988, pp. 46-55.

[Myers86] Brad A. Myers and William Buxton, "Creating Highly-Interactive and Graphical User Interfaces by Demonstration", Proceedings of SIGGRAPH 86, ACM Computer Graphics Vol 20, Number 4, pp 249-258, August 1986.

[Myers88] Brad A. Myers, "The Garnet User Interface Development Environment: A Proposal", CMU-CS-88-153, September 1988.

[Myers89] Brad A. Myers, Brad V. Zanden and Roger B. Dannenberg, "Creating Graphical Interactive Application Objects by Demonstration", UIST'89, Symposium on User Interface Software and Technology, November 1989.

[Pereira88] João Pereira, F. Reis, C. Vinagre and M. Rui Gomes, "Parallel Processing on a Transputer-Based Graphic Board",Third Eurographics Workshop on Graphics Hardware, Setembro 1988.

[Rosenthal82] D. Rosenthal, J. C. Michener, G. Pfaff, R. Kessener and M. Sabin, "The detailed semantics of graphics input devices", Computer Graphics 16(3), pp 33-38, July 1983.

[Scheifler86] Robert W. Scheifler and Jim Gettys, "The X Window System", ACM Transactions on Graphics 5(2) pp 79-109, April 1986.

[Schmucker86] Kurt J. Schmucker, "MacApp: An Application FrameWork", Byte pp 189-193, August 1986.

[Shneiderman 83] Ben Shneidreman, "Direct Manipulation: A Step Beyond Programming Languages", IEEE Computer 16(8) pp 57-69, August 1893.

[Steele84] Guy L. Steele (editor) "Common Lisp: The Language", Digital Press, 1984.

[Stroustrup86] B. Stroustrup, "The C++ Programming Language", Addison-Wesley Reading, Mass 1986.

[Webster89] B. F. Webster, "The NeXT Book", Addison-Wesley, 1989.

[X88] Xlib - C Language X Interface, the X Window System X11R3, May 1988.

[Pex88] - PEX - A 3D Extension for X, Version 3.00, April 1988.

List of Participants

J. Bangratz, Syseca Temps Reel, 315 Bureaux de la Colline, 92213 Saint-Cloud Cedex, FRANCE

L. Bass, SEI, 5000 Forbes Avenue, 15213 Pittsburgh PA, USA

M. Bordegoni, Progetto Finalizzato Robotica, Via Ampere, 56, 20131 Milan, ITALY

N. V. Carlsen, Dept. of Graphical Communication, Technical University of Denmark, Bldg. 116, DK-2800 Lyngby, DENMARK

R. Casteleiro, INESC, rua Alves Redol 9, apartado 10105, 1017 Lisboa Codex, PORTUGAL

G. Cockton, Department of Computer Science, University of Glasgow, Glasgow G12 8QQ, UK

U. Cugini, Progetto Finalizzato Robotica, Via Ampere, 56, 20131 Milan, ITALY

B. David, Ecole Centrale de Lyon, BP 163, 69131 Ecully Cedex, FRANCE

W. Doster, Daimler-Benz AG, Research Institute, Wilhelm-Runge Str. 11, 7900 Ulm, FRG

D.A. Duce, Rutherford Appleton Laboratory, Chilton, Didcot, Oxon OX11 0QX, UK

D. Ehmke, ZGDV, Wilhelminenstr. 7, 6100 Darmstadt, FRG

G. Faconti, CNUCE, Via S. Maria 36, 56100 Pisa, ITALY

R. Gimnich, IBM Germany, Heidelberg Scientific Centre, Tiergartenstrasse 15, Postfach 10 30 68, 6900 Heidelberg, FRG

M. Rui Gomes, INESC, rua Alves Redol 9, apartado 10105, 1017 Lisboa Codex, PORTUGAL

P. Grant, Department of Mathematics and Computer Science, University College of Swansea, Singleton Park, Swansea SA2 8PP, UK

J. Grollmann, Siemens AG, ZFE IS KOM 32, Postfach 83 09 53, 8000 München 83, FRG

R.A. Guedj, INT, 9 Rue Charles Fourier, 91011 Evry Cedex, FRANCE

N. Guimaraes, INESC, rua Alves Redol 9, apartado 10105, 1017 Lisboa Codex, PORTUGAL

P.J.W. ten Hagen, CWI, P.O. Box 4079, 1009 AB Amsterdam, THE NETHERLANDS

C.C. Hayball, STC Technology Ltd, London Road, Harlow, Essex CM17 9NA, UK

M. Herrmann, ECRC, Arabellastrasse 17, 8000 München 32, FRG

R.D. Hill, Bell Communication Research, 445 South Street, Room 2D-295, Morristown NJ 07960 - 1910, USA

E. Hollnagel, Computer Resources Intl. A/S, Bregneroedvej 144, DK-3460 Birkerod, DENMARK

G. Howell, Scottish HCI Centre, Mountbatten Building, Edinburgh EF1 2HT, UK

F.R.A. Hopgood, Rutherford Appleton Laboratory, Chilton, Didcot, Oxon OX11 0QX, UK

W. Huebner, ZGDV, Wilhelminenstr. 7, 6100 Darmstadt, FRG

P. Johnson, Department of Computer Science, Queen Mary and Westfield College, Mile End Road, London E1 4NS, UK

A.C. Kilgour, Department of Computer Science, Heriot-Watt University, 70 Grassmarket, Edinburgh EH1 2HJ, UK

L. van Klarenbosch, CWI, P.O. Box 4079, 1009 AB Amsterdam, THE NETHERLANDS

L. Larsson, Telelogic Programsystem AB, Teknikringen 2, 583 30 Linkoping, SWEDEN

E. Le Thieis, Syseca Temps Reel, 315 Bureaux de la Colline, 92213 Saint-Cloud Cedex, FRANCE

J.R. Lee, EdCAAD, University of Edinburgh, 20 Chambers Street, Edinburgh EH1 1JZ, UK

M. Martinez, Departamento de Arquitectura, Facultad de Informatica, Universidad Politecnica de Madrid, Urbanizacion Monteprincipe, 28660 Boadilla del Monte, Madrid, SPAIN

K. Molander, NMP-CAD, Box 1193, S-164 22 KISTA, SWEDEN

D. Morin, Syseca Temps Reel, 315 Bureaux de la Colline, 92213 Saint-Cloud Cedex, FRANCE

P. Munch, UNIRAS A/S, 376 Gladsaxevej, DK-2860 Soborg, DENMARK

F. Neelamkavil, Dept. of Computer Science, O'Reilly Institute, Trinity College, Dublin 2, IRELAND

F. Shevlin, Dept. of Computer Science, O'Reilly Institute, Trinity College, Dublin 2, IRELAND

D. Soede, CWI, P.O. Box 4079, 1009 AB Amsterdam, THE NETHERLANDS

M. Spenke, GMD, Postfach 1240, Schloss Birlinghoven, 5205 Sankt Augustin 1, FRG

P. Sturm, Department of Computer Science, University of Kaiserslautern, P.O. Box 3049, 6750 Kaiserslautern, FRG

D. Svanaes, Dept. of Informatics, The University of Trondheim, N-7055 Dragvoll, NORWAY

P. Townsend, Department of Mathematics and Computer Science, University College of Swansea, Singleton Park, Swansea SA2 8PP, UK

C. Villalobos, Andersen Consulting S.A., Raimundo Fernandez Villaverde, 65, 28003, Madrid, SPAIN

S. Wilson, Department of Computer Science, Queen Mary and Westfield College, Mile End Road, London E1 4NS, UK,

EurographicSeminars

Tutorials and Perspectives in Computer Graphics

Eurographics Tutorials '83. Edited by P. J. W. ten Hagen.
XI, 425 pages, 164 figs., 1984

User Interface Management Systems. Edited by G. E. Pfaff.
XII, 224 pages, 65 figs., 1985

Methodology of Window Management. Edited by F. R. A. Hopgood, D. A. Duce, E. V. C. Fielding, K. Robinson, A. S. Williams.
XV, 250 pages, 41 figs., 1985

Data Structures for Raster Graphics. Edited by L. R. A. Kessener, F. J. Peters, M. L.P. van Lierop. VII, 201 pages, 80 figs., 1986

Advances in Computer Graphics I. Edited by G. Enderle, M. Grave, F. Lillehagen.
XII, 512 pages, 168 figs., 1986

Advances in Computer Graphics II. Edited by F. R. A. Hopgood, R. J. Hubbold, D. A. Duce. X, 186 pages, 96 figs., 1986

Advances in Computer Graphics Hardware I. Edited by W. Straßer.
X, 147 pages, 76 figs., 1987

GKS Theory and Practice. Edited by P. R. Bono, I. Herman.
X, 316 pages, 92 figs., 1987

Intelligent CAD Systems I. Theoretical and Methodological Aspects.
Edited by P. J. W. ten Hagen, T. Tomiyama. XIV, 360 pages, 119 figs., 1987

Advances in Computer Graphics III. Edited by M. M. de Ruiter.
IX, 323 pages, 247 figs., 1988

Advances in Computer Graphics Hardware II. Edited by A. A. M. Kuijk, W. Straßer.
VIII, 258 pages, 99 figs., 1988

CGM in the Real World. Edited by A. M. Mumford, M. W. Skall.
VIII, 288 pages, 23 figs., 1988

Intelligent CAD Systems II. Implementational Issues. Edited by V. Akman, P. J. W. ten Hagen, P. J. Veerkamp. X, 324 pages, 114 figs., 1989

Advances in Computer Graphics IV. Edited by W. T. Hewitt, M. Grave, M. Roch.
XVI, 255 pages, 138 figs., 1991

Advances in Computer Graphics V. Edited by W. Purgathofer, J. Schönhut.
VIII, 223 pages, 101 figs., 1989

User Interface Management and Design. Edited by D. A. Duce, M. R. Gomes, F. R. A. Hopgood, J. R. Lee. VIII, 324 pages, 117 figs., 1991

In preparation:

Advances in Computer Graphics VI. Edited by G. Garcia, I. Herman. Approx. 465 pages, 1991

Advances in Object-Oriented Graphics I. Edited by E. Blake, P. Wisskirchen. Approx. 225 pages, 1991

Advances in Computer Graphics Hardware III. Edited by A. A. M. Kuijk. Approx. 225 pages, 1991

Advances in Computer Graphics Hardware IV. Edited by R. L. Grimsdale, W. Straßer. Approx. 290 pages, 1991

Intelligent CAD Systems III. Practical Experience and Evaluation. Edited by P. J. W. ten Hagen, P. J. Veerkamp. Approx. 280 pages, 1991